Object-Oriented
Ray Tracing in C++

Object-Oriented Ray Tracing in C++

NICHOLAS WILT

John Wiley & Sons, Inc.

New York • Chichester • Brisbane • Toronto • Singapore

Associate Publisher: Katherine Schowalter
Editor: Tim Ryan
Managing Editor: Jackie Martin
Editorial Production & Design: Electric Ink, Ltd.

This text is printed on acid-free paper.

Library of Congress Cataloging-in-Publication Data

Wilt, Nicholas.
    Object-oriented ray tracing in C++ / Nicholas Wilt.
        p.   cm.
    Includes bibliographical references and index.
    ISBN 0-471-30414-X (alk. paper). — ISBN 0-471-30415-8 (pbk.)
    1. Computer graphics. 2. C++ (Computer program language)
    3. Object-oriented programming (Computer science)   I. Title.
    T385.W56   1994
    006.6'6—dc20
                                                        93-20765
                                                        CIP

Printed in the United States of America
10 9 8 7 6 5 4 3 2 1

Contents

CHAPTER 2

Introduction to Ray Tracing   51

CHAPTER 3

The Shading Equation   61

CHAPTER 4

Different Types of Object   77

Chapter 5

Acceleration Techniques 147

Chapter 6

Texture Mapping 167

Acknowledgments

Many people have helped me in my struggle to complete this work. I would like to thank a subset of them, and I apologize in advance to those whom I neglect.

First I would like to thank my former thesis advisor, Prof. Scot Drysdale, for his help and encouragement while writing the thesis that evolved into this book.

Thanks also to Jeff Duntemann, for his early and continued encouragement of my programming and writing careers.

I would like to thank Eric Haines for an extremely constructive prepublication review. The book is much better for it. Eric also granted permission to incorporate portions of his Standard Procedural Database into my ray tracing class library.

I would like to thank David Kurlander for granting permission to use his figure illustrating Phong specular reflections.

My employers at Automatix, Inc., deserve special thanks for permitting me the opportunity to finish this book.

Thanks are due Amna Greaves—she knows why—and Leo Carayannopolous—he knows why—for their help at critical times in the book's development.

Finally, I must thank Robin for her constructive criticism, support, and tolerance.

The book wouldn't've been the same without you.

Introduction

Computers are capable of generating truly striking images using techniques such as ray tracing. Images generated using this technique are not only realistic in the sense that they can generate images almost indistinguishable from photographs; they can also be used to describe phenomena for scientific visualization, or to help mathematicians visualize four-dimensional objects. Ray tracing is particularly well-suited for many of these tasks.

This book is about ray tracing, a three-dimensional rendering technique. For a long time, ray tracing was the method of choice for photorealistic computer graphics. Although techniques such as radiosity have subverted its role as the premier method of photorealistic rendering, ray tracing remains important for several reasons. It can *directly* render a wide variety of objects such as fractals and algebraic surfaces, while many rendering techniques are limited to polygonalized approximations of these objects. Rather than rendering a sphere, for example, most rendering programs draw a conglomeration of triangles that looks like a sphere. Another reason ray tracing remains important is that it is used as a subroutine for other rendering methods, including radiosity.

Ray tracing has received a lot of attention, not all of it good. It has a reputation for being very compute- and memory-intensive, and for being extremely complicated. None of these reputations are deserved.

Ray tracing is less memory-intensive than most rendering techniques because it represents objects directly, rather than polygonalizing them. A direct representation usually requires less memory than a slew of triangles or other polygons.

Ray tracing was compute-intensive for the time when it was invented in 1980, but new algorithms and faster hardware make it feasible to ray trace images on inexpensive desktop computers.

Finally, like most profound ideas, ray tracing is a simple concept at heart. It is simple enough that many public-domain ray tracers have been written, and when a contest was run on the Internet to see who could write the smallest ray tracer, a number of the entries were less than 100 lines long!

Our treatment of ray tracing will begin with a discussion of 3D graphics and rendering in general. Readers who are familiar with 3D graphics may want to skip this material. Readers less familiar with 3D graphics will find ray tracing to be an excellent way to start. Although this book is not suitable as an introductory text on computer graphics, it can be used in conjunction with one. Since ray tracing is simple compared to traditional polygon rendering techniques, the reader can begin with ray tracing and move on to more complicated (and faster) rendering methods later.

Rather than describing ray tracing in a purely theoretical way, I will present the ideas behind it and describe OORT, a C++ class library for ray tracing. Readers should be familiar with C++ syntax before trying to understand OORT, or at the very least have a C++ reference handy so explanations of the syntax are readily available. Understanding inheritance and polymorphism, operator overloading, C++ scoping, references, and the use of the `const` keyword are particularly important.

Ray tracing has been an area of intensive research for more than a decade, and many exciting ideas have been described in the literature. Many ideas not implemented in OORT will be mentioned so that interested readers can follow up on their own. Many chapters end with suggestions for additions and improvements to OORT.

The Class Library

Most ray tracers are written in C and, because the C programming language is not designed for ray tracing, they include special "input languages" to describe the scene to be ray traced. OORT used to have its own input language, too; the parser was several thousand lines of C++. But once you develop a proprietary input language, you have to choose between providing a complete set of related tools (such as debuggers) and living without them. Instead of trying to provide a complete set of tools for a proprietary input language for OORT, I discarded the input language entirely and wrote the scene descriptions in C++. I have found writing the scene descriptions in straight C++ to be as readable as most ray tracer input languages, and it is much more powerful. Because usage of C++ is growing exponentially, there is a lot of market momentum for development tools. Powerful C++ compilers, debuggers, class browsers and other tools are already available, and more are being developed all the time. These tools can be used to debug scenes when the scene descriptions are written in C++.

Not providing a native input language for OORT does not preclude an input language, of course. Actually, I may have done the world a favor by not inventing Yet Another Ray Tracer Input Language. There are at least four other ray tracer input languages to choose from (those for QRT, DKBTrace, Rayshade, and VORT), and nothing prevents us from writing OORT parsers for those input languages. I have written parsers for subsets of the NFF and OFF file formats, as well.

OORT is designed to be easily extensible, so new primitives and features can be added with a minimum of effort. C++ has proven particularly well-suited to ray tracing implemention. Its language support for efficient operator over-loading, parameterized types, inheritance and polymorphism, and information hiding have proven particularly useful. Appendix A describes the C++ features that OORT uses heavily.

OORT is an ongoing project. I hope to continue to improve it on a number of fronts. I want to increase the number of ray-traceable primitives supported, increase the number of output file formats that it supports, make it more portable as C++ implementations converge, and write a Windows front-end to the ray tracer that uses the class library for rendering.

I have made the source code to OORT publicly available, on the condition that it not be redistributed for profit. Feel free to copy OORT in its entirety and give it to friends or upload it to bulletin boards. Feel free also to incorporate it into your own programs. If you redistribute OORT source code, distribute it in its entirety—and *do not* publish the source code for profit.

No software is error-free, and OORT is no exception. If you find a bug in OORT, let me know so I can incorporate a bug fix into a later release of the class library. I can be reached by mail in care of the publisher, or directly at CompuServe [75210,2455]. I also welcome suggestions, additions, and improvements to the class library, although I cannot respond to every suggestion or compensate contributors in any way.

Although Borland C++ 3.1 was used to develop the ray tracer, it should be relatively easy to port to any C++ compiler supporting the C++ 3.0 specification (including templates). One of my goals is to make OORT more portable in the future.

Typeface Conventions

B ook text is set in Times Roman. C++ keywords and the names of vectors are set as bold letters (e.g., **static**, $\mathbf{v_1}$). References to filenames and functions in OORT are set in Courier (e.g., `vector.cpp`, `Polygon::Precompute`).

Suggestions for Further Reading

Computer Graphics

[FOLE90]   Foley, James D., Andries van Dam, Steven K. Feiner, and John F. Hughes. *Computer Graphics*. Reading, MA: Addison–Wesley, 1990.

The definitive text on computer graphics.

[GLAS89a]   Glassner, Andrew, ed. *An Introduction to Ray Tracing*. London: Academic Press, 1989.

A collection of papers on ray tracing. This book will keep a ray tracer implementor busy for years.

[GLAS90]   Glassner, Andrew, ed. *Graphics Gems*. Boston: Academic Press, 1990.

A collection of small articles on different topics in computer graphics, including ray tracing and radiosity.

[ARVO91]   Arvo, James, ed. *Graphics Gems II*. Boston: Academic Press, 1991.

The second in the Gems series, similar to its predecessor.

[KIRK92]   Kirk, David, ed. *Graphics Gems III*. Boston: Academic Press, 1992.

The third in the Gems series, arguably the best.

[SPEER91]   Speer, L.R. A cross-indexed guide to the ray tracing literature. *Computer Graphics Forum* 10 (2), 145–174, June 1991.

C++ Programming

[COPL92]   Coplien, James O. *Advanced C++ Programming Styles and Idioms.* Reading: Addison–Wesley, 1992.

[ELLI90]   Ellis, Margaret and Bjarne Stroustrup. *The Annotated C++ Reference Manual.* Reading: Addison–Wesley, 1990.

[MEY92]   Meyers, Scott. *Effective C++.* Reading: Addison–Wesley, 1992.

[STRO91]   Stroustrup, Bjarne. *The C++ Programming Language*, 2nd ed. Reading: Addison–Wesley, 1991.

1

Introduction to 3D Graphics

Visual information dominates the sensory information that humans process. Because of our dependence on visual stimuli, computer graphics has proven to be a useful way to communicate tremendous amounts of information in a short amount of time. High-quality 2D computer graphics has become ubiquitous in the form of graphical user interfaces running on machines ranging from Macintoshes to IBM PC compatibles to a wide variety of UNIX machines. 3D graphics has been slower in coming because displaying 3D objects on the computer screen is more complicated than displaying 2D objects. 2D objects can be described very conveniently; a system knows exactly what to do with the video hardware if the programmer asks it to draw a line from (100, 75) to (200, 200). Describing what to display, and how to display it, is more complicated in the 3D case.

This chapter will introduce the reader to 3D graphics and describe some tools for 3D graphics that are widely used, such as simple linear algebra. Readers who are completely unfamiliar with 3D computer graphics will find this chapter to be a whirlwind introduction with suggested references for further reading. Readers more familiar with these concepts may find it convenient to refer to this chapter as needed.

1.1 The Rendering Pipeline

The rendering pipeline separates different tasks related to the display of photo-realistic images into a number of steps, each of which is taken care of by an entirely different system:

1. Modeling

2. Rendering

3. Quantization and Display

Modeling is the process of describing the "world" that is to be rendered. This is the step where objects, the eye location and other parameters of the rendering process are determined. OORT, the ray tracer developed for this book, has the same primitive modeling capabilities as other, more traditional ray tracers: users must describe the scene, then render the image at low resolution to see whether it looks right. Any problems that show themselves at low resolution must be fixed by changing the scene description. Once the image looks correct at low resolution, a final rendering can be done at high resolution and with antialiasing. The primary difference between this iterative process using OORT and using another ray tracer such as DKBTrace is that OORT does not have a built-in input language. For now, the scene descriptions must be written in C++ using calls to the class library.

Rendering is the process of taking the "world" from a modeller and creating a full-color image. The renderer needs a model of the world, an eye location, the *target resolution* (resolution of the computer display that the image will be shown on), and other parameters. The ray tracer developed for this book is strictly a renderer.

Quantization and display are the processes involved in taking the output from the renderer and drawing it on the computer display. Color quantization is for computers that can display only a limited number of colors on the display at a time. For such displays, a representative subset of the colors in the image must be chosen in order to display an approximation of the image.

It should be clear why these three steps are so clearly delineated. They are independent of each other, and are frequently taken care of by separate programs. A modeller might generate output in terms of quadric surfaces to be rendered. Then, depending on the renderer, it may render these quadrics directly or decompose them into polygons. This results in a full-color image that must be displayed, a machine-dependent process best left to a program separate from the renderer.

1.2 **2D Graphics and Imaging**

The computer screen is composed of a large number of screen elements (called *pixels* for *picture elements*) whose colors can be manipulated independently. By systematically changing the colors of different pixels on the screen, the computer can display rectangles, text, cursors, and other elements that should be familiar to anyone who has used a graphical user interface. The number of colors displayable by computers ranges from 2 (black and white) to 2^{24} (16,777,216). Computers that can display 256 or more colors are able to display convincing, realistic images that look almost like photographs. It is fairly easy to scan photographs and turn them into such images, or to install hardware so the computer can acquire them from a camera. It is much more difficult to program the computer to generate such an image all by itself: the computer must somehow model the three-dimensional objects mathematically, and once the model is defined, the computer must be programmed to render images of it.

The branch of computer graphics research that works to make computers generate realistic images is called *photorealism*. This is a misnomer, because it implies that photorealistic computer graphics is for generating images indistinguishable from real life. Actually, realism often takes a back seat to practicality and effectiveness of presentation. For example, the light sources in ray traced images are almost never physically correct (that is, the energy arriving from a light source is rarely attenuated by an amount proportional to the inverse square of the distance from the light source). Many applications for photorealistic computer graphics, including scientific visualization, do not require strict adherence to realism. Rather, they require only that the images communicate effectively.

1.3 **Colors**

Unlike most objects, computer displays generate light rather than reflecting it. The primary colors for objects that emit light are red, green and blue. Every color the computer can display can be described in terms of a combination of these colors.

The computer specifies colors by assigning a number to each of the primary colors. Colors are usually specified as 3-tuples, with each value ranging from 0–1. A value of 0 means that the primary color is not present at all; 1 means that the primary color is at maximum intensity. Using this scheme, black is (0, 0, 0) (listing red, green, and blue, in that order). White is (1, 1, 1). A mid-intensity gray is (0.5, 0.5, 0.5). Here are some typical color values:

```
          Red           (1, 0, 0)
          Green         (0, 1, 0)
          Blue          (0, 0, 1)
          Yellow        (1, 1, 0)
```

OORT includes a public-domain listing of colors ranging from aquamarine to brick red. They are listed in `colors.h`.

```
// =====================================================================
// colors.h: Header file containing all kinds of colors for OORT.
// =====================================================================

#define Black RGBColor(0, 0, 0)
#define White RGBColor(1, 1, 1)
#define Red RGBColor(1, 0, 0)
#define Green RGBColor(0, 1, 0)
#define Blue RGBColor(0, 0, 1)
#define Yellow RGBColor(1, 1, 0)
#define Cyan RGBColor(0, 1, 1)
#define Magenta RGBColor(1, 0, 1)
#define Aquamarine RGBColor(0.439216, 0.858824, 0.576471)
#define BlueViolet RGBColor(0.62352, 0.372549, 0.623529)
#define Brown RGBColor(0.647059, 0.164706, 0.164706)
#define CadetBlue RGBColor(0.372549, 0.623529, 0.623529)
#define Coral RGBColor(1.0, 0.498039, 0.0)
#define CornflowerBlue RGBColor(0.258824, 0.258824, 0.435294)
#define DarkGreen RGBColor(0.184314, 0.309804, 0.184314)
#define DarkOliveGreen RGBColor(0.309804, 0.309804, 0.184314)
#define DarkOrchid RGBColor(0.6, 0.196078, 0.8)
#define DarkSlateBlue RGBColor(0.419608, 0.137255, 0.556863)
#define DarkSlateGray RGBColor(0.184314, 0.309804, 0.309804)
#define DarkSlateGrey RGBColor(0.184314, 0.309804, 0.309804)
#define DarkTurquoise RGBColor(0.439216, 0.576471, 0.858824)
#define DimGray RGBColor(0.329412, 0.329412, 0.329412)
#define DimGrey RGBColor(0.329412, 0.329412, 0.329412)
#define Firebrick RGBColor(0.556863, 0.137255, 0.137255)
#define ForestGreen RGBColor(0.137255, 0.556863, 0.137255)
#define Gold RGBColor(0.8, 0.498039, 0.196078)
#define Goldenrod RGBColor(0.858824, 0.858824, 0.439216)
#define Gray RGBColor(0.752941, 0.752941, 0.752941)
#define GreenYellow RGBColor(0.576471, 0.858824, 0.439216)
#define Grey RGBColor(0.752941, 0.752941, 0.752941)
#define IndianRed RGBColor(0.309804, 0.184314, 0.184314)
#define Khaki RGBColor(0.623529, 0.623529, 0.372549)
```

Listing 1.1   `colors.h`

```
#define LightBlue RGBColor(0.74902, 0.847059, 0.847059)
#define LightGray RGBColor(0.658824, 0.658824, 0.658824)
#define LightGrey RGBColor(0.658824, 0.658824, 0.658824)
#define LightSteelBlue RGBColor(0.560784, 0.560784, 0.737255)
#define LimeGreen RGBColor(0.196078, 0.8, 0.196078)
#define Maroon RGBColor(0.556863, 0.137255, 0.419608)
#define MediumAquamarine RGBColor(0.196078, 0.8, 0.6)
#define MediumBlue RGBColor(0.196078, 0.196078, 0.8)
#define MediumForestGreen RGBColor(0.419608, 0.556863, 0.137255)
#define MediumGoldenrod RGBColor(0.917647, 0.917647, 0.678431)
#define MediumOrchid RGBColor(0.576471, 0.439216, 0.858824)
#define MediumSeaGreen RGBColor(0.258824, 0.435294, 0.258824)
#define MediumSlateBlue RGBColor(0.498039, 0.0, 1.0)
#define MediumSpringGreen RGBColor(0.498039, 1.0, 0.0)
#define MediumTurquoise RGBColor(0.439216, 0.858824, 0.858824)
#define MediumVioletRed RGBColor(0.858824, 0.439216, 0.576471)
#define MidnightBlue RGBColor(0.184314, 0.184314, 0.309804)
#define Navy RGBColor(0.137255, 0.137255, 0.556863)
#define NavyBlue RGBColor(0.137255, 0.137255, 0.556863)
#define Orange RGBColor(0.8, 0.196078, 0.196078)
#define OrangeRed RGBColor(1.0, 0.0, 0.498039)
#define Orchid RGBColor(0.858824, 0.439216, 0.858824)
#define PaleGreen RGBColor(0.560784, 0.737255, 0.560784)
#define Pink RGBColor(0.737255, 0.560784, 0.560784)
#define Plum RGBColor(0.917647, 0.678431, 0.917647)
#define Salmon RGBColor(0.435294, 0.258824, 0.258824)
#define SeaGreen RGBColor(0.137255, 0.556863, 0.419608)
#define Sienna RGBColor(0.556863, 0.419608, 0.137255)
#define SkyBlue RGBColor(0.196078, 0.6, 0.8)
#define SlateBlue RGBColor(0.0, 0.498039, 1.0)
#define SpringGreen RGBColor(0.0, 1.0, 0.498039)
#define SteelBlue RGBColor(0.137255, 0.419608, 0.556863)
#define Tan RGBColor(0.858824, 0.576471, 0.439216)
#define Thistle RGBColor(0.847059, 0.74902, 0.847059)
#define Turquoise RGBColor(0.678431, 0.917647, 0.917647)
#define Violet RGBColor(0.309804, 0.184314, 0.309804)
#define VioletRed RGBColor(0.8, 0.196078, 0.6)
#define Wheat RGBColor(0.847059, 0.847059, 0.74902)
#define YellowGreen RGBColor(0.6, 0.8, 0.196078)
```

Listing 1.1 `colors.h` *(continued)*

Computers can display colors only to a limited precision. Instead of using arbitrary real numbers, they use integers to denote how much of each primary color is present. For example, the integer range might be 0–255 (an 8-bit range). Then red is denoted by (255, 0, 0) rather than (1, 0, 0). If each of the primary colors gets 8 bits of precision, then there are 3·8 or 24 bits of precision for a color, or 2^{24} = 16,777,216 colors.

Most computers cannot set each pixel independently to one of these colors. More typically, computers have a palette of some number of colors that can be chosen from a wider set. A Super VGA display for the IBM PC, for example, can typically display 256 out of 218 colors (six bits for each primary). When this is the case, we must perform *color quantization* on the full-color image to choose a representative subset of the colors in the image. Once the representative colors have been chosen, each pixel in the full-color image is color-matched against the representative colors, and the pixel is replaced by the closest color.

Photorealistic renderers do not typically concern themselves with such constraints. Rather, they take input from the modeller and generate a full-color (24-bit) image. The process of displaying the image depends on the type of computer display, so it is left as a separate step. Most personal computer displays will need the full-color image to be quantized before display. The RAW2GIF program, described in Appendix D, will quantize your full-color images so they can be displayed.

1.4 Vectors

A location in 3D space can be conveniently described with three coordinates. We will use a Cartesian coordinate system with mutually perpendicular axes called X, Y, and Z. The X and Y coordinate axes should be familiar from high school mathematics classes. The X axis points to the right and the Y axis points upward. The Z axis is perpendicular to both X and Y. If you think about it, there are two choices for the direction Z points. We will be using the mathematical standard, called *right-handed.* (See Figure 1.1.) If you point your right index finger, point your thumb up so that it is perpendicular, and point the middle finger to the left so that it is perpendicular to your thumb and index finger, then your right hand describes the origin of the right-handed coordinate system. The thumb is the Y axis, the middle finger is the X axis, and the index finger is the Z axis. For the purpose of 3D computer graphics, the Z axis is thought of as pointing "out" of the screen, toward the user; this preserves the 2D coordinate system with the X axis pointing to the right and the Y axis pointing upward.

Because locations are so prevalent in computer graphics, it is often convenient to think of the three coordinates as a single unit. This unit is called a *vector.* The idea of a vector is much more general than the 3D vectors used in computer graphics; in linear algebra, vectors can be of any dimension. We will

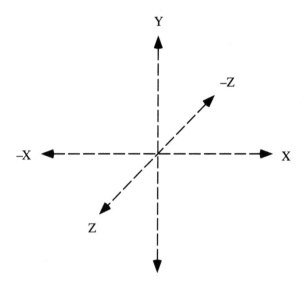

Figure 1.1   Right-handed coordinate axes.

draw upon linear algebra to help deal with the 3D vectors used in this book, but the reader need not be familiar with linear algebra to understand the book.

In linear algebra, a single number (component of a vector) is called a *scalar*. In this book, this term is used only to contrast with the term *vector*. A *vector* is a collection of 3 coordinates; a *scalar* is one of those coordinates. We will refer to the components of a vector V as $V.x$, $V.y$, and $V.z$. This notation is modelled after the C++ notation for structure member access.

1.5   Operations on Vectors

A vector describes a location in 3D space. When described in terms of X, Y and Z, vectors are usually thought of as pointing from the origin to that location. If you start at the origin, the vector describes how far you have to travel along the X, Y, and Z axes to get to that point. See Figure 1.2.

A vector can be negated. $-V$ is exactly as long as V (has the same magnitude) and points in the opposite direction. See Figure 1.3.

Vectors can be added; the sum of two vectors A and B is a vector that points to the location where you would end up if you started at the origin, walked to A, then walked along B from there. Vector addition is commutative (that is, $A + B = B + A$). Figure 1.4 shows a parallelogram that demonstrates

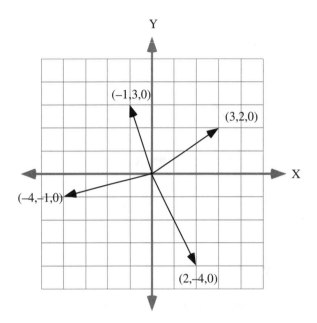

Figure 1.2   Vector.

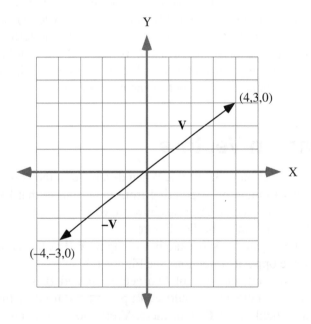

Figure 1.3   Negating a vector.

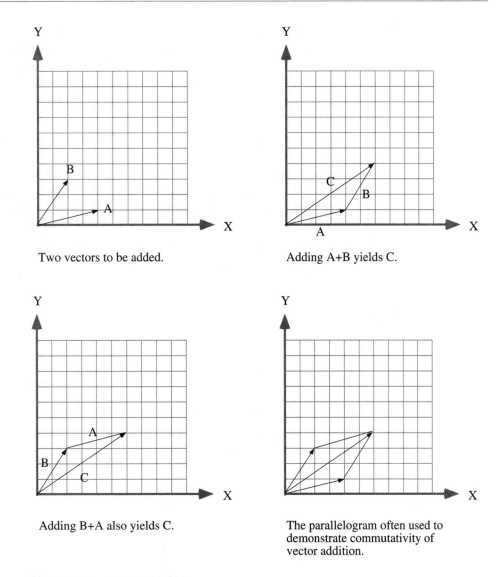

Two vectors to be added.

Adding A+B yields C.

Adding B+A also yields C.

The parallelogram often used to demonstrate commutativity of vector addition.

Figure 1.4 Vector addition.

this concept. You end up at the same point whether you apply **A** or **B** first. To implement vector addition, just add corresponding elements of each of the two vectors (see the implementation of `operator+=` in `vector.h`). See Figure 1.4.

Vectors can also be subtracted. Like subtraction of scalars, **A** – **B** is equivalent to adding **–B** to **A** (subtracting corresponding elements).

For the sake of consistency, I have implemented *vector multiplication* and *vector division*, which perform member-wise multiplication and division between the corresponding elements of two vectors. These operations are not really standard in linear algebra, but they have proven useful.

The magnitude is the Euclidean distance of the vector from the origin. The magnitude of a 3D vector (x, y, z) is given by:

$$\sqrt{x^2 + y^2 + z^2} \qquad (1.1)$$

In this book, the magnitude of a vector $\mathbf{V}$ is given as $\|\mathbf{V}\|$. This is to avoid confusion with the notation for absolute value ($|x|$ is the absolute value of a scalar x).

Another operation that can be performed on vectors is scalar multiplication. $s\mathbf{V}$ (where s is a scalar and $\mathbf{V}$ is a vector) is a vector with the same direction as $\mathbf{V}$ and magnitude $s\|\mathbf{V}\|$. Scalar multiplication is implemented by multiplying each coordinate of the vector by the scalar. See Figure 1.5.

The dot product is computed by summing the multiples of corresponding elements in two vectors. Thus, the dot product is a scalar. The dot product of two 3D vectors $\mathbf{V}_1$ and $\mathbf{V}_2$ is as follows:

$$\mathbf{V}_1 \cdot \mathbf{V}_2 = \mathbf{V}_1.x\mathbf{V}_2.x + \mathbf{V}_1.y\mathbf{V}_2.y + \mathbf{V}_1.z\mathbf{V}_2.z \qquad (1.2)$$

The dot product can be thought of as the length of the projection of $\mathbf{V}_1$ onto $\mathbf{V}_2$ (or vice versa). Note that the magnitude of a vector $\mathbf{V}$ can be computed as:

$$\|\mathbf{V}\| = \sqrt{\mathbf{V} \cdot \mathbf{V}} \qquad (1.3)$$

as well as the expression in (1.1).

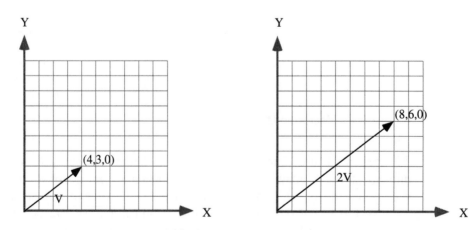

Figure 1.5   Scalar multiplication of a vector.

In 3D computer graphics, dot products are most useful when used in conjunction with the Law of Cosines. The Law of Cosines holds that for any two vectors $\mathbf{V}_1$ and $\mathbf{V}_2$:

$$\mathbf{V}_1 \cdot \mathbf{V}_2 = \|\,\mathbf{V}_1\,\|\|\,\mathbf{V}_2\,\|\cos\theta \tag{1.4}$$

where θ is the smallest angle between the two vectors. The Law of Cosines is most useful when $\mathbf{V}_1$ and $\mathbf{V}_2$ are normalized (have length of 1). That way, the dot product is exactly equal to $\cos\theta$.

The last vector operation we will discuss is the cross product. Taking the cross product of two 3D vectors yields another vector that is perpendicular to the first two. There are two candidates for this vector; they point in opposite directions perpendicular to the plane defined by the first two vectors. The vector returned by the cross product is determined by the *right-hand rule*: if you curve the fingers of your right hand in the direction of the first vector toward the second, your thumb points in the direction of the vectors' cross product. The cross product is not commutative (that is, $\mathbf{A}\times\mathbf{B}\neq\mathbf{B}\times\mathbf{A}$). Rather, $\mathbf{A}\times\mathbf{B}=-\mathbf{B}\times\mathbf{A}$. Intuitively, this makes sense: if you switch the vectors' order, your fingers curve in the opposite direction and point the other way.

The three-dimensional cross product of two vectors $\mathbf{V}_1$ and $\mathbf{V}_2$ is as follows:

$$\mathbf{V}_1 \times \mathbf{V}_2 = \left(\mathbf{V}_1.y\mathbf{V}_2.z - \mathbf{V}_1.z\mathbf{V}_2.y,\,\mathbf{V}_1.z\mathbf{V}_2.x - \mathbf{V}_1.x\mathbf{V}_2.z,\,\mathbf{V}_1.x\mathbf{V}_2.y - \mathbf{V}_1.y\mathbf{V}_2.x\right) \tag{1.5}$$

The cross product is often used to find a normal to a plane. For example, the cross product is used when computing the normal to a polygon (see Section 4.6).

Table 1.1 summarizes vector operations.

Implementation

Support for 3D vectors is encapsulated in the class `Vector3D` and implemented in `vector.h` and `vector.cpp`. The `Vector3D` class contains three 32-bit floating-point numbers named x, y, and z. The members of `Vector3D` are **public**, since many different classes need direct access to them.

Many operators are overloaded for `Vector3D`, including unary + and − and binary + and −. The ∗ and / operators are overloaded to perform memberwise multiplication and division, as well as scalar multiplication and division. Many of these binary operators are implemented in terms of their corresponding assignment operators (+=, −=, ∗=, and /= have all been overloaded for scalar and vector operations). The [ ] operator is overloaded to access the x, y, and z coordinates when indices of 0, 1, or 2 are given. The << operator has been overloaded so that `Vectors` can be written to `iostream` classes.

Operation	Example	Result	How Implemented
Addition	$\mathbf{v}_1 + \mathbf{v}_2$	Vector	Add corresponding elements.
Subtraction	$\mathbf{v}_1 + \mathbf{v}_2$	Vector	Subtract corresponding elements.
Multiplication	$\mathbf{v}_1 * \mathbf{v}_2$	Vector	Multiply corresponding elements.
Division	$\mathbf{v}_1 / \mathbf{v}_2$	Vector	Divide corresponding elements.
Multiplication	$s * \mathbf{v}$	Vector	Multiply elements of $\mathbf{v}$ by s.
Division	$\mathbf{v} / s$	Vector	Divide elements of $\mathbf{v}$ by s.
Magnitude	Magnitude($\mathbf{v}$)	Scalar	$\sqrt{x^2 + y^2 + z^2}$
Dot product	DotProd($\mathbf{v}_1, \mathbf{v}_2$)	Scalar	$\mathbf{v}_1.x * \mathbf{v}_2.x + \mathbf{v}_1.y * \mathbf{v}_2.y + \mathbf{v}_1.z * \mathbf{v}_2.z$
Cross product	CrossProd($\mathbf{v}_1, \mathbf{v}_2$)	Vector	See description on pg. xxx.`
Normalization	Normalize($\mathbf{v}$)	Vector	Divide $\mathbf{v}$ by its magnitude.
Cosine of angle between two vectors	$\dfrac{\mathbf{V}_1 \cdot \mathbf{V}_2}{\|\mathbf{V}_1\|\|\mathbf{V}_2\|}$	Scalar	Take the dot product and divide by the product of the vectors' magnitudes. If both vectors have magnitudes of 1, the division is not needed.
Angle between two vectors	$\cos^{-1}\left(\dfrac{\mathbf{V}_1 \cdot \mathbf{V}_2}{\|\mathbf{V}_1\|\|\mathbf{V}_2\|}\right)$	Scalar	Take the arccosine of the above.

Table 1.1 Vector Operations

There are a number of **friend** functions of `Vector3D` as well. `Magnitude` returns the magnitude of a vector. `Normalize` takes a vector and returns a unit vector with the same direction. `DotProd` and `CrossProd` compute the dot product and cross product of two vectors, respectively.

A number of nonstandard but useful vector operations have been implemented in OORT. The `Minimize` function, for example, replaces each component of a vector with the corresponding component of candidate if the candidate component is smaller. An analogous `Maximize` function takes the maximum of corresponding components. `Minimize` and `Maximize` are useful for finding the bounding box of a set of points. They are called frequently in `Object3D::BBox` implementations, which compute the bounding boxes of various primitives.

The last function in `Vector3D` that deserves mention is `Vector3D::ExtractVerts`. `Vector3D::ExtractVerts` is declared as follows:

```
void ExtractVerts(float *px, float *py, int which)
                  const;
```

The `which` parameter of this function should be 0, 1, or 2. If it is 0, the Y and Z components of the vector are written to `px` and `py`. If it is 1, the X and Z components are written. Otherwise, the X and Y components are written. By ignoring one of the vector coordinates, this operation implements an oblique parallel projection of the vector onto one of the coordinate planes. A number of applications for this function are found in OORT, especially in the polygon intersection routine.

```
// ====================================================================
// vector.h
//      Header file for Vector3D class in OORT.
//
//            The Object-Oriented Ray Tracer (OORT)
//            Copyright (C) 1993 by Nicholas Wilt.
//
// This software product may be freely copied and distributed in
// unmodified form but may not be sold.  A nominal distribution
// fee may be charged for media and handling by freeware and
// shareware distributors.  The software product may not be
// included in whole or in part into any commercial package
// without the express written consent of the author.
//
// This software product is provided as is without warranty of
// any kind, express or implied, including but not limited to
// the implied warranties of merchantability and fitness for a
// particular purpose.  The author assumes no liability for any
// alleged or actual damages arising from the use of this
// software.  The author is under no obligation to provide
// service, corrections or upgrades to the software.
//
// --------------------------------------------------------------
//
// Please contact me with questions, comments, suggestions or
// other input about OORT.  My Compuserve account number is
// [75210,2455] (Internet sites can reach me at
// 75210.2455@compuserve.com).
//                                     --Nicholas Wilt
// ====================================================================
```

Listing 1.2 `vector.h`

```
#ifndef __VECTOR__

#define __VECTOR__

// Forward-declare some other classes.
class Matrix;
class ostream;

class Vector3D {

public:
    float x, y, z;

    // constructors
    Vector3D() { }
    Vector3D(float X, float Y, float Z) { x = X; y = Y; z = Z; }
    Vector3D(float X) { x = y = z = X; }
    Vector3D(const Vector3D& v) { x = v.x; y = v.y; z = v.z; }

    // Functions to get at the vector components
    float& operator[] (int inx) {
        if (inx == 0)        return x;
        else if (inx == 1) return y;
        else                          return z;
    }
    const float& operator[] (int inx) const {
        if (inx == 0)        return x;
        else if (inx == 1) return y;
        else                          return z;
    }
    void ExtractVerts(float *px, float *py, int which) const;

    friend float Magnitude(const Vector3D& v);
    friend Vector3D Normalize(const Vector3D& A);

    // Rotate a normal vector.
    friend Vector3D PlaneRotate(const Matrix&, const Vector3D&);

    // Unary operators
    Vector3D operator+ () const;
    Vector3D operator- () const;
```

Listing 1.2 vector.h *(continued)*

```
    // Assignment operators
    Vector3D& operator+= (const Vector3D& A);
    Vector3D& operator-= (const Vector3D& A);
    Vector3D& operator*= (const Vector3D& A);
    Vector3D& operator*= (float A);
    Vector3D& operator/= (float A);

    // Binary operators
    friend Vector3D operator+ (const Vector3D& A, const Vector3D& B);
    friend Vector3D operator- (const Vector3D& A, const Vector3D& B);
    friend Vector3D operator* (const Vector3D& A, const Vector3D& B);
    friend Vector3D operator* (const Vector3D& A, float B);
    friend Vector3D operator* (float A, const Vector3D& B);
    friend Vector3D operator* (const Matrix&, const Vector3D&);
    friend Vector3D operator/ (const Vector3D& A, const Vector3D& B);

    friend int operator< (const Vector3D& A, const Vector3D& B);

    friend Vector3D operator/ (const Vector3D& A, float B);
    friend int operator== (const Vector3D& A, const Vector3D& B);
    friend float DotProd(const Vector3D& A, const Vector3D& B);
    friend Vector3D CrossProd (const Vector3D& A, const Vector3D& B);

    friend ostream& operator<< (const ostream& s, const Vector3D& A);

    friend void Minimize(Vector3D& min, const Vector3D& Candidate);
    friend void Maximize(Vector3D& max, const Vector3D& Candidate);
};

class RGBColor : public Vector3D {
public:
    RGBColor() { }
    RGBColor(float X, float Y, float Z) { x = X; y = Y; z = Z; }
    RGBColor(float X) { x = y = z = X; }
    RGBColor(const Vector3D& v) { x = v.x; y = v.y; z = v.z; }
    friend RGBColor NormalizeColor(const RGBColor& x);
};

inline float Magnitude(const Vector3D& v)
{
```

Listing 1.2 `vector.h` *(continued)*

```
    return sqrt(v.x*v.x + v.y*v.y + v.z*v.z);
}

inline Vector3D Normalize(const Vector3D& A)
{
    return A / Magnitude(A);
}

inline float DotProd (const Vector3D& A, const Vector3D& B)
{
    return A.x * B.x + A.y * B.y + A.z * B.z;
}

inline Vector3D Vector3D::operator+ () const
{
    return *this;
}

inline Vector3D Vector3D::operator- () const
{
    return Vector3D(-x, -y, -z);
}

inline Vector3D& Vector3D::operator+= (const Vector3D& A)
{
    x += A.x;   y += A.y;   z += A.z;
    return *this;
}

inline Vector3D& Vector3D::operator-= (const Vector3D& A)
{
    x -= A.x;   y -= A.y;   z -= A.z;
    return *this;
}

inline Vector3D& Vector3D::operator*= (float A)
{
    x *= A;   y *= A;   z *= A;
    return *this;
}
```

Listing 1.2 `vector.h` *(continued)*

```
inline Vector3D& Vector3D::operator/= (float A)
{
   x /= A;   y /= A;   z /= A;
   return *this;
}

inline Vector3D& Vector3D::operator*= (const Vector3D& A)
{
   x *= A.x;   y *= A.y;   z *= A.z;
   return *this;
}

inline Vector3D operator+ (const Vector3D& A, const Vector3D& B)
{
   return Vector3D(A.x + B.x, A.y + B.y, A.z + B.z);
}

inline Vector3D operator- (const Vector3D& A, const Vector3D& B)
{
   return Vector3D(A.x - B.x, A.y - B.y, A.z - B.z);
}

inline Vector3D operator* (const Vector3D& A, const Vector3D& B)
{
   return Vector3D(A.x * B.x, A.y * B.y, A.z * B.z);
}

inline Vector3D operator* (const Vector3D& A, float B)
{
   return Vector3D(A.x * B, A.y * B, A.z * B);
}

inline Vector3D operator* (float A, const Vector3D& B)
{
   return B * A;
}

inline Vector3D operator/ (const Vector3D& A, const Vector3D& B)
{
   return Vector3D(A.x / B.x, A.y / B.y, A.z / B.z);
}
```

Listing 1.2   `vector.h` *(continued)*

```
inline Vector3D operator/ (const Vector3D& A, float B)
{
    return Vector3D(A.x / B, A.y / B, A.z / B);
}

inline int operator< (const Vector3D& A, const Vector3D& B)
{
    return A.x < B.x && A.y < B.y && A.z < B.z;
}

// Might replace floating-point == with comparisons of
// magnitudes, if needed.
inline int operator== (const Vector3D& A, const Vector3D& B)
{
    return (A.x == B.x) && (A.y == B.y) && (A.z == B.z);
}

inline Vector3D CrossProd (const Vector3D& A, const Vector3D& B)
{
    return Vector3D(A.y * B.z - A.z * B.y,
                    A.z * B.x - A.x * B.z,
                    A.x * B.y - A.y * B.x);
}

// Compute a normalized version of a color (same hue, but less
   bright).
inline RGBColor NormalizeColor(const RGBColor& clr)
{
    if (clr.x > 1.0 || clr.y > 1.0 || clr.z > 1.0) {
        float max = clr.x;
        if (clr.y > max)
            max = clr.y;
        if (clr.z > max)
            max = clr.z;
        if (max != 0.0)
            return clr / max;
    }
    return clr;
}

#endif
```

Listing 1.2 `vector.h` *(continued)*

```
// =====================================================================
// vector.cpp
//          Vector3D support routines for OORT.
//
//                    The Object-Oriented Ray Tracer (OORT)
//                    Copyright (C) 1993 by Nicholas Wilt.
//
// This software product may be freely copied and distributed in
// unmodified form but may not be sold.  A nominal distribution
// fee may be charged for media and handling by freeware and
// shareware distributors.  The software product may not be
// included in whole or in part into any commercial package
// without the express written consent of the author.
//
// This software product is provided as is without warranty of
// any kind, express or implied, including but not limited to
// the implied warranties of merchantability and fitness for a
// particular purpose.  The author assumes no liability for any
// alleged or actual damages arising from the use of this
// software.  The author is under no obligation to provide
// service, corrections or upgrades to the software.
//
// -----------------------------------------------------------
//
// Please contact me with questions, comments, suggestions or
// other input about OORT.  My Compuserve account number is
// [75210,2455] (Internet sites can reach me at
// 75210.2455@compuserve.com).
//                                        --Nicholas Wilt
// =====================================================================

#include <iostream.h>
#include <math.h>
#include <stdio.h>
#include "matrix.h"
#include "vector.h"

// Overload << operator for C++-style output
```

Listing 1.3 `vector.cpp`

```
ostream&
operator<< (const ostream& s, const Vector3D& A)
{
      return s << "(" << A.x << ", " << A.y << ", " << A.z << ")";
}


// Given min a vector to minimize and a candidate vector, replace
// elements of min whose corresponding elements in Candidate are
// smaller.  This function is used for finding objects' bounds,
// among other things.
void
Minimize(Vector3D& min, const Vector3D& Candidate)
{
      if (Candidate.x < min.x)
            min.x = Candidate.x;
      if (Candidate.y < min.y)
            min.y = Candidate.y;
      if (Candidate.z < min.z)
            min.z = Candidate.z;
}


// Given min a vector to minimize and a candidate vector, replace
// elements of min whose corresponding elements in Candidate are
// larger.  This function is used for finding objects' bounds,
// among other things.
void
Maximize(Vector3D& max, const Vector3D& Candidate)
{
      if (Candidate.x > max.x)
            max.x = Candidate.x;
      if (Candidate.y > max.y)
            max.y = Candidate.y;
      if (Candidate.z > max.z)
            max.z = Candidate.z;
}


// Project the vector onto the YZ, XZ, or XY plane depending on which.
// which          Coordinate plane to project onto
```

Listing 1.3 `vector.cpp` *(continued)*

```
// 0                    YZ
// 1                    XZ
// 2                    XY
// This function is used by the polygon intersection code.

void
Vector3D::ExtractVerts(float *px, float *py, int which) const
{
       switch (which) {
             case 0:
                     *px = y;
                     *py = z;
                     break;
             case 1:
                     *px = x;
                     *py = z;
                     break;
             case 2:
                     *px = x;
                     *py = y;
                     break;
       }
}
```

Listing 1.3 `vector.cpp` *(continued)*

1.6 Transformations

Transformations are a common need in computer graphics. Transformations are ways to change objects systematically, moving, rotating, stretching, or compressing them. They can be thought of in two ways. They can be thought of as changing the object transformed, or changing the coordinate system the object is in. We will discuss both ways of thinking.

This section is intended as an introduction to the *idea* of transformations. Implementation will be discussed later in this chapter.

1.6.1 Translation

Translation is moving an object without changing its attitude or size. (See Figure 1.6.)

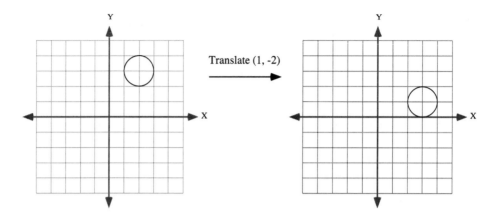

Figure 1.6 Translation.

Translation can be thought of either as moving the object or as moving the coordinate system that the object is in. Although you may find the first way of thinking more intuitive, sometimes it makes much more sense to think of transformations affecting the coordinate system when every object in the coordinate system is going to get transformed in the same way. For example, it is common to apply a *view transform* to the objects in the world before rendering. The view transform changes coordinate systems so that the "eye" is at the origin looking down the Z axis. That way, the rendering code does not need to worry about taking different eye locations and directions into account. After the view transform has been applied to every object in the scene, the eye location and direction are always the same no matter where the eye started out.

1.6.2 Scaling

Scaling is changing the size of an object in one or more dimensions. (See Figure 1.7.) Like translation, scaling can also be thought of as compressing or expanding the coordinate system rather than the object.

Note that scaling occurs with respect to the origin. A circle centered about the origin will not move after scaling; however, a circle centered at (x_0, y_0) will be centered at $(s_x x_0, s_y y_0)$ after scaling by (s_x, s_y).

1.6.3 Rotation

An object is rotated by a certain angle about an axis; this can be either a coordinate axis or an axis defined in some other way. Rotations always occur about the

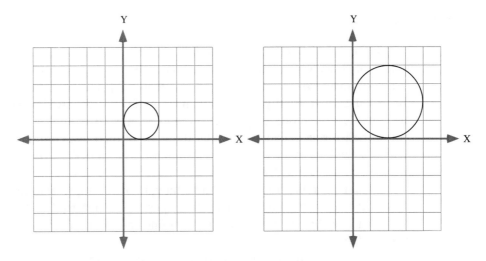

Scaling by 2 in X and Y. Note that the scaling occurs with respect to the origin.

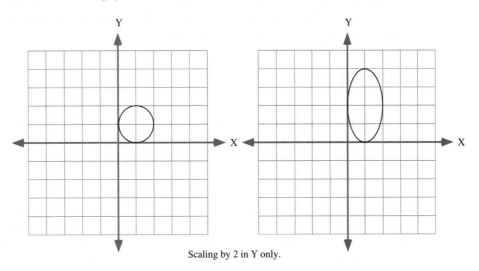

Scaling by 2 in Y only.

Figure 1.7 Scaling.

origin of the coordinate axes, so they are frequently combined with translations to move the coordinate axes to the point that must be rotated around. See Section 1.6.5 for a discussion of *concatenation*, the operation where transformations are applied in sequence.

1.6.4 Projection

Projections are defined by Foley, van Dam, Feiner, and Hughes as transformations that "transform points in a coordinate system of dimension n into points in a coordinate system of dimension less than n." [FOLE90] In the context of 3D graphics, that usually means transforming 3D points into 2D points. There are countless methods of projection, and interested readers are referred to Foley et al. for an exhaustive discussion. One of the most common projection methods (and the only one directly supported in OORT) is *oblique parallel projection* (see Figure 1.8).

Oblique parallel projection can be thought of as simply ignoring one coordinate. It is easy to visualize why this operation is referred to as "parallel": every point on the object falls in a parallel line onto the plane the object is being projected onto.

Perspective projection is often used by polygon rendering systems to project the 3D polygons in the scene onto a two-dimensional analog of the computer screen. Ray tracing performs the same operation in a different way, so perspective projections are not supported by OORT.

1.6.5 Concatenation

To get the expected results, it is often necessary to *concatenate* transformations, or apply more than one in sequence. Take, for example, a square that you would like to rotate by 45° (see Figure 1.9).

But just rotating the square about the axis by 45° will give an unexpected result (see Figure 1.10).

This is because the rotation is about the origin, not the object itself. To rotate the object about a certain point, you must translate the coordinate system to that point, perform the rotation, then translate the coordinate system back to where it was. This three-step operation will give the result shown in Figure 1.11.

The three-step operation to rotate the square in Figure 1.11 can really be thought of as a transformation in its own right. It is composed of simpler transformations concatenated together. The operation is called *concatenation* rather than *combination* because the order of transformations is important. Translating an object, then rotating it, almost always has a different result than rotating the object, then translating it (why?).

Fortunately, there is a compact and efficient way to deal with not only translation, rotation, and scaling, but the transformations that can be constructed by concatenating transformations.

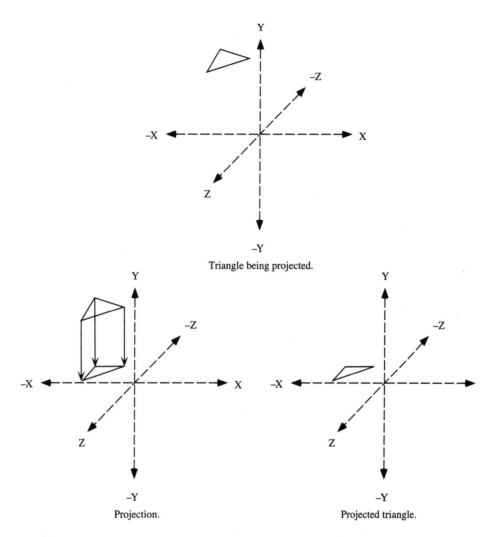

Figure 1.8 Oblique parallel projection onto the XZ plane (ignores Y coordinate).

1.7 Transformation Matrices

Computer graphicists have borrowed a tool from linear algebra to describe compactly all different types of transformation. This is the 4×4 transformation matrix. Matrices, like vectors, are a compact way to deal with several numbers as a unit. The numbers are laid out in rows and columns. By convention, the

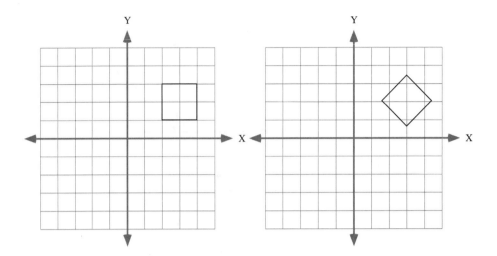

Figure 1.9 Desired rotation by 45˚.

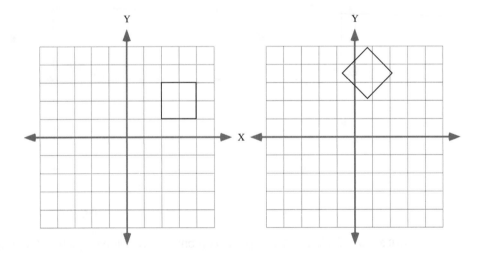

Figure 1.10 Result if the square is simply rotated.

number of rows in the matrix is given before the number of columns. Here is a 2×3 matrix:

$$\begin{bmatrix} 7 & 2 & 9 \\ 5 & 8 & 3 \end{bmatrix}$$

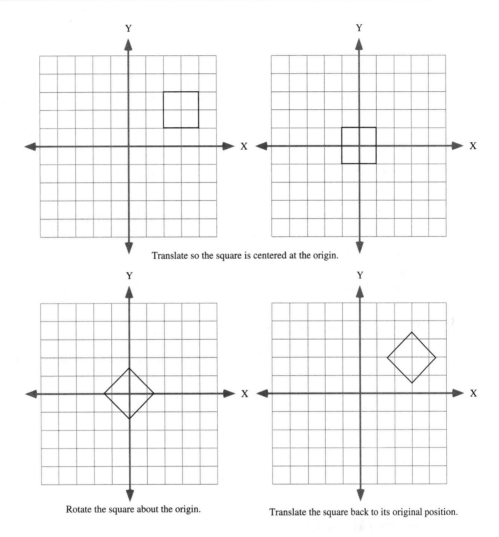

Figure 1.11 Concatenation.

Vectors can be thought of as matrices. They are matrices with one row (a *row vector*) or one column (a *column vector*).

1.7.1 Matrix Multiplication

The most important matrix operation is matrix multiplication. Matrix multiplication consists of multiplying and summing row and column elements of the two matrices. The number of columns in the right-hand matrix must be the same as the number of rows in the left-hand matrix. Multiplying an $M \times N$ matrix by an $N \times P$ matrix results in an $M \times P$ matrix.

Matrix multiplication works like this: for each row of the left matrix and each column of the right matrix, corresponding elements of each row and column are multiplied together and summed. Here, a 2×3 matrix is multiplied by a 3×2 matrix:

$$\begin{bmatrix} 5 & 2 & 4 \\ 7 & 8 & 5 \end{bmatrix} \begin{bmatrix} 1 & 3 \\ 9 & 8 \\ 3 & 1 \end{bmatrix} = \begin{bmatrix} 5 \cdot 1 + 2 \cdot 9 + 4 \cdot 3 & 5 \cdot 3 + 2 \cdot 8 + 4 \cdot 1 \\ 7 \cdot 1 + 8 \cdot 9 + 5 \cdot 3 & 7 \cdot 3 + 8 \cdot 8 + 5 \cdot 1 \end{bmatrix} = \begin{bmatrix} 43 & 35 \\ 94 & 90 \end{bmatrix}$$

Matrix multiplication is *not* commutative: $\mathbf{M_1 M_2} \neq \mathbf{M_2 M_1}$. Because of this, the terminology for matrix multiplication is slightly different than for commutative multiplication operations. If $\mathbf{M_1}$ is multiplied by $\mathbf{M_2}$ as follows: $\mathbf{M_1 M_2}$, then $\mathbf{M_2}$ is said to be *premultiplied* by $\mathbf{M_1}$. It is equally correct to say that $\mathbf{M_1}$ is *postmultiplied* by $\mathbf{M_2}$. It may be ambiguous, however, to say that "$\mathbf{M_1}$ is multiplied by $\mathbf{M_2}$."

1.7.2 Matrix Transposition

Transposing a matrix consists of swapping the rows and columns. Transposing an $M \times N$ matrix results in an $N \times M$ matrix. Matrix transposition is denoted by a superscript $\mathbf{T}$ after the matrix being transposed.

Here is a 2×3 matrix transposed:

$$\begin{bmatrix} 1 & 2 & 3 \\ 4 & 5 & 6 \end{bmatrix}^{\mathbf{T}} = \begin{bmatrix} 1 & 4 \\ 2 & 5 \\ 3 & 6 \end{bmatrix}$$

Square Matrices

Most of the matrices we deal with in ray tracing are *square*: they have the same number of rows and columns. In fact, most of the matrices we deal with are 4×4 matrices. The matrix properties discussed in the following section concentrate on square matrices.

1.7.3 Matrix Identity

The identity matrix is a square matrix with all elements 0 except the elements down the center diagonal, which contain 1. This matrix, when pre- or postmultiplied by another matrix, yields the same matrix it was multiplied by. Here is the 2×2 identity matrix:

$$\begin{bmatrix} 1 & 0 \\ 0 & 1 \end{bmatrix}$$

1.7.4 Matrix Inversion

A square matrix may have an inverse. A matrix, when multiplied by its inverse, yields the identity matrix. Not all square matrices have inverses.

One popular method for matrix inversion is called Gaussian elimination. This method consists of performing row operations in order to transform the matrix into an identity matrix. Performing the same row operations on an identity matrix will turn it into the inverse of the original matrix. In practice, the row operations are performed on both matrices at once.

Valid row operations are as follows:

1. Multiply a row by a nonzero constant.

2. Swap two rows.

3. Multiply a row by a nonzero constant and add it to another row.

If it is not possible to transform the original matrix into the identity matrix using these row operations, the matrix has no inverse. Below, the 2×2 matrix

$$\begin{bmatrix} 1 & 1 \\ 1 & 0 \end{bmatrix}$$

is inverted by placing the matrix on the left and the identity matrix on the right. The row operations performed on the left-hand matrix are also performed on the right-hand matrix. When the left-hand matrix is the identity matrix, the matrix on the right is the inverse of the original left-hand matrix. This is a common way to invert matrices by hand using Gaussian elimination.

$$\left[\begin{array}{cc|cc} 1 & 1 & 1 & 0 \\ 1 & 0 & 0 & 1 \end{array}\right]$$

First, the rows of the matrices are exchanged, yielding the following:

$$\left[\begin{array}{cc|cc} 1 & 0 & 0 & 1 \\ 1 & 1 & 1 & 0 \end{array}\right]$$

Now the upper row of the left-hand matrix is the same as the upper row of the identity matrix. We subtract the top row from the bottom row to arrive at the inverse matrix. (This is the same as multiplying the top row by a constant (−1) and adding it to the bottom row).

$$\left[\begin{array}{cc|cc} 1 & 0 & 0 & 1 \\ 0 & 1 & 1 & -1 \end{array}\right]$$

Note that pre- or postmultiplying the original matrix by its inverse yields the identity matrix.

1.7.5   Using Matrices to Transform Vectors

A vector may be transformed by premultiplying the column vector by a 4×4 transformation matrix, as follows. (Note: Many earlier graphics texts treat vectors as row vectors and transform them by postmultiplying by the matrix. If this is the case, the transformation matrices are transposed with respect to the matrices used in this book.)

$$\mathbf{V'} = \mathbf{MV} \tag{1.6}$$

In the above equation, $\mathbf{V'}$ and $\mathbf{V}$ are expressed in homogeneous coordinates. The homogeneous representation of a three-dimensional vector includes the three elements X, Y, and Z, plus a fourth element, W. A three-dimensional vector is converted to homogeneous coordinates by setting W to 1. To convert a homogeneous 3D vector back to a canonical 3D vector, divide X, Y, and Z by W.

Let's take an example. The matrix to scale by 2 in X, Y, and Z is as follows:

$$\begin{bmatrix} 2 & 0 & 0 & 0 \\ 0 & 2 & 0 & 0 \\ 0 & 0 & 2 & 0 \\ 0 & 0 & 0 & 1 \end{bmatrix}$$

Postmultiplying this matrix by the vector $\begin{bmatrix} 5 & 8 & 4 & 1 \end{bmatrix}^T$ results in the vector $\begin{bmatrix} 10 & 16 & 8 & 1 \end{bmatrix}^T$, as expected:

$$\begin{bmatrix} 2 & 0 & 0 & 0 \\ 0 & 2 & 0 & 0 \\ 0 & 0 & 2 & 0 \\ 0 & 0 & 0 & 1 \end{bmatrix} \begin{bmatrix} 5 \\ 8 \\ 4 \\ 1 \end{bmatrix} = \begin{bmatrix} 10 \\ 16 \\ 8 \\ 1 \end{bmatrix}$$

A more complicated example is rotation. The matrix for rotation about the Z axis is as follows:

$$R_z(\theta) = \begin{bmatrix} \cos\theta & -\sin\theta & 0 & 0 \\ \sin\theta & \cos\theta & 0 & 0 \\ 0 & 0 & 1 & 0 \\ 0 & 0 & 0 & 1 \end{bmatrix}$$

where is the angle to rotate by. Thus, the matrix for $=30°$ is as follows:

$$\begin{bmatrix} 0.8660 & -0.5 & 0 & 0 \\ 0.5 & 0.8660 & 0 & 0 \\ 0 & 0 & 1 & 0 \\ 0 & 0 & 0 & 1 \end{bmatrix}$$

Postmultiplying this matrix by the vector $\begin{bmatrix} 5 & 0 & 0 & 1 \end{bmatrix}^T$ yields $(5, 0, 0)$ rotated by 30°, as follows:

$$\begin{bmatrix} 0.8660 & -0.5 & 0 & 0 \\ 0.5 & 0.8660 & 0 & 0 \\ 0 & 0 & 1 & 0 \\ 0 & 0 & 0 & 1 \end{bmatrix} \begin{bmatrix} 5 \\ 0 \\ 0 \\ 1 \end{bmatrix} = \begin{bmatrix} 4.33 \\ 2.5 \\ 0 \\ 1 \end{bmatrix}$$

A graphical depiction of this process is shown in Figure 1.12.

Homogeneous coordinates are commonly used in projection-based rendering systems that use polygons. Since ray tracing does not use perspective projections for rendering, homogeneous coordinates are not used.

Identity

$$I = \begin{bmatrix} 1 & 0 & 0 & 0 \\ 0 & 1 & 0 & 0 \\ 0 & 0 & 1 & 0 \\ 0 & 0 & 0 & 1 \end{bmatrix} \qquad (1.8)$$

This matrix does not affect the vector. The function `IdentityMatrix` generates this matrix.

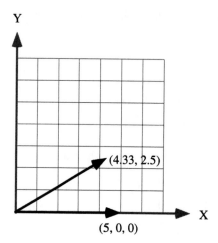

Figure 1.12 Vector rotated.

Translation

$$T(t_x, t_y, t_z) = \begin{bmatrix} 1 & 0 & 0 & t_x \\ 0 & 1 & 0 & t_y \\ 0 & 0 & 1 & t_z \\ 0 & 0 & 0 & 1 \end{bmatrix} \qquad (1.9)$$

This matrix translates the vector by the specified amounts in X, Y, and Z. Postmultiplying a vector **V** by **T**(t_x, t_y, t_z) yields the vector **V** + (t_x, t_y, t_z). The function `TranslationMatrix` generates this matrix.

Rotation

Rotation matrices vary with the axis of rotation. To rotate about the X axis, the matrix is as follows:

$$R_x(\theta) = \begin{bmatrix} 1 & 0 & 0 & 0 \\ 0 & \cos\theta & -\sin\theta & 0 \\ 0 & \sin\theta & \cos\theta & 0 \\ 0 & 0 & 0 & 1 \end{bmatrix} \qquad (1.10)$$

where is the angle to rotate by. The function `RotationXMatrix` generates this matrix.

To rotate about the Y axis, the matrix is as follows:

$$R_y(\theta) = \begin{bmatrix} \cos\theta & 0 & \sin\theta & 0 \\ 0 & 1 & 0 & 0 \\ -\sin\theta & 0 & \cos\theta & 0 \\ 0 & 0 & 0 & 1 \end{bmatrix}$$
(1.11)

The function `RotationYMatrix` generates this matrix.
To rotate about the Z axis, the matrix is as follows:

$$\begin{bmatrix} \cos\theta & -\sin\theta & 0 & 0 \\ \sin\theta & \cos\theta & 0 & 0 \\ 0 & 0 & 1 & 0 \\ 0 & 0 & 0 & 1 \end{bmatrix}$$
(1.12)

The function `RotationZMatrix` generates this matrix.
To rotate about an arbitrary axis, given by a unit vector (x, y, z), the matrix is as follows:

$$R_{axis}(x,y,z) = \begin{bmatrix} x^2 + \cos\theta(1-x^2) & xy(1-\cos\theta) - z\sin\theta & xz(1-\cos\theta) + y\sin\theta & 0 \\ xy(1-\cos\theta) + z\sin\theta & y^2 + \cos\theta(1-y^2) & yz(1-\cos\theta) - x\sin\theta & 0 \\ xz(1-\cos\theta) - y\sin\theta & yz(1-\cos\theta) + x\sin\theta & z^2 + \cos\theta(1-z^2) & 0 \\ 0 & 0 & 0 & 1 \end{bmatrix}$$
(1.13)

The function `RotationAxisMatrix` generates this matrix.
Foley et al. [FOLE90] point out some characteristics that all rotation matrices share. The upper left-hand 3×3 submatrix of all rotation matrices has the following characteristics:

1. Each row and column is a unit vector (has magnitude of 1).

2. Each row is perpendicular to the other two rows (this also pertains to the columns).

3. The 3×3 submatrix has a determinant of 1.

You can verify these properties for the matrices provided with OORT. They are especially useful when developing new rotation matrices.

Scaling

$$S(s_x, s_y, s_z) = \begin{bmatrix} s_x & 0 & 0 & 0 \\ 0 & s_y & 0 & 0 \\ 0 & 0 & s_z & 0 \\ 0 & 0 & 0 & 1 \end{bmatrix}$$

(1.14)

where s_x, sy, and s_z are the X, Y, and Z scale factors. The function ScaleMatrix generates this matrix.

1.7.6 Implementation

The Matrix class (defined in matrix.h and implemented in matrix.cpp) encapsulates a 4×4 transformation matrix as described above. The fundamental operations supported are member-wise addition and subtraction, matrix multiplication, and multiplication of a vector by a matrix.

The routine that multiplies Vector3D by Matrix converts the Vector3D to homogeneous coordinates before the multiplication. That is, they convert $[X \ Y \ Z]$ to $[X \ Y \ Z \ 1]$. After the Vector3D is transformed, it is converted back to a 3-tuple by dividing by the W coordinate of the homogeneous representation. All these conversions are less efficient than sticking with one representation, but in practice they do not impact performance because ray tracers do not spend much time transforming vectors.

```
// ======================================================================
// matrix.h
//      Header file for Matrix class in OORT.
//
//
//              The Object-Oriented Ray Tracer (OORT)
//              Copyright (C) 1993 by Nicholas Wilt.
//
// This software product may be freely copied and distributed in
// unmodified form but may not be sold.  A nominal distribution
// fee may be charged for media and handling by freeware and
// shareware distributors.  The software product may not be
// included in whole or in part into any commercial package
// without the express written consent of the author.
//
```

Listing 1.4 matrix.h

```
// This software product is provided as is without warranty of
// any kind, express or implied, including but not limited to
// the implied warranties of merchantability and fitness for a
// particular purpose.  The author assumes no liability for any
// alleged or actual damages arising from the use of this
// software.  The author is under no obligation to provide
// service, corrections or upgrades to the software.
//
// -----------------------------------------------------------
//
// Please contact me with questions, comments, suggestions or
// other input about OORT.  My Compuserve account number is
// [75210,2455] (Internet sites can reach me at
// 75210.2455@compuserve.com).
//                                          --Nicholas Wilt
// ===================================================================

#ifndef __MATRIX__

#define __MATRIX__

// Forward-declare some other classes
class Vector3D;
class ostream;

class Matrix {

public:
    float x[4][4];

    Matrix() { }

    // Assignment operators
    Matrix& operator+= (const Matrix& A);        // add-to
    Matrix& operator-= (const Matrix& A);        // subtract-from
    Matrix& operator*= (const Matrix& A);        // multiply by matrix
    Matrix& operator*= (float A);                // scale by scalar
    // Fundamental operations
    void Invert();                               // Invert the matrix
    void Transpose();                            // Transpose the matrix
    friend Matrix Invert(const Matrix& M);       // Invert a given matrix
```

Listing 1.4 `matrix.h` *(continued)*

```
    friend Matrix Transpose(const Matrix& M);   // Transpose a given matrix

    // Create various types of matrix.
    friend Matrix IdentityMatrix();
    friend Matrix ZeroMatrix();
    friend Matrix TranslationMatrix(const Vector3D& Location);
    friend Matrix RotationXMatrix(float Angle);
    friend Matrix RotationYMatrix(float Angle);
    friend Matrix RotationZMatrix(float Angle);
    friend Matrix RotationYPRMatrix(float Yaw, float Pitch, float
        Roll);
    friend Matrix RotationAxisMatrix(const Vector3D& axis, float
        Angle);

    friend Matrix ScaleMatrix(float X, float Y, float Z);
    friend Matrix GenRotation(const Vector3D& x, const Vector3D& y,
        const Vector3D& z);
    friend Matrix ViewMatrix(const Vector3D& LookAt, const Vector3D&
        Viewer, const Vector3D& Up);
    friend Matrix QuadricMatrix(float a, float b, float c, float d,
        float e, float f, float g, float h, float j, float k);
    friend Matrix MirrorX();
    friend Matrix MirrorY();
    friend Matrix MirrorZ();
    friend Matrix RotationOnly(const Matrix& x);

    // Binary operators
    friend Matrix operator+ (const Matrix& A, const Matrix& B);
    friend Matrix operator- (const Matrix& A, const Matrix& B);
    friend Matrix operator* (const Matrix& A, float B);
    friend Matrix operator* (const Matrix& A, const Matrix& B);
    friend class Vector3D operator* (const Matrix& M, const Vector3D&
        v);
    friend class Vector3D RotateOnly(const Matrix& M, const Vector3D&
        v);

    // Overloaded output operator.
    friend ostream& operator<< (ostream& s, const Matrix& M);
};

#endif
```

Listing 1.4   `matrix.h` *(continued)*

```
// ======================================================================
// matrix.cpp
//     Matrix routines for OORT.
//
//            The Object-Oriented Ray Tracer (OORT)
//            Copyright (C) 1993 by Nicholas Wilt.
//
// This software product may be freely copied and distributed in
// unmodified form but may not be sold.  A nominal distribution
// fee may be charged for media and handling by freeware and
// shareware distributors.  The software product may not be
// included in whole or in part into any commercial package
// without the express written consent of the author.
//
// This software product is provided as is without warranty of
// any kind, express or implied, including but not limited to
// the implied warranties of merchantability and fitness for a
// particular purpose.  The author assumes no liability for any
// alleged or actual damages arising from the use of this
// software.  The author is under no obligation to provide
// service, corrections or upgrades to the software.
//
// ----------------------------------------------------------
//
// Please contact me with questions, comments, suggestions or
// other input about OORT.  My Compuserve account number is
// [75210,2455] (Internet sites can reach me at
// 75210.2455@compuserve.com).
//                                       --Nicholas Wilt
// ======================================================================

#include <math.h>
#include <iomanip.h>
#include "matrix.h"
#include "vector.h"

// Invert the matrix using Gaussian elimination.  Not efficient,
// nor does it check for singular matrices.
void
Matrix::Invert()
{
    int i, j, k;
    Matrix Out = IdentityMatrix();

    for (i = 0; i < 4; i++) {
        if (x[i][i] != 1.0) {
```

Listing 1.5 matrix.cpp

```
              float divby = x[i][i];
              for (j = 0; j < 4; j++) {
                      Out.x[i][j] /= divby;
                      x[i][j] /= divby;
              }
       }
       for (j = 0; j < 4; j++) {
              if (j != i) {
                      if (x[j][i] != 0.0) {
                              float mulby = x[j][i];
                                for (k = 0; k < 4; k++) {
                                      x[j][k] -= mulby * x[i][k];
                                      Out.x[j][k] -= mulby * Out.x[i][k];
                                }
                      }
              }
       }
   }
   *this = Out;
}

// Invert the given matrix using the above inversion routine.
Matrix
Invert(const Matrix& M)
{
   Matrix InvertMe = M;
   InvertMe.Invert();
   return InvertMe;
}

// Transpose the matrix.
void
Matrix::Transpose()
{
   for (int i = 0; i < 4; i++)
      for (int j = i; j < 4; j++)
             if (i != j) {
                    float temp = x[i][j];
                    x[i][j] = x[j][i];
                    x[j][i] = temp;
             }
}

// Transpose the given matrix using the transpose routine above.
Matrix
```

Listing 1.5 `matrix.cpp` *(continued)*

```
Transpose(const Matrix& M)
{
   Matrix TransposeMe = M;
   TransposeMe.Transpose();
   return TransposeMe;
}

// Construct an identity matrix.
Matrix
IdentityMatrix()
{
   Matrix M;

   for (int i = 0; i < 4; i++)
      for (int j = 0; j < 4; j++)
            M.x[i][j] = (i == j) ? 1.0 : 0.0;
   return M;
}

// Construct a zero matrix.
Matrix
ZeroMatrix()
{
   Matrix M;
   for (int i = 0; i < 4; i++)
      for (int j = 0; j < 4; j++)
            M.x[i][j] = 0;
   return M;
}

// Construct a translation matrix given the location to translate to.
Matrix
TranslationMatrix(const Vector3D& Location)
{
   Matrix M = IdentityMatrix();
   M.x[3][0] = Location.x;
   M.x[3][1] = Location.y;
   M.x[3][2] = Location.z;
   return M;
}

// Construct a rotation matrix.  Rotates Angle radians about the
// X axis.
Matrix
RotationXMatrix(float Angle)
```

Listing 1.5 matrix.cpp *(continued)*

```
{
   Matrix M = IdentityMatrix();
   float Cosine = cos(Angle);
   float Sine = sin(Angle);
   M.x[1][1] = Cosine;
   M.x[2][1] = -Sine;
   M.x[1][2] = Sine;
   M.x[2][2] = Cosine;
   return M;
}

// Construct a rotation matrix.  Rotates Angle radians about the
// Y axis.
Matrix
RotationYMatrix(float Angle)
{
   Matrix M = IdentityMatrix();
   float Cosine = cos(Angle);
   float Sine = sin(Angle);
   M.x[0][0] = Cosine;
   M.x[2][0] = -Sine;
   M.x[0][2] = Sine;
   M.x[2][2] = Cosine;
   return M;
}

// Construct a rotation matrix.  Rotates Angle radians about the
// Z axis.
Matrix
RotationZMatrix(float Angle)
{
   Matrix M = IdentityMatrix();
   float Cosine = cos(Angle);
   float Sine = sin(Angle);
   M.x[0][0] = Cosine;
   M.x[1][0] = -Sine;
   M.x[0][1] = Sine;
   M.x[1][1] = Cosine;
   return M;
}

// Construct a yaw-pitch-roll rotation matrix.          Rotate Yaw
// radians about the XY axis, rotate Pitch radians in the
// plane defined by the Yaw rotation, and rotate Roll radians
// about the axis defined by the previous two angles.
```

Listing 1.5 matrix.cpp *(continued)*

```
Matrix
RotationYPRMatrix(float Yaw, float Pitch, float Roll)
{
    Matrix M;
    float ch = cos(Yaw);
    float sh = sin(Yaw);
    float cp = cos(Pitch);
    float sp = sin(Pitch);
    float cr = cos(Roll);
    float sr = sin(Roll);

    M.x[0][0] = ch*cr + sh*sp*sr;
    M.x[1][0] = -ch*sr + sh*sp*cr;
    M.x[2][0] = sh*cp;
    M.x[0][1] = sr*cp;
    M.x[1][1] = cr*cp;
    M.x[2][1] = -sp;
    M.x[0][2] = -sh*cr - ch*sp*sr;
    M.x[1][2] = sr*sh + ch*sp*cr;
    M.x[2][2] = ch*cp;
    for (int i = 0; i < 4; i++)
        M.x[3][i] = M.x[i][3] = 0;
    M.x[3][3] = 1;

    return M;
}

// Construct a rotation of a given angle about a given axis.
// Derived from Eric Haines's SPD (Standard Procedural
// Database).
Matrix
RotationAxisMatrix(const Vector3D& axis, float angle)
{
    Matrix M;
    double cosine = cos(angle);
    double sine = sin(angle);
    double one_minus_cosine = 1 - cosine;

    M.x[0][0] = axis.x * axis.x + (1.0 - axis.x * axis.x) * cosine;
    M.x[0][1] = axis.x * axis.y * one_minus_cosine + axis.z * sine;
    M.x[0][2] = axis.x * axis.z * one_minus_cosine - axis.y * sine;
    M.x[0][3] = 0;

    M.x[1][0] = axis.x * axis.y * one_minus_cosine - axis.z * sine;
    M.x[1][1] = axis.y * axis.y + (1.0 - axis.y * axis.y) * cosine;
```

Listing 1.5 `matrix.cpp` *(continued)*

```
   M.x[1][2] = axis.y * axis.z * one_minus_cosine + axis.x * sine;
   M.x[1][3] = 0;

   M.x[2][0] = axis.x * axis.z * one_minus_cosine + axis.y * sine;
   M.x[2][1] = axis.y * axis.z * one_minus_cosine - axis.x * sine;
   M.x[2][2] = axis.z * axis.z + (1.0 - axis.z * axis.z) * cosine;
   M.x[2][3] = 0;

   M.x[3][0] = 0;
   M.x[3][1] = 0;
   M.x[3][2] = 0;
   M.x[3][3] = 1;

   return M;
}


// Construct a scale matrix given the X, Y, and Z parameters
// to scale by.  To scale uniformly, let X==Y==Z.
Matrix
ScaleMatrix(float X, float Y, float Z)
{
   Matrix M = IdentityMatrix();

   M.x[0][0] = X;
   M.x[1][1] = Y;
   M.x[2][2] = Z;

   return M;
}

// Construct a rotation matrix that makes the x, y, z axes
// correspond to the vectors given.
Matrix
GenRotation(const Vector3D& x, const Vector3D& y, const Vector3D& z)
{
   Matrix M = IdentityMatrix();

   M.x[0][0] = x.x;
   M.x[1][0] = x.y;
   M.x[2][0] = x.z;
   M.x[0][1] = y.x;
   M.x[1][1] = y.y;
   M.x[2][1] = y.z;
   M.x[0][2] = z.x;
```

Listing 1.5 `matrix.cpp` *(continued)*

```
    M.x[1][2] = z.y;
    M.x[2][2] = z.z;

    return M;
}


// Construct a view matrix to rotate and translate the world
// given that the viewer is located at Viewer, looking at
// LookAt, and the up vector is UpL.  The transformation
// changes things around so the viewer is at the origin and
// looking down the -Z axis.
Matrix
ViewMatrix(const Vector3D& LookAt, const Vector3D& Viewer, const
    Vector3D& UpL)
{
    Matrix M = IdentityMatrix();
    Vector3D U, V, N;
    Vector3D Up = Normalize(UpL);

    N = Normalize(Viewer - LookAt);

    V = Up - LookAt;
    V -= N * DotProd(V, N);
    V = Normalize(V);
//  V = Normalize(Up - N * DotProd(Up, N));

    U = CrossProd(V, N);

    M.x[0][0] = U.x;
    M.x[1][0] = U.y;
    M.x[2][0] = U.z;
    M.x[0][1] = V.x;
    M.x[1][1] = V.y;
    M.x[2][1] = V.z;
    M.x[0][2] = N.x;
    M.x[1][2] = N.y;
    M.x[2][2] = N.z;

    M.x[3][0] = -DotProd(U, Viewer);
    M.x[3][1] = -DotProd(V, Viewer);
    M.x[3][2] = -DotProd(N, Viewer);

    return M;
}
```

Listing 1.5 `matrix.cpp` *(continued)*

```
// Construct a quadric matrix.          After Foley et al. pp. 528-529.
Matrix
QuadricMatrix(float a, float b, float c, float d, float e,
              float f, float g, float h, float j, float k)
{
    Matrix M;

    M.x[0][0] = a;  M.x[0][1] = d;  M.x[0][2] = f;  M.x[0][3] = g;
    M.x[1][0] = d;  M.x[1][1] = b;  M.x[1][2] = e;  M.x[1][3] = h;
    M.x[2][0] = f;  M.x[2][1] = e;  M.x[2][2] = c;  M.x[2][3] = j;
    M.x[3][0] = g;  M.x[3][1] = h;  M.x[3][2] = j;  M.x[3][3] = k;

    return M;
}

// Construct various "mirror" matrices, which flip coordinate
// signs in the various axes specified.
Matrix
MirrorX()
{
    Matrix M = IdentityMatrix();
    M.x[0][0] = -1;
    return M;
}

Matrix
MirrorY()
{
    Matrix M = IdentityMatrix();
    M.x[1][1] = -1;
    return M;
}

Matrix
MirrorZ()
{
    Matrix M = IdentityMatrix();
    M.x[2][2] = -1;
    return M;
}

Matrix
RotationOnly(const Matrix& x)
{
    Matrix M = x;
```

Listing 1.5 `matrix.cpp` *(continued)*

```
    M.x[3][0] = M.x[3][1] = M.x[3][2] = 0;
    return M;
}

// Add corresponding elements of the two matrices.
Matrix&
Matrix::operator+= (const Matrix& A)
{
    for (int i = 0; i < 4; i++)
        for (int j = 0; j < 4; j++)
            x[i][j] += A.x[i][j];
    return *this;
}

// Subtract corresponding elements of the matrices.
Matrix&
Matrix::operator-= (const Matrix& A)
{
    for (int i = 0; i < 4; i++)
        for (int j = 0; j < 4; j++)
            x[i][j] -= A.x[i][j];
    return *this;
}

// Scale each element of the matrix by A.
Matrix&
Matrix::operator*= (float A)
{
    for (int i = 0; i < 4; i++)
        for (int j = 0; j < 4; j++)
            x[i][j] *= A;
    return *this;
}

// Multiply two matrices.
Matrix&
Matrix::operator*= (const Matrix& A)
{
    Matrix ret = *this;

    for (int i = 0; i < 4; i++)
        for (int j = 0; j < 4; j++) {
            float subt = 0;
            for (int k = 0; k < 4; k++)
                subt += ret.x[i][k] * A.x[k][j];
```

Listing 1.5 `matrix.cpp` *(continued)*

```
            x[i][j] = subt;
        }
    return *this;
}


// Add corresponding elements of the matrices.
Matrix
operator+ (const Matrix& A, const Matrix& B)
{
    Matrix ret;

    for (int i = 0; i < 4; i++)
        for (int j = 0; j < 4; j++)
            ret.x[i][j] = A.x[i][j] + B.x[i][j];
    return ret;
}


// Subtract corresponding elements of the matrices.
Matrix
operator- (const Matrix& A, const Matrix& B)
{
    Matrix ret;

    for (int i = 0; i < 4; i++)
        for (int j = 0; j < 4; j++)
            ret.x[i][j] = A.x[i][j] - B.x[i][j];
    return ret;
}


// Multiply matrices.
Matrix
operator* (const Matrix& A, const Matrix& B)
{
    Matrix ret;

    for (int i = 0; i < 4; i++)
        for (int j = 0; j < 4; j++) {
            float subt = 0;
            for (int k = 0; k < 4; k++)
                subt += A.x[i][k] * B.x[k][j];
            ret.x[i][j] = subt;
        }
    return ret;
}
```

Listing 1.5 matrix.cpp *(continued)*

```cpp
// Transform a vector by a matrix.
Vector3D
operator* (const Matrix& M, const Vector3D& v)
{
    Vector3D ret;
    float denom;

    ret.x = v.x * M.x[0][0] + v.y * M.x[1][0] + v.z * M.x[2][0] +
        M.x[3][0];
    ret.y = v.x * M.x[0][1] + v.y * M.x[1][1] + v.z * M.x[2][1] +
        M.x[3][1];
    ret.z = v.x * M.x[0][2] + v.y * M.x[1][2] + v.z * M.x[2][2] +
        M.x[3][2];
    denom = M.x[0][3] + M.x[1][3] + M.x[2][3] + M.x[3][3];
    if (denom != 1.0)
        ret /= denom;
    return ret;
}

// Apply the rotation portion of a matrix to a vector.
Vector3D
RotateOnly(const Matrix& M, const Vector3D& v)
{
    Vector3D ret;
    float denom;

    ret.x = v.x * M.x[0][0] + v.y * M.x[1][0] + v.z * M.x[2][0];
    ret.y = v.x * M.x[0][1] + v.y * M.x[1][1] + v.z * M.x[2][1];
    ret.z = v.x * M.x[0][2] + v.y * M.x[1][2] + v.z * M.x[2][2];
    denom = M.x[0][3] + M.x[1][3] + M.x[2][3] + M.x[3][3];
    if (denom != 1.0)
        ret /= denom;
    return ret;
}

// Scale each element of the matrix by B.
Matrix
operator* (const Matrix& A, float B)
{
    Matrix ret;

    for (int i = 0; i < 4; i++)
        for (int j = 0; j < 4; j++)
            ret.x[i][j] = A.x[i][j] * B;
    return ret;
```

Listing 1.5 `matrix.cpp` *(continued)*

```
}

// Overloaded << for C++-style output.
ostream&
operator<< (ostream& s, const Matrix& M)
{
    for (int i = 0; i < 4; i++) {
        for (int j = 0; j < 4; j++)
              s << setprecision(2) << setw(10) << M.x[i][j];
        s << '\n';
    }
    return s;
}

// Rotate a direction vector...
Vector3D
PlaneRotate(const Matrix& tform, const Vector3D& p)
{
    // I sure hope that matrix is invertible...
    Matrix use = Transpose(Invert(tform));

    return RotateOnly(use, p);
}
```

Listing 1.5   `matrix.cpp` *(continued)*

1.8   3D Graphics on the 2D Screen: Projection

If we place an "eye" in the 3D world, and point it in a direction, we want the computer screen to reflect what the eye "sees." Some objects in the world may not be visible to the eye (objects behind the eye, for example). The region in 3D space that is visible to the eye starts at the eye and extends in whichever direction the eye is looking.

Because the computer screen is two-dimensional, we cannot display 3D objects directly. We must decide how to *project* the 3D scene onto the screen.

The most common method of projection is called *perspective projection.* The key to perspective projection is that objects closer to the eye are larger. In a perspective projection, the region visible to the eye starts at the point where the eye is located, and extends away in a three-dimensional trapezoid (see Figure 1.13). This construct is called the *viewing frustrum.*

Where does the computer screen fit into this? How do you go from the eye and the viewing frustrum to pixel colors?

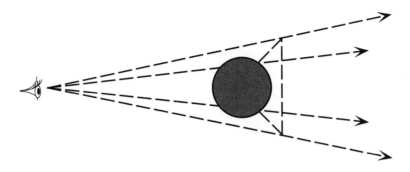

Figure 1.13   Viewing frustrum.

The viewing frustrum has a rectangular cross-section that is divided in the same way as the target screen resolution. If the output image is to have 1024×768 resolution, then the viewing frustrum is divided into 786,432 ($1024 \cdot 768$) smaller frustra that extend away from the eye in positions corresponding to the pixels on the target screen. In ray tracing, one or more rays are cast down each pixel's frustrum to find that pixel's color.

2

Introduction to Ray Tracing

R ay tracing is a technique for *rendering*. That means that it only concerns itself with drawing full-color pictures. What to draw a picture of and how to display the picture after it is generated are separate steps that the ray tracer does not worry about. Of course, we have to worry about these steps. "What to draw a picture of" is a synopsis of the modeling problem. For now, we describe models to the ray tracer by writing C++ programs and making calls into the OORT class library. Modeling using this technique is tedious, though no less tedious than using a traditional ray tracing input language. In the future, it may be possible to develop interactive programs that use faster rendering techniques to show the model during development.

For quantization and display, I've included the RAW2GIF program (described in Appendix E) to help quantize the full-color images that OORT generates. Any public-domain GIF-viewing program can be used to look at the results once RAW2GIF has been run on an image. The examples diskette contains a shareware GIF viewer that can be used for this purpose.

For more information on the mechanics of rendering with OORT, see Appendix E.

2.1 Overview of the Ray Tracing Process

Ray tracing is a very simple idea. As a rendering technique, it takes as input a 3D world to render, an eye location, the direction that the eye is looking, and a target resolution (resolution of the computer screen). This is all the information needed by the computer to render a "photograph" of the world as seen from the "eye." Thus, the output generated by the ray tracer is a full-color image at the target resolution. For every pixel on the computer screen, the ray tracer must determine a color to assign to that pixel.

Most renderers find pixel colors by projecting objects onto the computer screen (see Figure 2.1). There is a one-to-one correspondence between pixels in the target computer screen and the virtual screen in the world space.

In order to show more realistic images, we must remove the hidden lines and surfaces that are shown in Figure 2.1. Techniques to remove hidden surfaces vary widely. When it was invented, ray tracing offered one of the most innovative and intuitively pleasing ways to solve this problem.

Ray tracing works by casting rays from the eye, through the target screen and into the world. Typically, one ray is cast through each pixel in the computer screen and used to determine that pixel's color. The rays are intended to retrace the paths taken by beams of light arriving at the eye. The reason the rays are traced "backward" from the eye, where light is arriving, rather than "forward" from sources of light in the scene is that much of the light in a scene is uninteresting—it is bouncing around behind the eye, or is behind an opaque object where the eye cannot see it. By tracing rays from the eye, a lot of unnecessary work is avoided.

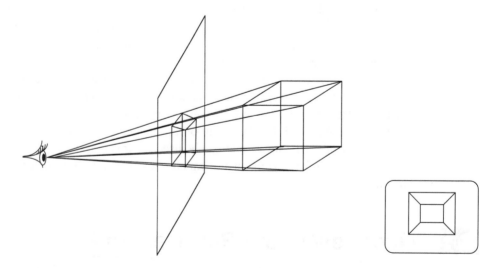

Figure 2.1 Projective rendering. Cube rendered at right (hidden lines and surfaces showing).

Determining the color at the nearest intersection point is one of the most interesting aspects of ray tracing. We will defer discussion of it until Chapter 3. Before we discuss how to compute the color at the nearest intersection point, we should discuss what a ray is and how it can be intersected with an object.

2.2 The Anatomy of a Ray

A ray can be described by two vectors: the location of the ray origin and a direction vector where the ray is headed. Every point **p** on the ray may be described parametrically, in terms of a variable t:

$$\mathbf{p} = \mathbf{loc} + t\mathbf{dir} \tag{2.1}$$

For $t = 0$, **p** lies on the origin (**loc**). As t increases, **p** moves along the ray, getting farther from the origin. If $t < 0$, the point is on the same line as the ray, but behind the ray origin. All objects that intersect the ray satisfy that equation for some t. Figure 2.2 depicts a ray and a few points along it.

The direction vector of a ray is typically normalized. This is useful for a number of reasons. Most importantly, if the ray direction is normalized, the ray parameter for a given point indicates that point's distance from the ray origin. Also, we can sometimes use the fact that the ray direction is normalized to write more efficient ray–object intersection routines (see the description of the Sphere intersection routine in Chapter 4 for an example).

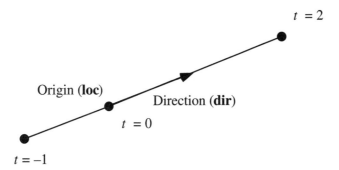

Figure 2.2   Anatomy of a ray. The dots signify points with ray parameters $t = -1$, $t = 0$ (the origin) and $t = 2$.

2.2.1 Ray Implementation

Rays are encapsulated by the Ray class in oort.h. The loc and dir members contain the ray's location and direction, respectively. The ll, ld, and dd members contain precomputed parameters of the ray (memberwise multiplications of loc by itself, loc by dir, and dir by itself). These precomputed parameters are needed for some intersection calculations, so they are computed just once for the ray and used by intersection routines thereafter.

The Extrap member function computes a point on the ray given a parameter. The Interp member function performs the converse: given a point guaranteed to be on the ray, it returns the corresponding parameter. The ApplyTransform applies a transform to the ray.

ReflectRay computes the reflected direction of a ray given the normal at the point where reflection is occurring. This function is used to compute specular reflections, as well as the direction of reflection for reflective objects.

One final note: Because only a limited number of classes need to access the members of Ray, all the data members are declared **private**. Thus, classes that need to access the Ray data must be declared **friends** of Ray. This includes classes that inherit from Object3D, classes that inherit from Surface, and the World class.

```
// ----------------------------------------------------------------
// Ray class.  A ray is defined by a location and a direction.
// The direction is always normalized (length == 1).
// ----------------------------------------------------------------
class Ray {
public:
   // constructors
   Ray(const Vector3D& wherefrom, const Vector3D& whichdir) {
      loc = wherefrom;
      dir = Normalize(whichdir);
      Precompute();
   }

   // ---------------------------------
   // Extrapolate ray given parameter
   // ---------------------------------
   Vector3D Extrap(float t) const {
      return loc + dir * t;
   }
```

Listing 2.1 Ray definition from oort.h

```
// ----------------------------------
// Return parameter given point on ray
// ----------------------------------
float Interp(Vector3D& x) const {
    for (int i = 0; i < 3; i++)
        if (fabs(dir[i]) > Limits::Small)
            return (x[i] - loc[i]) / dir[i];
    return 0;
}

// ----------------------------------
// Reflects direction of reflection for the ray,
// given the normal to the surface.
// ----------------------------------
Vector3D ReflectRay(const Vector3D& N) const {
    return N*2*DotProd(N, -dir) + dir;
}

void ApplyTransform(Matrix& tform) {
    loc = tform * loc;
    dir = RotateOnly(tform, dir);
    Precompute();
}
private:
    Vector3D loc, dir;          // Describes ray
    Vector3D ll, ld, dd;        // Various vectors with corresponding
                                // elements multiplied together.
    void Precompute() {
        ll = loc * loc;
        ld = loc * dir;
        dd = dir * dir;
    }

    friend class World;
    friend class AxisAlignedBox;
    friend class Object3D;
    friend class Sphere;
    friend class BoundingBox;
    friend class Planar;
    friend class Polygon;
    friend class Quadric;
    friend class Ellipsoid;
    friend class Algebraic;
```

Listing 2.1 Ray definition from oort.h *(continued)*

```
    friend class HallSurface;
    friend class DistributedHall;
};
```

Listing 2.1 Ray definition from `oort.h` *(continued)*

2.3 Intersection Calculations

If we have a 3D object we would like to intersect with a ray, all we need to do is plug equation (2.1) into the equation for the object. For example, the equation for a sphere of radius r and centered at (x_0, y_0, z_0) is as follows:

$$(x-x_0)^2 + (y-y_0)^2 + (z-z_0)^2 = r^2 \tag{2.2}$$

And, if we decompose the portions of vectors **loc** and **dir** in equation (2.1) into their X, Y, and Z components, the ray equation is as follows:

$$x = \mathbf{loc}.x + t\mathbf{dir}.x \tag{2.3a}$$

$$y = \mathbf{loc}.y + t\mathbf{dir}.y \tag{2.3b}$$

$$z = \mathbf{loc}.z + t\mathbf{dir}.z \tag{2.3c}$$

Now if we plug (2.3a–c) into (2.1), we get the following:

$$(\mathbf{loc}.x + t\mathbf{dir}.x - x_0)^2 + (\mathbf{loc}.y + t\mathbf{dir}.y - y_0)^2 + (\mathbf{loc}.z + t\mathbf{dir}.z - z_0)^2 = r^2 \tag{2.4}$$

Equation 2.4 looks complicated, but it is quite a bit simpler than it appears. It is a quadratic equation in t. To solve for t, we need only get equation (2.4) into the form

$$At^2 + Bt + C = 0 \tag{2.5}$$

and use the quadratic formula. As it turns out, for equation (2.4), the three coefficients A, B, and C are as follows:

$$A = \mathbf{dir} \cdot \mathbf{dir} \tag{2.6a}$$

$$B = \mathbf{loc} \cdot \mathbf{dir} \tag{2.6b}$$

$$C = \mathbf{loc} \cdot \mathbf{loc} - r^2 \tag{2.6c}$$

If the ray direction is normalized (has magnitude 1), then A is guaranteed to be equal to 1. As it turns out, it is very convenient for direction vectors to be normalized. Whenever a direction vector is used in OORT, it is normalized as soon as it is known to represent a direction vector. `Ray` directions are normalized in the constructors for `Ray` (`Ray::Ray`).

Take a look at `Sphere::NearestInt`, which implements the intersection calculation just discussed. The ray location and direction are combined with the sphere's origin and radius to compute the *B* and *C* coefficients to the quadratic equation (since *A* is guaranteed to be 1). Then the quadratic equation is solved. If the roots are imaginary, then the ray does not hit the sphere. If one or both roots are negative, the sphere intersects the line that the ray is on, but one or both intersections are behind the ray origin. If one of the roots is positive, then that root corresponds to an intersection of the ray with the sphere. `Sphere::NearestInt` passes back the smallest positive root, if there is one (Otherwise it returns 0, which means the ray did not intersect the sphere.) The smallest positive root is the object's nearest intersection along the ray.

Now, if we have a list of all the objects we want to ray trace, and intersection routines like `Sphere::NearestInt` that will return the nearest intersection of a ray with the object, it becomes very simple to find the nearest object along a ray: just traverse the list of objects and find the one with the smallest positive intersection. The problem with this approach is that it is slow. We will develop techniques for quickly finding nearest intersections in Chapter 5.

```
// Sphere intersection routine.
int
Sphere::NearestInt(Ray& ray, float& t, float maxt)
{
    float b, c, d;
    float t1, t2;
    Vector3D diff;

    Statistics::Intersections::Sphere++;

    diff = center - ray.loc;
    c = (float) DotProd(diff, diff) - radiussq;
    b = -2 * DotProd(diff, ray.dir);
    d = b*b - 4*c;

    if (d <= 0)
        return 0;

    d = sqrt(d);
```

Listing 2.2 `Sphere::NearestInt`

```
t1 = (-b+d)/2.0;
t2 = (-b-d)/2.0;

if (t1 < Limits::Threshold || t1 >= maxt)
    t1 = -1;
if (t2 < Limits::Threshold || t2 >= maxt)
    t2 = -1;
if (t1 < 0) {
    if (t2 < 0)
            return 0;
    t = t2;
}
else {
    if (t2 < 0)
            t = t1;
    else
            t = (t1 < t2) ? t1 : t2;
}
if (t2 < t1) {
    float temp = t1;
    t1 = t2;
    t2 = temp;
}
return t > Limits::Threshold;
}
```

Listing 2.2 `Sphere::NearestInt`

2.4 Objects, Inheritance, and Polymorphism

A ray tracer must be able to deal with a variety of three-dimensional objects. At the same time, the operations that must be performed on these objects are remarkably similar. When searching for the nearest intersection, for example, an intersection calculation must be performed with a ray and the nearest intersection (if any) returned. C++ contains language facilities ready-made to implement this sort of scenario. In OOP-speak they are called *inheritance* and *polymorphism.*

If you have read about inheritance and polymorphism, but have not had a chance to use them, you're probably familiar with descriptions of these object-oriented features that appeared in the trade press. Most of them describe applications for inheritance and polymorphism hypothetically ("Inheritance is really neat! It lets you declare a generic Car class, then inherit more specific Porsche and Audi classes from it...."). Ray tracing is laden with concrete applications for inheritance and polymorphism. When you want to intersect a ray with an object, you never care what kind of object it is—you just want to know whether the ray hits it and, if so, where the intersection occurs. This idea is implemented in the abstract `Object3D` class and the many classes that inherit from it. Other abstract classes that use this idea are `Texture` and `Light`. Polymorphism is the single most important feature of C++ for ray tracing implementation. Other important features of C++ that find application in ray tracing are described in Appendix A.

3
The Shading Equation

O nce the nearest intersection along a ray is determined, the color at the intersection point must be computed. Before you can compute the color, you have to decide on a shading model that describes how you compute the color at a point. Shading models can be ludicrously simple. A simple shading model used by some renderers for speed is one with no light sources, where light is ambient from all directions at all locations in the scene. The computation actually used to calculate the color is called the *shading equation*. The shading equation for the ambient-only shading model is as follows:

$$\text{Color} = k_a I_a$$

where k_a is the coefficient of ambient light reflection for the object being shaded and I_a is the intensity of the ambient light in the scene. Note that there are no shadows, since the ambient light is incident from all directions, and that no provision is made for reflective or transparent objects. Thus, this shading model has a simple shading equation that is fast to evaluate, but does not yield very realistic results.

Ray tracing implements a much more complex shading model. Glassner gives a good description of shading models for ray tracing [GLAS89b]. We will discuss the shading model and the associated shading equations that OORT uses, a simplified version of the Hall shading model described by Glassner.

3.1 Overview

The color at the intersection point is the sum of five different color components: ambient, diffuse, specular, reflected and transmitted. Each component models a different mode of light transport. The latter two are what set ray tracing apart from other rendering techniques; reflective and transparent objects are very difficult to model with other methods. Ray tracing also makes it very simple to render realistic shadows.

The components can be split into three categories.

- Approximation of diffuse interobject reflections:
  — Ambient component
- Components due to light sources:
  — Diffuse component
  — Specular component
- Components arrived at by recursion:
  — Reflected component
  — Transmitted component

The ambient component approximates the diffuse reflection of light between objects. That is, light bounces not only from light sources off objects, but between objects as well. Traditional ray tracing is not good at modeling these interobject reflections.

The second category, light from light sources reflected off the object, includes the diffuse and specular components. Like the ambient component, the diffuse component reflects light equally in all directions, but unlike the ambient component, it is attenuated according to the amount of light arriving from light sources at the point being shaded. The specular component models the sharp highlights of light sources on shiny objects such as apples or billiard balls.

These components are both caused by the light sources in the world, so the ray tracer must determine how much light is reaching the intersection point from light sources. This is done by casting a *shadow ray* from the intersection point toward each light source. If the ray hits an opaque object, the object blocks the light source from the intersection point (the intersection point is in shadow). If the ray hits a transparent object, the light must be attenuated by the object's coefficient of transparency.

The third category, components arrived at by recursion, includes the reflected and transmitted components. The reflected and transmitted components are computed by spawning a ray at the intersection point in the direction of reflection or transmission, finding the nearest object along that ray, and evaluating the shading equation at that intersection point. This process is analogous to casting a primary ray through a pixel. Since the nearest object intersected might also be reflective or transparent, yet another ray might be spawned. For this reason, ray tracers that support reflected or transparent objects are frequently referred to as *recursive ray tracers.*

It is easy to imagine scenes that cause ray tracers to recurse without limit. For example, two reflective objects might cause a ray to bounce between them indefinitely. This problem is typically dealt with by imposing a depth limit on the recursion. If the depth limit is reached, the ambient, diffuse and specular components are evaluated but the reflective and transparent components are not. The resulting error in the image is usually not noticeable.

Figure 3.1 depicts the general idea behind recursive ray tracing. It shows how a single ray fired from the eye causes more rays to be fired in order to evaluate the shading equation.

3.2 A Note on Color Coefficients

Every object has its own surface characteristics. An object might be a simple diffuse reflector, like a sheet of paper. Glass objects are almost perfectly transparent, slightly reflective, and exhibit specular reflection as well. In addition, objects can reflect or transmit selectively—a green object does not reflect the red components of incident light, for example. To describe the amount and type of a given component that is reflected or transmitted, we are given a *coefficient of reflection* (or *transmission*), an RGB triple that tells how much and what type of light is reflected or transmitted for each of the five components above.

Example: the coefficient of diffuse reflection for an object is (0, 0.8, 0.6), listing red, green, and blue in that order. White light falling on the object has an intensity of (0.8, 0.8, 0.8). Member-wise multiplication of the three elements yields a diffuse component of (0, 0.64, 0.48), a blue-green color.

3.3 Ambient Component

$$k_a I_a$$

k_a Coefficient of ambient reflection at the intersection point.

I_a Intensity of ambient light at the intersection point.

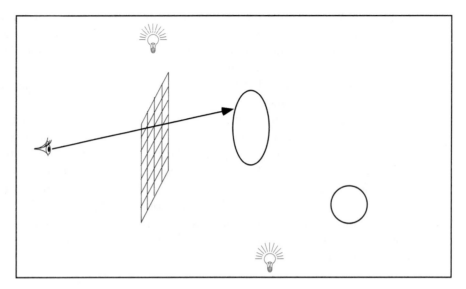

First, a primary ray is shot through the pixel we want to find the color of. Whatever color the ellipsoid is at the intersection point, that is the color of the pixel.

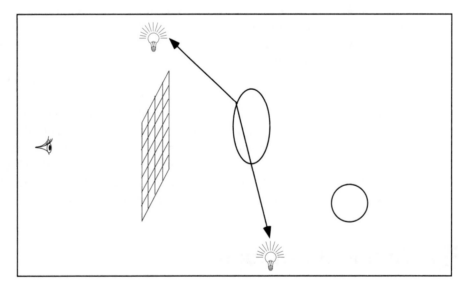

Shadow rays are fired at each light source from the intersection point. Light from the light sources is used to determine the diffuse and specular components of the shading equation.

Figure 3.1   Recursive ray tracing.

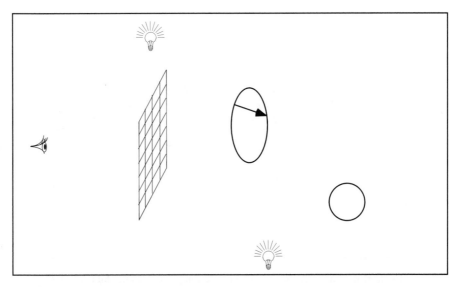

The ellipsoid is transparent, so a ray is fired in the direction of transmission to determine what light is shining through the intersection point.

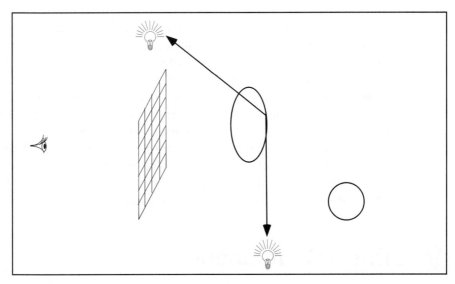

The ellipsoid hit itself again; whatever color the ellipsoid is at this intersection point is the color being transmitted at the first intersection point.

Figure 3.1   *(continued).*

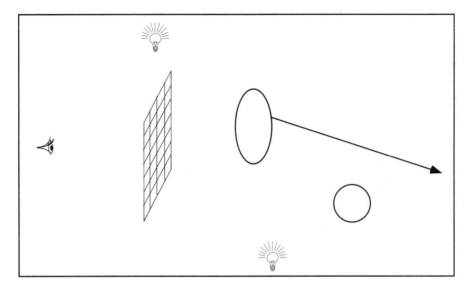

The transmitted ray at the second intersection point does not hit anything, so the recursion stops.

Figure 3.1 *(continued).*

The ambient component is intended to model the light diffusely reflected between objects in the scene. Like many ray tracers, OORT models this as light that is equally intense everywhere in the environment, incident from all directions and reflected equally in all directions. Another photorealistic rendering technique, "radiosity," computes a much better approximation of interobject reflections. The crudeness of the simple approximation above is why radiosity is a more realistic rendering technique for many types of scene.

In OORT, I_a is a constant everywhere in the environment (the Ambient member of the World class). k_a is the color of ambient light reflected by the object. Corresponding components of these two colors are multiplied together to find the ambient contribution to the shading equation.

3.4 Diffuse Component

$$k_d \sum I_j (\mathbf{L}_j \cdot \mathbf{N})$$

k_d Coefficient of diffuse reflection at the intersection point.

N   Normal to object at intersection point.

L$_j$ Direction vector pointing from intersection point toward light source.

I$_j$ Intensity of light arriving at intersection point from light source.

The diffuse and specular components, unlike the others, are directly attributable to the light sources in the world. The diffuse and specular components due to each light source are computed separately and summed. Both the specular and diffuse components require the intensity of each light source at the intersection point. This is determined by casting a shadow ray at the light source from the intersection point. If the ray hits an opaque object, the point is in shadow and the diffuse and specular components due to that light source are zero. If the ray hits any transparent objects, the light arriving at the intersection point must be attenuated by those objects' coefficients of transparency. See Figure 3.2.

The diffuse component models the object's reflection of the light sources in all directions. The intensity of this reflection depends on how directly the object "faces" the light source.

This measure is given by the angle between the object's normal **N** at the intersection point and the direction to the light source **L**$_j$. The attenuation of this reflection varies as the cosine of the angle: if the angle is 0, the reflection is not attenuated, and if the angle is 90 degrees or more, the light source is not reflected at all. If the vectors **N** and **L**$_j$ are normalized (have a magnitude of 1), the cosine of the angle between them is their dot product, resulting in the expression above.

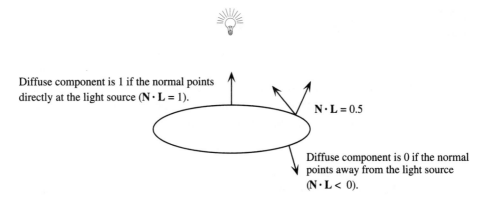

Figure 3.2   Different cases when computing the diffuse component due to a light source.

3.5 Specular Component

$$k_s \sum I_j (\mathbf{L}_j \cdot \mathbf{R})^\alpha$$

k_s Coefficient of specular reflection for the object.
I_j Intensity of light from the jth light source at the intersection point.
$\mathbf{L}_j$ Direction toward the jth light source.
$\mathbf{R}$ Direction of perfect reflection of the incident ray.
α Specularity, a measure of the sharpness of the specular highlight (ranges from three to several hundred).

The specular component models the object's sharp reflection of light sources. A specularly reflective object reflects without attenuation when the light source is in exactly the direction of perfect reflection. (See the next section on how to compute this direction.) The intensity of this reflection drops off exponentially as the direction toward the light source and the direction of perfect reflection coincide less. In the Phong shading model used by OORT, the cosine of the angle between the two vectors $\mathbf{L}_j$ and $\mathbf{R}$ is used as the base for the exponent.

Specular reflection is used to model the shiny highlights on objects such as apples or billiard balls; the larger α is, the sharper the highlight. Plate 1 illustrates the effects of different coefficients of specular reflection and different specularities.

Note that the Phong model used by OORT is only one of many ways to approximate specular reflection. Foley et al. [FOLE90] contains a good overview of other shading models.

3.6 Reflected Component

$$k_r I_r$$

I_r is computed by casting a ray in the direction of reflection at the intersection point, finding the nearest intersection and evaluating the shading equation there.

The reflected ray direction $\mathbf{R}$ is given by

$$\mathbf{R} = 2(-\mathbf{I} \cdot \mathbf{N})\mathbf{N} + \mathbf{I} \tag{3.1}$$

where $\mathbf{I}$ is the direction of the incident ray and $\mathbf{N}$ is the direction of the normal to the object at the intersection point. Figure 3.3 depicts this computation.

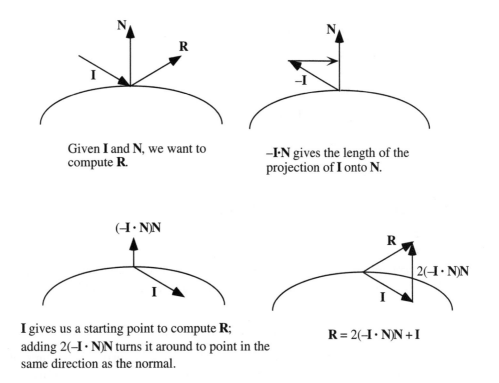

Given **I** and **N**, we want to compute **R**.

−**I**·**N** gives the length of the projection of **I** onto **N**.

I gives us a starting point to compute **R**; adding 2(−**I** · **N**)**N** turns it around to point in the same direction as the normal.

$$\mathbf{R} = 2(-\mathbf{I} \cdot \mathbf{N})\mathbf{N} + \mathbf{I}$$

Figure 3.3 Computing the direction of perfect reflection.

After the reflected ray is cast and the color in the direction of reflection is found, it is multiplied by the object's coefficient of reflectivity and added into the shading equation.

3.7 Transmitted Component

$$k_t I_t$$

The transmitted component of the shading equation is similar to the reflected component. A ray is spawned to find the color in the direction of transmission and then multiplied by the object's coefficient of transparency. The only difference between the reflected and transmitted components is the spawned ray's direction. When light intersects a boundary, it is deflected by an amount depending on the indices of refraction with respect to vacuum of the two media.

Figure 3.4 depicts the situation when an incident ray is transmitted by an object. **I**, **N**, and **R** are the incident, normal and transmitted rays. The incident

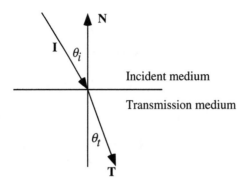

Figure 3.4   Transmission of a ray.

medium and transmission medium have indices of refraction that are specified by the user. The amount of deflection is expressed by Snell's Law:

$$\frac{\sin \theta_i}{\sin \theta_t} = \frac{\eta_t}{\eta_i} \qquad (3.2)$$

Here, $_i$ and $_t$ are the indices of refraction with respect to vacuum of the incident and transmission media. Snell's Law shows that the radio of these indices of refraction is important. As it turns out, **T** can be computed using the ratio:

$$\eta_{it} = \frac{\eta_i}{\eta_t} \qquad (3.3)$$

T is a linear combination of **I** and **N**:

$$\mathbf{T} = \alpha \mathbf{I} + \beta \mathbf{N} \qquad (3.4)$$

Glassner [GLAS89b] gives geometric and algebraic derivations of α and β. The solutions are as follows.

$$\alpha = \eta_{it}$$
$$\beta = \eta_{it} \cos \theta_i - \sqrt{1 + \eta_{it}^2 (\cos^2 \theta_i - 1)} \qquad (3.5)$$

$\cos \theta_i = \mathbf{N} \cdot \mathbf{I}$, so T can be written as follows.

$$\mathbf{T} = \eta_{it} \mathbf{I} + [\eta_{it}(-\mathbf{N} \cdot \mathbf{I}) - \sqrt{1 + \eta_{it}^2((\mathbf{N} \cdot \mathbf{I})^2 - 1)}]\mathbf{N} \qquad (3.6)$$

If the expression under the radical is negative, then total internal reflection has occurred. Total internal reflection is when light *reflects* off the interface between the media instead of transmitting through it. In this case, OORT does not add a transmitted component to the shading equation expression.

Once the direction for the transmitted ray has been computed, the color in that direction is found exactly as with a primary or reflected ray.

3.8 Implementation

Several classes make up OORT's support for evaluating the shading equation (see Table 3.1). To extend OORT's capabilities in a certain area, you have to "hook into" the class hierarchy in the right place. Adding a new type of light source or object to OORT is a simple matter: just inherit from Light or Object3D and overload the necessary member functions. Adding a more fundamental capability, such as uniform spatial subdivision (a ray tracing acceleration technique described in Chapter 5), would take more thought and effort.

The reader is encouraged to examine HallSurface::ComputeColor, the routine in surface.cpp that computes the shading equation.

First, the intersection point and direction of the normal are perturbed (if a bump map is in effect). Then the return value is initialized to black (0, 0, 0). If an ambient texture is available, its color at the intersection point is computed, multiplied member-wise by the amount of ambient light available, and added to the return value. If a diffuse or specular texture is available, the coefficients of diffuse and specular reflection are precomputed and stored in the Surface by the BeginShadeLight member function. Then, World::DiffuseLight is called to compute the amount of light due to light sources at the intersection point.

Class	Function
Light	Encapsulates a variety of light sources.
Object3D	Encapsulates a variety of objects.
ShadingInfo	Encapsulates the information needed to shade a point, such as the location of the point and the direction of the incident ray.
Surface	Encapsulates the shading model evaluation.
Texture	This class computes a color coefficient based on a location.
World	This class contains all the information needed to render a scene, such as the objects in the scene, the locations of light sources and the location of the viewer.

Table 3.1   OORT classes for shading

```
// ---------------------------------------------------------
// Surface
//     Surface computes the color at an intersection point
//     using the information in a ShadingInfo structure.
// ---------------------------------------------------------

class Surface {
public:
    virtual ~Surface() { }
    virtual void ApplyTransform(const Matrix&) = 0;
    virtual void PreMulTransform(const Matrix&) = 0;
    virtual Surface *Dup() const = 0;

    virtual int Transparent() = 0;
    virtual RGBColor Transmitted(Vector3D&) = 0;
    virtual void BeginShadeLight(Vector3D& loc) = 0;
    virtual RGBColor ShadeLight(ShadingInfo& shade, Vector3D& dir) = 0;

    virtual RGBColor ComputeColor(ShadingInfo& shade, int depth) = 0;
};

class HallSurface : public Surface {
public:
    HallSurface() {
        NewNormal = 0;
        Ambient = Diffuse = Specular = Reflect = Transmit = 0;
    }

    virtual void SetBumpMap(BumpMap *);
    virtual void SetAmbient(Texture *);
    virtual void SetDiffuse(Texture *);
    virtual void SetSpecular(Texture *, float);
    virtual void SetTransmit(Texture *, float);
    virtual void SetReflect(Texture *);

    virtual void ApplyTransform(const Matrix&);
    virtual void PreMulTransform(const Matrix&);
    virtual Surface *Dup() const;
    virtual int Transparent();
    virtual RGBColor Transmitted(Vector3D&);
```

Listing 3.1 Surface

```
    virtual RGBColor ComputeColor(ShadingInfo& shade, int depth);

    virtual void BeginShadeLight(Vector3D& loc);
    virtual RGBColor ShadeLight(ShadingInfo& shade, Vector3D& dir);
protected:
    BumpMap *NewNormal;           // Bump map

    Texture *Ambient;             // Ambient-reflected light
    Texture *Diffuse;             // Diffuse color of the object

    Texture *Specular;            // Index of specular reflection
    float specnum;                // Specularity factor

    Texture *Transmit;            // How much light is transmitted
    float index;                  // Index of refraction for object

    Texture *Reflect;             // How much light is reflected

    RGBColor diffuse, specular;   // Computed when BeginShadeLight() called
};
```

Listing 3.1 `Surface` *(continued)*

```
RGBColor
HallSurface::ComputeColor(ShadingInfo& shade, int depth)
{
    if (NewNormal)
        NewNormal->PerturbNormal(shade);

    RGBColor AmtLight = RGBColor(0);

    if (Ambient)
        AmtLight += Ambient->GetColor(shade.p) *
                shade.world->GetAmbientLight();

    if (Diffuse || Specular) {
        BeginShadeLight(shade.p);
        AmtLight += shade.world->DiffuseLight(shade, this);
    }
```

Listing 3.2 `HallSurface::ComputeColor`

```
    if (shade.world->HitDepthLimit(depth))
        return AmtLight;

    if (Reflect) {
        Ray ReflectedRay(shade.p, shade.ray->ReflectRay(shade.normal));
        Statistics::ReflectedRays++;
        AmtLight += Reflect->GetColor(shade.p) *
                shade.world->FindColor(ReflectedRay, depth+1);
    }

    if (Transmit) {
        Vector3D normal = shade.normal;
        float gamma, dot, sqrterm;

        Statistics::TransmittedRays++;

            dot = DotProd(shade.normal, -shade.incident);
            if (dot > 0)
                    gamma = 1 / index;
            else {
                    gamma = index;
                    dot = -dot;
                    normal = -normal;
            }
            sqrterm = 1.0 - gamma*gamma*(1.0 - dot*dot);

        // Check for total internal reflection.
        // Do nothing if it applies.
            if (sqrterm > 0) {
                    sqrterm = gamma*dot - sqrt(sqrterm);
                    Ray TransmittedRay = Ray(shade.p,
                        normal*sqrterm + shade.incident*gamma);
                    AmtLight += Transmitted(shade.p) *
                        shade.world->FindColor(TransmittedRay,
    depth+1);
            }
    }
    return AmtLight;
}
```

Listing 3.2   `HallSurface::ComputeColor` *(continued)*

If the depth limit has been reached, the reflective and transmitted components are not computed. Otherwise, the reflected direction is computed using `Ray::ReflectRay`, and a new ray is spawned with its origin at the intersection point. `World::FindColor`, the same routine used to compute the color of a pixel, is called to compute the color in the direction of reflection. This color is multiplied by the coefficient of reflection at the intersection point.

Finally, if the object is transparent, a ray is spawned in the direction of transmission and `World::FindColor` is called. `ComputeColor` checks the sign of the dot product between the direction of the incident ray and the surface normal to determine whether the incident ray is entering or leaving the object (line 29).

Each component of the shading equation is multiplied by its coefficient of attenuation. These coefficients are RGB triples returned by `Texture` classes. Chapter 6 discusses texture mapping and the `Texture` class in detail.

3.9 Exercises

1. Try adding Glassner's simple model for fog and haze [GLAS90] to OORT. The idea is that after a certain distance, colors gradually blend into the color of the fog (usually a light gray). At another, larger distance, colors are assumed to have been overwhelmed by the fog. If we are given a distance d that colored light traveled in the fog, the fog affects the light as follows:

$$clr' = \alpha \cdot fog + (1 - \alpha \cdot clr)$$

$$\alpha = clamp(0, 1, \frac{d - d_{near}}{d_{far} - d_{near}})$$

where d_{near} is the distance light must travel before the attenuation begins; d_{far} is the distance where the fog overwhelms the color of the light; clr is the color being attenuated and fog is the color of the fog.

(Note: more realistic simulations of fog and haze may be found in Hall [HALL89].)

2. Currently, rays in OORT travel through vacuum. Even at the juncture of a transparent object, the ray is bent at the intersection point and immediately reenters vacuum. Vacuum does not attenuate light with distance, and it always has an index of refraction of 1. What would be involved in adding other media to the ray tracer?

Different Types
of Object

Ray tracing is a technique that can accommodate a wide variety of objects. In order to render them, we have to provide two fundamental operations: ray intersection and normal computation. This chapter will describe how to intersect a ray with each type of object supported by OORT, and how to compute the normal to each type of object. We will also describe a number of other operations, such as how to transform each type of object.

4.1 Overview

OORT encapsulates different types of object in a class called `Object3D`. The `Object3D` class itself does not contain much information, but it provides a framework for objects that can be ray traced. Member functions of `Object3D` allow clients of OORT to intersect with, find the normal of, and otherwise deal with objects in a uniform way. This overview describes the operations that must be supported by a class that inherits from `Object3D`. All of the objects described in this chapter inherit from `Object3D`, so to understand the source code in this chapter you should read the following sections on `Object3D`.

4.1.1 Intersection

Intersection is a computation that determines whether a given ray hits the object and, if so, computes the locations of the intersections. As discussed in Section 2.1, the parameterized equation for a ray, where the equations for x, y, and z are separated in terms of a single variable t, is as follows:

$$x = \mathbf{loc}.x + t\mathbf{dir}.x \qquad (4.1a)$$

$$y = \mathbf{loc}.y + t\mathbf{dir}.y \qquad (4.1b)$$

$$z = \mathbf{loc}.z + t\mathbf{dir}.z \qquad (4.1c)$$

In general, intersecting a ray with an object involves plugging equations (4.1a–c) into the equation for the object and solving for t. There is a close relationship between the number of solutions for t and the number of times a ray can intersect a primitive. For example, an infinite plane is a first-degree implicit surface, and the equation to solve for t is linear and always has a solution. This reflects the fact that a line *always* hits an infinite plane. Of course, if t is negative, then the intersection is "behind" the ray origin and the ray misses.

In some cases, such as polygons and bounding boxes, more involved computation is necessary. We will begin with some of the simpler primitives supported by OORT, then move on to more complicated ones. After reading the detailed description of how to perform the intersection calculation and compute the normal, the reader can look at the relevant source code of OORT to see how the calculations are actually implemented.

Even if there are positive solutions for t, the ray might be considered to miss the object. Most ray tracers impose lower and upper bounds on valid parameters of intersection. The lower bound is a small, positive number (typically 0.001 or even smaller) to prevent rays from hitting the objects that spawned them when casting secondary rays. Without this lower bound, floating-point errors cause shadow rays cast from an object to appear to intersect the object they originated on. The resulting image makes the object look pockmarked, as some shadow rays cast from the object cause the object to shadow itself.

A number of factors might impose an upper bound on the object's parameter of intersection. When searching for the nearest intersection (casting a primary or secondary ray), the nearest intersection found so far is used as an upper bound on the parameter of intersection. Objects farther away than the nearest-so-far are not interesting, since only the nearest object along the ray must be shaded. When casting a shadow ray, however, the maximum parameter of intersection is equal to the distance to the light source. This is because objects beyond the light source cannot obscure the light.

Implementation

Three member functions of `Object3D` deal with intersection calculations.

```
virtual int NearestInt(Ray& ray, float& t, float maxt) = 0;
```

This function intersects the object with the given ray. If the ray hits the object, the function returns a nonzero integer and sets `t` to the parameter of the nearest intersection along the ray. The `NearestInt` will not return an intersection if all the intersections with the object have parameters less than `Limits::Threshold` or greater than `maxt`. When calling `Object3D::NearestInt`, `maxt` is typically set to the nearest intersection so far, or in the case of shadow rays, the distance to the light source.

```
virtual SpanList *FindAllIntersections(Ray& ray) = 0;
```

This function computes *all* the intersections of the object with the ray given. This operation is required only if you wish to do CSG on the object. See Chapter 8 for details.

```
virtual int HitAtAll(Ray& ray, float maxt);
```

This function only seeks to determine whether the ray hits the object; it does not return the parameter of intersection. It is called by `World::FindAtten`, which casts a shadow ray in the `World`. Since it doesn't usually matter *where* an object intersects a shadow ray, but only whether the object and the ray intersect, `HitAtAll` implementations can sometimes be more efficient.

There are not many situations where the `HitAtAll` computation is more efficient than the `NearestInt` computation. Because of this, `HitAtAll` is implemented for `Object3D`—it just calls `NearestInt`. For objects with more efficient `HitAtAll` implementations, the function can be overloaded, but it will work fine if it is not.

4.1.2 Finding the Normal

Besides intersecting a ray with an object, we have to know how to compute the normal to an object at a given point. The normal is a vector that points at right angles away from the surface. It is important for computing the various contributions to the shading equation. For the purposes of shading, the normal should be *normalized* (have a magnitude of 1).

In computer graphics, surface normals tell which way an object "faces." A countertop has a normal that points uniformly upward at all points on the surface—and so does the polygon that would be used to model such a countertop in computer graphics. In contrast, the surface normal to a sphere always points directly away from the center of the sphere, so the normal is different at every point on the sphere.

For implicit surfaces such as planes and spheres, the direction of the normal is given by the gradient of the function for the surface. The function for a plane, $f(x,y,z) = Ax + By + Cz + D$, has a gradient of (A, B, C); as we shall see, that vector corresponds also to the normal to the plane, which is constant at all points on the plane. A sphere of radius r, centered at (x_0, y_0, z_0), has the implicit function $f(x,y,z) = (x - x_0)^2 + (y - y_0)^2 + (z - z_0)^2 - r^2$. The gradient for this function is $(2x - 2x_0, 2y - 2y_0, 2z - 2z_0)$, which points directly away from the center of the sphere for all points (x,y,z). Of course, the gradient vector must be normalized before use in the shading equations.

Implementation

`Object3D::FindNormal` is declared as follows.

```
virtual Vector3D FindNormal(const Vector3D&) = 0;
```

This function computes the normal to the object at a given intersection point. This is usually a simple operation (`Planar::FindNormal` and `Sphere::FindNormal` are both one-line functions). The return value is guaranteed to be of magnitude 1, so `FindNormal` implementations often call `Normalize` on the vector before returning it.

4.1.3 Transformations

Different objects are transformed in different ways, so `Object3D` provides a virtual function that transforms the object according to a transformation matrix.

```
virtual void ApplyTransform(Matrix& tform) = 0;
```

This function applies the given 4×4 transformation matrix to the object.

4.1.4 `PtDistance` and `IsInside`

These functions are declared as follows:

```
virtual float PtDistance(Vector& x) = 0;
virtual int IsInside(Vector&);
```

PtDistance is supposed to give a distance measure from a given point to the nearest point on the surface. Following the convention established by implicit surfaces, points "inside" the surface should have a negative distance. For implicit surfaces, the existing PtDistance implementations generally throw the vector through the implicit surface's function. For a plane, this gives exactly the distance to the plane. For a quadric (other than spheres), this gives a value that varies with the square of the distance.

IsInside returns nonzero if the given point is "inside" the surface. Object3D implements IsInside in terms of PtDistance (since PtDistance is guaranteed to return a negative distance for points inside the surface). However, more efficient implementations of IsInside can overload the default implementation given by Object3D.

4.1.5 Bounding Volumes

OORT implements a ray tracing efficiency scheme based on bounding boxes. To help OORT's World class generate bounding volume hierarchies, Object3D provides a function that returns the bounding box of the object.

```
virtual AxisAlignedBox BBox() const;
```

BBox returns an AxisAlignedBox, which is a six-sided box with sides parallel to the coordinate planes. Object3D provides a default implementation of BBox that returns an unbounded box. This tells OORT that the object is not bounded and that it cannot be included in the bounding volume hierarchy. For some primitives, such as Planes, Quadrics, and other unbounded primitives, this is a reasonable default. For bounded primitives, overloading the default BBox implementation allows the primitive to participate in the accelerated ray tracing made possible by bounding volume hierarchies.

4.1.6 Other Member Functions of Object3D

```
virtual void CountMe() const;
```

This function increments a global variable corresponding to the type of object. For example, Sphere::CountMe increments Statistics::Objects::Sphere. This member function is intended to help count the number of each type of object in the scene.

```
virtual void Describe(int ind) const;
```

This function indents `ind` spaces, then prints a description of the object to the standard C++ stream `cout`.

```
virtual Object3D *Dup() const;
```

This function creates a duplicate instance of the object and returns a pointer to the duplicate.

```
int Flags();
```

This function returns the `Flags` integer for the object. Although objects are supposed to be treated uniformly, sometimes you need to know certain things about an object. The least significant bits of the `Flags` integer can have the following values:

Define	Value	Meaning
BOUNDING	1	Object is a bounding volume.
CSG	2	Object is a CSG primitive.
AGGREGATE	4	Object is an `Aggregate`.

Thus, to tell whether an object is a bounding volume, call `Flags` and check the return value as follows:

```
if (objs->Flags() & BOUNDING) {
    // Object is a bounding volume
}
else {
    // Object is not a bounding volume
}
```

```
class Object3D {
public:
   // Constructors set flags and color.
   Object3D(int F = 0): surf(0), flags(F) { }
   Object3D(Surface *NewColor, int F):
      surf(NewColor), flags(F) { }

   // Make destructor explicitly virtual so it can be overloaded.
   virtual ~Object3D() { }

   Surface *ReturnColor() const { return surf; }
   int Flags() const { return flags; }
```

Listing 4.1   `Object3D` class definition

```
void OverrideColor(Surface *NewColor) { surf = NewColor; }
// NearestInt returns 1 if the ray hits the object; it passes back
// the parameter of intersection in t.  maxt specifies the maximum
// allowable value for the parameter of intersection; if the only
// intersections with the object are of greater parameter than maxt,
// no intersection is returned.
virtual int NearestInt(Ray& ray, float& t, float maxt) = 0;

// FindAllIntersections returns a pointer to a SpanList that
// contains all the spans where the ray passes through the
// object.  This is primarily used for CSG.
virtual SpanList *FindAllIntersections(Ray& ray) = 0;

// Returns the normal to the object at the given intersection point.
virtual Vector3D FindNormal(const Vector3D& p) = 0;

// Returns the sum of the object's ambient, diffuse, specular,
// reflective, and transparent components.
//
// This was unneeded (the World class knew how to do this stuff
// in FindColor) until hypertexture objects came along.  Since
// these objects get shaded quite a bit differently from other
// objects, ShadeObject has a default implementation for all
// objects that gets overloaded by the SoftObject (hypertexture)
// class.
virtual RGBColor ShadeObject(World&, Ray&, Vector3D&, int);

// Returns the number of children the object has.  This is defined
// to be 0, except for bounding volumes.
virtual int NumChildren() { return 0; }

// Apply an arbitrary 3D 4x4 matrix to the object.
virtual void ApplyTransform(const Matrix& tform) = 0;

// Applies a given transform to the Surface structure associated
// with the object.
virtual void TransformSurface(SurfaceList& clist, const Matrix&
tform);

// Return a duplicate of the object.
virtual Object3D *Dup() const = 0;
```

Listing 4.1 Object3D **class definition** *(continued)*

```
    // Return nonzero if the given point is inside the object, 0 if not.
    virtual int IsInside(Vector3D& v);
    // Return nonzero if the given ray intersects the object with
    // parameter of intersection less than maxt.  This is frequently
    // more efficient to implement than find-nearest-intersection.
    virtual int HitAtAll(Ray& ray, float maxt);

    // Return a measure of how far inside the object the given point is.
    // This distance is 0 on the object's surface, negative if inside the
    // object, or positive if outside the object.  If the number is
    // positive or negative, it should reflect how far inside or outside
    // the object the given point is.

    // This function is used strictly by the SoftObject hypertexture class.
    virtual float PtDistance(Vector3D& v) = 0;

    // Writes a brief description of the object, indenting by the given
    // number of spaces first.
    virtual void Describe(int ind) const = 0;

    // Returns bounding box of object.    Unbounded by default.
    virtual AxisAlignedBox BBox() const {
        return AxisAlignedBox(Vector3D(-MAXFLOAT), Vector3D(MAXFLOAT));
    }

    virtual void CountMe() const = 0;

    friend World;
protected:
    Surface *surf;      // Object surface.
private:
    int flags;          // Flags: see just above for #define's
};
```

Listing 4.1 Object3D **class definition** *(continued)*

```
// =====================================================================
// object3d.cpp
//     Support routines for Object3D class.
//
//         The Object-Oriented Ray Tracer (OORT)
//         Copyright (C) 1993 by Nicholas Wilt.
//
// This software product may be freely copied and distributed in
// unmodified form but may not be sold.  A nominal distribution
// fee may be charged for media and handling by freeware and
// shareware distributors.  The software product may not be
// included in whole or in part into any commercial package
// without the express written consent of the author.
//
// This software product is provided as is without warranty of
// any kind, express or implied, including but not limited to
// the implied warranties of merchantability and fitness for a
// particular purpose.  The author assumes no liability for any
// alleged or actual damages arising from the use of this
// software.  The author is under no obligation to provide
// service, corrections or upgrades to the software.
//
// -----------------------------------------------------------
//
// Please contact me with questions, comments, suggestions or
// other input about OORT.  My Compuserve account number is
// [75210,2455] (Internet sites can reach me at
// 75210.2455@compuserve.com).
//                              --Nicholas Wilt
// =====================================================================

#include "oort.h"
#include "world.h"


// ==========================================================
// Object3D::ShadeObject
//     Called by World when it is determined that the
//     object was the closest along the given ray.
// ==========================================================
RGBColor
Object3D::ShadeObject(World& world, Ray& ray, Vector3D& Intersection,
   int depth)
{
   ShadingInfo shade;
```

Listing 4.2 from object3d.cpp

```
    shade.p = Intersection;
    shade.normal = FindNormal(Intersection);
    shade.incident = ray.dir;
    shade.reflected = ray.ReflectRay(shade.normal);
    shade.obj = this;
    shade.ray = &ray;
    shade.world = &world;
    return surf->ComputeColor(shade, depth);
}

int
Object3D::HitAtAll(Ray& ray, float maxt)
{
    float tempt;
    return NearestInt(ray, tempt, maxt) != 0;
}

int
Object3D::IsInside(Vector3D& v)
{
    float dist = PtDistance(v);
    return dist < 0 || fabs(dist) < Limits::Small;
}

void
Object3D::TransformSurface(SurfaceList& clist, const Matrix& tform)
{
    if (flags & BOUNDING) {
        ((BoundingVolume *) this)->TransformSurface(clist, tform);
    }
    else if (! (flags & CSG)) {
        if (surf && ! clist.SurfaceThere(surf)) {
            clist.AddToList(surf);
            surf->PreMulTransform(tform);
        }
    }
}

int
SurfaceList::SurfaceThere(Surface *probe)
{
    for (Iterator sc(*this); sc.Valid(); sc.GotoNext()) {
        if (sc.Contents() == probe)
            return 1;
    }
```

Listing 4.2   from `object3d.cpp` *(continued)*

```
        return 0;
}

void
ObjectList::TransformList(const Matrix& Transform)
{
    for (Iterator sc(*this); sc.Valid(); sc.GotoNext())
        sc.Contents()->ApplyTransform(Transform);
}

void
ObjectList::TransformSurfaces(SurfaceList& clist, const Matrix&
    Transform)
{
    for (Iterator sc(*this); sc.Valid(); sc.GotoNext())
        sc.Contents()->TransformSurface(clist, Transform);
}
```

Listing 4.2 from `object3d.cpp` *(continued)*

4.2 Planes

The plane is the general first-degree implicit surface. The equation for a plane is:

$$Ax + By + Cz + D = 0 \qquad (4.2)$$

Taken as a vector, the coefficients (A, B, C) compose the normal to the plane. If the vector (A, B, C) is normalized, $|D|$ is the distance from the origin to the nearest point on the plane.

Intersection

To intersect a plane with a ray, plug equations (4.1a–c) into equation (4.2) and solve for t:

$$A(\textbf{loc}.x + t\textbf{dir}.x) + B(\textbf{loc}.y + t\textbf{dir}.y) + C(\textbf{loc}.z + t\textbf{dir}.z) + D = 0 \qquad (4.3)$$

$$t = \frac{-D - A\textbf{loc}.x - B\textbf{loc}.y - C\textbf{loc}.z}{A\textbf{dir}.x + B\textbf{dir}.y + C\textbf{dir}.z} \qquad (4.4)$$

If (A, B, C) is thought of as the normal $\textbf{N}$ to the plane, this can be formulated in terms of dot products:

$$t = \frac{-D - \textbf{N} \cdot \textbf{loc}}{\textbf{N} \cdot \textbf{dir}} \qquad (4.5)$$

Finding the Normal

The normal to all planar objects is precomputed, so `Planar::FindNormal` just returns that normal.

Transformations

To transform an infinite plane, the rotation portion of the matrix is applied to the normal. This gives the first three parameters (A, B, C) of the new plane's equation. The fourth parameter, D, is computed by transforming the point nearest the origin on the original plane, then plugging that point into the equation for the new plane and solving for D. See the implementation of `Planar::Apply-Transform`.

`PtDistance` and `IsInside`

Assuming that the normal is of unit length, the distance to the plane at (x, y, z) is:

$$Ax + By + Cz + D \tag{4.6}$$

or, in vector notation:

$$\mathbf{N} \cdot \mathbf{p} + D \tag{4.7}$$

This gives the signed distance to the plane.

Bounding boxes

Since no finite bounding box can enclose an infinite plane, the default implementation of `BBox()` provided by `Object3D` is satisfactory. It simply returns an infinitely large bounding box.

Although infinite planes are unbounded, some planar objects are not. The `Ring` and `Polygon` classes overload the `BBox()` member function so they can participate in acceleration techniques based on bounding volume hierarchies.

Implementation

There are a variety of planar objects supported by OORT. Besides infinite planes implemented by `Plane`, rings and polygons are planar. The `Planar` class implements many member functions needed by these objects. For example, `Planar::NearestInt` can be used by derived classes to compute the parameter of intersection with the plane (though they may impose additional constraints on the point in order for an intersection to occur). `Planar:`

:ApplyTransform applies a transform to the plane (though derived classes may need to perform additional work to apply a transform to themselves). Planar::Normal returns the normal to the plane, and none of the classes that inherit from Planar have had to overload that function yet. For more information, see the descriptions of rings and polygons below.

The Listings for the Planar and Plane classes are given here.

```
// ------------------------------------------------------------
// Planar
//     Root of a hierarchy of planar objects (infinite plane,
//     polygon, ring).
// ------------------------------------------------------------
class Planar : public Object3D {
public:
    Planar(Surface *NewColor);
    Planar(float A, float B, float C, float D, Surface *NewColor);
    Planar(const Vector3D& norm, float D, Surface *NewColor);
    virtual ~Planar() { }

    virtual int NearestInt(Ray& Ray, float& t, float maxt);
    virtual SpanList *FindAllIntersections(Ray& ray);
    virtual Vector3D FindNormal(const Vector3D& Intersection);
    virtual void ApplyTransform(const Matrix& tform);
    virtual Object3D *Dup() const = 0;
    virtual void Describe(int ind) const = 0;
    virtual float PtDistance(Vector3D& v);
    virtual void CountMe() const = 0;
protected:
    Vector3D Normal;          // a, b, c of plane equation
    float d;                  // d of plane equation
    int bad;                  // nonzero if normal is of
                              // zero length.
};


// ------------------------------------------------------------
// Plane
//     Infinite plane.
// ------------------------------------------------------------
class Plane : public Planar {
public:
```

Listing 4.3 Planar and Plane definitions

```
    Plane(float A, float B, float C, float D, Surface *NewColor);
    Plane(const Vector3D& norm, float D, Surface *NewColor):
        Planar(norm, D, NewColor) { }

    virtual int NearestInt(Ray& Ray, float& t, float maxt);
    virtual Object3D *Dup() const;
    virtual void Describe(int ind) const;
    virtual void CountMe() const { Statistics::Objects::Plane++; }
};
```

Listing 4.3   `Planar` and `Plane` definitions   *(continued)*

```
// =======================================================================
// plane.cpp
//      Plane support routines for OORT.
//
//          The Object-Oriented Ray Tracer (OORT)
//          Copyright (C) 1993 by Nicholas Wilt.
//
// This software product may be freely copied and distributed in
// unmodified form but may not be sold.  A nominal distribution
// fee may be charged for media and handling by freeware and
// shareware distributors.  The software product may not be
// included in whole or in part into any commercial package
// without the express written consent of the author.
//
// This software product is provided as is without warranty of
// any kind, express or implied, including but not limited to
// the implied warranties of merchantability and fitness for a
// particular purpose.  The author assumes no liability for any
// alleged or actual damages arising from the use of this
// software.  The author is under no obligation to provide
// service, corrections or upgrades to the software.
//
// ---------------------------------------------------------------
//
// Please contact me with questions, comments, suggestions or
// other input about OORT.  My Compuserve account number is
// [75210,2455] (Internet sites can reach me at
```

Listing 4.4   `Planar` and `Plane` implementations

```
// 75210.2455@compuserve.com).
//          --Nicholas Wilt
// ================================================================

#include "oort.h"

Planar::Planar(Surface *NewColor): Object3D(NewColor, 0)
{
   bad = 1;
}

Planar::Planar(float A, float B, float C, float D, Surface *NewColor):
   Object3D(NewColor, 0)
{
   Normal = Vector3D(A, B, C);
   d = D;
   float mag = Magnitude(Normal);
   bad = fabs(mag) < Limits::Small;
   if (! bad) {
      Normal /= mag;
      d /= mag;
   }
}

Planar::Planar(const Vector3D& norm, float D, Surface *NewColor):
   Object3D(NewColor, 0)
{
   Normal = norm;
   d = D;
   float mag = Magnitude(Normal);
   bad = fabs(mag) < Limits::Small;
   if (! bad) {
      Normal /= mag;
      d /= mag;
   }
}

int
Planar::NearestInt(Ray& ray, float& t, float maxt)
{
   if (bad)
```

Listing 4.4 `Planar` and `Plane` implementations *(continued)*

```
        return 0;

    float dot = DotProd(Normal, ray.dir);

    // Watch for near-zero denominator
    if (fabs(dot) < Limits::Small) {
        return 0;
    }

    t = (-d - DotProd(Normal, ray.loc)) / dot;

    return t > Limits::Threshold && t < maxt;
}

SpanList *
Planar::FindAllIntersections(Ray& ray)
{
    float dot = DotProd(Normal, ray.dir);

    if (fabs(dot) == 0) {
        // Ray is parallel; if ray is in the plane, it intersects
        // the plane infinitely far away in both directions; otherwise
        // it intersects the ray not at all, because it is parallel.
        if (DotProd(Normal, ray.loc) + d < Limits::Small) {
            SpanList *ret = new SpanList(Span(-Limits::Infinity, this,
                Limits::Infinity, this));
            return ret;
        }
        else return 0;
    }

    float t = (-d - DotProd(Normal, ray.loc)) / dot;

    if (dot < 0)
        return new SpanList(Span(t, this, Limits::Infinity, this));
    else {
        if (t < Limits::Threshold)
            return 0;
        return new SpanList(Span(-Limits::Infinity, this, t, this));
    }
}
```

Listing 4.4   Planar and Plane implementations *(continued)*

```
Vector3D
Planar::FindNormal(const Vector3D& v)
{
    return Normal;
}

void
Planar::ApplyTransform(const Matrix& tform)
{
    Vector3D v = Normal * -d;
    Normal = Normalize(RotateOnly(tform, Normal));
    d = -DotProd(tform * v, Normal);
}

float
Planar::PtDistance(Vector3D& v)
{
    return DotProd(v, Normal) + d;
}

// =====================================================================
// Plane implementations
// =====================================================================

Plane::Plane(float A, float B, float C, float D, Surface *NewColor):
    Planar(A, B, C, D, NewColor)
{ }

int
Plane::NearestInt(Ray& ray, float& t, float maxt)
{
    Statistics::Intersections::Plane += 1;
    return Planar::NearestInt(ray, t, maxt);
}


Object3D *
Plane::Dup() const
{
    return new Plane(Normal.x, Normal.y, Normal.z, d, surf);
```

Listing 4.4 Planar and Plane implementations *(continued)*

```
}

void
Plane::Describe(int ind) const
{
    indent(ind);
    cout << "Plane: " << setprecision(3) << Normal.x << "x + ";
    cout << Normal.y << "y + " << Normal.z << "z + " << d << " = 0\n";
}
```

Listing 4.4   `Planar` and `Plane` implementations   *(continued)*

4.3   Rings

Rings are planar objects with a center, an inner radius, and an outer radius. The area between the inner and outer radii is considered to be inside the ring. Since a ring is a subset of a plane, the `Ring` class inherits from `Planar`. Intersecting a ring involves first intersecting with the ring's plane, then computing the distance of the intersection point to the center of the ring. If the distance falls between the inner and outer radii of the ring, then the ray intersects the ring.

Because the `Planar` class implements almost all of the functionality needed to implement `Rings`, the `Ring` implementation is almost trivial.

```
// -----------------------------------------------------------------
// Ring
//     A circular, concentric ring.
// -----------------------------------------------------------------
class Ring : public Planar {
public:
    Ring(float A, float B, float C, float D,
        const Vector3D& _center, float _inner, float _outer,
        Surface *NewColor);
    Ring(const Vector3D& norm, float D,
        const Vector3D& _center, float _inner, float _outer,
        Surface *NewColor);
    virtual int NearestInt(Ray& ray, float& t, float maxt);
    virtual void ApplyTransform(const Matrix& tform);
    virtual Object3D *Dup() const;
    virtual void Describe(int ind) const;
    virtual void CountMe() const { Statistics::Objects::Ring++; }
private:
```

Listing 4.5   `Ring` definition

```
    Vector3D center;
    float inner, outer;
};
```

Listing 4.5 Ring definition *(continued)*

```
// =====================================================================
// Ring implementations
// =====================================================================

Ring::Ring(float A, float B, float C, float D,
           const Vector3D& _center, float _inner, float _outer,
           Surface *surf):
    Planar(A, B, C, D, surf), center(_center), inner(_inner),
    outer(_outer)
{
}

Ring::Ring(const Vector3D& norm, float D,
           const Vector3D& _center, float _inner, float _outer,
           Surface *surf):
    Planar(norm, D, surf), center(_center), inner(_inner),
    outer(_outer)
{
}

int
Ring::NearestInt(Ray& ray, float& t, float maxt)
{
    // Count ring intersection
    Statistics::Intersections::Ring += 1;

    // If we miss the plane, we miss the ring.
    if (Planar::NearestInt(ray, t, maxt)) {
        // If we hit the plane, we have to be between the two radii
        // to hit the ring.
        float dist = Magnitude(ray.Extrap(t) - center);
        return dist >= inner && dist <= outer;
    }
    return 0;
}

void
```

Listing 4.6 Ring implementation

```
Ring::ApplyTransform(const Matrix& tform)
{
    Planar::ApplyTransform(tform);
    center = tform * center;
}

Object3D *
Ring::Dup() const
{
    return new Ring(Normal, d, center, inner, outer, surf);
}

void
Ring::Describe(int ind) const
{
    indent(ind);
    cout << "Ring: plane normal " << Normal << ", dist " << d;
    cout << ", inner rad " << inner << ", outer rad " << outer << '\n';
}
```

Listing 4.6 Ring implementation *(continued)*

4.4 Spheres

A sphere is the 3D analog of a circle: the set of points equidistant from a given point. It has a particularly easy intersection calculation, and the normal is easy to compute. If the center is at (x_0, y_0, z_0) and the radius is r, the equation for a sphere is:

$$(x - x_0)^2 + (y - y_0)^2 + (z - z_0)^2 = r^2 \qquad (4.8)$$

Plugging the implicit equations for x, y and z from (4.1) into (4.8) yields

$$(\mathbf{loc}.x + t\mathbf{dir}.x - x_0)^2 + (\mathbf{loc}.y + t\mathbf{dir}.y - y_0)^2 + (\mathbf{loc}.z + t\mathbf{dir}.z - z_0)^2 = r^2 \qquad (4.9)$$

Equation 4.9 is a quadratic equation in t. To solve for t, we need only get equation (4.9) into the form

$$At^2 + Bt + C = 0 \qquad (4.10)$$

and use the quadratic formula. As it turns out, for equation (4.9), the three coefficients A, B, and C are as follows:

$$A = \mathbf{dir} \cdot \mathbf{dir} \qquad (4.11a)$$

$$B = \mathbf{loc} \cdot \mathbf{dir} \qquad\qquad (4.11b)$$

$$C = \mathbf{loc} \cdot \mathbf{loc} - r^2 \qquad\qquad (4.11c)$$

If the ray direction vector is normalized, then A is guaranteed to be 1. Not coincidentally, the Ray constructors make sure to normalize the direction.

Finding the Normal

To compute the normal at a point on the sphere, just subtract the vector given ($\mathbf{V}$) from the sphere center ($\mathbf{C}$) and normalize:

$$\mathbf{N} = \frac{\mathbf{V} - \mathbf{C}}{|\mathbf{V} - \mathbf{C}|} \qquad\qquad (4.12)$$

Transformations

Because C++ does not let classes change their identity at runtime, OORT does not let you turn Spheres into non-Spheres by means of transformations. For example, you can't scale a sphere to turn it into an ellipsoid. To deal with spheres more generally, work with them as Quadrics. Creating a quadric sphere and transforming it into an ellipsoid works fine, because ellipsoids are quadrics as well. See the description of quadrics in the next section.

Because the sphere cannot be transformed into another object, only the center point of the sphere is affected by the transformation.

PtDistance and IsInside

PtDistance at a point $\mathbf{V}$ is equal to $\| \mathbf{V} - \mathbf{C} \| - R$, where R is the radius of the sphere and $\mathbf{C}$ is the center point. This distance has a linear relationship with the distance to the center of the sphere.

The default IsInside implementation is used, since Sphere::PtDistance is just as efficient as Sphere::IsInside would be.

Bounding Box

The bounding box of a sphere is given by the minimum $(\mathbf{C} - (r, r, r))$ and the maximum $(\mathbf{C} + (r, r, r))$.

```
// -------------------------------------------------------------------
// Sphere
//              Derived from Object3D.
// -------------------------------------------------------------------

class Sphere : public Object3D {
public:
    Sphere(const Vector3D& NewCenter, float NewRadius, Surface
    *NewColor);

    virtual int NearestInt(Ray& Ray, float& t, float maxt);
    virtual SpanList *FindAllIntersections(Ray& ray);
    virtual Vector3D FindNormal(const Vector3D& intersection);
    virtual void ApplyTransform(const Matrix& tform);
    virtual Object3D *Dup() const;
    virtual void Describe(int ind) const;
    virtual int IsInside(Vector3D& v);
    virtual float PtDistance(Vector3D& v);
    virtual AxisAlignedBox BBox() const;
    virtual void CountMe() const { Statistics::Objects::Sphere++; }
private:
    Vector3D center;            // location of sphere's center
    float radius;               // radius
    float radiussq;             // radius^2 (precomputed for efficiency)
};
```

Listing 4.7 Sphere definition

```
// ===================================================================
// sphere.cpp
//      Sphere support routines for OORT.
//
//          The Object-Oriented Ray Tracer (OORT)
//          Copyright (C) 1993 by Nicholas Wilt.
//
// This software product may be freely copied and distributed in
// unmodified form but may not be sold.  A nominal distribution
// fee may be charged for media and handling by freeware and
// shareware distributors.  The software product may not be
// included in whole or in part into any commercial package
// without the express written consent of the author.
//
// This software product is provided as is without warranty of
```

Listing 4.8 Sphere implementation

```
// any kind, express or implied, including but not limited to
// the implied warranties of merchantability and fitness for a
// particular purpose.  The author assumes no liability for any
// alleged or actual damages arising from the use of this
// software.  The author is under no obligation to provide
// service, corrections or upgrades to the software.
//
// -----------------------------------------------------------
//
// Please contact me with questions, comments, suggestions or
// other input about OORT.  My Compuserve account number is
// [75210,2455] (Internet sites can reach me at
// 75210.2455@compuserve.com).
//                                    --Nicholas Wilt
// ===================================================================

#include "oort.h"

// Sphere constructor.   Takes center, radius, color.
Sphere::Sphere(const Vector3D& C, float R, Surface *clr):
  Object3D(clr, 0), center(C), radius(R)
{
    radiussq = radius*radius;
}

// Sphere intersection routine.
int
Sphere::NearestInt(Ray& ray, float& t, float maxt)
{
    float b, c, d;
    float t1, t2;
    Vector3D diff;

    Statistics::Intersections::Sphere++;

    diff = center - ray.loc;
    c = (float) DotProd(diff, diff) - radiussq;
    b = -2 * DotProd(diff, ray.dir);
    d = b*b - 4*c;

    if (d <= 0)
       return 0;

    d = sqrt(d);
    t1 = (-b+d)/2.0;
```

Listing 4.8 Sphere implementation *(continued)*

```
    t2 = (-b-d)/2.0;

    if (t1 < Limits::Threshold || t1 >= maxt)
        t1 = -1;
    if (t2 < Limits::Threshold || t2 >= maxt)
        t2 = -1;
    if (t1 < 0) {
        if (t2 < 0)
            return 0;
        t = t2;
    }
    else {
        if (t2 < 0)
            t = t1;
        else
            t = (t1 < t2) ? t1 : t2;
    }
    if (t2 < t1) {
        float temp = t1;
        t1 = t2;
        t2 = temp;
    }
    return t > Limits::Threshold;
}

SpanList *
Sphere::FindAllIntersections(Ray& ray)
{
    float b, c, d;
    float t1, t2;
    Vector3D diff;

    Statistics::Intersections::Sphere++;

    diff = center - ray.loc;
    c = (float) DotProd(diff, diff) - radiussq;
    b = -2 * DotProd(diff, ray.dir);
    d = b*b - 4*c;

    if (d <= 0)
        return 0;

    d = sqrt(d);
    t1 = (-b+d)/2.0;
    t2 = (-b-d)/2.0;
```

Listing 4.8 Sphere implementation *(continued)*

```
      // If both parameters are less than threshold, return no-intersection.
      if (t1 < Limits::Threshold && t2 < Limits::Threshold)
          return 0;

      if (t1 > t2)
          Swap(t1, t2);
      if (t1 < 0) {
          if (IsInside(ray.loc))
              return new SpanList(Span(t1, this, t2, this));
          else
              return new SpanList(Span(t2, this, Limits::Infinity, this));
      }
      return new SpanList(Span(t1, this, t2, this));
}


// Sphere normal-finding routine.
Vector3D
Sphere::FindNormal(const Vector3D& intersection)
{
    return(Normalize(intersection - center));
}


// Apply transform to sphere.  Only center point is affected.
void
Sphere::ApplyTransform(const Matrix& tform)
{
    center = tform * center;
}


// Duplicate sphere.
Object3D *
Sphere::Dup() const
{
    return(new Sphere(center, radius, surf));
}


int
Sphere::IsInside(Vector3D& v)
{
    Vector3D diff = v - center;
    return Magnitude(diff) < radiussq;
}


float
Sphere::PtDistance(Vector3D& v)
```

Listing 4.8 Sphere implementation *(continued)*

```
{
    Vector3D diff = v - center;
    return DotProd(diff, diff) - radiussq;
}

// Describe sphere.   Indent spaces first.
void
Sphere::Describe(int ind) const
{
    indent(ind);
    cout << "Sphere: center at " << center << ", radius " << radius <<
    ".\n";
}

AxisAlignedBox
Sphere::BBox() const
{
    return AxisAlignedBox(Vector3D(center - Vector3D(radius)),
                    Vector3D(center + Vector3D(radius)));
}
```

Listing 4.8   `Sphere` implementation *(continued)*

4.5   Quadrics

A quadric surface is a second-degree *implicit surface*. An implicit surface is one whose points can be expressed as an equation in *x*, *y*, and *z*. (The plane, described in Section 4.2, is a first-degree implicit surface.) A completely general quadric is expressed in the following equation:

$$Ax^2 + By^2 + Cz^2 + 2Dxy + 2Eyz + 2Fxz + 2Gx + 2Hy + 2Jz + K = 0 \qquad (4.13)$$

It can also be expressed in the form of a matrix equation, as follows:

$$[x \quad y \quad z \quad 1] \begin{bmatrix} a & d & f & g \\ d & b & e & h \\ f & e & c & j \\ g & h & j & k \end{bmatrix} \begin{bmatrix} x \\ y \\ z \\ 1 \end{bmatrix} = 0 \qquad (4.14)$$

Many familiar shapes are quadric surfaces, including spheres, ellipsoids, cylinders, cones, paraboloids, and hyperboloids. Several taxonomies, with equations for the various types of surface [CYCH92] and techniques for their intersection [GLAS89a], are available for quadric surfaces. Figure 4.1 depicts a number of quadrics.

All of the quadric equations in Table 4.1 specify quadrics aligned along the Y axis except for the ellipsoid (which does not have a principal axis). Also, all of the quadric equations above specify quadrics that are centered on the origin. To generate a quadric that is not aligned along the Y axis, or one that is not centered at the origin, it is easiest to create a canonical quadric and transform it.

Intersecting With A Quadric

Although the quadric intersection calculation is more complicated than that for a sphere, it is similar in spirit: the coefficients A, B, and C of the quadratic equation must be computed, and the resulting equation solved for t. See `Quadric::NearestInt` in `quadric.cpp` for the particulars.

Finding the Normal

The normal to a quadric surface (indeed, the normal to any implicit surface) is equal to the *gradient* at the point given. The gradient of a function $f(x, y, z)$ is a vector

$$\left(\frac{\partial f}{\partial x}, \frac{\partial f}{\partial y}, \frac{\partial f}{\partial z} \right) \tag{4.15}$$

Quadric Type	Equation	Assumptions
Cone	$\dfrac{x^2}{a^2} - y^2 + \dfrac{z^2}{c^2} = 0$	Principal axis lengths $2a$ and $2c$ at a unit distance from the apex.
Cylinder	$\dfrac{x^2}{a^2} + \dfrac{z^2}{c^2} - 1 = 0$	With principal axis lengths $2a$ and $2c$.
Ellipsoid	$\dfrac{x^2}{a^2} + \dfrac{y^2}{b^2} + \dfrac{z^2}{c^2} - 1 = 0$	Axis lengths of a, b, and c along the principal directions x, y, and z.
Hyperboloid	$\dfrac{x^2}{a^2} - \dfrac{y^2}{b^2} + \dfrac{z^2}{c^2} - 1 = 0$	Principal axis vertex distances of 2a and 2c at the origin, and b determining the asymptotes.
Paraboloid	$\dfrac{x^2}{a^2} + \dfrac{z^2}{c^2} - 4fy = 0$	Principal axis lengths 2a and 2c at twice the focal length f.

Table 4.1   Equations for different types of quadric.

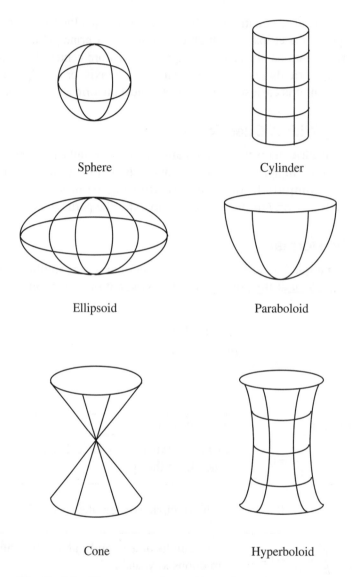

Figure 4.1 Taxonomy of quadric surfaces.

For those who don't feel like computing the partial derivatives of (4.13), or those who are unfamiliar with partial derivatives, this evaluates to:

$$(2Ax + Dy + Fz + G, 2By + Dx + Ez + H, 2Cz + Ey + Fx + J) \qquad (4.16)$$

Transformations

An arbitrary 4×4 transformation matrix may be applied to a quadric. This operation is best described in matrix notation. If $\mathbf{Q}$ denotes the quadric matrix before transformation, and $\mathbf{Q'}$ denotes the quadric matrix of the transformed quadric, the quadric is transformed by a transformation matrix $\mathbf{M}$ as follows [FOLE90]:

$$\mathbf{Q'} = \mathbf{M}^{-1} \cdot \mathbf{Q} \cdot \left(\mathbf{M}^{-1}\right)^{\mathrm{T}} \tag{4.17}$$

Since many types of quadric have less complicated equations than the general form (equation 4.13), these quadrics have simpler intersection calculations than the one necessary for a general quadric.

`PtDistance` and `IsInside`

`PtDistance` simply takes the given point (x,y,z) and plugs it into the implicit function of the quadric. This function meets the requirement that the return value be negative "inside" the surface, 0 on the surface, and positive "outside" the surface, but the "distance" it measures is not the distance from the point to the surface.

The default `IsInside` implementation provided by `Object3D` is used by `Quadric`.

Bounding Boxes

Quadrics are assumed to be unbounded. Most quadrics are; the only type of quadric that is bounded is the ellipsoid. To allow ellipsoids to participate in accelerated ray tracing, I wrote an `Ellipsoid` class that inherits from `Quadric`. The constructor takes X, Y, and Z radii for the ellipsoid and calls `Quadric::Quadric` with the correct coefficients to create a correctly-sized ellipsoid centered about the origin. `Ellipsoid::Ellipsoid` also creates a bounding box, and whenever the ellipsoid is transformed, the bounding box is transformed as well. The resulting bounding box is not very "tight," and depending on the transformations applied it can be *very* loose. Consider what would happen if you rotated the ellipsoid 45 degrees, then rotated it back again. The bounding box would increase greatly in size with each transformation, even though the transformations yield the original ellipsoid.

4.6 Polygons

Polygons are the bread and butter of most 3D computer graphics systems because they are easy to manipulate in hardware. Ray tracing is not well-suited

```
// ------------------------------------------------------------------
// Quadric
//     These are defined by the equation:
//     Ax^2 + By^2 + Cz^2 + 2Dxy + 2Eyz + 2Fxz + 2Gx + 2Hy + 2Jz + K = 0
//
//     It is useful to reformulate this into a 4x4 3D transformation
//     matrix for some operations, such as transformations.
// ------------------------------------------------------------------
class Quadric : public Object3D {
public:
    Quadric(float a, float b, float c, float d, float e, float f,
            float g, float h, float j, float k, Surface *NewColor);

    virtual int NearestInt(Ray& Ray, float& t, float maxt);
    virtual SpanList *FindAllIntersections(Ray& ray);
    virtual Vector3D FindNormal(const Vector3D& Intersection);
    virtual void ApplyTransform(const Matrix& tform);
    virtual Object3D *Dup() const;
    virtual void Describe(int ind) const;
    virtual float PtDistance(Vector3D& v);
    virtual void CountMe() const { Statistics::Objects::Quadric++; }
private:
    Matrix mat;                      // Quadric matrix
    double A, B, C, D, E, F, G, H, J;        // Temporaries

    void Precompute();
    void ComputeABC(Ray& ray, double *a, double *b, double *c) const;

    friend Algebraic;
};


// ------------------------------------------------------------------
// Ellipsoid
//     These are quadrics that can be bounded by bounding boxes.
//
// ------------------------------------------------------------------
class Ellipsoid : public Quadric {
public:
    Ellipsoid(float Xrad, float Yrad, float Zrad, Surface *NewColor);
    virtual void ApplyTransform(const Matrix& tform);
    virtual Object3D *Dup() const;
    virtual void Describe(int ind) const;
    virtual void CountMe() const { Statistics::Objects::Ellipsoid++; }
    virtual AxisAlignedBox BBox() const;
private:
```

Listing 4.9   Quadric and Ellipsoid definitions

```
   float a, b, c;
   AxisAlignedBox bbox;
};
```

Listing 4.9 Quadric **and** Ellipsoid **definitions** *(continued)*

```
// =====================================================================
// quadric.cpp
//     Quadric support routines for OORT.
//
//       The Object-Oriented Ray Tracer (OORT)
//       Copyright (C) 1993 by Nicholas Wilt.
//
// This software product may be freely copied and distributed in
// unmodified form but may not be sold.  A nominal distribution
// fee may be charged for media and handling by freeware and
// shareware distributors.  The software product may not be
// included in whole or in part into any commercial package
// without the express written consent of the author.
//
// This software product is provided as is without warranty of
// any kind, express or implied, including but not limited to
// the implied warranties of merchantability and fitness for a
// particular purpose.  The author assumes no liability for any
// alleged or actual damages arising from the use of this
// software.  The author is under no obligation to provide
// service, corrections or upgrades to the software.
//
// -----------------------------------------------------------
//
// Please contact me with questions, comments, suggestions or
// other input about OORT.  My Compuserve account number is
// [75210,2455] (Internet sites can reach me at
// 75210.2455@compuserve.com).
//                                 --Nicholas Wilt
// =====================================================================

#include "oort.h"
```

Listing 4.10 Quadric **and** Ellipsoid **implementations**

```
// Quadric constructor.  For now, we just take the equation and color
// and plug them into the matrix.  Later, more sophisticated
// methods of making quadrics such as Ellipsoids may be added.
Quadric::Quadric(float a, float b, float c, float d, float e, float f,
            float g, float h, float j, float k, Surface *clr) :
            Object3D (clr, 0)
{
   mat = QuadricMatrix(a, b, c, d, e, f, g, h, j, k);
   Precompute();
}


void
Quadric::ComputeABC(Ray& ray, double *a, double *b, double *c) const
{
   *a = mat.x[0][0] * ray.dd.x +
       mat.x[1][1] * ray.dd.y +
       mat.x[2][2] * ray.dd.z +
       D * ray.dir.x * ray.dir.y +
       E * ray.dir.y * ray.dir.z +
       F * ray.dir.x * ray.dir.z;
   *b = A * ray.ld.x +
       B * ray.ld.y +
       C * ray.ld.z +
       D * (ray.loc.x * ray.dir.y + ray.loc.y * ray.dir.x) +
       E * (ray.loc.y * ray.dir.z + ray.loc.z * ray.dir.y) +
       F * (ray.loc.x * ray.dir.z + ray.loc.z * ray.dir.x) +
       G * ray.dir.x +
       H * ray.dir.y +
       J * ray.dir.z;
   *c = mat.x[0][0] * ray.ll.x +
       mat.x[1][1] * ray.ll.y +
       mat.x[2][2] * ray.ll.z +
       D * ray.loc.x * ray.loc.y +
       E * ray.loc.y * ray.loc.z +
       F * ray.loc.x * ray.loc.z +
       G * ray.loc.x +
       H * ray.loc.y +
       J * ray.loc.z +
       mat.x[3][3];
```

Listing 4.10 Quadric and Ellipsoid implementations *(continued)*

```
}

// Quadric intersection routine.  Find the nearest intersection,
// if any.  Slow and ugly, but serviceable.
int
Quadric::NearestInt(Ray& ray, float& t, float maxt)
{
   double a, b, c, d;
   float t1, t2;

   Statistics::Intersections::Quadric++;
   ComputeABC(ray, &a, &b, &c);

   d = b * b - 4 * a * c;
   if (d <= 0)
      return 0;

   d = sqrt(d);
   a += a;
   if (fabs(a) < Limits::Small)
      return 0;
   t1 = (-b + d) / a;
   if (t1 >= maxt)
      t1 = -1;
   t2 = (-b - d) / a;
   if (t2 >= maxt)
      t2 = -1;

   if (t1 < 0) {
      if (t2 < 0)
         return 0;
      t = t2;
   }
   else {
      if (t2 < 0)
         t = t1;
      else
         t = (t1 < t2) ? t1 : t2;
   }
```

Listing 4.10 Quadric and Ellipsoid implementations *(continued)*

```
   return t > Limits::Threshold;
}

SpanList *
Quadric::FindAllIntersections(Ray& ray)
{
   double a, b, c, d;
   float t1, t2;

   Statistics::Intersections::Quadric += 1;
   ComputeABC(ray, &a, &b, &c);
   d = b * b - 4 * a * c;
   if (d <= 0)
      return 0;
   d = sqrt(d);
   a += a;
   if (fabs(a) < Limits::Small)
         return 0;
   t1 = (-b + d) / a;
   t2 = (-b - d) / a;

   // If both parameters are less than threshold, return no-
   intersection.
   if (t1 < Limits::Threshold && t2 < Limits::Threshold)
      return 0;

   // And if either parameter is near zero, assume self-intersection
   // and return no-intersection.
   if (fabs(t1) < Limits::Threshold || fabs(t2) < Limits::Threshold)
      return 0;
   if (t1 > t2)
      Swap(t1, t2);
   if (t1 < 0) {
      if (IsInside(ray.loc))
         return new SpanList(Span(t1, this, t2, this));
      else
         return new SpanList(Span(t2, this, Limits::Infinity, this));
   }
   return new SpanList(Span(t1, this, t2, this));
```

Listing 4.10 Quadric and Ellipsoid implementations *(continued)*

```
}

// Quadric normal-finder.  Again, slow and ugly.
Vector3D
Quadric::FindNormal(const Vector3D& intersection)
{
    Vector3D Direction(      A * intersection.x +
                       D * intersection.y +
                       F * intersection.z + G,
                       B * intersection.y +
                       D * intersection.x +
                       E * intersection.z + H,
                       C * intersection.z +
                       F * intersection.x +
                       E * intersection.y + J);
    return Normalize(Direction);
}

// Apply a transform to a quadric.
void
Quadric::ApplyTransform(const Matrix& tform)
{
    Matrix Inverted = Invert(tform);
    Matrix Transposed = Transpose(Inverted);

    mat = Inverted * mat * Transposed;

    Precompute();
}

// Precompute some useful values related to the quadric.
void
Quadric::Precompute()
{
    int i, j;
    float min = 1;

    for (i = 0; i < 4; i++)
        for (j = 0; j < 4; j++)
```

Listing 4.10 Quadric and Ellipsoid implementations *(continued)*

```
            if (fabs(mat.x[i][j]) > 1e-6 &&
                fabs(mat.x[i][j]) < min /*&&
                fabs(mat.x[i][j] > 0.001)*/)
               min = fabs(mat.x[i][j]);
    mat *= 1 / min;
    A = 2 * mat.x[0][0];
    B = 2 * mat.x[1][1];
    C = 2 * mat.x[2][2];
    D = mat.x[0][1] + mat.x[1][0];
    E = mat.x[1][2] + mat.x[2][1];
    F = mat.x[2][0] + mat.x[0][2];
    G = mat.x[3][0] + mat.x[0][3];
    H = mat.x[1][3] + mat.x[1][3];
    J = mat.x[2][3] + mat.x[3][2];
}


// Duplicate the quadric.
Object3D *
Quadric::Dup() const
{
    return new Quadric(*this);
}


float
Quadric::PtDistance(Vector3D& v)
{
    return mat.x[0][0] * v.x * v.x +
           mat.x[1][1] * v.y * v.y +
           mat.x[2][2] * v.z * v.z +
           D * v.x * v.y +
           E * v.y * v.z +
           F * v.x * v.z +
           G * v.x +
           H * v.y +
           J * v.z + mat.x[3][3];
}


// Describe a quadric.   Indent by the given amount first.
void
```

Listing 4.10 Quadric and Ellipsoid implementations *(continued)*

```
Quadric::Describe(int ind) const
{
   indent(ind);
   cout << setprecision(7) << "Quadric: " << A << ", " << B << ", ";
   cout << C << ", " << D << ", " << E << ", " << F << ", " << G;
   cout << ", " << H << ", " << J << ", " << mat.x[3][3] << '\n';
}



// =====================================================================
// Ellipsoid
//    Derived from Quadric.  However, because ellipsoids are
//    bounded, we can surround our ellipsoid with a loose bounding
//    volume and move the bounding volume around whenever the
//    ellipsoid is transformed.
// =====================================================================

Ellipsoid::Ellipsoid(float Xrad, float Yrad, float Zrad, Surface
   *NewColor):
   Quadric(1/(Xrad*Xrad), 1/(Yrad*Yrad), 1/(Zrad*Zrad),
      0, 0, 0, 0, 0, 0, -1, NewColor)
{
   a = Xrad;    // Needed only when Dup() is called.
   b = Yrad;
   c = Zrad;
   bbox = AxisAlignedBox(Vector3D(-a, -b, -c), Vector3D(a, b, c));
}


void
Ellipsoid::ApplyTransform(const Matrix& tform)
{
   bbox = Transform(bbox, tform);
   Quadric::ApplyTransform(tform);
}


Object3D *
Ellipsoid::Dup() const
{
   return new Ellipsoid(a, b, c, surf);
```

Listing 4.10 Quadric and Ellipsoid implementations *(continued)*

```
}

void
Ellipsoid::Describe(int ind) const
{
    indent(ind);
    cout << "Ellipsoid: (" << a << ", " << b << ", " << c << ")\n";
}

AxisAlignedBox
Ellipsoid::BBox() const
{
    return bbox;
}
```

Listing 4.10   `Quadric` and `Ellipsoid` implementations *(continued)*

to rendering collections of polygons. There are two motivations for supporting polygons in a ray tracer. First, many modelers produce polygons as output, rather than higher-level primitives that can be decomposed into polygons as needed. Second, while polygons are slow to render, some types of object are even slower, and it is most efficient to decompose these objects into collections of polygons before rendering.

A polygon is a collection of points in a plane. It is usually specified by a list of endpoints, and the points enclosed are inside the polygon. In computer graphics, polygons are usually thought of as "facing" a particular direction. Such polygons are visible only from one side—the side the polygon normal points toward. It is common to adopt a convention of ordering the vertices to specify the direction a polygon is facing. In OORT, as in many rendering systems, the vertices are considered to be given in *clockwise* order, as seen from the visible side of the polygon.

A polygon is considered to lie in a plane, and one of the many values precomputed for a polygon is the plane equation. As was explained in Section 4.2, the normal to a plane is part of the plane equation. Given that the vertices are in clockwise order when viewed from the direction the normal is facing, the normal can be computed from the first three vertices $\mathbf{v}_0, \mathbf{v}_1, \mathbf{v}_2$ as follows:

$$\mathbf{N} = (\mathbf{v}_0 - \mathbf{v}_1) \times (\mathbf{v}_2 - \mathbf{v}_1) \tag{4.18}$$

If **N** has length 0, then the three vertices are collinear and do not define a plane. Also, if there are more than four vertices, they may not lie in a plane. A more robust technique for computing the normal to the polygon takes all the vertices into account. Foley et al. describe such a technique [FOLE90, 476-477].

Once **N** has been computed, the value D for the plane equation can be computed from any one of the points. Again, a technique taking all the polygon vertices into account is more robust.

Intersection

The straightforward polygon intersection calculation can be divided into two parts: intersection with the plane that the polygon resides in, and a check to see whether the intersection point on the plane lies within the polygon. The first step is performed by calling `Planar::NearestInt` to compute the parameter of intersection with the plane of the polygon (if any).

Determining whether the intersection point lies within the polygon can be reduced from a three-dimensional problem to a two-dimensional problem by applying a parallel projection to the polygon vertices onto one of the coordinate planes. This operation amounts to ignoring one of the X, Y, or Z components of each vertex. The technique is most robust if we ignore the component of the normal that has the largest magnitude. For example, if a polygon has a normal (0, 1, 0), pointing directly along the Y axis, then it should be projected onto the XZ plane by ignoring the Y component of each vertex. The function `Vector3D::ExtractVerts` performs the projection. Although the two coordinates passed back have the same values they did before the projection, they are no longer in the 3D world coordinate system. To emphasize this transition, the two coordinates are subsequently referred to as U and V. Which coordinate of X, Y or Z is assigned to U and which to V does not matter, as long as the projection is done consistently for all the points projected.

The UV projection can be precomputed, though OORT does not do so. Instead, OORT precomputes whether the X, Y or Z component should be ignored and uses `Vector3D::ExtractVerts` to perform the projection inline.

Once the plane to project the polygon onto has been decided, a two-dimensional point-in-polygon test must be performed. There are a number of techniques for doing this test; there are even different criteria for deciding when a point is in a polygon. These criteria only disagree about polygons with crossing edges (e.g., the star in Figure 4.2), so we will not greatly concern ourselves with the differences between them. The criterion used by OORT is called the "odd parity" rule. If a ray (a 2D geometric ray, not to be confused with the rays cast

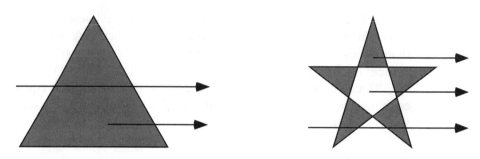

Figure 4.2 Point-in-polygon test

during ray tracing) that starts at the intersection point intersects an odd number of polygon edges, then the intersection point is inside the polygon. Otherwise it is outside. See Figure 4.2.

Optimizing Polygon Intersection

The slowest part of a polygon intersection routine is the test for odd parity. Fortunately, the odd parity test is a last resort. If we can determine that the ray misses the polygon before the odd parity test has to be performed, we can return no-intersection and skip it altogether.

The first opportunity to return no-intersection early comes immediately after the plane intersection test. If the intersection point is behind the ray origin (has a negative parameter of intersection) or is close to zero (indicating self-intersection of the ray with the object that spawned it), then the routine returns no-intersection.

Then comes one more opportunity to return no-intersection before the odd-parity test. This optimization is due to Woo [WOO90]. We can project the intersection point onto the same plane that the polygon vertices are projected onto and check to see whether it is within the bounding rectangle of the projected vertices. If it is not, then the intersection point cannot possibly be within the polygon and we can return no-intersection. In OORT, `Polygon:` `:Precompute` computes the bounding rectangle of the projected vertices and stores it in `umin`, `vmin`, `umax`, `vmax`. `Polygon:` `:NearestInt` checks the projected intersection point against these values before the odd-parity test.

Because of these techniques of rejecting an intersection early, only a small fraction of polygon intersection calculations actually require the odd parity test to be performed. The odd parity test itself involves casting a geometric ray from the projected intersection point in the +U direction of the UV plane that the polygon is projected onto. This ray is tested against each edge of the polygon in turn; if it crosses an edge, a count is incremented. If the count is odd after the last edge has been tested against the ray, then the intersection point is considered to have fallen within the polygon.

To check the ray against a given edge, the endpoints (u_1, v_1) and (u_2, v_2) of the edge are translated so that the intersection point is at the origin. Then four cases must be checked to determine whether the 2D ray intersects the edge:

1. If v_1 and v_2 have the same sign, the ray misses the edge.

2. If u_1 and u_2 are both negative, the ray misses the edge.

3. If u_1 and u_2 are both positive, the ray hits the edge (since v_1 and v_2 have already been determined to have different signs).

4. Otherwise, the intersection between the geometric ray and the polygon edge must be computed as follows:

$$t = \frac{-v_1}{v_2 - v_1}$$

(4.19)

After computing t, the ray intersects the edge if $u_1 + t(u_2 u_1) > 0$.

Figure 4.3 depicts these four cases and how they are resolved. The point is considered to be inside the polygon if the ray intersected an odd number of polygon edges.

Interested readers can refer to `int_lineseg` in `polygon.cpp` to see the actual implementation of this ray-edge intersection calculation. It takes care of a few implementation issues we have not mentioned. For example, equation (4.19) can overflow on the divide if the magnitude of $|v_2 - v_1|$ is not checked.

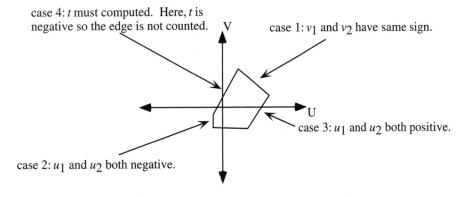

case 4: t must computed. Here, t is negative so the edge is not counted.

V

case 1: v_1 and v_2 have same sign.

U

case 3: u_1 and u_2 both positive.

case 2: u_1 and u_2 both negative.

Figure 4.3 Edge cases during odd parity test.

Finding the Normal

The normal to a polygon is precomputed and set by the `Polygon::Precompute`. It is returned by `Planar::FindNormal`.

Transformations

A polygon is transformed by transforming each of the vertices.

PtDistance and IsInside

The `Planar` implementations of these functions are used by `Polygon`.

Bounding Boxes

The bounding box of a polygon is found by computing the smallest axis-aligned box that encloses all of the polygon's vertices.

```
// -------------------------------------------------------------
// Polygon
//     Derived from Planar.
//     Much of the information in this class is precomputed to speed
//     intersection calculations.
// -------------------------------------------------------------
class Polygon : public Planar {
public:
   Polygon(): Planar(0) { }
   Polygon(int NewNumVerts, Vector3D *NewVertices, Surface *NewColor);
   Polygon(const Polygon& x);

   virtual ~Polygon();
   virtual int NearestInt(Ray& Ray, float& t, float maxt);
   virtual void ApplyTransform(const Matrix& tform);
   virtual Object3D *Dup() const;
   virtual void Describe(int ind) const;
   virtual AxisAlignedBox BBox() const;
   virtual void CountMe() const { Statistics::Objects::Polygon++; }
protected:
   int NumVerts;          // Number of vertices
   Vector3D *Vertices;    // Pointer to an array of NumVerts vertices
   // Projection information
```

Listing 4.11 `Polygon` definition

```
    int which;               // Which coordinate to ignore in projection
    float umin, umax;        // Bounding box of projection
    float vmin, vmax;        //

    void Precompute();       // Computes projection and some other stuff
};
```

Listing 4.11   `Polygon` definition   *(continued)*

```
// =====================================================================
// polygon.cpp
//     Polygon support routines for OORT.
//
//       The Object-Oriented Ray Tracer (OORT)
//       Copyright (C) 1993 by Nicholas Wilt.
//
// This software product may be freely copied and distributed in
// unmodified form but may not be sold.  A nominal distribution
// fee may be charged for media and handling by freeware and
// shareware distributors.  The software product may not be
// included in whole or in part into any commercial package
// without the express written consent of the author.
//
// This software product is provided as is without warranty of
// any kind, express or implied, including but not limited to
// the implied warranties of merchantability and fitness for a
// particular purpose.  The author assumes no liability for any
// alleged or actual damages arising from the use of this
// software.  The author is under no obligation to provide
// service, corrections or upgrades to the software.
//
// --------------------------------------------------------
//
// Please contact me with questions, comments, suggestions or
// other input about OORT.  My Compuserve account number is
// [75210,2455] (Internet sites can reach me at
// 75210.2455@compuserve.com).
//                            --Nicholas Wilt
// =====================================================================

// Polygon constructor
Polygon::Polygon(int NewNumVerts,     // number of vertices
```

Listing 4.12   `Polygon` implementation   *(continued)*

```
              Vector3D *NewVertices,   // vertices
              Surface *NewSurface):    // polygon surface
   Planar(NewSurface)
{
   NumVerts = NewNumVerts;             // copy given info
   Vertices = new Vector3D[NumVerts];
   for (int i = 0; i < NumVerts; i++)
      Vertices[i] = NewVertices[i];
   Precompute();                       // precompute
}

Polygon::Polygon(const Polygon& x): Planar(x.surf)
{
   Vertices = new Vector3D[NumVerts = x.NumVerts];
   for (int i = 0; i < NumVerts; i++)
      Vertices[i] = x.Vertices[i];
   Precompute();
}

// Polygon destructor
Polygon::~Polygon()
{
   delete[] Vertices;
}

// Precompute various parameters about the polygon:
//     The plane equation (including normal)
//     which component of the normal is dominant (needed
//            for intersection routine)
//     Bounding rectangle of projection (used by intersection
//            routine to eliminate intersections)
//     Overall bounding box of polygon (used by intersection
//            routine to intersect with ray bounding boxes)
void
Polygon::Precompute()
{
   int i;                      // Index variable
   float max;                  // Maximum component of normal
   Vector3D minvert, maxvert;  // Bounds of polygon

   // Compute the plane equation of the polygon.
   Vector3D xprod = CrossProd(Vertices[2] - Vertices[1],
                     Vertices[0] - Vertices[1]);
   if (fabs(Magnitude(xprod)) > Limits::Small) {
      bad = 0;
```

Listing 4.12 Polygon implementation *(continued)*

```
        Normal = Normalize(xprod);
    }
    else {
        bad = 1;
        return;
    }
    d = -DotProd(Normal, Vertices[0]);

    // Precompute which.  which is 0 if the normal is dominant
    // in the X direction, 1 if the Y direction, 2 if the Z direction.

    which = 0;                      // Assume we'll ignore X for now
    max = fabs(Normal.x);
    if (fabs(Normal.y) > max) {     // Check to see if we ignore Y
        max = fabs(Normal.y);       // Yes, ignore Y instead
        which = 1;
    }
    if (fabs(Normal.z) > max)       // Check to see if we ignore Z
        which = 2;                  // Yep

    // Compute bounding rectangle of projection.  This is fairly
    // successful at rejecting nonintersections.
    Vertices[0].ExtractVerts(&umin, &vmin, which);
    umax = umin;
    vmax = vmin;
    for (i = 1; i < NumVerts; i++) {
        float tempx, tempy;

        Vertices[i].ExtractVerts(&tempx, &tempy, which);
        if (tempx < umin)
            umin = tempx;
        else if (tempx > umax)
            umax = tempx;
        if (tempy < vmin)
            vmin = tempy;
        else if (tempy > vmax)
            vmax = tempy;
    }
}

#ifdef ASM
extern "C" int int_lineseg(float, float, float, float, float, float);
#else
// int_lineseg returns 1 if the given line segment intersects a 2D
// ray travelling in the positive X direction.   This is used in the
```

Listing 4.12 Polygon **implementation** *(continued)*

```
// Jordan curve computation for polygon intersection.
int
int_lineseg(float px, float py, float u1, float v1, float u2, float
    v2)
{
    float t;
    float ydiff;

    u1 -= px; u2 -= px;          // translate line
    v1 -= py; v2 -= py;

    if ((v1 > 0 && v2 > 0) ||
        (v1 < 0 && v2 < 0) ||
        (u1 < 0 && u2 < 0))
         return 0;

    if (u1 > 0 && u2 > 0)
        return 1;

    ydiff = v2 - v1;
    if (fabs(ydiff) < Limits::Small) {       // denominator near 0
        if (((fabs(v1) > Limits::Small) ||
            (u1 > 0) || (u2 > 0)))
            return 0;
        return 1;
    }

    t = -v1 / ydiff;               // Compute parameter

    return (u1 + t * (u2 - u1)) > 0;
}
#endif

// Polygon intersection routine.
int
Polygon::NearestInt(Ray& ray, float& t, float maxt)
{
    int count;
    float u, v, u1, v1, u2, v2;
    int i;

    Statistics::Intersections::Polygon++;
    if (Planar::NearestInt(ray, t, maxt)) {
        // Project the intersection point onto the coordinate plane
        // specified by which.
```

Listing 4.12 `Polygon` implementation *(continued)*

```
        ray.Extrap(t).ExtractVerts(&u, &v, which);

        // Reject intersection if outside projected bounding rectangle
        if (u < umin || u > umax || v < vmin || v > vmax)
            return 0;

        // We're stuck with the Jordan curve computation.  Count number
        // of intersections between the line segments the polygon
comprises
        // with a ray originating at the point of intersection and
        // travelling in the positive X direction.

        count = 0;
        Vertices[NumVerts - 1].ExtractVerts(&u1, &v1, which);

        for (i = 0; i < NumVerts; i++) {
            Vertices[i].ExtractVerts(&u2, &v2, which);
            count += int_lineseg(u, v, u1, v1, u2, v2) != 0;

            u1 = u2;
            v1 = v2;
        }

        // We hit polygon if number of intersections is odd.
        return count & 1;
    }
    return 0;
}

// Apply transform to a polygon: transform each vertex, then
// re-precompute all the precomputed information.
void
Polygon::ApplyTransform(const Matrix& tform)
{
    for (int i = 0; i < NumVerts; i++)
        Vertices[i] = tform * Vertices[i];
    Precompute();
}

// Duplicate a polygon.
Object3D *
Polygon::Dup() const
{
    return new Polygon(NumVerts, Vertices, surf);
}
```

Listing 4.12 `Polygon` implementation *(continued)*

```
// Print out vertices of polygon.
void
Polygon::Describe(int ind) const
{
    int i;

    indent(ind);
    cout << "Polygon.  Vertices: ";
    for (i = 0; i < NumVerts; i++) {
        cout << Vertices[i];
        if (i < NumVerts-1)
            cout << ", ";
    }
    cout << '\n';
}

AxisAlignedBox
Polygon::BBox() const
{
    int i;
    Vector3D min = Vertices[0];
    Vector3D max = Vertices[0];

    for (i = 1; i < NumVerts; i++) {
        Minimize(min, Vertices[i]);
        Maximize(max, Vertices[i]);
    }
    // Make sure the bounding box isn't flat.
    Vector3D diff = min - max;
    for (i = 0; i < 3; i++)
        if (fabs(diff[i]) < Limits::Threshold) {
            min[i] -= Limits::Threshold;
            max[i] += Limits::Threshold;
        }
    return AxisAlignedBox(min, max);
}
```

Listing 4.12 `Polygon` **implementation** *(continued)*

4.7 Bounding Boxes

Axis-aligned bounding boxes are popular because they are easy to compute and intersect with a ray, because it is easy to compute the intersection or union of two bounding boxes, and because whether a point is inside the bounding box can be determined very quickly. The major disadvantage with axis-aligned bounding boxes is that they are not very "tight": they may occupy much more space than the objects they enclose. Other types of bounding volume that have been described are spheres [WHIT80] and slabs [KAY86].

Intersection

The bounding box is completely described by two vectors, **min** and **max**. **min** and **max** are the bounding box's closest and farthest points from the origin. The bounding box can be thought of as the intersection of six half-spaces defined by six planes. In terms of the **min** and **max** vectors, the plane equations for the six planes defining the bounding box are as follows:

$$x = \textbf{min}.x \tag{4.20a}$$

$$x = \textbf{max}.x \tag{4.20b}$$

$$y = \textbf{min}.y \tag{4.20c}$$

$$y = \textbf{max}.y \tag{4.20d}$$

$$z = \textbf{min}.z \tag{4.20e}$$

$$z = \textbf{max}.z \tag{4.20f}$$

The six planes correspond of three pairs of planes that are parallel to each other. It is necessary to compute the parameter of intersection of each of these pairs of planes. For the x component, the two parameters of intersection with a ray of origin **loc** and direction **dir** are as follows:

$$t_1 = \frac{\textbf{min}.x - \textbf{loc}.x}{\textbf{dir}.x} \tag{4.21a}$$

$$t_2 = \frac{\textbf{max}.x - \textbf{loc}.x}{\textbf{dir}.x} \tag{4.21b}$$

If **dir**.x is close to zero, then the ray is nearly parallel to the two planes and t_1 and t_2 both diverge. This situation does not preclude intersecting the bounding box, however. If the ray origin loc falls within the bounding box extents for the X component (**min**.$x <$ **loc**.$x <$ **max**.x), the ray might still hit the bounding box.

Once the two parameters of intersection are computed for the X component, the smaller one is assigned to a temporary xmin and the larger is assigned to xmax. The same calculation must be performed in the Y and Z dimensions, and the ray tracer winds up with six variables: xmin, xmax, ymin, ymax, zmin, and zmax.

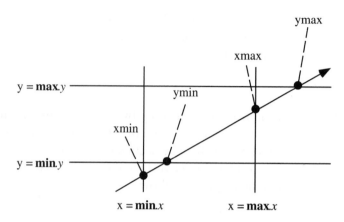

Figure 4.4   2D analog of bounding box intersection.

Two of these six variables are the parameters of intersection with the ray, if it intersects the bounding box at all. The smaller parameter of intersection, `tmin`, is the *maximum* of (`xmin`, `ymin`, `zmin`). The larger parameter of intersection, `tmax`, is the *minimum* of (`xmax`, `ymax`, `zmax`). Figure 4.4 depicts a two-dimensional analog of this operation. If `tmax` is negative, then the ray misses the bounding box. Otherwise, if `tmin` is negative, the ray origin lies within the bounding box and the parameter of nearest intersection is `tmax`. If `tmin` is positive, it is the parameter of nearest intersection with the bounding box.

Note that if the ray is nearly parallel to one or two of the coordinate planes, then the ray origin must be checked against the bounding box extents. If the ray origin is not within the bounding box extents, then the ray does not hit the bounding box. Otherwise, it *might* hit the bounding box. If so, the minimum and maximum for that coordinate are set to –MAXFLOAT and MAXFLOAT to signify that the ray intersects the two planes at negative and positive infinity. When `tmin` is computed, it is not possible for it to assume –MAXFLOAT because `tmin` is the maximum of `minx`, `miny`, and `minz`, and at least one of those values will be greater than –MAXFLOAT. Similarly, `tmax` cannot assume a value of MAXFLOAT because one of `maxx`, `maxy`, `maxz` will be less than MAXFLOAT.

Finding the Normal

No function should ever attempt to compute the normal to a bounding box. That operation is reserved for visible objects. `BoundingVolume::FindNormal` prints an error and exits if it is called.

Transformations

A bounding box may be transformed by transforming each of its eight corner points, then finding the smallest axis-aligned box that encloses them. Anything that was enclosed in the original bounding box, then transformed, will still be enclosed in the resulting box if this procedure is used. Of course, the bounding box will be much looser after the transformation; rotating a bounding box, for example, usually greatly increases the volume it encloses.

Implementation Notes

`BoundingVolume` is a class derived from `Object3D` that encompasses all types of bounding volume. For now, of course, there is only one type of bounding volume in OORT. So `BoundingBox` inherits from `BoundingVolume` and implements the various intersection and other functions required of it.

Since axis-aligned boxes (also called *voxels* or *rectangular prisms*) are a useful concept in their own right, they are implemented as a separate class (`AxisAlignedBox`). `AxisAlignedBox` implements many operations that are defined on axis-aligned boxes, including intersection and union. Since `BoundingBox` inherits from `AxisAlignedBox`, it inherits all of the member functions that support these operations.

```
// -------------------------------------------------------
// AxisAlignedBox class.
//    This is a box in 3-space, defined by min and max
//    corner vectors.
// -------------------------------------------------------

class AxisAlignedBox {
public:
   // Constructors.
   AxisAlignedBox() { }
   AxisAlignedBox(const Vector3D& Min, const Vector3D& Max): min(Min),
   max(Max) { }

   // Read-only access to min and max vectors.
   Vector3D Min() const;
   Vector3D Max() const;

   // Return whether the box is unbounded.  Unbounded boxes appear
   // when unbounded objects such as quadric surfaces are included.
```

Listing 4.13 `AxisAlignedBox`, `BoundingVolume` **and** `BoundingBox` **definitions**

```
    int Unbounded() const;

    // Expand the axis-aligned box to include the given object.
    void Include(const Vector3D& newpt);
    void Include(const AxisAlignedBox& bbox);

    // Overlap returns 1 if the two axis-aligned boxes overlap.
    friend int Overlap(const AxisAlignedBox&, const AxisAlignedBox&);

    // Returns the smallest axis-aligned box that includes all points
    // inside the two given boxes.
    friend AxisAlignedBox Union(const AxisAlignedBox& x, const
    AxisAlignedBox& y);

    // Returns the intersection of two axis-aligned boxes.
    friend AxisAlignedBox Intersect(const AxisAlignedBox& x, const
    AxisAlignedBox& y);

    friend AxisAlignedBox Transform(const AxisAlignedBox& box, const
    Matrix& tform);

    virtual float SurfaceArea() const;
    int ComputeMinMaxT(Ray& ray, float *tmin, float *tmax) const;

    friend class Ray;
protected:
    Vector3D min, max;
};

inline int
Overlap(const AxisAlignedBox& x, const AxisAlignedBox& y)
{
    if (x.max.x < y.min.x ||
        x.min.x > y.max.x ||
        x.max.y < y.min.y ||
        x.min.y > y.max.y ||
        x.max.z < y.min.z ||
        x.min.z > y.max.z) {
        return 0;
    }
    return 1;
}

inline AxisAlignedBox
```

Listing 4.13 `AxisAlignedBox`, `BoundingVolume` **and** `BoundingBox` **definitions** *(continued)*

```
Intersect(const AxisAlignedBox& x, const AxisAlignedBox& y)
{
   if (x.Unbounded())
      return y;
   else if (y.Unbounded())
      return x;
   AxisAlignedBox ret = x;
   if (Overlap(ret, y)) {
      Maximize(ret.min, y.min);
      Minimize(ret.max, y.max);
      return ret;
   }
   else          // Null intersection.
      return AxisAlignedBox(Vector3D(0), Vector3D(0));
}


inline AxisAlignedBox
Union(const AxisAlignedBox& x, const AxisAlignedBox& y)
{
   Vector3D min = x.min;
   Vector3D max = x.max;
   Minimize(min, y.min);
   Maximize(max, y.max);
   return AxisAlignedBox(min, max);
}
inline AxisAlignedBox
Transform(const AxisAlignedBox& box, const Matrix& tform)
{
   AxisAlignedBox ret(Vector3D(MAXFLOAT), Vector3D(-MAXFLOAT));
   ret.Include(tform * Vector3D(box.min.x, box.min.y, box.min.z));
   ret.Include(tform * Vector3D(box.min.x, box.min.y, box.max.z));
   ret.Include(tform * Vector3D(box.min.x, box.max.y, box.min.z));
   ret.Include(tform * Vector3D(box.min.x, box.max.y, box.max.z));
   ret.Include(tform * Vector3D(box.max.x, box.min.y, box.min.z));
   ret.Include(tform * Vector3D(box.max.x, box.min.y, box.max.z));
   ret.Include(tform * Vector3D(box.max.x, box.max.y, box.min.z));
   ret.Include(tform * Vector3D(box.max.x, box.max.y, box.max.z));
   return ret;
}


// ------------------------------------------------------------------
// BoundingVolume
//    This abstract class is derived from Object3D.  It contains a
//    list of other objects (those contained in the bounding
```

Listing 4.13 AxisAlignedBox, BoundingVolume and BoundingBox definitions *(continued)*

```
//     volume).  Member functions to manipulate the list are
//     provided.
// ----------------------------------------------------------------
class BoundingVolume: public Object3D {
public:
   BoundingVolume() : Object3D(BOUNDING) { }
   virtual int NumChildren() { return contents.ListCount(); }
   virtual Vector3D FindNormal(const Vector3D& intersection) = 0;
   virtual void ApplyTransform(const Matrix& tform) = 0;
   virtual void TransformSurface(SurfaceList& clist, const Matrix&
   tform);
   virtual SpanList *FindAllIntersections(Ray& ray) = 0;
   virtual Object3D *Dup() const = 0;
   virtual void Describe(int ind) const = 0;
   virtual float PtDistance(Vector3D& v) = 0;
   virtual AxisAlignedBox BBox() const = 0;
   virtual void CountMe() const = 0;

   virtual float SurfaceArea() const = 0;

   virtual void AddObject(const Object3D& NewObj); // add new instance
   of object
   virtual void AddObject(Object3D *NewObj);       // put object in
   list
   virtual ObjectList *List() { return &contents; }
   friend World;

protected:
   ObjectList contents;       // Contents of bounding volume

};


// ----------------------------------------------------------------
// BoundingBox
//     Derived multiply from BoundingVolume and AxisAlignedBox, this
//     class encapsulates the axis-aligned bounding boxes used by
//     OORT.
// ----------------------------------------------------------------
class BoundingBox : public BoundingVolume, public AxisAlignedBox {
public:
   BoundingBox(): BoundingVolume(),
      AxisAlignedBox(Vector3D(MAXFLOAT), Vector3D(-MAXFLOAT)) { }
   BoundingBox(const Vector3D& Min, const Vector3D& Max):
```

Listing 4.13 AxisAlignedBox, BoundingVolume **and** BoundingBox **definitions**
(continued)

```
        BoundingVolume(),
            AxisAlignedBox(Min, Max) { }
        BoundingBox(AxisAlignedBox& x): BoundingVolume(), AxisAlignedBox(x)
        { }

        virtual SpanList *FindAllIntersections(Ray& ray);
        virtual int NearestInt(Ray& ray, float& t, float maxt);
        virtual Vector3D FindNormal(const Vector3D& intersection);
        virtual void ApplyTransform(const Matrix& tform);
        virtual Object3D *Dup() const;
        virtual int IsInside(Vector3D& v);
        virtual float PtDistance(Vector3D& v);
        virtual void Describe(int ind) const;
        virtual AxisAlignedBox BBox() const;
        virtual void CountMe() const { Statistics::Objects::BBox++; }
        virtual float SurfaceArea() const;

        virtual void AddObject(const Object3D&);
        virtual void AddObject(Object3D *);

        friend class Quadric;
        friend class Ray;
private:
        int ComputeMinMaxT(Ray& ray, float *tmin, float *tmax);
};
```

Listing 4.13 AxisAlignedBox, BoundingVolume **and** BoundingBox **definitions**
(continued)

```
// ====================================================================
// bbox.cpp
//      Bounding box-related routines.
//
//          The Object-Oriented Ray Tracer (OORT)
//          Copyright (C) 1993 by Nicholas Wilt.
//
// This software product may be freely copied and distributed in
// unmodified form but may not be sold.  A nominal distribution
// fee may be charged for media and handling by freeware and
// shareware distributors.  The software product may not be
// included in whole or in part into any commercial package
// without the express written consent of the author.
//
// This software product is provided as is without warranty of
```

Listing 4.14 BoundingBox **implementation**

```
// any kind, express or implied, including but not limited to
// the implied warranties of merchantability and fitness for a
// particular purpose.  The author assumes no liability for any
// alleged or actual damages arising from the use of this
// software.  The author is under no obligation to provide
// service, corrections or upgrades to the software.
//
// ------------------------------------------------------------
//
// Please contact me with questions, comments, suggestions or
// other input about OORT.  My Compuserve account number is
// [75210,2455] (Internet sites can reach me at
// 75210.2455@compuserve.com).
//                             --Nicholas Wilt
// ============================================================

#include "oort.h"

// AxisAlignedBox implementations
Vector3D
AxisAlignedBox::Min() const
{
    return min;
}

Vector3D
AxisAlignedBox::Max() const
{
    return max;
}
int
AxisAlignedBox::Unbounded() const
{
    return min == Vector3D(-MAXFLOAT) || max == Vector3D(-MAXFLOAT);
}

void
AxisAlignedBox::Include(const Vector3D& newpt)
{
    Minimize(min, newpt);
    Maximize(max, newpt);
}

void
AxisAlignedBox::Include(const AxisAlignedBox& bbox)
```

Listing 4.14 BoundingBox implementation *(continued)*

```
{
    Minimize(min, bbox.min);
    Maximize(max, bbox.max);
}

extern "C" int bboxint(const Vector3D *minmax,
                       const Vector3D *locdir,
                       float *tmin, float *tmax);

// ComputeMinMaxT computes the minimum and maximum parameters
// of intersection with the ray; it returns 1 if the ray hits
// the bounding box and 0 if it does not.
int
AxisAlignedBox::ComputeMinMaxT(Ray& ray, float *tmin, float *tmax)
    const
{
#ifndef ASM
    float t1, t2;
    float minx, maxx, miny, maxy, minz, maxz;
    if (fabs(ray.dir.x) < 0.001) {
        if (min.x < ray.loc.x && max.x > ray.loc.x) {
            minx = -MAXFLOAT;
            maxx = MAXFLOAT;
        }
        else
            return 0;
    }
    else {
        t1 = (min.x - ray.loc.x) / ray.dir.x;
        t2 = (max.x - ray.loc.x) / ray.dir.x;
        if (t1 < t2) {
            minx = t1;
            maxx = t2;
        }
        else {
            minx = t2;
            maxx = t1;
        }
        if (maxx < 0)
            return 0;
    }

    if (fabs(ray.dir.y) < 0.001) {
        if (min.y < ray.loc.y && max.y > ray.loc.y) {
            miny = -MAXFLOAT;
```

Listing 4.14   BoundingBox implementation *(continued)*

```
            maxy = MAXFLOAT;
         }
         else
            return 0;
      }
   else {
      t1 = (min.y - ray.loc.y) / ray.dir.y;
      t2 = (max.y - ray.loc.y) / ray.dir.y;
      if (t1 < t2) {
         miny = t1;
         maxy = t2;
      }
      else {
         miny = t2;
         maxy = t1;
      }
      if (maxy < 0)
         return 0;
   }

   if (fabs(ray.dir.z) < 0.001) {
      if (min.z < ray.loc.z && max.z > ray.loc.z) {
         minz = -MAXFLOAT;
         maxz = MAXFLOAT;
      }
      else
         return 0;
   }
   else {
      t1 = (min.z - ray.loc.z) / ray.dir.z;
      t2 = (max.z - ray.loc.z) / ray.dir.z;
      if (t1 < t2) {
         minz = t1;
         maxz = t2;
      }
      else {
         minz = t2;
         maxz = t1;
      }
      if (maxz < 0)
         return 0;
   }

   *tmin = minx;
   if (miny > *tmin)
```

Listing 4.14 BoundingBox implementation *(continued)*

```
        *tmin = miny;
    if (minz > *tmin)
        *tmin = minz;

    *tmax = maxx;
    if (maxy < *tmax)
        *tmax = maxy;
    if (maxz < *tmax)
        *tmax = maxz;
#else
    if (! bboxint(&min, &ray.loc, tmin, tmax))
        return 0;
#endif
    return 1;
}

int
BoundingBox::NearestInt(Ray& ray, float& t, float maxt)
{
    float tmin, tmax;

    Statistics::Intersections::BBox++;

    if (! AxisAlignedBox::ComputeMinMaxT(ray, &tmin, &tmax))
        return 0;
    if (tmax < tmin)
        return 0;
    if (tmin < 0) {
        // No intersection if both parameters are negative
        if (tmax < 0)
            return 0;
        // The ray hit the bounding box
        // tmax is parameter of intersection
        t = (tmax < maxt) ? tmax : maxt;
    }
    else {
        // The ray hit the bounding box
        // with parameter tmin.
        t = (tmin < maxt) ? tmin : maxt;
    }
    return 1;
}

SpanList *
BoundingBox::FindAllIntersections(Ray& ray)
```

Listing 4.14 BoundingBox implementation *(continued)*

```
{
   cerr << "BoundingBox::FindAllIntersections called\n";
   exit(1);
   return 0;
}

void
BoundingBox::ApplyTransform(const Matrix &tform)
{
   AxisAlignedBox bbox(Vector3D(MAXFLOAT), Vector3D(-MAXFLOAT));

   for (ObjectList::Iterator sc(contents); sc.Valid(); sc.GotoNext())
   {
      sc.Contents()->ApplyTransform(tform);
      bbox = Union(bbox, sc.Contents()->BBox());
   }
   min = bbox.Min();
   max = bbox.Max();
}

Vector3D
BoundingBox::FindNormal(const Vector3D& intersection)
{
   cerr << "BoundingBox::FindNormal called\n";
   return Vector3D(0);
}

Object3D *
BoundingBox::Dup() const
{
   BoundingBox *ret = new BoundingBox;

   for (ObjectList::Iterator sc(contents); sc.Valid(); sc.GotoNext())
      ret->AddObject(sc.Contents()->Dup());

   return ret;
}

int
BoundingBox::IsInside(Vector3D& v)
{
   return ! (v.x < min.x ||
             v.x > max.x ||
             v.y < min.y ||
             v.y > max.y ||
```

Listing 4.14   BoundingBox implementation *(continued)*

```
                        v.z < min.z ||
                        v.z > max.z);
}

float
BoundingBox::PtDistance(Vector3D& v)
{
    cerr << "BoundingBox::PtDistance called\n";
    exit(2);
    return 0;
}

void
BoundingBox::Describe(int ind) const
{
    ObjectList::Iterator sc(contents);

    indent(ind);
    cout << setprecision(2) << "Bounding box (" << min.x << ", ";
    cout << min.y << ", " << min.z << ")-(" << max.x << ", ";
    cout << max.y << ", " << max.z << ") contains:\n";
    while (sc.Valid()) {
        sc.Contents()->Describe(ind + 2);
        sc.GotoNext();
    }
}

void
BoundingVolume::AddObject(const Object3D& NewObj)
{
    contents.AddToList(NewObj.Dup());
}

void
BoundingVolume::AddObject(Object3D *NewObj)
{
    contents.AddToList(NewObj);
}

void
BoundingVolume::TransformSurface(SurfaceList& clist, const Matrix&
    tform)
{
    ObjectList::Iterator sc(contents);
```

Listing 4.14   BoundingBox implementation *(continued)*

```
    while (sc.Valid()) {
        sc.Contents()->TransformSurface(clist, tform);
        sc.GotoNext();
    }
}

float
AxisAlignedBox::SurfaceArea() const
{
    Vector3D ext = max - min;
    return 2 * (ext.x * ext.y +
            ext.x * ext.z +
            ext.y * ext.z);
}

float
BoundingBox::SurfaceArea() const
{
    return AxisAlignedBox::SurfaceArea();
}

AxisAlignedBox
BoundingBox::BBox() const
{
    return AxisAlignedBox(Min(), Max());
}

void
BoundingBox::AddObject(const Object3D& NewObj)
{
    BoundingVolume::AddObject(NewObj);
    Include(NewObj.BBox());
}

void
BoundingBox::AddObject(Object3D *NewObj)
{
    BoundingVolume::AddObject(NewObj);
    Include(NewObj->BBox());
}
```

Listing 4.14 `BoundingBox` implementation *(continued)*

4.8 Aggregate Objects

Aggregates are not objects unto themselves, they are simply containers for objects that have been grouped together. Having a single `Aggregate` that contains a group of objects is convenient when the group of objects must be transformed together.

Before rendering, OORT scans the object list for `Aggregates` and breaks them down into the component objects.

The Sphereflake and Sierpinski's Tetrahedron, recursively defined objects shown in Plates 7 and 8, are implemented as classes that inherit from `Aggregate`.

`Aggregate::AddObject` takes a pointer to an object that is to be added to the `Aggregate`.

Most operations that can be performed on objects should never be performed on `Aggregates`; however, `ApplyTransform` applies the given transform to every object in the `Aggregate`. This allows groups of objects to be transformed together.

```
// =======================================================================
// sphflake.cpp
//     Implementation file for SphereFlake class.
//     The code for this file is derived from balls.c in Eric
//     Haines's public domain Standard Procedural Database (SPD).
//     For more information on the SPD, see his article "A Proposal
//     For Standard Graphics Environments" in the November 1987
//     issue of IEEE Computer Graphics & Applications.
//
//
//         The Object-Oriented Ray Tracer (OORT)
//         Copyright (C) 1993 by Nicholas Wilt.
//
// This software product may be freely copied and distributed in
// unmodified form but may not be sold.  A nominal distribution
// fee may be charged for media and handling by freeware and
// shareware distributors.  The software product may not be
// included in whole or in part into any commercial package
// without the express written consent of the author.
//
// This software product is provided as is without warranty of
// any kind, express or implied, including but not limited to
// the implied warranties of merchantability and fitness for a
```

Listing 4.15 `balls.cpp`

```
// particular purpose.  The author assumes no liability for any
// alleged or actual damages arising from the use of this
// software.  The author is under no obligation to provide
// service, corrections or upgrades to the software.
//
// -----------------------------------------------------------
//
// Please contact me with questions, comments, suggestions or
// other input about OORT.  My Compuserve account number is
// [75210,2455] (Internet sites can reach me at
// 75210.2455@compuserve.com).
//                                --Nicholas Wilt
// ===========================================================================

#include "oort.h"
#include "utils.h"

// Declare some globals that are static within the class.
Vector3D SphereFlake::objset[9];
int SphereFlake::objset_computed = 0;

void
SphereFlake::CreateObjSet(Vector3D passbk[9])
{
    int num_set, num_vert;
    Vector3D axis, temp_pt, trio_dir[3];
    Matrix mx;

    double dist = 1 / sqrt(2);
    trio_dir[0] = Vector3D(dist, dist, 0);
    trio_dir[1] = Vector3D(dist, 0, -dist);
    trio_dir[2] = Vector3D(0, dist, -dist);
    axis = Normalize(Vector3D(1, -1, 0));
    mx = RotationAxisMatrix(axis, asin(2.0 / sqrt(6)));
    for (num_vert = 0; num_vert < 3; num_vert++)
       trio_dir[num_vert] = mx * trio_dir[num_vert];
    for (num_set = 0; num_set < 3; num_set++) {
       mx = RotationZMatrix(num_set*2*M_PI/3);
       for (num_vert = 0; num_vert < 3; num_vert++)
          objset[3*num_set+num_vert] = mx * trio_dir[num_vert];
    }
}

void
SphereFlake::AddSphere(const Vector3D& center, float rad, const
```

Listing 4.15 `balls.cpp` *(continued)*

```
      Vector3D& dir, int depth, Surface *surf)
{
    if (! depth--)
        return;
    AddObject(new Sphere(center, rad, surf));
    Matrix mulby;

    if (dir.z >= 1)
        mulby = IdentityMatrix();
    else if (dir.z <= -1)
        mulby = RotationYMatrix(M_PI);
    else {
        Vector3D axis = Normalize(CrossProd(Vector3D(0, 0, 1), dir));
        float ang = acos(DotProd(axis, Vector3D(0, 0, 1)));
        mulby = RotationAxisMatrix(axis, ang);
    }
    double scale = rad * (1.0 + 1.0/3.0);
    for (int num_vert = 0; num_vert < 9; num_vert++) {
        Vector3D child_pt = mulby * objset[num_vert] * scale + center;
        Vector3D child_dir = (child_pt - center) / scale;
        AddSphere(child_pt, rad / 3, child_dir, depth, surf);
    }
}

SphereFlake::SphereFlake(const Vector3D& center, float rad, const
    Vector3D& dir, int depth, Surface *surf)
{
    if (! objset_computed) {
        CreateObjSet(objset);
        objset_computed = 1;
    }
    AddSphere(center, rad, dir, depth, surf);
}
```

Listing 4.15 `balls.cpp` *(continued)*

```
// ======================================================================
// stetra.cpp
//     Implementation file for STetrahedron class.
//     The code for this file is derived from tetra.c in Eric
//     Haines's public domain Standard Procedural Database (SPD).
//     For more information on the SPD, see his article "A Proposal
//     For Standard Graphics Environments" in the November 1987
//     issue of IEEE Computer Graphics & Applications.
//
//
//         The Object-Oriented Ray Tracer (OORT)
//         Copyright (C) 1993 by Nicholas Wilt.
//
// This software product may be freely copied and distributed in
// unmodified form but may not be sold.  A nominal distribution
// fee may be charged for media and handling by freeware and
// shareware distributors.  The software product may not be
// included in whole or in part into any commercial package
// without the express written consent of the author.
//
// This software product is provided as is without warranty of
// any kind, express or implied, including but not limited to
// the implied warranties of merchantability and fitness for a
// particular purpose.  The author assumes no liability for any
// alleged or actual damages arising from the use of this
// software.  The author is under no obligation to provide
// service, corrections or upgrades to the software.
//
// ----------------------------------------------------------
//
// Please contact me with questions, comments, suggestions or
// other input about OORT.  My Compuserve account number is
// [75210,2455] (Internet sites can reach me at
// 75210.2455@compuserve.com).
//                              --Nicholas Wilt
// ======================================================================

#include "oort.h"
#include "utils.h"

STetrahedron::STetrahedron(int depth, float mag, Surface *surf)
{
    CreateTetra(depth, Vector3D(0), mag, surf);
}
```

Listing 4.16 stetra.cpp

```
// Create tetrahedrons recursively
void
STetrahedron::CreateTetra(int depth, const Vector3D& center, float
   mag, Surface *surf)
{
    int    num_face, num_vert, swap, vert_ord[3];
    int x_dir, y_dir, z_dir;
    Vector3D dir;
    Vector3D face_pt[3], obj_pt[4];
    Vector3D sub_center;

    if ( depth <= 1 ) {
        /* Output tetrahedron */

        /* find opposite corners of a cube which form a tetrahedron */
        for ( num_vert = 0, x_dir = -1 ; x_dir <= 1 ; x_dir += 2 ) {
            for ( y_dir = -1 ; y_dir <= 1 ; y_dir += 2 ) {
                for ( z_dir = -1 ; z_dir <= 1 ; z_dir += 2 ) {
                    if ( x_dir*y_dir*z_dir == 1 ) {
                        Vector3D dir(x_dir, y_dir, z_dir);
                        obj_pt[num_vert] = center + dir * mag;
                        ++num_vert ;
                    }
                }
            }
        }

        /* find faces and output */
        for ( num_face = 0 ; num_face < 4 ; ++num_face ) {
            /* output order:
             *    face 0:  points 0 1 2
             *    face 1:  points 3 2 1
             *    face 2:  points 2 3 0
             *    face 3:  points 1 0 3
             */
            for ( num_vert = 0 ; num_vert < 3 ; ++num_vert ) {
                vert_ord[num_vert] = (num_face + num_vert) % 4 ;
            }
            if ( num_face%2 == 1 ) {
                swap = vert_ord[0] ;
                vert_ord[0] = vert_ord[2] ;
                vert_ord[2] = swap ;
            }

            for ( num_vert = 0 ; num_vert < 3 ; ++num_vert )
```

Listing 4.16   `stetra.cpp` *(continued)*

```
            face_pt[num_vert] = obj_pt[vert_ord[num_vert]];
         AddObject(new Polygon(3, face_pt, surf));
      }
   }
   else {
      /* Create sub-tetrahedra */

      /* find opposite corners of a cube to form sub-tetrahedra */
      for ( x_dir = -1 ; x_dir <= 1 ; x_dir += 2 ) {
         for ( y_dir = -1 ; y_dir <= 1 ; y_dir += 2 ) {
            for ( z_dir = -1 ; z_dir <= 1 ; z_dir += 2 ) {
               if ( x_dir*y_dir*z_dir == 1 ) {
                  Vector3D dir(x_dir, y_dir, z_dir);
                  Vector3D subcenter = center + dir * mag / 2.0;
                  CreateTetra(depth - 1, subcenter, mag / 2, surf);
               }
            }
         }
      }
   }
}
```

Listing 4.16 `stetra.cpp` *(continued)*

4.9 Exercises

1. Define a class, derived from `Quadric`, that simplifies creating a specific type of quadric (e.g., `Cylinder`). Because the class inherits from `Quadric`, the class need only have a constructor that takes the object parameters (for a cylinder, these might be the major and minor radii) and calls `Quadric::Quadric` with the correct coefficients. If desired, you can also overload the `NearestInt` member function to make ray tracing these primitives more efficient.

2. Planes and polygons are "one-sided" in OORT—that is, they can only be seen from the side that the normal faces toward. What would it take to add two-sided planes and polygons? How much code could be shared between one-sided and two-sided versions of the two classes?

3. Implement a more robust method of computing the plane equation for a polygon.

4. The point-in-polygon test described in Section 4.5 is O(N) in the number of vertices. For convex polygons, it is possible to reduce this runtime to O(lgN)

by using a technique related to binary search (see Preparata and Shamos [PREP85], p. 43). Is a faster point-in-polygon test worth implementing in a ray tracer?

5. The ray-triangle intersection calculation is much more efficient than the ray-polygon intersection calculation (see Snyder and Barr [SNYD87] for an efficient ray-triangle intersection calculation). Triangles are a common output medium for many modeling and tessellation algorithms, as well. What would be involved in adding support for triangles to OORT? Is it worth doing?

6. What would be involved in adding another type of bounding volume to OORT?

7. A generalization of the rectangular prism is the *hypercube*, a concept that extends the idea of a rectangle (in 2D) or rectangular prism (in 3D) to higher dimensions. What uses might a general hypercube class have in OORT?

5

Acceleration Techniques

Since naive ray tracing is prohibitively slow, many methods of fast ray tracing have been described in the literature. OORT implements a number of these to make it go faster. It does not implement a number of promising techniques that we will describe and give references for. In addition, OORT specifically does not implement a number of techniques that do not combine well with the ones already implemented.

Besides the references given in the discussions below, Arvo and Kirk [ARVO89] give an excellent overview of ray tracing acceleration techniques.

5.1 Bounding Volumes and Hierarchies

Some types of object are easier to intersect with a ray than others. This observation led to one of the earliest ray tracing acceleration techniques: "bounding volumes." The idea of a bounding volume takes advantage of the fact that rays usually miss the objects they are tested against. By enclosing complicated objects in invisible bounding volumes that are easy to intersect with, the intersection calculation with the complicated object can be avoided if the ray misses the bounding volume. Of course, if the ray pierces the bounding volume, the ray has to be intersected with the interior object anyway, but this happens rarely enough in practice that bounding volumes make a lot of sense.

For bounding volumes, OORT uses axis-aligned bounding boxes because they are simple to compute, simple to intersect, and have simple closure properties. Section 4.7 describes the intersection calculation of a bounding box.

Once the idea of a bounding volume is mastered, it is simple to imagine nesting bounding volumes in one another so that all the bounded objects in the world are enclosed in one large bounding volume. This *root* bounding volume contains a number of bounding volumes, each of which contains bounding volumes or primitive objects. This idea is called a *bounding volume hierarchy*. A well-designed hierarchy can yield enormous performance improvements. The problem with bounding volume hierarchies is that they are not convenient for a user to specify. That drawback is addressed by techniques for generating bounding volume hierarchies automatically.

5.2 Automatic Bounding Volume Hierarchy Generation

In order to generate a bounding volume hierarchy automatically, we must invent a way to estimate the "cost" of a hierarchy: the number of intersections needed to find the nearest intersection along a ray. In computer science, a function to estimate costs is frequently called a *heuristic*. (For example, the function used by a chess program to evaluate a board configuration is also called a heuristic.)

Actually, *two* heuristics must be defined for automatic bounding volume hierarchy generation. The first evaluates the effectiveness of a hierarchy, while the second approximates an optimal hierarchy in the first heuristic. The second heuristic is necessary because the number of possible hierarchies grows exponentially as the number of objects in the world. Thus, it is not feasible to find the optimal bounding volume hierarchy using a nontrivial heuristic.

Goldsmith and Salmon propose a method of automatic bounding volume hierarchy generation [GOLD87]. First, they define a heuristic to estimate a hierarchy's cost. To define this heuristic, they make a number of reasonable assumptions. They assume that all objects in the hierarchy require the same amount of computation to intersect with a ray. They also assume that the bounding volumes are convex; this implies that the probability of a ray striking the bounding volume is proportional to its surface area [STON75, as cited by Goldsmith and Salmon]. Finally, since rays that do not hit the root bounding volume require only one intersection calculation, Goldsmith and Salmon restrict their attention to rays that pierce the root bounding volume. We can use these assumptions to define a hierarchy cost heuristic.

If a ray hits the root bounding volume BV_r, the conditional probability that it will also hit an inner bounding volume BV_i is proportional to A_i/A_r, where A_i and A_r are the surface areas of BV_i and BV_r. Since intersection computations will be performed on all objects inside BV_i if BV_i is struck by the ray, BV_i's contribution to the overall estimated cost of the hierarchy is kA_i/A_r, where k is the number of objects inside BV_i. The overall estimated cost of a bounding volume hierarchy is the sum of each bounding volume's contribution. This cost is an estimate of the number of intersection calculations that will be performed if a ray intersects the root bounding volume.

The algorithm to construct a hierarchy proceeds incrementally, adding one object to the hierarchy at a time. For each object, it starts at the root and chooses the bounding volume that will increase least in surface area if the object is added to it. The subtree rooted at that bounding volume is recursively considered until a terminal node is reached. This process approximates the hierarchy cost heuristic described above. The decision of whether to add the object to the leaf node (increase the number of objects in the bounding volume) or to create a new bounding volume is based on which will least increase the overall estimated cost of the hierarchy. If a new node is created and added to the parent of the terminal node just found, it increases by one the number of objects to intersect with if the parent is struck, and the new bounding volume's contribution to the overall cost must be considered. On the other hand, adding the object to an existing bounding volume increases the number of objects in it by one and may increase that bounding volume's surface area. Figure 5.1 depicts this dilemma and the ways it is resolved by the algorithm in two cases.

Everywhere surface area is mentioned in the above discussion, a function proportional to surface area may be substituted. For axis-aligned bounding boxes, the surface area is $2wh + 2wd + 2hd$ where w, h, and d are the width, height and depth. An expression that is proportional to this one, but simpler to compute, is $w(h + d) + hd$.

OORT implements Goldsmith and Salmon's technique faithfully, including possible drawbacks, such as its emphasis on axis-aligned bounding boxes for bounding volumes. The implementation is in `hier.cpp`.

5.3 Optimizing Shadow Rays

Since every primary ray and secondary ray causes the shading equation to be computed (with a shadow ray cast at every light source), the number of shadow rays cast is typically much larger than the number of other types of ray. Optimizing shadow ray casting therefore has a disproportionate impact on the

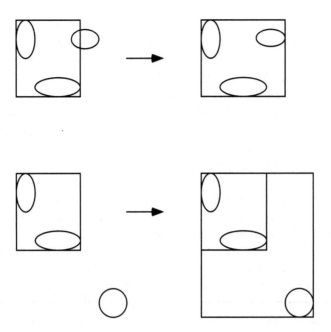

Figure 5.1 Goldsmith–Salmon automatic BVH generation.

```cpp
// Compute increase in bounding box volume if the bounding box of
// an object and another bounding box are union'ed.
// If the bounding boxes are disjoint, the increase should be 0.
static float
BBoxIncrease(const Object3D *candidate, const AxisAlignedBox& bbox)
{
    AxisAlignedBox cbbox = candidate->BBox();
    return Union(cbbox, bbox).SurfaceArea() - bbox.SurfaceArea();
}

// Given a list of objects and a bounding box, return a manipulator
// pointing at the element whose bounding box increases least in
// volume when the bounding box is union'ed with it.
static ObjectList::Manipulator *
MinVolumeIncrease(ObjectList *x, const AxisAlignedBox& bbox)
{
    ObjectList::Manipulator sc(*x);
    ObjectList::Manipulator ret(*x);
    float minincrease = BBoxIncrease(ret.Contents(), bbox);
    while (sc.Valid()) {
```

Listing 5.1 subset of `hier.cpp`

```
        float tempincrease = BBoxIncrease(sc.Contents(), bbox);
        if (tempincrease < minincrease) {
            minincrease = tempincrease;
            ret = sc;
        }
        sc.GotoNext();
    }
    return new ObjectList::Manipulator(ret);
}

static int
HeuristicIncrease(Object3D *candidate,
                const AxisAlignedBox& bbox,
                float *increase,
                const SimpleStack<ObjectList::Manipulator *>& stk)
{
    // Precompute some important stuff and assign to local vars.
    int k = candidate->NumChildren();
    AxisAlignedBox cbbox = candidate->BBox();

    // Compute surface area of the union of the candidate's bbox
    // and the new object's bbox.
    float newsa = Union(bbox, cbbox).SurfaceArea();

    // Compute the new heuristic value if you add the object
    // directly to the bbox.
    float addbbox = newsa * (k + 1);

    // Compute the new heuristic value if you replace the existing
    // bbox with one that contains the old one plus the object
    // being added.
    float replacebbox = 2 * newsa + k * cbbox.SurfaceArea();

    // Declare the integer return value.  It will be set in the
    // following if statement.
    int ret;

    // Decide whether to add the object directly to the bbox, or
    // keep the old bbox and enclose it in a new bounding volume
    // that also encloses the object being added.
    if (addbbox < replacebbox) {
        // Keep the old bounding box, add an object to it.
        *increase = addbbox;
        ret = 0;
    }
```

Listing 5.1   subset of `hier.cpp` *(continued)*

```
    else {
        // Replace the old bounding box.
        *increase = replacebbox;
        ret = 1;
    }

    // Declare a stack iterator to nondestructively examine the
    // contents of the stack.
    SimpleStack<ObjectList::Manipulator *>::Iterator stksc(stk);

    stksc.GotoNext();      // (we've already taken care of TOS)

    while (stksc.Valid()) {
        int numchildren = stksc.Contents()->Contents()->NumChildren();
        *increase += numchildren * Union(stksc.Contents()->
            Contents()->BBox(),
                                  bbox).SurfaceArea();
        stksc.GotoNext();
    }
    return ret;
}

// Add an object to a hierarchy using Goldsmith and Salmon's
// technique of automatic bounding volume hierarchy generation.
void
AddNewObject(ObjectList *root, Object3D *addme)
{
    SimpleStack<ObjectList::Manipulator *> stk;
    AxisAlignedBox bbox = addme->BBox();
    ObjectList *curlist = root;
    int flags;

    do {
        stk.Push(MinVolumeIncrease(curlist, bbox));
        flags = stk.Top()->Contents()->Flags();
        if (flags & BOUNDING)
            curlist = ((BoundingVolume *) stk.Top()->Contents())->List();
    } while (flags & BOUNDING);

    // Make a copy of the stack so we can compute the bounds later.
    SimpleStack<ObjectList::Manipulator *> cpystk = stk;
    ObjectList::Manipulator *min;
    int minmethod, tempmethod;
    float minincrease, tempincrease;
    min = stk.Top();
```

Listing 5.1 subset of `hier.cpp` *(continued)*

```
minmethod = HeuristicIncrease(stk.Top()->Contents(), bbox,
    &minincrease, stk);
while (! stk.Empty()) {
    tempmethod = HeuristicIncrease(stk.Top()->Contents(), bbox,
        &tempincrease, stk);
    if (tempincrease < minincrease) {
        min = stk.Top();
        minincrease = tempincrease;
        minmethod = tempmethod;
    }
    stk.Pop();
}
if (minmethod || (! (min->Contents()->Flags() & BOUNDING))) {
    // Replace old node in the tree with a bounding box.
    BoundingBox *newbbox = new BoundingBox;
    newbbox->AddObject(min->Contents());
    newbbox->AddObject(addme);
    min->ReplaceContents(newbbox);
}
else {
    // Just add the new object to the bounding box.
    ((BoundingVolume *) min->Contents())->AddObject(addme);
}
while (! cpystk.Empty()) {
    if (cpystk.Top()->Contents()->Flags() & BOUNDING) {
        BoundingBox *innernode = (BoundingBox *) cpystk.Top()-
>Contents();
        innernode->Include(bbox);
    }
    cpystk.Pop();
}
}
```

Listing 5.1   subset of `hier.cpp` *(continued)*

overall speed of the ray tracer. Techniques for optimizing shadow rays concentrate on a feature of shadow rays not shared by other types of ray: any opaque object between the intersection point and the light source places the intersection point in shadow. Intersection testing can cease as soon as an opaque object is detected between the intersection point and the light source.

Haines and Greenberg describe a preprocessing technique that dramatically increases the speed of shadow ray casting [HAIN86]. Each light source is enclosed in a *light buffer*, an axis-aligned box whose sides are divided into rectangles. (See Figure 5.2.) Each rectangle has a list of objects "visible" to the light source through it. When a shadow ray is cast at the light source, it pierces

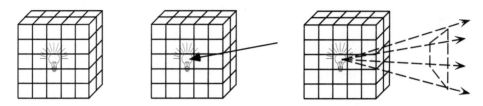

Figure 5.2 Light buffer.

the light buffer through one of these rectangles. Only the objects associated with that rectangle's list need be tested for intersection with the shadow ray.

The authors also describe *shadow caching*, a simpler optimization that can be implemented easily (and is implemented in OORT). When a shadow ray is cast at a light source, any opaque object found is cached with the light source. The next time a shadow ray is cast at the light source, it is first intersected with the cached object. If the ray intersects the cached object, the intersection point is in shadow and no other intersection tests need be performed. Otherwise, the shadow ray is computed normally (possibly resulting in a different opaque object being cached).

5.4 Assembler Optimization

The obvious candidates for assembler optimization in a ray tracer are the ray-object intersection computations. The routine that stands out is the bounding box intersection routine. With the advent of automatic bounding volume hierarchy generation, the program spends a large amount of time computing rays' intersections with bounding boxes. Rewriting OORT's bounding box intersection routine required only a few hours, and afforded the program a 20–40% speedup. This is not a stellar speedup, but it makes a difference of hours for long traces.

```
; *************************************************************
; bboxa.asm
;     386-specific assembler for bounding box intersection.
; Copyright (C) 1993 by Nicholas Wilt.      All rights reserved.
; *************************************************************

.MODEL    LARGE,C

.386
```

Listing 5.2 bboxa.asm

```
        .CODE

        ; Given the min and max vectors for an axis-aligned bounding
        ; box, and the direction and location of a ray, compute the
        ; two intersections of the ray with the bounding box.
        ; If the ray misses the bounding box, the function returns 0.
        ; Otherwise the function returns 1 and the two parameters
        ; of intersection are written to tmin and tmax.

        ; int bboxint(Vector *min, Vector *max,
        ;       Vector *dir, Vector *loc,
        ;       float *tmin, float *tmax);

                PUBLIC    bboxint

LARGENUM        DD      100000.0

bboxint PROC    USES DS SI DI
ARG    MINMAX:DWORD,LOCDIR:DWORD,TMIN:DWORD,TMAX:DWORD
        lds    si,MINMAX     ; DS:SI <- min
        les    di,LOCDIR     ; ES:DI <- max
        mov    cx,3          ; Three times we do this
@@Do3:  fld    dword ptr es:[di+12] ; Get dir element
        fld    st            ; dir.x dir.x
        fabs                 ; abs(dir.x) dir.x
        ftst                 ; Compare abs to zero
        fstsw  ax            ;
        fstp   st            ; dir.x
        sahf                 ;
        jne    @@NotZero     ; dir.x not zero
        fstp   st            ; Clear dir.x from stack
        fld    dword ptr es:[di]
        fcom   dword ptr [si] ; Compare to min.x
        fstsw  ax            ;
        sahf                 ;
        jb     @@NoInt       ; Hope still alive for -MAX to MAX
        fcomp  dword ptr [si+12] ; Compare to max.x
        fstsw  ax            ;
        sahf                 ;
        ja     @@LoopRet0    ;
        fld    LARGENUM      ; Load maxt (LARGENUM)
        fld    st            ;
        fchs                 ; Load mint (-LARGENUM)
        fxch                 ; Exchange them so max is TOS
        jmp    short @@Loop3
```

Listing 5.2   bboxa.asm *(continued)*

```
@@NoInt:
        fstp      st              ; Clear TOS
@@LoopRet0:
        xor       ax,ax           ; Return zero.
        sub       cx,3            ; Subtract cx from 3
        neg       cx              ;
        and       cx,3            ;
        shl       cx,1            ;
        jz        @@Done          ; Jump if stack already clear
@@ClearStack:
        fstp      st              ; Clear stack
        loop      @@ClearStack    ;    (loop until done)
@@Done: jmp       @@Return        ; Long jump to return
@@NotZero:                        ; dir.x on TOS
        fld       dword ptr [si+12] ; max.x dir.x
        fsub      dword ptr es:[di] ; (max.x - loc.x) dir.x
        fdiv      st,st(1)        ; t2 dir.x
        fld       dword ptr [si]    ; min.x t2 dir.x
        fsub      dword ptr es:[di] ; (min.x - loc.x) (max.x - loc.x) dir.x
        fdivrp    st(2),st        ; t1 t2
        fcom      st(1)           ; If ST < ST(1), swap
        fstsw     ax              ;
        sahf                      ;
        ja        @@Max           ; Jump if greater
        fxch                      ; ST <- max(ST, ST(1))
@@Max:    ftst                    ; If max is less than zero, no intersection.
        fstsw     ax              ;
        sahf                      ;
        jae       @@Loop3         ;
        dec       cx              ;
        jmp       short @@LoopRet0
@@Loop3:
        add       si,4            ; Increment pointers properly
        add       di,4            ;
        add       bx,4            ;
        add       dx,4            ;
        dec       cx              ; Loop until done
        jnz       @@Do3           ;
; At this point the coprocessor stack has six max/min pairs.
; ST(0) max.z
; ST(1) min.z
; ST(2) max.y
; ST(3) min.y
; ST(4) max.x
; ST(5) min.x
```

Listing 5.2 bboxa.asm *(continued)*

```
                ; Find min of max's and max of min's.
        fcom        st(2)           ; Compare max.z to max.y
        fstsw       ax              ;
        sahf                        ;
        jb          @@MaxZMaxY      ;
        fxch        st(2)           ;
@@MaxZMaxY:
        fcom        st(4)           ; Compare min(max.z, max.y) to max.x
        fstsw       ax              ;
        sahf                        ;
        jb          @@MaxMaxX   ;
        fxch        st(4)           ;
@@MaxMaxX:                          ; ST is now min(min(max.z, max.y), max.x)
        fxch                        ; ST is now min.z
        fcom        st(3)           ; Compare min.z to min.y
        fstsw       ax              ;
        sahf                        ;
        ja          @@MinZMinY      ;
        fxch        st(3)           ;
@@MinZMinY:
        fcom        st(5)           ; Compare max(min.z, min.y) to min.x
        fstsw       ax              ;
        sahf                        ;
        ja          @@MinMinX   ;
        fxch        st(5)           ;
@@MinMinX:                          ; ST now max of mins, ST(1) min of max's
        fxch        st(5)           ; ST(5) is now max of mins
        fxch                        ; ST now min of maxs
        fxch        st(4)           ; ST(4) now min of maxs
        fstp        st              ; Clear coprocessor stack
        fstp        st              ;
        fstp        st              ;
        fstp        st              ;
        lds         si,TMAX         ; Pass back tmin
        fstp        dword ptr [si]      ;
        lds         si,TMIN     ;
        fstp        dword ptr [si]      ;
        mov         ax,1            ;
@@Return:
        ret
bboxint ENDP

        END
```

Listing 5.2 `bboxa.asm` *(continued)*

5.5 Kay-Kajiya Bounding Volume Hierarchy Traversal

The obvious code to traverse a bounding volume hierarchy is shown in Figure 5.3.

Note that if a bounding volume's nearest intersection is beyond the nearest intersection found so far, the bounding volume's contents need not be considered. Kay and Kajiya [KAY86] developed a method of bounding volume hierarchy traversal that considers the closest bounding volumes first, on the assumption that these bounding volumes are more likely to contain the closest intersection. Since bounding volumes beyond the closest intersection need not be considered, Kay and Kajiya's hierarchy traversal technique is likely to halt intersection testing sooner than the naive traversal outlined in Figure 5.3.

Pseudocode for this traversal technique is shown in Figure 5.4.

Kay-Kajiya hierarchy traversal proffers a tradeoff. For the added cost of maintaining a priority queue (essentially, sorting the bounding volumes in increasing order of parameter of intersection), the algorithm reduces the number of intersection calculations performed. In my experience, the tradeoff is a favorable one.

Note that Kay-Kajiya hierarchy traversal speeds up finding the *nearest* intersection, an acceleration that does not apply to shadow rays. When casting a shadow ray, the object is to find *any* intersection with an opaque object, not the nearest intersection. `World::FindAtten`, the function that implements shadow ray casting in OORT, uses the naive hierarchy traversal technique in Figure 5.3.

5.6 Techniques That Do Not Work Well

Not all techniques that have been described in the literature work well together. I had high hopes for many of the techniques described in this section, but for

Find-Nearest(*ray*, *root*)
if (*ray* intersects *root* and intersection is closer than nearest-so-far)
    if (*root* is bounding volume)
        for each object *obj* in *root*
            Find-Nearest(*ray*, *obj*)
   else
        update nearest intersection found so far.

Figure 5.3 Traversal technique.

Find-Nearest(*ray*, *root*)
if (*ray* intersects *root*)
    Insert all members of *root* into PQ, using *root*'s nearest intersection
        point as the key.
while (PQ not empty) do
    Extract minimum object *obj* from PQ
    if (*obj*'s key is farther than the nearest intersection found so far)
        No objects remain that could be closer. Terminate.
    if (*ray* intersects *obj*)
        if (*obj* is a bounding volume)
            Insert all objects inside *obj* into PQ, using *obj*'s nearest
                intersection point as the key.
        else
            Update nearest intersection with results from *obj*.
Return nearest intersection.

Note   the PQ data structure is a priority queue of bounding volumes keyed by
their parents' nearest intersection with the ray.

Figure 5.4   Psedocode for Kay-Kajiya hierarchy traversal.

one reason or another they all fell short of expectations. They are described here because I want to warn readers away from improvements to OORT that have already been tried and did not work well. Section 5.7 describes some techniques that I believe would greatly improve OORT's efficiency.

5.6.1 Ray Boxes

Ray boxes are like bounding volumes in reverse. Instead of enclosing objects in bounding volumes that have to be pierced by the ray before you need to bother intersecting with their contents, why not enclose the ray in a bounding volume that has to be intersected? This idea is attributed to Snyder and Barr [SNYD87]. It appears to lend itself well to a bounding volume hierarchy scheme, because every time a bounding volume is intersected, the parameters of intersection can be used to compute a ray box. Then, the ray box is intersected with the bounding box of each primitive in the bounding volume. Only objects whose bounding boxes overlap that of the ray box need to be further intersected with the ray.

This scheme has a few disadvantages. Unlike a bounding volume hierarchy, it does not decrease the total number of intersection calculations. It only strives to make intersection calculations more efficient on average. The ray box-bounding box intersection calculation requires at most six floating-point comparisons (a trivial computation compared to even the simplest intersection calculation), so even a small number of successful rejections would result in a speedup because a successful rejection is so much faster than a full intersection calculation. In my experiments, when all the bounded objects in a scene are enclosed in a single bounding box, 98 percent of the intersection calculations attempted are successfully rejected by one of those six comparisons. The speedup is tremendous compared to a naive ray tracing scheme.

But ray boxes do not appear to combine well with a bounding volume hierarchy generated by Goldsmith and Salmon's technique. When the two techniques are combined, the ray box intersection rejection rate plummets from 98 percent to less than 50 percent. That means all six initial comparisons are being wasted half the time.

Ray boxes are an investment that may not pay off because whenever a ray pierces a bounding volume, a new ray box must be computed. Computing a new ray box costs six floating-point comparisons to order the ray box vertices correctly. In an automatically generated hierarchy, there are many bounding volumes, so ray boxes are constantly being recomputed. Since rays aren't rejected by the ray boxes frequently enough to offset this investment, they are not worth doing in this context.

5.6.2 Last–Nearest Caching

Last–nearest caching appears to be a folk algorithm in ray tracing. It works like this: Whenever a reflected or transmitted ray is cast, the reflective or transparent object remembers the nearest object found along that ray. Next time a ray is spawned from that object, the ray is tested for intersection with the object that was the nearest last time a ray was spawned. Because of coherence, the object is assumed to have a good chance of being the closest object again. If it intersects the ray, it makes a good upper bound to apply to the parameters of intersection with the ray for other objects. The idea can be applied to primary rays as well, if the eye is considered an object that spawns rays.

I tested this idea in OORT and had little success. Although the last–nearest test often succeeded in establishing the upper bound desired, it had a marginal impact on the overall performance of the ray tracer.

5.7 Other Techniques

Many speedup techniques that have been described in the literature have not been implemented in OORT. We don't have room to describe or even mention all the techniques that have been described, but we can discuss a few promising ones.

5.7.1 Spatial Subdivision

Spatial subdivision contrasts nicely with the bounding volume hierarchies used by OORT. Instead of enclosing objects in bounding boxes, spatial subdivision techniques divide the space occupied by the world into axis-aligned rectangular prisms (frequently called *voxels*, the three-dimensional analog to pixels). The ray tracer must precompute a list of objects that intersect each voxel (see Figure 5.5). Then, whenever a ray is cast, the voxels it intersects are traversed in order. The first voxel where the ray hits an object contains the nearest intersection along the ray.

Spatial subdivision schemes come in two flavors: uniform and nonuniform. Uniform spatial subdivision [FUJI86] involves dividing space into equal-sized voxels, while nonuniform spatial subdivision [GLAS84] uses voxels of different sizes. Uniform spatial subdivision requires less computation to traverse the voxels, but nonuniform spatial subdivision can take the placement of objects in the world into account when building the voxel set.

One problem that is faced by uniform spatial subdivision techniques is sometimes called the "teapot in a football stadium problem," where a small, complicated object is placed in a large scene. If the subdivision is fine enough to ray trace the "teapot" efficiently, it requires a prohibitive amount of space to store enough voxels to encompass the "football stadium." Several methods spring to mind to address this problem. One is to place the objects in each voxel into a bounding volume hierarchy. Another is to impose *another* spatial subdivision inside voxels that contain too many objects. Nested spatial subdivisions are described by Jevans and Wyvill [JEVA89].

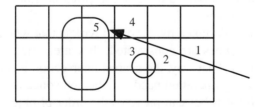

Figure 5.5   Uniform spatial subdivision.

5.7.2 Ray Classification

Arvo and Kirk [ARVO87] describe a technique for efficient ray casting that is based on the five degrees of freedom of a ray (three for the location and two for the direction). Using this idea, a ray can be completely described as a 5D vector, and a collection of rays can be bounded by a five-dimensional hypercube. Each hypercube contains a candidate list of objects that can be intersected by any ray inside it.

To begin with, six root hypercubes are defined, one for each of the six axis directions (+X, −X, +Y, etc.). Each of these hypercubes also bounds every ray origin (the eye, plus every bounded object in the scene). The candidate list for each of these six root hypercubes is the list of all bounded objects.

Each root hypercube is the root of a hyper-octree, analogous to a binary tree where each node has 32 (2^5) children rather than 2. To trace a ray, the hyper-octree is traversed from the root corresponding to the ray's principal direction. Once a root node of the hyper-octree has been reached, the ray's nearest intersection with all the objects in its candidate list is computed. The nodes of the hyper-octree are not precomputed. Because only a small fraction of the possible ray origins and directions are ever needed for a given run of the ray tracer, Arvo and Kirk recommend using lazy evaluation to compute only the nodes of the hyper-octree that are needed.

The criterion for whether to subdivide a hypercube is the number of objects in its candidate list. If a hypercube's candidate list contains too many objects, the hypercube is subdivided and 32 child nodes are added to the tree. In the spirit of the lazy evaluation, however, only the candidate list for the child needed for the ray is computed.

The candidate list for a child hypercube is a subset of the candidate list of its parent. To construct the candidate list for a hypercube, each object in its parent's candidate list must be checked to see whether it falls within the child's bounds. Rather than trying to use the exact bounds of the child's hypercube, the set of ray origins and ray directions are enclosed in a bounding cone, and each object to be tested is enclosed in a bounding sphere. The sphere-cone test is an approximation, but it is much faster and less complicated than the exact inside/outside test for the hypercube.

One other optimization undertaken by Arvo and Kirk is that when the candidate lists for the root hypercubes are constructed, they are sorted along that hypercube's principal direction. That way, the nearest intersection is likely to be found more quickly. This sorting operation need only be done once for each root hypercube, since the child hypercubes can preserve the order of objects in their own candidate lists.

5.7.3 Statistical Techniques

Not all improvements to ray tracing involve making ray casting faster. Many methods attempt to cast fewer rays. Any number of techniques have been described to cast fewer rays while maintaining high-quality output. Most of these [DIPP85, LEE85, MITC87, MITC91] were inspired by distribution ray tracing, which involves casting more than one ray to compute a single pixel value. Akimoto et al. describe a technique designed to cast fewer primary rays [AKIM91].

Distribution ray tracing requires a formidable amount of time if implemented naively, but can be almost as efficient as naive ray tracing if statistical optimizations are used. The statistical optimizations in OORT were inspired by Mitchell [MITC87, MITC91] and are described in Chapter 7.

5.7.4 Adaptive Depth Control

In our introduction to recursive ray tracing, we pointed out that some scenes with many reflective or transparent objects will cause rays to bounce around the scene indefinitely. A common solution to this problem is to impose a fixed depth limit on the ray tracer's recursion: if the depth limit is reached, no secondary ray is traced from the intersection point to evaluate the shading equation.

As it turns out, fixed depth limits cause the ray tracer to waste a lot of time casting rays that barely contribute to the scene. This is because each secondary ray's color is attenuated by the coefficient of reflection or transmission at the intersection point. Glass is only slightly reflective ($k_r \approx 0.2$), so the contributions from rays reflected between two glass objects quickly become insignificant as the first coefficient is applied (0.2), then the second (0.04), then the third (0.008). The fixed depth limit of a ray tracer is usually set to accommodate the machine stack without taking into account whether the secondary rays being cast will contribute to the scene.

Schemes for adaptive depth control such as the one described by Hall et al. [HALL83] strive to avoid casting secondary rays that do not contribute to the scene. This is done by tracking the maximum contribution a secondary ray could make to the scene; if the contribution is smaller than a preset threshold, the recursion is discontinued.

5.7.5 Mailboxes

Arnaldi et al. coined the term *mailbox* for a place to store an intersection calculation [ARNA87]. That way, a ray–object intersection can be avoided if it has already been done. Bounding volume hierarchy schemes like OORT uses do not need mailboxes, but spatial subdivision techniques mandate them. Many objects span across more than one voxel in a spatial subdivision scheme. Without remembering the results of intersection calculations, a ray traversing those voxels might cause many intersection calculations with the same object. By designing a data structure to remember intersection results, these redundant intersection calculations can be avoided.

5.7.6 Parallelism

Ray tracing is a "trivially parallelizable" problem, in that once the problem (the scene to be rendered) has been described, any number of computers can independently work on the solution (the resulting image) in parallel without communicating intermediate results to one another. Fractal generation and factoring large composite numbers are similar problems. In theory, having N computers work on the image will be N times as fast.

In practice, there is an upper limit to the number of computers that will increase the speed of the rendering. This is because every machine that will participate in the computation must get a description of the scene to be rendered. Since this takes time, if there are too many computers it may take more time to distribute the scene description than it takes to render the scene. Another problem is balancing the load on each computer. Some parts of the image are easier to render than others, and computers that were given easy parts will finish earlier than their counterparts. Since computers that finish early could have been working on other parts of the image, parallel ray tracers are faced with the problem of *load balancing* to ensure that every computer participating in the calculation performs useful work throughout.

Practically speaking, these concerns are academic if the infrastructure to implement a parallel ray tracer is in place. One common infrastructure suitable for parallel ray tracing implementation is a group of networked computers. This would work best if a client–server model were used. Each machine with some spare time to spend ray tracing would announce itself on the network as a ray tracing server. Then, any programs that were aware of this facility and wanted ray tracing to be done could contact the ray tracing servers on the network and distribute the problem among them.

Another infrastructure that will become common in the near future is symmetric multiprocessing. A machine built for symmetric multiprocessing has a number of processors that share the same virtual memory address space. Such a system could have different processors working on different parts of the image at the same time. Upcoming systems such as Windows NT will have transparent support for symmetric multiprocessing.

5.8 Exercises

1. How much effort would be required to make OORT support another type of bounding volume? What types of bounding volume would make sensible additions, and why?

2. Think of some improvements to the heuristics defined by Goldsmith and Salmon. Try implementing them; do they improve the algorithm's performance?

3. OORT does not implement one technique described by Goldsmith and Salmon. Late in the construction of the hierarchy, bounding boxes near the root will tend not to increase in surface area at all, forcing the heuristic to choose randomly between subtrees to investigate. Goldsmith and Salmon suggest that it would be better to investigate *all* such subtrees and choose between them only when discrepancies in the heuristic start to appear. What would it take to implement this modification? Try implementing it. Does it improve the algorithm's performance?

4. How would the technique of Goldsmith and Salmon have to change if other types of bounding volume were supported by OORT?

5. What would be involved in adding light buffers to OORT to replace the shadow caching scheme now being used? If your design is feasible, implement it.

6. Design and implement one of the ray tracing efficiency schemes described in Section 5.7. Is it faster than before? If so, by how much?

6

Texture Mapping

6.1 Introduction

Texture mapping is a way to make simple objects appear complicated without paying the price of modeling the complexity directly. For example, a simple sphere can be made to look like a beach ball by systematically varying the color of the sphere. This process is much simpler and more efficient than trying to define each square on the beach ball as a separate object.

For a while, the simple idea of "map a two-dimensional picture onto a three-dimensional object" encompassed all of texture mapping. But complexity can be added to objects in other ways. Perlin [PERL85] and Peachey [PEAC85] independently proposed the idea of *solid texturing*, where a texture is thought of as a function of points in 3D space rather than a function of 2D points mapped onto 3D surfaces. Solid textures make it possible to render realistic wood, marble, and other solid materials. Because the solid textures are defined in 3D space, they make objects look like they were carved out of the materials being emulated.

Another generalization of texture mapping is *bump mapping*, first discussed by Blinn [BLIN78]. Instead of varying the color of a point depending on the position, bump mapping involves changing the normal at a point. As the name implies, bump mapping makes it possible to make smooth objects look irregular—bumpy, rippled or wrinkled.

Another technique for adding complexity to objects is *displacement mapping*. Rather than varying the color or normal at a point depending on the position, displacement mapping changes the intersection point itself. Ray tracing is not well-suited to displacement mapping, so the technique is not covered in detail here. For more information see Cook [COOK84b] and Upstill [UPST90].

In OORT, the `Texture` and `BumpMap` abstract classes implement texture and bump mapping using a host of primitives, including noise (`NoiseMaker`), color maps (`ColorMap`), and inverse mappings (`Mapping`).

`HallSurface::ShadeObject`, the function responsible for shading, invokes a bump map and textures on a given intersection point in order. First, the normal is changed if a bump map is in effect. Then, a texture is used to compute the coefficient for each color component needed by the shader. Up to five textures are invoked, one each for the ambient, diffuse, specular, reflective, and transparent components.

6.2 Bump Mapping

`BumpMap`, the class that implements bump mapping, is defined in `bump.h`. The abstract definition of `BumpMap` is shown in Listing 6.1.

`BumpMap::PerturbNormal` is expected to change the normal in the `ShadingInfo` structure based on information in that structure, including the intersection point, input direction of the normal, and direction of the incident ray.

```
// ================================================================
// BumpMap
//    Takes the ShadingInfo for a point--direction of the
//    incident ray, intersection point, normal and other
//    information--and modifies the intersection point or
//    the normal, or both.
// ================================================================

class BumpMap {
public:
    virtual ~BumpMap() { }
    virtual void PerturbNormal(ShadingInfo& shade) = 0;
    virtual BumpMap *Dup() const = 0;
    virtual void ApplyTransform(const Matrix& tform) { }
    virtual void PreMulTransform(const Matrix& tform) { }
};
```

Listing 6.1 BumpMap definition

Many bump maps take other bump maps as parameters. For example, `ReverseNormal` gives another bump map a chance to perturb the normal before it reverses the normal's direction. The user can combine different bump maps to get the desired effect.

6.3 Texture Mapping

A texture is a way to compute the color of a point in 3D space. As discussed in Section 3.2, textures are used to compute the coefficients of reflection and transmission for all five components of the shading equation.

The definition of a `Texture` in OORT is given in Listing 6.2.

`Texture::GetColor` takes a point in 3D space and returns the texture color at that point. To compute the color at a point, the texture may have to transform the point, apply an inverse mapping, transform the point again, use a solid noise generator to get a position-dependent, random-seeming value, and use a color map to take a value and map it to a color.

```
// --------------------------------------------------------
// Texture
//     Implements various methods of taking intersection
//     points on objects and turning them into colors.
// --------------------------------------------------------

class Texture {
public:
    Texture() { reference = IdentityMatrix(); }
    Texture(const Matrix& ref): reference(ref) { }
    virtual ~Texture() { }

    virtual void ApplyTransform(const Matrix& tform);
    virtual void PreMulTransform(const Matrix& tform);

    virtual RGBColor GetColor(const Vector3D&) const = 0;
    virtual Texture *Dup() const = 0;

protected:
    Matrix reference;      // Matrix to apply to intersection points

    virtual Vector3D PreprocessVector(const Vector3D& x) const;
};
```

Listing 6.2   `Texture` definition

The simplest implementation is `PureColor::GetColor`, which returns the same color at all points.

Different textures take different parameters as input. `PureColor` takes a color as input. `Checkerboard` takes two textures as input, so it can use one texture or the other depending on which checkerboard square is called for. That way, the user is not limited to putting pure colors in the checkerboard.

6.4 Low-Level Support for Texture Mapping

Many tools are used by texture mapping. Inverse mappings, noise functions, and color maps all provide pieces of the puzzle to make texture mapping possible.

6.4.1 Inverse Mappings

Inverse mappings are an important component in the traditional model of texture mapping as a way to map 2D images onto 3D objects. OORT implements a wide variety of inverse mappings in the `Mapping` class. Like `BumpMap`, `Mapping` has a very simple definition (see Listing 6.3).

```
// ==================================================================
// mapping.h
//    Header file for inverse mappings.
//
//       The Object-Oriented Ray Tracer (OORT)
//       Copyright (C) 1993 by Nicholas Wilt.
//
// This software product may be freely copied and distributed in
// unmodified form but may not be sold.  A nominal distribution
// fee may be charged for media and handling by freeware and
// shareware distributors.  The software product may not be
// included in whole or in part into any commercial package
// without the express written consent of the author.
//
// This software product is provided as is without warranty of
// any kind, express or implied, including but not limited to
// the implied warranties of merchantability and fitness for a
// particular purpose.  The author assumes no liability for any
// alleged or actual damages arising from the use of this
// software.  The author is under no obligation to provide
// service, corrections or upgrades to the software.
```

Listing 6.3 Mapping definition

```
//
// -------------------------------------------------------------
//
// Please contact me with questions, comments, suggestions or
// other input about OORT.  My Compuserve account number is
// [75210,2455] (Internet sites can reach me at
// 75210.2455@compuserve.com).
//                                      --Nicholas Wilt
// =============================================================


// -------------------------------------------------------------
// Mapping
//      Implements various methods of taking 3D points and
//      turning them into 2D points.
// -------------------------------------------------------------

class Mapping {
public:
    Mapping() { }
    virtual ~Mapping() { }
    virtual Mapping *Dup() const = 0;
    virtual Vector3D Map3DTo2D(const Vector3D& v) const = 0;
};

// -------------------------------------------------------------
// CircularMapping
//      Maps onto a circle of arbitrary radius centered
//      about the origin.
// -------------------------------------------------------------
class CircularMapping : public Mapping {
public:
    CircularMapping(float Radius = 1);
    Mapping *Dup() const;
    Vector3D Map3DTo2D(const Vector3D& v) const;
private:
    float radius;
};



// -------------------------------------------------------------
// ConicalMapping
//      Maps onto a cone.
// -------------------------------------------------------------
class ConicalMapping : public Mapping {
public:
```

Listing 6.3 Mapping definition *(continued)*

```
   ConicalMapping(float rad0, float radh, float height);
   Mapping *Dup() const;
   Vector3D Map3DTo2D(const Vector3D& v) const;
private:
   float rad0, radh, height;
};


// ------------------------------------------------------------
// CylindricalMapping
//     Maps onto a cylinder centered on the Y axis.
// ------------------------------------------------------------
class CylindricalMapping : public Mapping {
public:
   CylindricalMapping(float radius, float height);
   Mapping *Dup() const;
   Vector3D Map3DTo2D(const Vector3D& v) const;
private:
   float radius, height;
};


// ------------------------------------------------------------
// ProjectionMapping
//     Projects the input vector onto the XY coordinate plane.
// ------------------------------------------------------------
class ProjectionMapping : public Mapping {
public:
   Mapping *Dup() const;
   Vector3D Map3DTo2D(const Vector3D& v) const;
};


// ------------------------------------------------------------
// QuadrilateralMapping
//     Maps points onto a quadrilateral.
// ------------------------------------------------------------
class QuadrilateralMapping : public Mapping {
public:
   QuadrilateralMapping(const Vector3D *Pts);
   Mapping *Dup() const;
   Vector3D Map3DTo2D(const Vector3D& v) const;
private:
   Vector3D pts[4];
   Vector3D Na, Nb, Nc, Nd;
```

Listing 6.3 Mapping definition *(continued)*

```
    float Du0, Du1, Du2, Dv0, Dv1, Dv2;
    int uaxespar, vaxespar;
    Vector3D Qux, Quy, Qvx, Qvy;
    float Dux, Duy, Dvx, Dvy;
};


// ------------------------------------------------------------
// SphericalMapping
//    Maps points onto a sphere centered about an arbitrary point.
// ------------------------------------------------------------
class SphericalMapping : public Mapping {
public:
    SphericalMapping(Vector3D _center = Vector3D(0));
    Mapping *Dup() const;
    Vector3D Map3DTo2D(const Vector3D& v) const;
private:
    Vector3D center;
};
```

Listing 6.3 Mapping definition *(continued)*

The most important function in Mapping, Map3DTo2D, takes a vector and maps it to a 2D parameter space. The return value has 0 for a Z component; the X and Y components are both in the range [0, 1].

All of the mappings except parallel projection are from Haines [HAIN89].

I should note that all of the mapping implementations assume a canonical form of the object to map onto. For example, the circular and spherical mappings assume that you are mapping onto an object centered at the origin; the cylindrical mapping assumes you are mapping onto a cylinder aligned with the Y axis. If the canonical form is not satisfactory, you have to transform the input points to the coordinate system of the mapping. You can do this by setting the reference matrix in the Texture. See Section 6.9 for a discussion of these and other implications of the reference matrix in the Texture class.

Circular

The circular mapping is a 2D→2D mapping, so the Z coordinate of the input vector is ignored. The U coordinate of the mapping is the angle about the Z axis, mapped to the range [0, 1]. The V coordinate of the mapping is the radius from the (X, Y) origin, mapped to the range [0, 1] so that 0 is at the origin and 1 is the radius of the circle. See Figure 6.1.

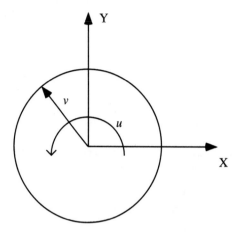

Figure 6.1 Circular mapping.

The equations are as follows. Listing 6.4 shows the implementation for `CircularMapping::Map3DTo2D`.

$$u' = \frac{\cos^{-1}(\dfrac{X}{\sqrt{X^2 + Y^2}})}{2\pi} \tag{6.1a}$$

$$u = 1 - u', Y < 0$$
$$= u', otherwise \tag{6.1b}$$

$$v = \sqrt{\frac{X^2 + Y^2}{R^2}} \tag{6.1c}$$

```
// -------------------------------------------------------------
// CircularMapping
//     Maps onto a circle centered about the origin.
// -------------------------------------------------------------

CircularMapping::CircularMapping(float _radius)
{
    radius = _radius;
}

Mapping *
```

Listing 6.4 `CircularMapping::Map3DTo2D`

```
CircularMapping::Dup() const
{
    return new CircularMapping(radius);
}

Vector3D
CircularMapping::Map3DTo2D(const Vector3D& v) const
{
    float mag = posmod(hypot(v.x, v.y), radius);
    float u = acos(posmod(v.x, radius)) / (2 * M_PI);
    return Vector3D((v.y < 0) ? 1 - u : u,
                    mag,
                    0);
}
```

Listing 6.4 `CircularMapping::Map3DTo2D` *(continued)*

Spherical

The spherical mapping maps a point onto a sphere. The U and V coordinates of the mapping are the latitude and longitude on the sphere, mapped to the range [0, 1]. (See Figure 6.2.) The sphere is assumed to be oriented so that its

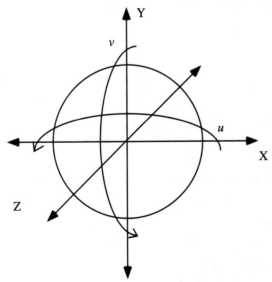

Both *u* and *v* are normalized to the range [0, 1].

Figure 6.2 Spherical mapping.

north pole is pointing in the +Y direction, and the origin of the longitude measure is assumed to point in the +X direction. If you want to map points to a sphere that is not oriented in this way, you must transform the point before passing it to the spherical mapping.

$$\phi = \cos^{-1} X' \tag{6.2a}$$

$$v = \frac{\phi}{\pi} \tag{6.2b}$$

$$u' = \frac{\cos^{-1} X'}{\sin \phi} \tag{6.2c}$$

$$u = u', Z' > 0$$
$$= 1 - u', otherwise \tag{6.2d}$$

```
// ------------------------------------------------------------
// SphericalMapping
//     Maps onto a sphere centered about any point.
// ------------------------------------------------------------

SphericalMapping::SphericalMapping(Vector3D _center)
{
    center = _center;
}

Mapping *
SphericalMapping::Dup() const
{
    return new SphericalMapping(center);
}

Vector3D
SphericalMapping::Map3DTo2D(const Vector3D& v) const
{
    Vector3D unit = Normalize(v - center);
    float phi = acos(unit.y);
    float theta = unit.x / sqrt(1 - unit.y * unit.y);
    if (fabs(theta) > 1)
        return Vector3D(0, phi / M_PI, 0);
    theta = acos(theta) / (2 * M_PI);
    if (unit.z > 0)
```

Listing 6.5 `SphericalMapping::Map3DTo2D`

```
        return Vector3D(theta, phi / M_PI, 0);
    else
        return Vector3D(1 - theta, phi / M_PI, 0);
}
```

Listing 6.5 `SphericalMapping::Map3DTo2D` *(continued)*

Cylindrical

The cylindrical mapping is mapped onto a canonical cylinder centered along the Y axis. The V coordinate of the mapping is set to the Y coordinate of the input point. The U coordinate of the mapping is the angle about the Y axis, mapped to the range [0, 1].

$$v = \frac{Y}{C_h} \tag{6.3a}$$

$$u' = \frac{\cos^{-1}\dfrac{X}{C_r}}{2\pi} \tag{6.3b}$$

$$u = \begin{cases} 1 - u', & Z < 0 \\ u', & otherwise \end{cases} \tag{6.3c}$$

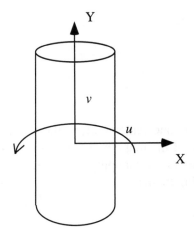

Figure 6.3   Cylindrical mapping

```
// -----------------------------------------------------------
// CylindricalMapping
//          Maps points onto a cylinder centered about the Y axis.
// -----------------------------------------------------------

CylindricalMapping::CylindricalMapping(float _radius, float _height)
{
        radius = _radius;
        height = _height;
}

Mapping *
CylindricalMapping::Dup() const
{
        return new CylindricalMapping(radius, height);
}

Vector3D
CylindricalMapping::Map3DTo2D(const Vector3D& v) const
{
        float u = acos(v.x / Magnitude(v)) / (2 * M_PI);
        return Vector3D( (v.y < 0) ? 1 - u : u,
                                    posmod(v.y, height),
                                    0);
}
```

Listing 6.6   `CylindricalMapping::Map3DTo2D`

Conical

The conical mapping is mapped onto a cone centered along the Y axis. Like the cylindrical mapping, the V coordinate of the mapping is set to the Y coordinate of the input point and the U coordinate of the mapping is the angle about the Y axis, mapped to the range [0, 1]. See Figure 6.4.

$$v = \frac{Y}{C_h}$$

(6.4a)

$$u' = \frac{\cos^{-1}\left(\dfrac{X}{\left(C_{r0} + \left(C_{rh} - C_{r0}\right)\dfrac{Z}{C_h}\right)}\right)}{2\pi} \tag{6.4b}$$

$$u = \begin{cases} 1 - u', & Z < 0 \\ u', & otherwise \end{cases} \tag{6.4c}$$

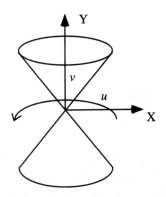

Figure 6.4   Conical mapping.

```
// ----------------------------------------------------------
// ConicalMapping
//     Maps points onto a cone centered about the Y axis.
// ----------------------------------------------------------
ConicalMapping::ConicalMapping(float _rad0, float _radh, float
    _height)
{
    rad0 = _rad0;
    radh = _radh;
    height = _height;
}

Mapping *
ConicalMapping::Dup() const
{
```

Listing 6.7   `ConicalMapping::Map3DTo2D`

```
    return new ConicalMapping(rad0, radh, height);
}

Vector3D
ConicalMapping::Map3DTo2D(const Vector3D& v) const
{
    float tempv = posmod(v.y, height);
    float denom = rad0 + (radh - rad0) * tempv;

    if (fabs(denom) < Limits::Small)
        return Vector3D(0, tempv, 0);

    float u = acos(fmod(v.x, denom)) / (2 * M_PI);

    return Vector3D( (v.z < 0) ? 1 - u : u,
                    tempv,
                    0);
}
```

Listing 6.7 `ConicalMapping::Map3DTo2D` *(continued)*

Simple Projection

This mapping applies an oblique parallel projection to the input point. It assumes that you are projecting onto the XY plane, so it just sets the Z coordinate of the input point to zero. See Listing 6.8 for the implementation of `ProjectionMapping::Map3DTo2D`.

```
// ----------------------------------------------------------
// ProjectionMapping
// Projects points onto the XY coordinate plane.
// ----------------------------------------------------------

Mapping *
ProjectionMapping::Dup() const
{
    return new ProjectionMapping;
}

Vector3D
ProjectionMapping::Map3DTo2D(const Vector3D& v) const
{
    return Vector3D(v.x, v.y, 0);
}
```

Listing 6.8 `ProjectionMapping::Map3DTo2D`

Quadrilateral

The quadrilateral mapping uses a two-dimensional coordinate system with coordinates ranging from 0–1 such that you can specify any point on a convex quadrilateral. (See Figure 6.5.) The four points of the quadrilateral are denoted $\mathbf{P}_0$, $\mathbf{P}_1$, $\mathbf{P}_2$ and $\mathbf{P}_3$. Given these four points, the following values are precomputed:

$$\mathbf{P}_a = \mathbf{P}_0 - \mathbf{P}_2 + \mathbf{P}_3 - \mathbf{P}_1$$
$$\mathbf{P}_b = \mathbf{P}_2 - \mathbf{P}_0$$
$$\mathbf{P}_c = \mathbf{P}_1 - \mathbf{P}_0$$
$$\mathbf{P}_d = \mathbf{P}_0$$
$$\mathbf{N}_a = \mathbf{P}_a \times \mathbf{P}_n$$
$$\mathbf{N}_c = \mathbf{P}_c \times \mathbf{P}_n$$
$$D_{u0} = \mathbf{N}_c \cdot \mathbf{P}_d$$
$$D_{u1} = \mathbf{N}_a \cdot \mathbf{P}_d + \mathbf{N}_c \cdot \mathbf{P}_b$$
$$D_{u2} = \mathbf{N}_d \cdot \mathbf{P}_b \tag{6.5}$$

If $D_{u2} = 0$, the u axes are parallel and u is computed as follows:

$$u = \frac{\mathbf{N}_c \cdot \mathbf{p} - D_{u0}}{D_{u1} - \mathbf{N}_a \cdot \mathbf{p}} \tag{6.6}$$

Otherwise, the following values are precomputed:

$$\mathbf{Q}_{ux} = \frac{\mathbf{N}_a}{2D_{u2}} \tag{6.7a}$$

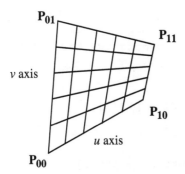

P_{01}

P_{11}

v axis

P_{10}

u axis

P_{00}

Figure 6.5 Quadrilateral mapping.

$$D_{ux} = \frac{-D_{u1}}{2D_{u2}}$$

(6.7b)

$$\mathbf{Q}_{uy} = \frac{-\mathbf{N}_c}{D_{u2}}$$

(6.7c)

$$D_{uy} = \frac{D_{u0}}{D_{u2}}$$

(6.7d)

and u is computed as follows. First, two values K_a and K_b are computed:

$$K_a = D_{ux} + \mathbf{p} \cdot \mathbf{Q}_{ux}$$
$$K_b = D_{uy} + \mathbf{p} \cdot \mathbf{Q}_{uy}$$

(6.8)

If $K_b < K_a^2$, the point is not within the quadrilateral. Otherwise, two values u_0 and u_1 are computed:

$$u_0 = K_a - \sqrt{K_a^2 - K_b}$$
$$u_1 = K_a + \sqrt{K_a^2 - K_b}$$

(6.9)

If both u_0 and u_1 are within the valid range [0, 1], the quadrilateral is not convex. Otherwise, one of u_0 and u_1 will be in the valid range; this is the value we return.

To compute v, we go through a process exactly analogous to computing u. See the implementation of Quadrilateral (Listing 6.9) for the particulars.

```
// --------------------------------------------------------
// QuadrilateralMapping
//     Maps onto an arbitrary quadrilateral.
// --------------------------------------------------------
QuadrilateralMapping::QuadrilateralMapping(const Vector3D *Pts)
{
    for (int i = 0; i < 4; i++)
        pts[i] = Pts[i];
    Vector3D Pa = pts[0] - pts[3] + pts[2] - pts[1];
    Vector3D Pb = pts[3] - pts[0];
    Vector3D Pc = pts[1] - pts[0];
    Vector3D Pd = pts[0];
    Vector3D Pn = -Normalize(CrossProd(pts[2] - pts[1],
```

Listing 6.9 Quadrilateral implementation

```
                                    pts[0] - pts[1]));
    Na = CrossProd(Pa, Pn);
    Nb = CrossProd(Pb, Pn);
    Nc = CrossProd(Pc, Pn);
    Nd = CrossProd(Pd, Pn);
    Du0 = DotProd(Nc, Pd);
    Du1 = DotProd(Na, Pd) + DotProd(Nc, Pb);
    Du2 = DotProd(Na, Pb);
    Dv0 = DotProd(Nb, Pd);
    Dv1 = DotProd(Na, Pd) + DotProd(Nb, Pc);
    Dv2 = DotProd(Na, Pc);
    uaxespar = fabs(Du2) < Limits::Small;
    if (! uaxespar) {
        Qux = Na / (2 * Du2);
        Dux = -Du1 / (2 * Du2);
        Quy = -Nc / Du2;
        Duy = Du0 / Du2;
    }
    vaxespar = fabs(Dv2) < Limits::Small;
    if (! vaxespar) {
        Qvx = Na / (2 * Dv2);
        Dvx = -Dv1 / (2 * Dv2);
        Qvy = -Nb / Dv2;
        Dvy = Dv0 / Dv2;
    }
}


Mapping *
QuadrilateralMapping::Dup() const
{
    return new QuadrilateralMapping(pts);
}


Vector3D
QuadrilateralMapping::Map3DTo2D(const Vector3D& x) const
{
    float u, v;
    if (uaxespar)
        u = (DotProd(Nc, x) - Du0) / (Du1 - DotProd(Na, x));
    else {
        float Ka = Dux + DotProd(Qux, x);
        float Kb = Duy + DotProd(Quy, x);
        if (Kb <= Ka*Ka) {
            float u0 = Ka - sqrt(Ka*Ka - Kb);
            float u1 = Ka + sqrt(Ka*Ka - Kb);
```

Listing 6.9 Quadrilateral implementation *(continued)*

```
        u = u0;
        if (! InRange((float) 0, (float) 1, u0))
            u = u1;
    }
    else u = 0;
}
if (vaxespar)
    v = (DotProd(Nb, x) - Dv0) / (Dv1 - DotProd(Na, x));
else {
    float Ka = Dvx + DotProd(Qvx, x);
    float Kb = Dvy + DotProd(Qvy, x);
    if (Kb <= Ka*Ka) {
        float v0 = Ka - sqrt(Ka*Ka - Kb);
        float v1 = Ka + sqrt(Ka*Ka - Kb);
        v = v0;
        if (! InRange((float) 0, (float) 1, v0))
            v = v1;
    }
    else v = 0;
}
return Vector3D(u, v, 0);
}
```

Listing 6.9   `Quadrilateral` implementation *(continued)*

6.4.2   Noise

Noise is an important component of texture mapping and its relatives. Random variations in color are important to many texture mapping applications, but the randomness must be carefully controlled. It is especially important to be able to generate a random number given a position in space, and to generate random numbers that are close to one another when given positions that are close to one another. Similarly, it is important to be able to generate random vectors that vary slowly but randomly with position.

In OORT, an abstract base class called `NoiseMaker` contains member functions that can be used to generate noise values, both scalar and vector.

`NoiseMaker::Noise` takes a point and returns the noise value at that point. The noise value is random for uncorrelated points, but for points within one unit of each other it varies slowly. For example, if you call `Noise` with the coordinates (1, 1, 1) and (3, 3, 3), it will return two uncorrelated random numbers between 0 and 1. However, if you call it with the coordinates (1, 1, 1) and (1.1, 1.1, 1.1), the values returned will be very similar.

`NoiseMaker::DNoise` takes a point and returns a noise *vector*. The noise vector has the same properties as the noise value, in that it changes slowly but randomly for different locations in space. The default implementation of this function is as described by Perlin: the location is passed to `Noise` three times, but translated by a large constant vector so the noise values are uncorrelated.

`NoiseMaker::Turbulence` takes a point and computes Perlin's suggested implementation for turbulence, as follows:

$$Turbulence = \sum_{i=1}^{n} abs(\frac{1}{2^i} Noise(2^i x)) \qquad (6.10)$$

In the equation above, n is a measure of the turbulence. The larger n is, the more "turbulent" the results returned will be.

`NoiseMaker::DTurbulence` is a vector-valued function analogous to `Turbulence`. It is defined similarly, but uses the vector-valued *DNoise* function instead of *Noise*.

Since all of the member functions of `NoiseMaker` are virtual, they can be overloaded by classes inheriting from them. Currently, `PerlinNoise` is the only implementation of a `NoiseMaker`.

Perlin proposed a popular noise-generation algorithm [PERL89]. The components of a `PerlinNoise` noise generator are as follows:

- N, the number of elements in the precomputed arrays **P** and **G**. In practice, Perlin suggests using N = 256.

- **P**, an array of integers that contains a random permutation of the integers from 0 to N–1.

- **G**, an array of integers that contains a precomputed random distribution of unit vectors.

The components of a noise value at a given point depend on the noise values of *lattice points* in the point's neighborhood. These lattice points are located at the integer values that bracket each coordinate of the point. For example, the point (1.3, 2.5, 0.6) is bracketed in X by 1 and 2, in Y by 2 and 3, and in Z by 0 and 1. The noise value is a weighted average of the noise values at each of the eight lattice points corresponding to the input point. Using the above example, the noise values at (1, 2, 0), (1, 2, 1), (1, 3, 0), (1, 3, 1), (2, 2, 0), (2, 2, 1), (2, 3, 0), (2, 3, 1) would be averaged as follows:

$$Noise = \sum_{i=\lfloor x \rfloor}^{\lfloor x \rfloor + 1} \sum_{j=\lfloor y \rfloor}^{\lfloor y \rfloor + 1} \sum_{k=\lfloor z \rfloor}^{\lfloor z \rfloor + 1} \Omega_{i,j,k}(x-i, y-j, z-k) \qquad (6.11)$$

where

$$\Omega_{i,j,k}(u,v,w) = \omega(u)\omega(v)\omega(w)(\Gamma_{i,j,k} \cdot (u,v,w)) \tag{6.12}$$

Perlin chooses $\omega(t)$ to be a cubic weighting function, as follows:

$$\omega(t) = 2|t|^3 - 3|t|^2 + 1 \text{ if } |t| < 1,$$
$$= 0, \text{ otherwise.} \tag{6.13}$$

A plot of $\omega(t)$ as it ranges from 0 to 1 is seen in Figure 6.6.

$\Gamma_{i,j,k}$ is a pseudorandom gradient vector at the lattice point (i, j, k). That's what **G**, the precomputed array of vectors, is for: rather than calling the random number generator to generate this vector, Perlin indexes into the precomputed array as follows:

$$\Gamma_{i,j,k} = \mathbf{G}(\phi(i + \phi(j + \phi(k)))) \tag{6.14}$$

where $(i) = \mathbf{P}[i \bmod N]$.

Each element in **G** is arrived at by generating each coordinate in the range $[-1, 1]$ and rejecting any resulting vectors with magnitude greater than 1. Otherwise the vector is normalized and added to the table. See `PerlinNoise::Initialize` for the implementation.

In animation and other contexts, it is important that the precomputed elements of a `NoiseMaker` be held constant. Otherwise, the textures in an animation will change radically from frame to frame. That is why `PerlinNoise` has

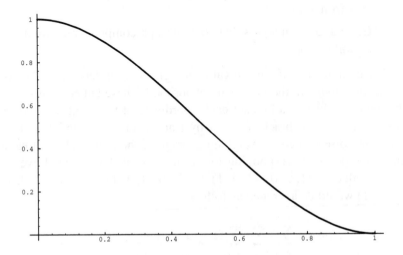

Figure 6.6 Hermite weighting function.

a constructor that takes a seed for the pseudorandom number generator. Given the same seed, `PerlinNoise` will generate the same precomputed data for **P** and **G**, as long as the same implementation of *rand()* is used.

`NoiseMaker` is implemented separately from `PerlinNoise` because noise algorithms other than Perlin's might be useful. Lewis [LEW89] surveys a number of solid noise functions and presents two algorithms as well.

```
// ------------------------------------------------------------
// NoiseMaker
//      Implements solid noise functions.  Given a solid
//      noise function (Noise), NoiseMaker implements a
//      vector-valued noise function (DNoise), a turbulence
//      function, and a vector-valued turbulence function.
// ------------------------------------------------------------

// ------------------------------------------------------------
// This vector is used to formulate vector-valued noise
// functions in terms of the scalar-valued noise function
// (see NoiseMaker::DNoise).
// ------------------------------------------------------------
#define BIGVECT Vector3D(1000.2, 1000.5, 1000.8)

class NoiseMaker {
public:
   NoiseMaker() { }
   virtual ~NoiseMaker() { }

   // Pure virtual Noise function.
   virtual float Noise(const Vector3D& x) = 0;

   // Vector3D-valued noise function, formulated in terms of the
   // scalar-valued noise function.
   virtual Vector3D DNoise(const Vector3D& x) {
      return Vector3D(Noise(x - BIGVECT), Noise(x), Noise(x + BIGVECT));
   }

   // Scalar and vector turbulence functions, formulated in terms of
   // the scalar-valued noise function.
   virtual float Turbulence(const Vector3D& x);
   virtual Vector3D DTurbulence(const Vector3D& x);
};

// ------------------------------------------------------------
```

Listing 6.10 Definitions for `NoiseMaker, PerlinNoise`

```
// PerlinNoise
//      Implements the solid noise function described in
//      Ken Perlin's "Hypertexture," SIGGRAPH '89, pg. 253.
// ----------------------------------------------------------

#define NUM_NOISE_POINTS 4096

class PerlinNoise : public NoiseMaker {
public:
    PerlinNoise();
    PerlinNoise(int seed);
    virtual ~PerlinNoise();
    virtual float Noise(const Vector3D& x);
private:
    Vector3D *G;      // An array of unit vectors uniformly distributed
                      // about the unit sphere.
    int *P;              // An array containing a random permutation of
                      // 0..NUM_NOISE_POINTS-1.

    // Hermite curve interpolation function.
    float w(float t) {
        t = fabs(t);
        if (t < 1)
            return t*t*(-3 + 2*t) + 1;
        else
            return 0;
    }

    // Truncate x to fit within the randomly permuted table, then
    // return the corresponding randomly permuted value.
    int Phi(long x) {
        return P[labs(x) & (NUM_NOISE_POINTS - 1)];
    }

    // 3D hashing function; given the truncated values of a vector
    // in 3-space, return the randomized vector corresponding to the
    // position.
    Vector3D Gamma(long i, long j, long k) {
        return G[Phi(i+Phi(j+Phi(k)))];
    }

    // Do a Hermite interpolation in the three dimensions.
    float Omega(const Vector3D& A, long x, long y, long z) {
        float dot = DotProd(Gamma(x, y, z), Vector3D(fabs(A.x),
            fabs(A.y), fabs(A.z)));
```

Listing 6.10   Definitions for `NoiseMaker`, `PerlinNoise` *(continued)*

```
        return w(A.x)*w(A.y)*w(A.z)*dot;
    }

    // Allocates and computes G and P.
    void Initialize();

};
```

Listing 6.10 Definitions for `NoiseMaker`, `PerlinNoise` *(continued)*

```
// DNoise (defined in header), Turbulence and DTurbulence are
// invariant with the type of noise.

// Turbulence: Sum noise values scaled by progressively smaller
//             values until the scale value goes under 0.1.
float
NoiseMaker::Turbulence(const Vector3D& p)
{
    float scale;
    float value;
    float ret;

    ret = 0;
    for (scale = 1.0; scale > 0.1; scale *= 0.5) {
        value = Noise(p / scale);
        ret += fabs(value) * scale;
    }
    return ret;
}

// DTurbulence: Vector3D-valued turbulence function.
Vector3D
NoiseMaker::DTurbulence(const Vector3D& p)
{
    Vector3D value;
    Vector3D ret;
    float scale;

    ret = Vector3D(0);
    for (scale = 1.0; scale >= 0.01; scale *= 0.5) {
        value = DNoise(p / scale);
        ret += value * scale;
    }
```

Listing 6.11 `PerlinNoise` implementation

```
      return ret;
}

// -----------------------------------------------------------------
// The PerlinNoise class implements the noise function defined in
// Ken Perlin's article "Hypertexture" on pg. 253 of the SIGGRAPH '89
// Proceedings.
// -----------------------------------------------------------------

void
PerlinNoise::Initialize()
{
    int i, j;

    P = new int[NUM_NOISE_POINTS];
    G = new Vector3D[NUM_NOISE_POINTS];
    for (i = 0; i < NUM_NOISE_POINTS; i++)
       P[i] = i;
    for (i = 0; i < NUM_NOISE_POINTS; i++) {
        int inx = rand() % NUM_NOISE_POINTS;
        int temp = P[inx];
        P[inx] = P[i];
        P[i] = temp;
    }
    for (i = 0; i < NUM_NOISE_POINTS; i++) {
        G[i] = Vector3D(1);
        while (Magnitude(G[i]) > 1) {
            for (j = 0; j < 3; j++) {
                int num = rand();
                if (num & (RAND_MAX+1 >> 1))
                    num |= RAND_MAX + 1;
                G[i][j] = (float) num / RAND_MAX;
            }
            G[i] = Normalize(G[i]);
        }
    }
}

PerlinNoise::PerlinNoise()
{
    Initialize();
}

PerlinNoise::PerlinNoise(int seed)
{
```

Listing 6.11 PerlinNoise implementation *(continued)*

```
    srand(seed);
    Initialize();
}

PerlinNoise::~PerlinNoise()
{
    delete P;
    delete G;
}

float
PerlinNoise::Noise(const Vector3D& p)
{
    long fx, fy, fz;
    long i, j, k;
    float subt;

    fx = p.x;
    fy = p.y;
    fz = p.z;

    subt = 0;
    for (i = fx; i <= fx + 1; i++)
        for (j = fy; j <= fy + 1; j++)
            for (k = fz; k <= fz + 1; k++)
                subt += Omega(p - Vector3D(i, j, k), i, j, k);

    subt += 0.5;
    if (subt <= 0)
        return 0;
    else if (subt > 1)
        return 1;
    return subt;
}
```

Listing 6.11 `PerlinNoise` implementation *(continued)*

6.4.3 Color Maps

Color maps, like noise, are an aid to texture mapping. A color map takes a number and maps it to a color. Typically, the number is obtained from a noise generator (see Section 6.4.2). In OORT, color maps are implemented by a class called `ColorMap`. See the definition in Listing 6.12.

The color map contains a number of entries. Each color map entry is asked whether it can handle the value given; the first one that can is asked to compute a color based on the value. It is up to the user of the color map to ensure that no two entries overlap. If they do, whichever happens to be the first in the color map's list will take precedence.

Although the high-level implementation is extremely general, the only implementations I have provided are simple. See the listing of `colormap.h`.

```
// -----------------------------------------------------
// ColorMap
//
//          Provides a way to map a value in the range [0, 1] to
//          an RGB triple.  The ColorMapEntries specify ranges
//          within [0, 1]; given a value in its range, a given
//          ColorMapEntry uses the value to interpolate between
//          the colors in the ColorMapEntry.
// -----------------------------------------------------

// Forward declaration.
class ColorMapEntry;

class ColorMap {
public:
       ColorMap() {
              num_entries = 0;
              entries = new ColorMapEntry*[max_entries = 2];
       }
       ~ColorMap();

       void AddEntry(ColorMapEntry *);
       RGBColor ComputeColor(float value);
private:
       int num_entries, max_entries;
       ColorMapEntry **entries;
};
```

Listing 6.12 `ColorMap` definition

6.5 Solid Texturing

Solid texturing is a simple idea that was independently proposed by Peachey [PEAC85] and Perlin [PERL85]. Solid texturing uses tools like noise and color maps to define an object's texture in all space. To determine a color at a point in 3D space, for example, a solid texture might perform the following steps:

- Transform the location so that it is close to the origin.

```
// ----------------------------------------------------------
// ColorMapEntry
//           Encapsulates an entry in the color map.  A
//           ColorMapEntry has to provide two basic operations:
//                - Tell whether a given value is within the
//                  bounds of the color map entry.  This is
//                  implemented by the IsInside member function.
//                - Compute a color given that value.  This is
//                  implemented by the ComputeColor member function.
// ----------------------------------------------------------
class ColorMapEntry {
public:
      ColorMapEntry() { }
      ColorMapEntry(float s, float e): start(s), end(e) { }
      virtual ~ColorMapEntry() { }

      // Compute color inside this entry given the value.
      virtual RGBColor ComputeColor(float value) const = 0;

      // Duplicate a color map entry.
      virtual ColorMapEntry *Dup() const = 0;

      // Given a value, return nonzero if it's within this entry's
bounds.
      int IsInside(float value) {
            return value >= start && value <= end;
      }
protected:
      float start, end;
      float fract(float value) {
            return (value - start) / (end - start);
      }
};
```

Listing 6.13 `ColorMapEntry` definition

- Scale the location so that it maps to values that are close to each other; this readies the location to be passed to the solid noise function.
- Call `PerlinNoise::Noise` to get a position-dependent pseudorandom value between 0 and 1.
- Pass the noise value to a color map to compute the color corresponding to the noise value.

The resulting color is returned as the color at the input location.

The Textures example, described in Appendix F, illustrates how to use a variety of solid textures. The rendered example image may be found in Plate 6.

6.6 Texture Mapping and Transformations

Transformations have some important roles with respect to textures and their relatives. The values returned by noise functions depend on the positions passed to them, so if the same object is going to be depicted in different locations, it is imperative to transform the points passed to the texture so that the same relative positions are passed into the noise function. Otherwise, the texture on an object will appear to depend on its position.

Transformations are especially important in the context of animation. Without translating an object's texture to the same location for every frame, the object's texture will change with every frame as values passed to the noise function vary with the object's position.

Transformations are also important when inverse mappings are used. Most inverse mappings require the texture to be translated and rotated into the canonical coordinate system when the inverse mapping is applied.

All textures contain a matrix called `reference` that is used to place the texture correctly before applying an inverse mapping.

6.7 Exercises

1. Implement some new types of texture. One good reference is Steve Upstill's *The RenderMan Companion* [UPST90].

2. Implement a new inverse mapping (for example, one for an ellipsoid).

3. Implement a new bump map.

4. Can you think of any flaws in Perlin's noise function (Hint: what value does it return when the coordinates of the input point are all integers)?

5. Implement a noise function other than Perlin's. Try rendering the same solid textures using different noise functions. How do they change?

6. Rectangles and checkerboards are not the only interesting patterns that can be mapped onto 3D objects. Try implementing some other interesting pattern, like a pattern of hexagons. In contrast to a checkerboard, which can tile two textures, a field of hexagons can tile three textures.

Chapter 15

7

Distribution Ray Tracing

Distribution ray tracing[1] is a technique pioneered by Cook et al. [COOK84a] that can generate a variety of effects when applied in different ways. OORT implements a number of these effects: antialiasing of primary rays, soft shadows cast by extended light sources, blurry reflections and translucency. Other effects described by Cook et al. include depth of field and motion blur.

7.1 Theoretical Basis

Naive ray tracing, which casts a single ray through each pixel to determine its color, can suffer from undesirable artifacts that appear in the image because of interactions between the rays being traced and the scene that is being rendered. In computer graphics, these undesirable artifacts are known collectively as *aliasing*.

Aliasing can arise in any problem where samples must be taken at points. Figure 7.1 shows a one-dimensional function being point-sampled at regular intervals. Because the frequency of the samples is smaller than the frequency of

---

[1] Distribution ray tracing was originally called *distributed ray tracing*, but this term has fallen out of favor because it can be confused with distributing a ray tracing computation over a network. Other names for the technique include *probabilistic ray tracing* and *stochastic ray tracing*.

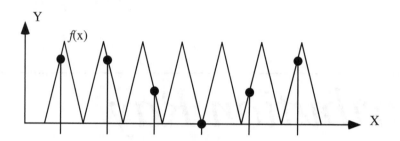

Figure 7.1   Aliasing in one dimension.

the function being sampled, whoever is doing the samples winds up with a very wrong idea of what the function looks like.

In ray tracing, the two-dimensional function of screen color is being sampled. Aliasing artifacts include banding and the notorious *jaggies* (jagged edges along pixel boundaries). If animation is being produced, you have to worry about temporal aliasing artifacts. (Small objects may blink in and out of existence in consecutive frames, for example.)

If you are restricted to a point-sampling technique such as ray tracing, the only way to combat aliasing is to increase the frequency of the samples. In the context of Figure 7.1, that might mean taking three samples per horizontal unit instead of one. In the context of ray tracing, that means firing more than one ray through each pixel. This is much more computationally expensive than naive ray tracing, and much of that work goes to waste because most pixels do not require antialiasing. We will discuss adaptive supersampling techniques in the next section; for now, we will discuss an ingenious methodology for antialiasing described by Cook et al. [COOK84a, COOK89].

Cook [COOK89] noted that the human eye is not normally subject to aliasing, and proposed using the distribution of photoreceptors as a model for antialiasing in ray tracing. Yellott [YELL83] studied the distribution of extrafoveal photoreceptors in the Rhesus monkey, which is similar to that of the human eye. Yellott found the receptors to be arranged in a minimum-distance Poisson distribution, a random distribution in which no two samples are within a given distance of each other. By using this distribution as a model for placing the samples when ray tracing, the desirable antialiasing effects of the eye can be emulated by the rendering program.

Two problems arise when using a true Poisson distribution for ray tracing samples. First, the minimum-distance Poisson distribution is difficult to compute. The only algorithms to compute minimum-distance Poisson distributions directly involve *dart-throwing*, or taking random samples until no two samples are within the "hard disk" radius.

The other problem with randomly placed rays is that each sample's contribution to neighboring pixels is difficult to compute. (In fact, this computation remains an open problem [COOK89].) To alleviate these problems, Cook approximates the Poisson distribution by sampling a regular grid and jittering each sample by a random amount. This technique causes aliasing artifacts to be replaced by the more tolerable artifacts of noise. Compared to a Poisson distribution of samples, generating the jittered samples and computing their contributions to the overall pixel value is simple and efficient.

If we were to implement Cook's jittered supersampling directly, then generating an antialiased image would work as follows. Instead of casting one ray through the center of each pixel, we would divide each pixel into a group of N×M rectangular subpixels and cast a ray through a random location in each subpixel. The resulting colors would then be averaged to find the pixel color.

The problem with this scheme is that it requires NM rays to be cast for every pixel. Most pixels do not require that many rays to be cast to be sampled properly, so this naive technique wastes a lot of computer time. A host of techniques [DIPP85, LEE85, MITC87, MITC91] have been invented to minimize the number of rays cast while preserving the antialiasing capabilities of supersampling. These techniques are known collectively as *adaptive supersampling*. OORT implements a hybrid scheme for adaptive supersampling. We will describe it first in the context of primary rays, then in the context of other types of ray.

7.2 Adaptively Supersampling Primary Rays

Techniques for adaptive supersampling have a common framework. First, they "test the waters" to see whether antialiasing is required. If it is, they take samples until some criterion is met (or some maximum number of samples are taken). Then, the samples are reconstructed somehow to give the final result of the sampling. Criteria to determine whether further antialiasing is required range from variance [DIPP85] to contrast [MITC87]. The most common technique for reconstructing the samples is simply to average the samples that fall within each pixel. (This is called *box filtering*.)

OORT provides a technique for statistical optimization based on the papers by Mitchell [MITC87, MITC91]. It works by taking a minimum number of samples, then evaluating the samples against a criterion to determine whether more samples are needed. If the samples don't show much variation, OORT assumes that they are representative of the function being sampled. If the samples show a lot of variation, OORT will take more samples until the maximum number of samples have been taken. In all cases, the samples are averaged to give the final result (see Figure 7.2).

To implement this scheme, we need two tools. First, we need a way of getting more samples incrementally and maintaining an approximation to the Poisson minimum-distance distribution. Second, we need a way of deciding whether more samples are needed.

Mitchell [MITC91] gives a technique for taking a variable number of samples and maintaining an approximation to the minimum-distance Poisson distribution. For each sample that must be taken, some number of candidate samples are generated. Of the candidates, the one with the largest minimum distance to the samples already in place is used. Although there is a chance that two samples will wind up close together using this technique, the possibility is exceedingly small if we use enough candidate samples (Mitchell suggests ten).

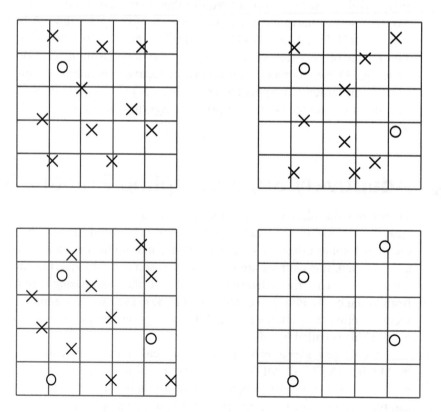

Figure 7.2   Incremental sample generation.

Mitchell [MITC87] contends that contrast is a good criterion for determining whether more samples are required. The contrast of a number of samples is as follows:

$$C = \frac{I_{MAX} - I_{MIN}}{I_{MAX} + I_{MIN}}$$

(7.1)

This value is computed for the red, green, and blue channels of the samples. Then each of the red, green, and blue contrasts is compared to a threshold. More samples are required if any of the three contrasts is above the threshold. Mitchell gives thresholds of 0.4, 0.3, and 0.6 for red, green, and blue (reflecting the relative strengths of human photoreceptors).

The parameters to this adaptive antialiasing algorithm, then, are as follows:

- Minimum number of samples to take.
- Maximum number of samples to take.
- Contrast threshold (default (0.4, 0.3, 0.6) per Mitchell).
- Number of candidates to consider before taking a sample.

The adaptive supersampling of primary rays is invoked by calling `World::SetAntiAliasMode` to set the `World`'s antialiasing mode to `Adaptive`. `World::PixelColor` generates the samples for the pixel using the progressive algorithm described by Mitchell; once the minimum number of samples has been taken, it calls a global function called `MoreRays` to determine whether more rays are needed. `MoreRays` computes the contrast given above and compares it against a tolerance; if any of the color channels fail to meet the tolerance, `MoreRays` returns 1, indicating that more rays are needed to sample the function properly. The algorithm stops sampling a given pixel as soon as the contrast criterion is met, or when the maximum number of samples has been taken.

Listing 7.1 shows the implementation for `World::PixelColor`, the function that samples a pixel. If the `Adaptive` mode is selected, `World::PixelColor` will adaptively supersample the pixel using the technique just described.

7.3 Distributing Shadow Rays

Because they can be partially occluded, extended light sources cast "soft" shadows, or *penumbrae*. This effect can be simulated by distributing shadow rays

```
RGBColor
World::PixelColor(float xtarg, float ytarg)
{
    RGBColor ret;

    switch (mode) {
        case None:
            Vector3D target(xtarg + ScreenWidth / HorzRes / 2,
                            ytarg + ScreenHeight / VertRes / 2,
                            -ScreenDist);
            Statistics::PrimaryRays += 1;
            ret = FindColor(Ray(Vector3D(0), target), 0);
            break;
        case Adaptive:
            {
                RGBColor Imin(MAXFLOAT), Imax(-MAXFLOAT), Intens(0);
                Vector3D *pts = new Vector3D[MaxSamples];
                int i;

                for (i = 0; i < MaxSamples; i++) {
                    pts[i] = NewSample(pts, i);

                    Vector3D target = pts[i];
                    target *= Vector3D(ScreenWidth / HorzRes, ScreenHeight /
                        VertRes, 0);
                    target += Vector3D(xtarg, ytarg, -ScreenDist);

                    Statistics::PrimaryRays += 1;
                    RGBColor clr = FindColor(Ray(Vector3D(0), target), 0);
                    Intens += clr;
                    clr = NormalizeColor(clr);
                    Minimize(Imin, clr);
                    Maximize(Imax, clr);

                    if (i >= MinSamples) {
                        if (i >= MaxSamples)
                            break;
                        if (! MoreRays(Imin, Imax, ContrastThreshold))
                            break;
                    }

                }
                delete[] pts;
                Statistics::RayPixHist[i - 1] += 1;
                ret = Intens / (i + 1);
```

Listing 7.1 World::PixelColor

```
        }
    }
    return ret;
}
```

Listing 7.1 `World::PixelColor`   *(continued)*

over extended light sources. In OORT, the only type of extended light source is rectangular. As with primary rays, ray targets are randomly chosen on the light source using the progressive algorithm described by Mitchell. `MoreRays` is called to determine when enough samples have been taken. The samples are averaged to find the occlusion of the light source at the intersection point.

See the implementation of `RectangularLight::ShadowLight` in Listing 7.2, which is very similar to `World::PixelColor`.

7.4 Distributing Reflected and Transmitted Rays

Reflected and transmitted rays are distributed the same way. A cone of possible directions that spawned rays can take is centered on the direction of perfect

```
RGBColor
RectangularLight::ShadowLight(ShadingInfo& shade, Surface *surf)
{
    RGBColor Imin(MAXFLOAT), Imax(-MAXFLOAT), Intens(0);
    Vector3D *pts = new Vector3D[MaxSamples];

    for (int i = 0; i < MaxSamples; i++) {
        pts[i] = NewSample(pts, i);

        Vector3D target = pts[i];
        target *= Vector3D(width, height, 0);
        target -= Vector3D(width / 2, height / 2, 0);
        target = applied * target;
        RGBColor clr = ShadowRay(shade, target, surf);
        Intens += clr;
        clr = NormalizeColor(clr);
        Minimize(Imin, clr);
        Maximize(Imax, clr);
```

Listing 7.2 `RectangularLight::ShadowLight`

```
    if (i >= MinSamples) {
        if (i >= MaxSamples)
            break;
        if (! MoreRays(Imin, Imax, ContrastThreshold))
            break;
    }
}
delete[] pts;
Statistics::RayPixHist[i - 1] += 1;
return Intens / (i + 1);
}
```

Listing 7.2 `RectangularLight::ShadowLight` *(continued)*

reflection or transmission. Samples are taken from the circular cross-section of this cone, using Mitchell's progressive algorithm to ensure that they are far apart.

The size of the cone is given by a parameter θ. Figure 7.3 shows the cone of possible directions for a reflected ray. Plate 3 shows a number of spheres that reflect with a variety of blurriness.

7.5 Implementation

The adaptive ray distribution scheme is implemented separately for primary, shadow, and secondary rays. Two global functions are used to help in this distribution. `MinDist` computes the distance of a given vector to the nearest in an

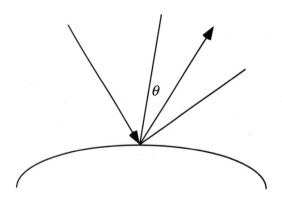

Figure 7.3 Cone of possible directions for a reflected ray.

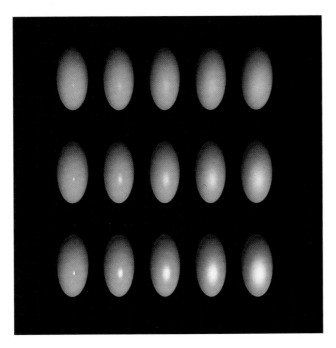

Specular Reflection

Specular reflection models the sharp highlights as seen on apples, billiard balls, and other shiny objects. From left to right, the spheres have increasing specular exponents (3, 5, 10, 27, 200). From top to bottom, the spheres have increasing coefficients of specular reflection, so that they reflect more brightly (0.1, 0.25, 0.5). This image is used with permission from David Kurlander [FOLE90, Fig. 16.10]. This image was generated by the example program F.1 in Appendix F.

Constructive Solid Geometry

This simple demonstration of constructive solid geometry shows the three fundamental CSG operations: difference (top), intersection (middle), and union (bottom). In each case, the two objects combined are shown on the left and the combination is shown on the right. At the bottom, the two spheres are transparent to better show that the union is one object with two lobes, rather than two objects that overlap each other. This image was generated by the example program F.2 in Appendix F.

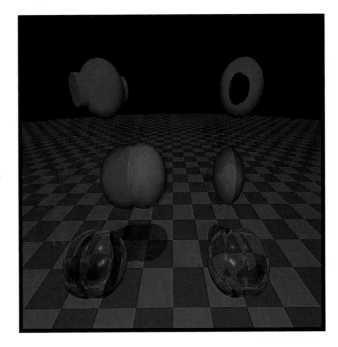

Blurry Reflection

These five spheres evince blurry reflection, as described in Chapter 8. The spheres reflect more blurrily from left to right. The entire scene, including the viewer, is enclosed in a checkered sphere. This image was generated by the example program F.3 in Appendix F.

Quadric Surfaces

Several important quadric surfaces are shown here. Clockwise from the ellipsoid (on the right) are the paraboloid, hyperboloid of one sheet, cylinder, and cone. This image was generated by the example program F.4 in Appendix F.

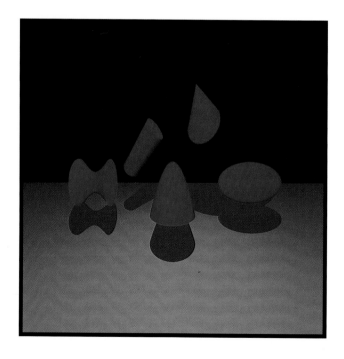

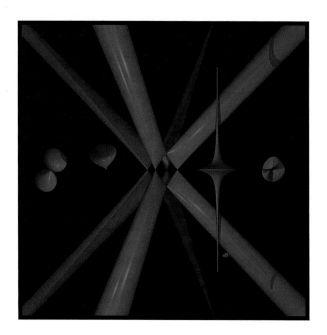

Algebraic Surfaces

From left to right, this image shows Steiner's surface, the quartic cylinder, Kummer's surface, the piriform, and the Lemniscate of Gerano. All of the surfaces shown are quartic (fourth-degree) surfaces. This image was generated by the example program F.5 in Appendix F.

Textures

This image shows a table textured with the WoodUpstill texture. The marbles on the table have a variety of textures applied to them, including wood, marble, and cloudy sky. The floor is an infinite plane checkered with white and blue marble. This image was generated by the example program F.6 in Appendix F.

Sphereflake

The Sphereflake is a recursively defined object composed of spheres. This Sphereflake is shown encased in a glass sphere. This image was generated by the example program F.7 in Appendix F.

Sierpinski's Tetrahedron

Sierpinski's Tetrahedron is a fractal object composed of triangles. The tetrahedron shown here contains 4096 triangles. This image was generated by the example program F.8 in Appendix F.

array of vectors. `MoreRays` applies the contrast criterion to a set of colors, and returns nonzero if more rays are needed.

Primary rays are distributed by `World::PixelColor`. The decision whether to distribute the rays or use the naive technique is given by the `AntiAliasModes` **enum** in `World`. `World::SetAntiAliasMode` can be called with `Naive` or `Adaptive` to set the antialiasing mode. Other member functions of `World` (`SetSamples`, `SetNumCandidates`, and `SetContrastThreshold`) are used to set the other parameters of the distribution scheme.

In the case of shadow ray distribution, each light source is responsible for sampling itself. Directional light sources are infinitely far away, and can only be sampled with a single ray. Similarly, point light sources are infinitely small and only one shadow ray can be used. However, rectangular light sources (and any other type of extended light source the reader may care to add) cause more than one shadow ray to be fired at themselves. The constructor for `RectangularLight` takes the parameters for the adaptive ray distribution (minimum and maximum numbers of samples, number of candidates, and contrast threshold).

Distributing reflected and transmitted rays is handled by `DistributedHall::SampleSpace`. Rays are cast down the cone of possible directions, treating all directions within the cone equally. Member functions of `DistributedHall` (`SetMinSamples`, `SetMaxSamples`, `SetCandidates`, and `SetThreshold`) let you set up the parameters for the adaptive ray distribution.

7.6 Future Work

OORT does not yet support two of the effects originally described by Cook et al. [COOK84a]. Depth-of-field is an effect that can be generated by distributing primary rays over a lens. The pinhole camera model usually used in computer graphics is frequently more desirable than simulating a camera lens, because every object is in focus. However, having the option of simulating depth-of-field would be advantageous.

The other effect described in [COOK84a] is motion blur. This effect would be more difficult to add to the existing implementation, which lacks animation support.

8

Advanced Primitives

8.1   Constructive Solid Geometry

Constructive solid geometry (CSG) is a way to make complicated objects by performing Boolean operations on simple ones. The three commonly cited CSG combinations are *union*, *intersection*, and *difference*. The union, intersection and difference operations are illustrated in Plate 2. Multiple CSG operations can be expressed as a tree, with the CSG operations as interior nodes and the objects being operated on as leaf nodes. Figure 8.1 depicts the tree for a "pie slice" (intersection of two planes) being subtracted from a sphere.

Ray tracing presents an extremely simple method for rendering CSG objects. Roth [ROTH82] describes how to decompose intersection with a CSG object into a one-dimensional problem along the ray. After computing all intersections of the ray with each object, the spans where the ray traverses the object are combined, depending on whether the union, intersection, or difference of the objects is being taken. The combinations for a sphere and a cylinder are shown in Figure 8.2.

Implementation

The `CSGObject` class, which derives from `Object3D`, roots a small hierarchy that contains the `CSGUnion`, `CSGIntersection` and `CSGDifference` classes (which inherit from `CSGObject`). Each of these classes encapsulates an interior node in a CSG tree (the union, intersection, or

207

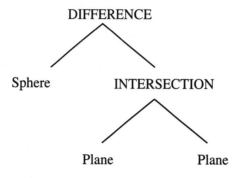

Figure 8.1   CSG tree.

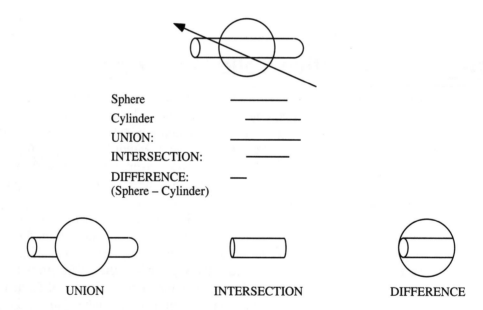

Figure 8.2   Performing CSG with a ray.

difference of two objects). If you want to intersect more than two objects, you must create multiple CSGIntersection instances that contain references to each other. To intersect with a CSG object, FindAllIntersections is called on the two objects that are being operated on. The resulting SpanLists are combined, and if any spans remain, the SpanList that contains them is returned.

The classes in the CSGObject hierarchy use the Span and SpanList classes heavily. Span encapsulates the span of a ray's traversal through an object. SpanList encapsulates a Heap of Spans. span.cpp contains functions to manipulate Spans; in particular, MergeUnion, MergeIntersection and MergeDifference take two SpanLists and combine them into one (the union, intersection, or difference of the two parameters). These three functions destroy the SpanLists passed in. They return 0 if no SpanList can be generated (for example, if two disjoint spans are passed to MergeIntersection).

```cpp
class Span {
public:
    Span() { }
    Span(float _tmin, Object3D *_omin, float _tmax, Object3D *_omax)
    {
        tmin = _tmin;  omin = _omin;
        tmax = _tmax;  omax = _omax;
    }
    friend int Compare(const Span& x, const Span& y) {
        if (x.tmin < y.tmin)
            return -1;
        else if (y.tmin < x.tmin)
            return 1;
        else return 0;
    }
    friend int Overlap(const Span& x, const Span& y) {
        if (x.tmin > y.tmax || x.tmax < y.tmin)
            return 0;
        else return 1;
    }

    friend CSGObject;
    friend World;
    friend InverseRayObject;

    friend class AlgQuadric;

    // These functions each take a pair of SpanLists, operate
    // on them and return a new SpanList according to the
    // operation (union, intersection, difference) being
    // performed.  The SpanList arguments are destroyed.
    friend SpanList *MergeUnion(SpanList *, SpanList *);
    friend SpanList *MergeIntersection(SpanList *, SpanList *);
```

Listing 8.1 Definitions of Span and SpanList

```
    friend SpanList *MergeDifference(SpanList *, SpanList *);
private:
    float tmin, tmax;
    Object3D *omin, *omax;
};

class SpanList {
public:
    SpanList() { }
    SpanList(Span& x) { spans.Insert(x); }
    void AddSpan(const Span& x) { spans.Insert(x); }
    Span ExtractMinSpan() { return spans.ExtractMin(); }
    int NumSpans() const { return spans.N(); }
private:
    Heap<Span> spans;
};
```

Listing 8.1 Definitions of `Span` and `SpanList` *(continued)*

```
// ====================================================================
// span.cpp
//     MergeIntersection, MergeDifference and MergeUnion functions
//     take two SpanLists and merge them according to a CSG
//     operation.
//
//         The Object-Oriented Ray Tracer (OORT)
//         Copyright (C) 1993 by Nicholas Wilt.
//
// This software product may be freely copied and distributed in
// unmodified form but may not be sold.  A nominal distribution
// fee may be charged for media and handling by freeware and
// shareware distributors.  The software product may not be
// included in whole or in part into any commercial package
// without the express written consent of the author.
//
// This software product is provided as is without warranty of
// any kind, express or implied, including but not limited to
// the implied warranties of merchantability and fitness for a
// particular purpose.  The author assumes no liability for any
// alleged or actual damages arising from the use of this
// software.  The author is under no obligation to provide
// service, corrections or upgrades to the software.
//
// --------------------------------------------------------------
```

Listing 8.2 `span.cpp`

```cpp
// Please contact me with questions, comments, suggestions or
// other input about OORT.  My Compuserve account number is
// [75210,2455] (Internet sites can reach me at
// 75210.2455@compuserve.com).
//                              --Nicholas Wilt
// ===================================================================

#include "oort.h"

SpanList *
MergeIntersection(SpanList *A, SpanList *B)
{
    SpanList *ret;
    Span *workingA, *workingB;

    if (! A || ! B) {
        if (A)
            delete A;
        if (B)
            delete B;
        return 0;
    }

    ret = new SpanList;
    workingA = workingB = 0;
    while (A->NumSpans() && B->NumSpans()) {
        if (! workingA)
            workingA = new Span(A->ExtractMinSpan());
        if (! workingB)
            workingB = new Span(B->ExtractMinSpan());
        if (Overlap(*workingA, *workingB)) {
            Span addme = *workingA;

            if (workingB->tmin > workingA->tmin) {
                addme.tmin = workingB->tmin;
                addme.omin = workingB->omin;
            }
            if (workingB->tmax < workingA->tmax) {
                addme.tmax = workingB->tmax;
                addme.omax = workingB->omax;
            }
            ret->AddSpan(addme);
            // Eliminate the span with the smaller max parameter
            if (workingA->tmax < workingB->tmax) {
                delete workingA;
```

Listing 8.2 `span.cpp` *(continued)*

```
               workingA = 0;
            }
            else {
               delete workingB;
               workingB = 0;
            }
         }
         else {   // Spans are disjoint, eliminate the one with min parameter
            if (workingA->tmin < workingB->tmin) {
               delete workingA;
               workingA = 0;
            }
            else {
               delete workingB;
               workingB = 0;
            }
         }
      }
      if (workingA)
         delete workingA;
      if (workingB)
         delete workingB;
      delete A;
      delete B;
      if (ret->NumSpans())
         return ret;
      else {
         delete ret;
         return 0;
      }
}

SpanList *
MergeUnion (SpanList *A, SpanList *B)
{
   SpanList *ret;
   Span *workingA, *workingB, *addme;

   if (! A)
     return B;
   if (! B)
     return A;
   ret = new SpanList;
   workingA = workingB = addme = 0;
   while(A->NumSpans() || B->NumSpans()) {
```

Listing 8.2 span.cpp *(continued)*

```
    if (! workingA)
        workingA = new Span(A->ExtractMinSpan());
    if (! workingB)
        workingB = new Span(B->ExtractMinSpan());
    if (addme) {          // Compare against addme if there
        if (Overlap(*workingA, *addme)) {     // A overlaps addme?
            if (workingA->tmin < addme->tmin) {
                addme->tmin = workingA->tmin;
                addme->omin = workingA->omin;
            }
            if (workingA->tmax > addme->tmax) {
                addme->tmax = workingA->tmax;
                addme->omax = workingA->omax;
            }
            delete workingA;
            workingA = 0;
        }
        else if (Overlap(*workingB, *addme)) {   // B overlaps addme?
            if (workingB->tmin < addme->tmin) {
                addme->tmin = workingB->tmin;
                addme->omin = workingB->omin;
            }
            if (workingB->tmax > addme->tmax) {
                addme->tmax = workingB->tmax;
                addme->omax = workingB->omax;
            }
            delete workingB;
            workingB = 0;
        }
        else {                    // Neither overlaps addme, so addme
            ret->AddSpan(*addme); // must be disjoint.
            delete addme;
            addme = 0;
        }
    }
    else {        // No addme to compare to, compare A and B
        if (Overlap(*workingA, *workingB)) {
            addme = workingA;
            if (workingB->tmin < addme->tmin) {
                addme->tmin = workingB->tmin;
                addme->omin = workingB->omin;
            }
            if (workingB->tmax > addme->tmax) {
                addme->tmax = workingB->tmax;
                addme->omax = workingB->omax;
```

Listing 8.2 `span.cpp` *(continued)*

```
                }
                workingA = 0;
                delete workingB;
                workingB = 0;
            }
            else {          // Disjoint, add the minimum
                if (workingA && workingB) {     // Compare if both there
                    if (workingA->tmin < workingB->tmin) {
                        ret->AddSpan(*workingA);
                        delete workingA;
                        workingA = 0;
                    }
                    else {
                        ret->AddSpan(*workingB);
                        delete workingB;
                        workingB = 0;
                    }
                }
                else {                              // One SpanList is exhausted
                    if (workingA) {
                        ret->AddSpan(*workingA);
                        delete workingA;
                        workingA = 0;
                    }
                    else {
                        ret->AddSpan(*workingB);
                        delete workingB;
                        workingB = 0;
                    }
                }
            }
        }
    }
    delete A;
    delete B;
    if (addme) {
        ret->AddSpan(*addme);
        delete addme;
    }
    return ret;
}

SpanList *
MergeDifference (SpanList *A, SpanList *B)
{
```

Listing 8.2 span.cpp *(continued)*

```
    SpanList *ret;
    Span *workingA, *workingB;

    if (! A) {
        if (B)
            delete B;
        return 0;
    }

    if (! B)
        return A;

    ret = new SpanList;
    workingA = workingB = 0;
    while (A->NumSpans() && B->NumSpans()) {
        if (! workingA)
            workingA = new Span(A->ExtractMinSpan());
        if (! workingB)
            workingB = new Span(B->ExtractMinSpan());

        if (Overlap(*workingA, *workingB)) {

            int switchon = (workingA->tmin < workingB->tmin) << 1 |
                        (workingA->tmax < workingB->tmax);

            switch (switchon) {
              case 0:
                  /* Have to clip A with B, add A to the SpanList, and
                     delete A */
                  workingA->tmin = workingB->tmax;
                  workingA->omin = workingB->omax;
                  delete workingB;
                  workingB = 0;
                  break;
              case 1: /* workingA encompasses workingB */
                  delete workingA;
                  workingA = 0;
                  break;
              case 2: /* workingB encompasses workingA */
                  ret->AddSpan(Span(     workingA->tmin, workingA->omin,
                                  workingB->tmin, workingB->omin));
//                  ret->AddSpan(Span(workingA->min, workingB->min));
                  workingA->tmin = workingB->tmax;
                  workingA->omin = workingB->omax;
                  delete workingB;
```

Listing 8.2 span.cpp *(continued)*

```
                    workingB = 0;
                    break;
                case 3:
                    workingA->tmax = workingB->tmin;
                    workingA->omax = workingB->omin;
                    delete workingA;
                    workingA = 0;
                    break;
            }
        }
        else { // Spans are disjoint, eliminate the one with min parameter
            if (workingA->tmin < workingB->tmin) {
                ret->AddSpan(*workingA);
                delete workingA;
                workingA = 0;
            }
            else {
                delete workingB;
                workingB = 0;
            }
        }
    }

    while (A->NumSpans())
        ret->AddSpan(A->ExtractMinSpan());
    delete A;
    delete B;

    if (workingA) {
        ret->AddSpan(*workingA);
        delete workingA;
    }

    if (workingB)
        delete workingB;

    if (ret->NumSpans())
        return ret;
    else {
        delete ret;
        return 0;
    }
}
```

Listing 8.2 span.cpp *(continued)*

Many operations on CSG objects can be implemented by the CSGObject class and need not be overloaded by CSGIntersection, CSGUnion or CSGDifference. For example, CSGObject::ApplyTransform applies a transform to the left and right child objects. CSGObject::NearestInt calls FindAllIntersections on the CSG object, then looks for the minimum intersection in the SpanList returned.

```
// ---------------------------------------------------------------
// CSGObject hierarchy
//     CSGObject and its descendents, CSGUnion, CSGIntersection and
//     CSGDifference, implement objects for constructive solid
//     geometry.
// ---------------------------------------------------------------

class CSGObject: public Object3D {
public:
    CSGObject() : Object3D(CSG) { left = right = 0; }
    CSGObject(Object3D *Left, Object3D *Right);

    virtual int NearestInt(Ray& Ray, float& t, float maxt);
    virtual SpanList *FindAllIntersections(Ray& ray) = 0;
    virtual Vector3D FindNormal(const Vector3D& Intersection);
    virtual void ApplyTransform(const Matrix& tform);
    virtual Object3D *Dup() const = 0;
    virtual void Describe(int ind) const = 0;
    virtual IsInside(Vector3D& v) = 0;
    virtual float PtDistance(Vector3D& v) = 0;
    virtual AxisAlignedBox BBox() const;
    virtual void CountMe() const = 0;
protected:
    Object3D *left, *right;      // Left and right nodes

    Object3D *nearest;           // Last child object intersected.
};

// ---------------------------------------------------------------
// CSGUnion
//     Derived from CSGObject.
// ---------------------------------------------------------------
class CSGUnion : public CSGObject {
public:
    CSGUnion(Object3D *Left, Object3D *Right):
        CSGObject(Left, Right) { }
```

Listing 8.3   Definitions of CSGObject and its descendants

```
    virtual SpanList *FindAllIntersections(Ray& ray);
    virtual Object3D *Dup() const;
    virtual int IsInside(Vector3D& v);
    virtual int HitAtAll(Ray& ray, float maxt);
    virtual float PtDistance(Vector3D& v);
    virtual void Describe(int ind) const;
    virtual void CountMe() const;
};


// ----------------------------------------------------------------
// CSGIntersection
//     Derived from CSGObject.
// ----------------------------------------------------------------
class CSGIntersection : public CSGObject {
public:
    CSGIntersection(Object3D *Left, Object3D *Right):
        CSGObject(Left, Right) { }

    virtual SpanList *FindAllIntersections(Ray& ray);
    virtual Object3D *Dup() const;
    virtual int IsInside(Vector3D& v);
    virtual float PtDistance(Vector3D& v);
    virtual void Describe(int ind) const;
    virtual void CountMe() const;
    virtual AxisAlignedBox BBox() const;
};


// ----------------------------------------------------------------
// CSGDifference
//     Derived from CSGObject.
// ----------------------------------------------------------------
class CSGDifference : public CSGObject {
public:
    CSGDifference(Object3D *Left, Object3D *Right) :
        CSGObject(Left, Right) { }

    virtual SpanList *FindAllIntersections(Ray& ray);
    virtual Object3D *Dup() const;
    virtual int IsInside(Vector3D& v);
    virtual float PtDistance(Vector3D& v);
    virtual void Describe(int ind) const;
    virtual void CountMe() const;
};
```

Listing 8.3 Definitions of `CSGObject` **and its descendants** *(continued)*

```
// ======================================================================
// csg.cpp
//      Constructive Solid Geometry implementation.
//
//          The Object-Oriented Ray Tracer (OORT)
//          Copyright (C) 1993 by Nicholas Wilt.
//
// This software product may be freely copied and distributed in
// unmodified form but may not be sold.  A nominal distribution
// fee may be charged for media and handling by freeware and
// shareware distributors.  The software product may not be
// included in whole or in part into any commercial package
// without the express written consent of the author.
//
// This software product is provided as is without warranty of
// any kind, express or implied, including but not limited to
// the implied warranties of merchantability and fitness for a
// particular purpose.  The author assumes no liability for any
// alleged or actual damages arising from the use of this
// software.  The author is under no obligation to provide
// service, corrections or upgrades to the software.
//
// ----------------------------------------------------------
//
// Please contact me with questions, comments, suggestions or
// other input about OORT.  My Compuserve account number is
// [75210,2455] (Internet sites can reach me at
// 75210.2455@compuserve.com).
//                              --Nicholas Wilt
// ======================================================================

#include <iostream.h>
#include "oort.h"

// ----------------------------------------------------------------
//      CSGObject routines.
//      These provide united support for the three CSG primitives,
//      union, intersection and difference.
//      Many functions are the same for all three (thus in CSGObject).
// ----------------------------------------------------------------

CSGObject::CSGObject(Object3D *Left, Object3D *Right) : Object3D(CSG)
{
    left = Left;
    right = Right;
```

Listing 8.4 `csg.cpp`

```
    if ((left->ReturnColor() && left->ReturnColor()->Transparent()) ||
        (right->ReturnColor() && right->ReturnColor()->Transparent())) {
        HallSurface *newsurf = new HallSurface;
        newsurf->SetTransmit(new PureColor(RGBColor(1)), 1.3);
        OverrideColor(newsurf);
    }
}

int
CSGObject::NearestInt(Ray& ray, float& t, float maxt)
{
    SpanList *tmp = FindAllIntersections(ray);
    if (tmp) {
        Span min = tmp->ExtractMinSpan();
        int ret;
        t = 0;

        // Find first intersection greater than Limits::Threshold
        while (t < Limits::Threshold) {
            if (min.omin) {
                ret = 1;
                nearest = min.omin;
                OverrideColor(min.omin->ReturnColor());
                min.omin = 0;
                t = min.tmin;
            }
            else {
                ret = 1;
                nearest = min.omax;
                OverrideColor(min.omax->ReturnColor());
                t = min.tmax;
                if (! tmp->NumSpans())
                    break;
                min = tmp->ExtractMinSpan();
            }
        }

        // If nearest int is too close, return no-intersection.
        if (t < Limits::Threshold || t >= maxt) {
            nearest = 0;
            ret = 0;
        }

        delete tmp;
        return ret;
```

Listing 8.4 csg.cpp *(continued)*

```
   }
   return 0;
}

Vector3D
CSGObject::FindNormal(const Vector3D& Intersection)
{
   if (nearest)
      return nearest->FindNormal(Intersection);
   cerr << "CSGObject::FindNormal called\n";
   exit(1);
   return Vector3D(0);
}

void
CSGObject::ApplyTransform(const Matrix& tform)
{
   left->ApplyTransform(tform);
   right->ApplyTransform(tform);
}

AxisAlignedBox
CSGObject::BBox() const
{
   AxisAlignedBox ret(Vector3D(MAXFLOAT), Vector3D(-MAXFLOAT));

   ret.Include(left->BBox());
   ret.Include(right->BBox());
   return ret;
}

void
CSGObject::CountMe() const
{
   left->CountMe();
   right->CountMe();
}

// ----------------------------------------------------------------
//    CSGUnion routines.
// ----------------------------------------------------------------

SpanList *
CSGUnion::FindAllIntersections(Ray& ray)
{
```

Listing 8.4 csg.cpp *(continued)*

```
    SpanList *leftint = left->FindAllIntersections(ray);
    SpanList *rightint = right->FindAllIntersections(ray);
    return MergeUnion(leftint, rightint);
}

Object3D *
CSGUnion::Dup() const
{
    return new CSGUnion(left->Dup(), right->Dup());
}

int
CSGUnion::IsInside(Vector3D& v)
{
    return left->IsInside(v) && right->IsInside(v);
}

int
CSGUnion::HitAtAll(Ray& ray, float maxt)
{
    return left->HitAtAll(ray, maxt) || right->HitAtAll(ray, maxt);
}

float
CSGUnion::PtDistance(Vector3D& v)
{
    float d1 = left->PtDistance(v);
    float d2 = right->PtDistance(v);
    return (d1 < d2) ? d1 : d2;
}

void
CSGUnion::Describe(int ind) const
{
    indent(ind);   cout << "CSGUnion:\n";
    indent(ind+2);   cout << "Left:\n";
    left->Describe(ind+4);
    indent(ind+2);   cout << "Right:\n";
    right->Describe(ind+4);
}

void
CSGUnion::CountMe() const
{
    Statistics::Objects::CSGUnion += 1;
```

Listing 8.4   csg.cpp   *(continued)*

```
    CSGObject::CountMe();
}

// -----------------------------------------------------------------
//     CSGIntersection routines.
// -----------------------------------------------------------------

SpanList *
CSGIntersection::FindAllIntersections(Ray& ray)
{
    SpanList *leftint = left->FindAllIntersections(ray);

    if (leftint) {
        SpanList *rightint = right->FindAllIntersections(ray);
        return MergeIntersection(leftint, rightint);
    }
    return 0;
}

Object3D *
CSGIntersection::Dup() const
{
    return new CSGIntersection(left->Dup(), right->Dup());
}

int
CSGIntersection::IsInside(Vector3D& v)
{
    return left->IsInside(v) && right->IsInside(v);
}

float
CSGIntersection::PtDistance(Vector3D& v)
{
    float d1 = left->PtDistance(v);
    float d2 = right->PtDistance(v);
    if (d1 < 0 && d2 < 0)              // If inside both, return min
        return (d1 < d2) ? d2 : d1;    // distance estimate
    else {
        if (d1 < 0)                    // If inside left, return that
            return d1;                 // distance estimate
        else if (d2 < 0)               // If inside right, return that
            return d2;                 // distance estimate
        else
            return (d1 < d2) ? d1 : d2;   // Else return min estimate
```

Listing 8.4 csg.cpp *(continued)*

```
    }
}

void
CSGIntersection::Describe(int ind) const
{
    indent(ind); cout << "CSGIntersection:\n";
    indent(ind+2);  cout << "Left:\n";
    left->Describe(ind+4);
    indent(ind+2);  cout << "Right:\n";
    right->Describe(ind+4);
}

AxisAlignedBox
CSGIntersection::BBox() const
{
    return Intersect(left->BBox(), right->BBox());
}

void
CSGIntersection::CountMe() const
{
    Statistics::Objects::CSGIntersection += 1;
    CSGObject::CountMe();
}

// ----------------------------------------------------------------
//    CSGDifference routines.
// ----------------------------------------------------------------

SpanList *
CSGDifference::FindAllIntersections(Ray& ray)
{
    SpanList *leftint = left->FindAllIntersections(ray);

    if (leftint) {
        SpanList *rightint = right->FindAllIntersections(ray);
        return MergeDifference(leftint, rightint);
    }
    return 0;
}

Object3D *
CSGDifference::Dup() const
{
```

Listing 8.4   csg.cpp *(continued)*

```
      return new CSGDifference(left->Dup(), right->Dup());
}

int
CSGDifference::IsInside(Vector3D& v)
{
    return left->IsInside(v) && ! right->IsInside(v);
}

float
CSGDifference::PtDistance(Vector3D& v)
{
    float d1 = left->PtDistance(v);
    float d2 = right->PtDistance(v);
    if (d2 < 0)          // Inside right node--so not inside object
        return d2;
    if (d1 < 0)          // Inside left node--so inside object
        return (-d1 < d2) ? d1 : -d2;

    // Not inside either of the constituent objects, return nearest
    // distance estimate.
    return (d1 < d2) ? d1 : d2;
}

void
CSGDifference::Describe(int ind) const
{
    indent(ind);   cout << "CSGDifference:\n";
    indent(ind+2);   cout << "Left:\n";
    left->Describe(ind+4);
    indent(ind+2);   cout << "Right:\n";
    right->Describe(ind+4);
}

void
CSGDifference::CountMe() const
{
    Statistics::Objects::CSGDifference += 1;
    CSGObject::CountMe();
}
```

Listing 8.4   csg.cpp *(continued)*

Optimizations

When evaluating a Boolean expression, you don't necessarily need to evaluate all of the expressions to know the correct answer. Because both inputs to an AND operator must be TRUE for the answer to be TRUE, the answer must be FALSE if the first input is FALSE. Similarly, because both inputs to an OR operator must be FALSE for the answer to be FALSE, the answer must be TRUE if the first input is TRUE. Evaluating Boolean expressions like this is called *short-circuit evaluation*.

We can use a similar idea to short-circuit the intersection calculations with CSG objects. Since hitting the left object is mandatory if the ray is to hit an Intersection or Difference at all, you can return no-intersection if the left object is missed by the ray. Similarly, if you are performing a *hit-at-all* test on the Union of two objects, you need not test the right object if the left is hit. Hitting the left object is sufficient to return a TRUE result for the hit-at-all test.

Because the left object is always tested, but the right object might not be, try to make the left-hand objects simpler than the right ones in `CSGUnion` and `CSGIntersection` objects. That way, if a computation is short-circuited, the more expensive intersection test is avoided.

Using CSG

Besides combining simple objects to create complicated ones, CSG can be used to place bounds on unbounded surfaces. For example, most quadric surfaces, including cylinders, paraboloids, and hyperboloids, extend to infinity in at least one direction. The best way to place bounds on such a surface is to intersect it with planes. For example, to create a cylinder of unit radius, aligned with the Y axis, you might call the Utilities library as follows:

```
Object3D *cyl = MakeCylinder(1, 1, surf);
```

To truncate this cylinder so that it extends from $Y = -1$ to $+\infty$ in the Y direction, intersect it with a plane that points downward (i.e., in the $-Y$ direction):

```
cyl = new CSGIntersection(cyl, new Plane(Vector3D(0,
    -1, 0), -1, surf));
```

The direction of the plane's normal vector is highly relevant to the behavior of this intersection. *Only portions of the ray that the normal points away from are included in the resulting object.*

To truncate the cylinder again, so that it is completely bounded and extends from $Y = -1$ to $Y = 5$, intersect it with a plane to points upward as well:

```
cyl = new CSGIntersection(cyl, new Plane(Vector3D(0,
    1, 0), -5, surf));
```

See the code for the Quadrics example image for a good example of how to bound quadrics with planes.

Shading CSG Objects

Only the leaf objects within the CSG tree can be shaded. It does not make sense to try to shade an interior node, since it does not contain any surface characteristics. Once a CSG object has detected an intersection, then, it sets its own surface characteristics to those of the child object that was intersected. That way, subsequent shading calculations (e.g., computing the normal, texture mapping) will be performed using the correct leaf object.

CSG can be used to expose parts of an object that normally would not be exposed. A `Plane` can be used to cut a sphere in half, for example, revealing the inner hemisphere. The normal vectors on that inner hemisphere all point away from the viewer, and unless we do something about it, the diffuse and specular components will be shaded black.

The solution is to use the `TwoSided` bump map. `TwoSided` ensures that the normal to the object faces toward the incident ray (RenderMan contains a similar function called **faceforward** [UPST90]). `TwoSided` can be combined with other bump maps (it applies the bump map to the normal before reversing it).

The CSGDemo example illustrates many of these ideas. In addition, the Quadrics demo uses CSG extensively to bound quadric surfaces.

8.2 Algebraic Surfaces

Algebraic surfaces are a generalization of the more familiar planes and quadric surfaces. An infinite plane is a first-degree implicit surface with the equation:

$$Ax + By + Cz + D = 0 \tag{8.1}$$

The surface is called *first-degree* because the sum of the exponents on the X, Y, and Z components of the equation is never greater than 1. Similarly, a quadric is a second-degree implicit surface with the equation:

$$Ax^2 + By^2 + Cz^2 + 2Dxy + 2Eyz + 2Fxz + 2Gx + 2Hy + 2Jz + K = 0 \tag{8.2}$$

The sum of the exponents on the X, Y, and Z components of the equation is never greater than 2. A generalized algebraic surface has an implicit representation of arbitrary degree:

$$\sum_i \sum_j \sum_k c_{ijk} x^i y^j z^k = 0 \tag{8.3}$$

Besides the more familiar planes and quadric surfaces, examples of algebraic surfaces are toruses, Steiner's surface and Kummer's surface. The Utilities library contains a number of functions to create algebraic surfaces (see Section B.2). Von Seggern [SEGG93] discusses algebraic surfaces in some detail and gives equations and sketches of them. Plate 5 displays a number of algebraic surfaces.

Intersecting with an Algebraic Surface

The most straightforward way to intersect with an algebraic surface is by plugging the equation for the ray into the implicit equation for the surface. This results in a polynomial expression in t. For example, plugging the ray equation into the equation for the cubic cusp catastrophe ($z^3 + xz + y = 0$) results in the following:

$$\left(\mathbf{loc}.z + t\mathbf{dir}.z\right)^3 + \left(\mathbf{loc}.x + t\mathbf{dir}.x\right)\left(\mathbf{loc}.z + t\mathbf{dir}.z\right) + \left(\mathbf{loc}.y + t\mathbf{dir}.y\right) = 0 \qquad (8.4)$$

This is a cubic equation in t. The points where the ray intersects the surface correspond to the roots of the polynomial. The smallest positive root is the closest intersection along the ray. When the polynomials involved can be of arbitrary degree, finding the roots of those polynomials can be very involved. We will discuss polynomials and how to find the roots of arbitrary polynomials in the following sections.

Computing the Normal

As with first- and second-degree implicit surfaces, computing the normal to an algebraic surface involves computing the gradient vector to the surface at the given point, as follows:

$$N = \left(\frac{\partial f}{\partial x}, \frac{\partial f}{\partial y}, \frac{\partial f}{\partial z}\right) \qquad (8.5)$$

For example, the normal to the cubic cusp catastrophe $z^3 + xz + y = 0$ is as follows:

$$\left(z, 1, 3z^2 + x\right) \qquad (8.6)$$

Of course, the gradient vector must be normalized so that it has unit length.

Transforming Algebraic Surfaces

For complex objects such as algebraic surfaces, it is less complicated to transform a ray than it is to transform the object. For such objects, the object itself is kept in some simple canonical form. (For example, an elliptical torus centered at the origin.) Then, whenever a ray is to be intersected with the object, it is transformed into the object's canonical coordinate system. If there is an intersection, the intersection point is transformed back from the object's canonical coordinate system.

In OORT, objects that are kept in a canonical coordinate system are called `InverseRayObjects`. `InverseRayObject` is an abstract class that overloads the `ApplyTransform` member function of `Object3D`, but leaves all other functions unimplemented. Objects such as `Algebraic` surfaces, which are to be kept in canonical coordinate systems, may derive from `InverseRayObject`. Then, before intersecting with the object, the ray is transformed into the object's canonical coordinate system. Any intersections with the object are transformed back into the world coordinate system before being returned.

Bounded Algebraic Surfaces

Some algebraic surfaces are bounded. For example, a torus in the XZ plane with minor radius 10 and major radius 100 is bounded by (–110, –10, –110) and (110, 10, 110). Bounded algebraic surfaces can inherit from the `Algebraic` class, keep track of the bounding box in object space (not canonical space) and overload the `BBox()` member function. See the `Torus` class, which works exactly like this.

Implementation

Listings 8.5 and 8.6 contain the definition and implementation of the `Algebraic` class and its derivatives. The `Torus` class, which inherits from `Algebraic`, implements elliptical toruses (toruses with an elliptical cross-section rather than a circular one). The `AlgQuadric` class implements quadric surfaces (described in Section 4.5) using the `Algebraic` code. This is useful only for debugging purposes, since the `Quadric` class is much more efficient.

```
// ----------------------------------------------------------------
// Algebraic surface
//     Derived from Object3D.
//     This defines a generalized, implicit surface.
// ----------------------------------------------------------------

// forward-declare Polynomial class
class Polynomial;

class Algebraic : public InverseRayObject {
public:
```

Listing 8.5 `Algebraic` and `Torus` definition

```
   Algebraic(): InverseRayObject(0) { }
   Algebraic(Surface *clr): InverseRayObject(clr, 0) { }
   Algebraic(const Quadric& q);

   virtual int NearestInt(Ray& Ray, float& t, float maxt);
   virtual SpanList *FindAllIntersections(Ray& ray);
   virtual Vector3D FindNormal(const Vector3D& intersection);
   virtual Object3D *Dup() const;
   virtual void Describe(int ind) const;
   virtual float PtDistance(Vector3D& v);
   virtual void CountMe() const { Statistics::Objects::Algebraic++; }

   void AddTerm(double c, int i, int j, int k);
protected:
   virtual Polynomial RayToPoly(Ray& ray);
private:
   class Term {
      double c;
      int i, j, k;
   public:
      Term(double _c, int _i, int _j, int _k):
         c(_c), i(_i), j(_j), k(_k) { }
      friend int operator==(const Term& A, const Term& B) {
         return (A.i == B.i && A.j == B.j && A.k == B.k);
      }
      friend Algebraic;
   };

   class TermList : public SimpleList<Term *> { };

   TermList terms;
};

// ------------------------------------------------------------------
// Torus
//    Derived from Algebraic.
// ------------------------------------------------------------------
class Torus : public Algebraic {
public:
   Torus(float a, float b, float c, Surface *clr);
   virtual void ApplyTransform(const Matrix&);
   virtual AxisAlignedBox BBox() const;
private:
   BoundingBox bbox;
};
```

Listing 8.5 Algebraic and Torus definition *(continued)*

```
// ======================================================================
// alg.cpp
//     Implementation file for algebraic surfaces.
//
//        The Object-Oriented Ray Tracer (OORT)
//        Copyright (C) 1993 by Nicholas Wilt.
//
// This software product may be freely copied and distributed in
// unmodified form but may not be sold.  A nominal distribution
// fee may be charged for media and handling by freeware and
// shareware distributors.  The software product may not be
// included in whole or in part into any commercial package
// without the express written consent of the author.
//
// This software product is provided as is without warranty of
// any kind, express or implied, including but not limited to
// the implied warranties of merchantability and fitness for a
// particular purpose.  The author assumes no liability for any
// alleged or actual damages arising from the use of this
// software.  The author is under no obligation to provide
// service, corrections or upgrades to the software.
//
// ----------------------------------------------------------
//
// Please contact me with questions, comments, suggestions or
// other input about OORT.  My Compuserve account number is
// [75210,2455] (Internet sites can reach me at
// 75210.2455@compuserve.com).
//                                  --Nicholas Wilt
// ======================================================================

#include "oort.h"
#include "poly.h"

Ray
InverseRayObject::InvertRay(Ray& ray)
{
   Ray ret = ray;
   ret.ApplyTransform(inv);
   return ret;
}

Vector3D
InverseRayObject::InvertPt(const Vector3D& v)
{
```

Listing 8.6 Algebraic and Torus implementation

```
      return inv * v;
}

Vector3D
InverseRayObject::InvRotatePt(const Vector3D& v)
{
    return RotateOnly(inv, v);
}

Ray
InverseRayObject::TransformRay(Ray& ray)
{
    Ray ret = ray;
    ret.ApplyTransform(mat);
    return ret;
}

Vector3D
InverseRayObject::TransformPt(const Vector3D& v)
{
    return mat * v;
}

Vector3D
InverseRayObject::RotatePt(const Vector3D& v)
{
    return RotateOnly(mat, v);
}

// Given a list of spans in the object's canonical space, transform
// it into a list of spans in world space.
void
InverseRayObject::ApplyTransform(const Matrix& tform)
{
    mat *= tform;
    inv = Invert(tform) * inv;
}

Algebraic::Algebraic(const Quadric& q):
    InverseRayObject(q.ReturnColor())
{
    float eps = 1e-8;
    if (fabs(q.mat.x[0][0]) > eps) AddTerm(q.mat.x[0][0], 2, 0, 0);
    if (fabs(q.mat.x[1][1]) > eps) AddTerm(q.mat.x[1][1], 0, 2, 0);
    if (fabs(q.mat.x[2][2]) > eps) AddTerm(q.mat.x[2][2], 0, 0, 2);
```

Listing 8.6 Algebraic and Torus implementation *(continued)*

```
        if (fabs(q.mat.x[3][3]) > eps) AddTerm(q.mat.x[3][3], 0, 0, 0);
        if (fabs(q.D) > eps) AddTerm(q.D, 1, 1, 0);
        if (fabs(q.E) > eps) AddTerm(q.E, 0, 1, 1);
        if (fabs(q.F) > eps) AddTerm(q.F, 1, 0, 1);
        if (fabs(q.G) > eps) AddTerm(q.G, 1, 0, 0);
        if (fabs(q.H) > eps) AddTerm(q.H, 0, 1, 0);
        if (fabs(q.J) > eps) AddTerm(q.J, 0, 0, 1);
}

// Returns x^y.  Should be faster than calling pow(), since
// this function only works when y is an integer.
double
intpow(double x, unsigned int y)
{
    double ret = 1;
    double mulby = x;
    while (y) {
        if (y & 1)
            ret *= mulby;
        mulby *= x;
        y >>= 1;
    }
    return ret;
}

void
Algebraic::AddTerm(double c, int i, int j, int k)
{
    for (TermList::Iterator sc(terms); sc.Valid(); sc.GotoNext()) {
        if (*sc.Contents() == Term(c, i, j, k)) {
            sc.Contents()->c += c;
            return;
        }
        sc.GotoNext();
    }
    // Detach iterator from list
    sc.Detach();
    terms.AddToList(new Term(c, i, j, k));
}

static int
compare_doubles(const void *A, const void *B)
{
    const double *a = (const double *) A;
    const double *b = (const double *) B;
```

Listing 8.6 Algebraic **and** Torus **implementation** *(continued)*

```
    if (*a < *b)
        return -1;
    else if (*b < *a)
        return 1;
    return 0;
}

Polynomial
Algebraic::RayToPoly(Ray& ray)
{
    Polynomial ret;
    for (TermList::Iterator sc(terms); sc.Valid(); sc.GotoNext()) {
        Term *t = sc.Contents();
        Polynomial addme;
        addme.AddElm(0, 1);
        if (t->i) addme *= Triangle(ray.dir.x, ray.loc.x, t->i);
        if (t->j) addme *= Triangle(ray.dir.y, ray.loc.y, t->j);
        if (t->k) addme *= Triangle(ray.dir.z, ray.loc.z, t->k);
        ret += t->c * addme;
    }
    return ret;
}

int
Algebraic::NearestInt(Ray& cpyme, float& t, float maxt)
{
    float tempt = maxt;
    int ret = 0;
    Ray ray = InvertRay(cpyme);

    Statistics::Intersections::Algebraic++;

    // Compute polynomial
    Polynomial solveme = RayToPoly(ray);

    // Find the roots and sort them in ascending order
    int rootcount;
    double *roots;
    rootcount = solveme.FindRealRoots(&roots);

    if (rootcount) {
        for (int i = 0; i < rootcount; i++) {
            // Transform each parameter back into world space
            if (roots[i] > Limits::Threshold && roots[i] < tempt) {
                tempt = roots[i];
```

Listing 8.6 Algebraic and Torus implementation *(continued)*

```
            ret = 1;
        }
    }
    t = tempt;
    delete[] roots;
    }
    return ret;
}

// Compute all intersections with the algebraic surface.
SpanList *
Algebraic::FindAllIntersections(Ray& cpyme)
{
    Ray ray = InvertRay(cpyme);
    SpanList *ret = 0;

    Statistics::Intersections::Algebraic++;

    Polynomial solveme = RayToPoly(ray);

    int rootcount;
    double *roots;
    rootcount = solveme.FindRealRoots(&roots);

    if (rootcount) {
        float tmin, tmax;
        Object3D *omin, *omax;
        int i;

        qsort(roots, rootcount, sizeof(double), compare_doubles);
        omin = omax = 0;
        for (i = 0; i < rootcount; i++) {
            if (fabs(roots[i]) < Limits::Threshold)
                return 0;
            if (roots[i] > Limits::Threshold)
                break;
        }
        // If every parameter is negative, return no-intersection.
        if (i == rootcount)
            return 0;
        omin = omax = this;
        if (IsInside(cpyme.loc)) {
            if (i != 0) {
                tmin = roots[i - 1];
                tmax = roots[i++];
```

Listing 8.6 Algebraic and Torus implementation *(continued)*

```
            }
        else {
            tmin = -Limits::Infinity;
            tmax = roots[i++];
        }
    }
    else {
        tmin = roots[i++];
        if (i == rootcount)
            tmax = Limits::Infinity;
        else
            tmax = roots[i++];
    }
    ret = new SpanList;
    while (i < rootcount) {
        if (omin && omax) {
            ret->AddSpan(Span(tmin, omin, tmax, omax));
            omin = omax = 0;
        }
        if (omin) {
            tmax = roots[i++];
            omax = this;
        }
        else {
            tmin = roots[i++];
            omin = this;
        }
    }
    if (omin && omax)
        ret->AddSpan(Span(tmin, omin, tmax, omax));
    else if (omin)
        ret->AddSpan(Span(tmin, omin, Limits::Infinity, this));
}
if (ret) {
    if (ret->NumSpans())
        return ret;
    delete ret;
}
return 0;
}

Vector3D
Algebraic::FindNormal(const Vector3D& xformme)
{
    Vector3D x = InvertPt(xformme);
```

Listing 8.6 `Algebraic` and `Torus` implementation *(continued)*

```
      Vector3D ret(0);

      for (TermList::Iterator sc(terms); sc.Valid(); sc.GotoNext()) {
         Term *t = sc.Contents();
         Vector3D addme(0);
         if (t->i) {
            float subt = intpow(x.x, t->i - 1) *
                        intpow(x.y, t->j) *
                        intpow(x.z, t->k);
            addme += Vector3D(t->i * subt, 0, 0);
         }
         if (t->j) {
            float subt = intpow(x.y, t->j - 1) *
                        intpow(x.x, t->i) *
                        intpow(x.z, t->k);
            addme += Vector3D(0, t->j * subt, 0);
         }
         if (t->k) {
            float subt = intpow(x.z, t->k - 1) *
                        intpow(x.x, t->i) *
                        intpow(x.y, t->j);
            addme += Vector3D(0, 0, t->k * subt);
         }
         ret += t->c * addme;
      }
//   ret = Normalize(PlaneRotate(mat, ret));
      return Normalize(RotateOnly(mat, ret));
}

Object3D *
Algebraic::Dup() const
{
   Algebraic *ret = new Algebraic;
   for (TermList::Iterator sc(terms); sc.Valid(); sc.GotoNext()) {
      Term *t = sc.Contents();
      ret->AddTerm(t->c, t->i, t->j, t->k);
   }
   return (Object3D *) ret;
}

void
Algebraic::Describe(int ind) const
{
   for (TermList::Iterator sc(terms); sc.Valid(); sc.GotoNext()) {
      Term *t = sc.Contents();
```

Listing 8.6   Algebraic and Torus implementation *(continued)*

```
            cout << t->c << " * x^" << t->i << "y^" << t->j << "z^" <<
                t->k << " + ";
        }
        Term *t = sc.Contents();
        if (t)
            cout << t->c << " * x^" << t->i << "y^" << t->j << "z^" <<
                t->k << '\n';
}

float
Algebraic::PtDistance(Vector3D& v)
{
    Vector3D x = InvertPt(v);
    float ret = 0;

    for (TermList::Iterator sc(terms); sc.Valid(); sc.GotoNext()) {
        Term *t = sc.Contents();
        ret += t->c * intpow(x.x, t->i) *
                      intpow(x.y, t->j) *
                      intpow(x.z, t->k);
    }
    return ret;
}

void
Torus::ApplyTransform(const Matrix& tform)
{
    bbox = Transform(bbox, tform);
    Algebraic::ApplyTransform(tform);
}

AxisAlignedBox
Torus::BBox() const
{
    return Transform(bbox, inv);
}


// Torus constructor.
Torus::Torus(float a, float b, float r, Surface *clr) :
        Algebraic(clr),
        bbox(Vector3D(-r-a, -b, -r-a), Vector3D(r+a, b, r+a))
{
    float p = (a*a) / (b*b);
    float a0 = 4 * r * r;
```

Listing 8.6 Algebraic and Torus implementation *(continued)*

```
        float b0 = r*r - a*a;
        AddTerm(1, 4, 0, 0);                // x^4
        AddTerm(1, 2, 0, 2);                // x^2z^2
        AddTerm(p, 2, 2, 0);                // px^2y^2
        AddTerm(b0, 2, 0, 0);               // b0x^2

        AddTerm(1, 2, 0, 2);                // x^2z^2
        AddTerm(1, 0, 0, 4);                // z^4
        AddTerm(p, 0, 2, 2);                // py^2z^2
        AddTerm(b0, 0, 0, 2);               // b0z^2

        AddTerm(p, 2, 2, 0);                // px^2y^2
        AddTerm(p, 0, 2, 2);                // py^2z^2
        AddTerm(p*p, 0, 4, 0);              // p*p*y^4
        AddTerm(b0*p, 0, 2, 0);             // b0*p*y^4

        AddTerm(b0, 2, 0, 0);               // b0*x^2
        AddTerm(b0, 0, 0, 2);               // b0*z^2
        AddTerm(b0*p, 0, 2, 0);             // b0*p*y^2
        AddTerm(b0*b0, 0, 0, 0);            // b0^2

        AddTerm(-a0, 2, 0, 0);              // -a0*x^2
        AddTerm(-a0, 0, 0, 2);              // -a0*z^2
}

// AlgQuadric: a class solely intended to help debug Algebraics.
// It's a second-degree Algebraic that uses Algebraic code to
// do everything Quadrics can do right now.

// I put this in when developing algebraics, and didn't feel
// like deleting it (too useful a debugging tool). I might
// delete it after algebraics have matured a little.

AlgQuadric::AlgQuadric(float a, float b, float c, float d, float e,
            float f, float g, float h, float j, float k,
            Surface *surf): q(a, b, c, d, e, f, g, h, j, k, surf),
            Algebraic(Quadric(a, b, c, d, e, f, g, h, j, k, surf))
{
}

void
AlgQuadric::ApplyTransform(const Matrix& tform)
{
    Algebraic::ApplyTransform(tform);
    q.ApplyTransform(tform);
```

Listing 8.6 Algebraic and Torus implementation *(continued)*

```
}


SpanList *
AlgQuadric::FindAllIntersections(Ray& ray)
{
    float eps = 1e-3;
    SpanList *me = Algebraic::FindAllIntersections(ray);
    SpanList *you = q.FindAllIntersections(ray);

    if ((! me) || (! you)) {
        if (me) {
            me = new SpanList;
        }
        else if (you) {
            you = new SpanList;
        }
        else return 0;
    }

    if (me->NumSpans() == you->NumSpans()) {
        SpanList *ret = new SpanList;
        while (me->NumSpans()) {
            Span memin = me->ExtractMinSpan();
            Span youmin = you->ExtractMinSpan();
            if (fabs(memin.tmin - youmin.tmin) > eps ||
                fabs(memin.tmax - youmin.tmax) > eps) {
                ret->AddSpan(youmin);
            }
            ret->AddSpan(memin);
        }
        delete me;
        delete you;
        return ret;
    }
    else {
        return 0;
    }
}
```

Listing 8.6 `Algebraic` **and** `Torus` **implementation** *(continued)*

8.2.1 The `Polynomial` Class

To help manipulate algebraic surfaces, I wrote a `Polynomial` class that encapsulates one-variable polynomials of arbitrary degree. The polynomial is represented as:

- The *order*. This is the maximum exponent of the polynomial.

- The *coefficients*. There are *order*+1 coefficients, including the constant (exponent 0).

There is a constructor to create a `Polynomial` instantly from an array of coefficients. For example, the polynomial $x^2 + 2x + 3$ can be created as follows:

```
double coeff[3] = {3, 2, 1};
//Declare Polynomial poly = x² + 2x + 3
Polynomial poly(2, coeff);
```

Note that the coefficients are given in increasing degree, so the constant is *coeff*[0] and the largest coefficient is *coeff*[*order*]. This is intended to be mnemonic; *coeff*[i] is the coefficient for x_i.

`Polynomials` can also be created incrementally by adding in coefficients one at a time. The default `Polynomial` constructor creates a `Polynomial` with no coefficients, and the `AddElm` member function can be used to add in a coefficient with a given exponent.

Many operators have been overloaded to work with the `Polynomial` class, including addition, subtraction, negation, multiplication by `Polynomials`, and multiplication by floating-point numbers (doubles). One of the more involved operations is polynomial modulus (operator%), which computes the remainder of the division of one polynomial by another. The operation will work only if the polynomial being divided into is of higher degree.

The definition and implementation of `Polynomial` are given in listings 8.7 and 8.8. The method for finding the real roots of a polynomial, which is at the heart of the ray-algebraic surface intersection calculation, is detailed next.

```
// =====================================================================
// poly.h
//    Header file for Polynomial class.
//
//       The Object-Oriented Ray Tracer (OORT)
//       Copyright (C) 1993 by Nicholas Wilt.
//
```

Listing 8.7 `Polynomial` definition

```
// This software product may be freely copied and distributed in
// unmodified form but may not be sold.  A nominal distribution
// fee may be charged for media and handling by freeware and
// shareware distributors.  The software product may not be
// included in whole or in part into any commercial package
// without the express written consent of the author.
//
// This software product is provided as is without warranty of
// any kind, express or implied, including but not limited to
// the implied warranties of merchantability and fitness for a
// particular purpose.  The author assumes no liability for any
// alleged or actual damages arising from the use of this
// software.  The author is under no obligation to provide
// service, corrections or upgrades to the software.
//
// ------------------------------------------------------------
//
// Please contact me with questions, comments, suggestions or
// other input about OORT.  My Compuserve account number is
// [75210,2455] (Internet sites can reach me at
// 75210.2455@compuserve.com).
//                              --Nicholas Wilt
// ================================================================


// ----------------------------------------------------------
// Polynomial
//      Implements an arbitrary-degree polynomial.
// ----------------------------------------------------------
class Polynomial {
public:
    // Maximum power of 10 to search for.
    // Default is 32.
    static int MAXPOW;

    // A coefficient smaller than SMALL_ENOUGH is
    // considered to be zero.  Default is 1e-12.
    static double SMALL_ENOUGH;

    // Smallest relative error we want.
    // Default is 1e-8.
    static double RELERROR;

    // Maximum number of iterations.
    // Default is 800.
```

Listing 8.7 `Polynomial` definition *(continued)*

```
static int MAXIT;

// Default constructor doesn't allocate any memory.
Polynomial() { ord = 0; coeff = 0; }

// This constructor allocates memory and copies the
// coefficients given.
Polynomial(int Order, double *Coeff);

// Copy constructor.
Polynomial(const Polynomial&);

// Assignment operator.
Polynomial& operator=(const Polynomial&);

// Destructor.
~Polynomial();

// Add an element to the polynomial
void AddElm(int deg, double x);

// Evaluate polynomial in terms of given x
double Evaluate(double x) const;

int SturmSequence(Polynomial **);

// Root-finding

// Finds the number of roots given the Sturm sequence
friend int NumRoots(Polynomial *sseq, int, int *, int *);
friend int NumChanges(Polynomial *sseq, int, double);
friend void SBisect(Polynomial *, int, double, double, int, int,
    double *);

// Returns all real roots (allocates passbk using operator new,
// then returns the root count).  No memory is allocated if there
// are no real roots.
int FindRealRoots(double **passbk);

// Unary operators
Polynomial operator+ () { return *this; }    // unary plus
Polynomial operator- ();                     // unary minus
friend Polynomial Normalize(const Polynomial&);  // Make
    coeff[ord-1]==1
friend Polynomial Derivative(const Polynomial&); // Manufactures
```

Listing 8.7 `Polynomial` definition *(continued)*

```
        derivative
    Polynomial& operator+= (const Polynomial&);     // Add another
        polynomial
    Polynomial& operator*= (const Polynomial&);     // Multiply by a
        polynomial
    Polynomial& operator*= (double);                // Scale by double

    // Binary operators
    friend Polynomial operator+ (const Polynomial&, const Polynomial&);
    friend Polynomial operator- (const Polynomial&, const Polynomial&);
    friend Polynomial operator* (const Polynomial&, const Polynomial&);
    friend Polynomial operator* (const Polynomial&, double&);
    friend Polynomial operator* (double, const Polynomial&);
    friend Polynomial operator% (const Polynomial&, const Polynomial&);

    friend ostream& operator<< (ostream& x, const Polynomial& y);
protected:
    int ord;            // Order of polynomial
    double *coeff;      // Coefficients.

    int ModRF(double a, double b, double *val);

};

// Returns the polynomial (ax+b)^t.
Polynomial Triangle(double a, double b, int t);

extern "C" int SolveQuadric(double[], double[]);
extern "C" int SolveCubic(double[], double[]);
extern "C" int SolveQuartic(double[], double[]);
```

Listing 8.7 `Polynomial` definition *(continued)*

```
// ===================================================================
// poly.cpp
//     Implementation file for Polynomial class.
//
//         The Object-Oriented Ray Tracer (OORT)
//         Copyright (C) 1993 by Nicholas Wilt.
//
// This software product may be freely copied and distributed in
// unmodified form but may not be sold.  A nominal distribution
// fee may be charged for media and handling by freeware and
```

Listing 8.8 `Polynomial` implementation

```
// shareware distributors.  The software product may not be
// included in whole or in part into any commercial package
// without the express written consent of the author.
//
// This software product is provided as is without warranty of
// any kind, express or implied, including but not limited to
// the implied warranties of merchantability and fitness for a
// particular purpose.  The author assumes no liability for any
// alleged or actual damages arising from the use of this
// software.  The author is under no obligation to provide
// service, corrections or upgrades to the software.
//
// ------------------------------------------------------------
//
// Please contact me with questions, comments, suggestions or
// other input about OORT.  My Compuserve account number is
// [75210,2455] (Internet sites can reach me at
// 75210.2455@compuserve.com).
//                              --Nicholas Wilt
// ====================================================================

#include <stdio.h>
#include <mem.h>
#include <math.h>
#include <iostream.h>
#include <stdlib.h>

#include "poly.h"

int Polynomial::MAXPOW = 32;
double Polynomial::SMALL_ENOUGH = 1e-12;
double Polynomial::RELERROR = 1e-8;
int Polynomial::MAXIT = 800;

Polynomial::Polynomial(int Order, double *Coeff)
{
    ord = Order;
    coeff = new double[ord+1];
    memcpy(coeff, Coeff, (ord+1)*sizeof(double));
}

Polynomial::Polynomial(const Polynomial& a)
{
    ord = a.ord;
    while (ord > 0 && a.coeff[ord] == 0.0)
```

Listing 8.8 `Polynomial` implementation *(continued)*

```
         ord--;
      coeff = new double[ord+1];
      memcpy(coeff, a.coeff, (ord+1)*sizeof(double));
}


Polynomial&
Polynomial::operator=(const Polynomial& x)
{
   if (coeff)
      delete[] coeff;
   ord = x.ord;
   while (ord > 0 && fabs(x.coeff[ord]) < SMALL_ENOUGH)
      ord--;
   coeff = new double[ord+1];
   memcpy(coeff, x.coeff, (ord+1)*sizeof(double));
   return *this;
}


// ----------------------------------------------------------
// Destructor frees the coefficient array.
// ----------------------------------------------------------
Polynomial::~Polynomial()
{
   delete[] coeff;
   coeff = 0;
}


// ----------------------------------------------------------
// Add a new coefficient (of given order) to the polynomial
// ----------------------------------------------------------
void
Polynomial::AddElm(int Order, double x)
{
   if (! coeff) {
      ord = Order;
      coeff = new double[ord+1];
      memset(coeff, 0, ord*sizeof(double));
      coeff[ord] = x;
   }
   else {
      if (Order > ord) {
         double *temp = new double[Order+1];
         memcpy(temp, coeff, (ord+1)*sizeof(double));
         if (Order-1 > ord)
            memset(temp+ord+1, 0, (Order-ord-1)*sizeof(double));
```

Listing 8.8 `Polynomial` implementation *(continued)*

```
                temp[ord = Order] = x;
                delete[] coeff;
                coeff = temp;
            }
        else
                coeff[Order] += x;
    }
}

// ------------------------------------------------------------
// Evaluate polynomial at a given point.
// ------------------------------------------------------------
double
Polynomial::Evaluate(double x) const
{
    int inx = ord+1;
    double ret = coeff[--inx];

    while (inx > 0)
        ret = x * ret + coeff[--inx];
    return ret;
}

// ------------------------------------------------------------
// Negate a polynomial.
// ------------------------------------------------------------
Polynomial
Polynomial::operator-()
{
    for (int i = 0; i <= ord; i++)
        coeff[i] = -coeff[i];
    return *this;
}

// ------------------------------------------------------------
// Transforms a polynomial so the first coefficient
// (coefficient of largest term) is equal to 1.
// ------------------------------------------------------------
Polynomial
Normalize(const Polynomial& x)
{
    double divby = fabs(x.coeff[x.ord]);
    if (divby == 1)
        return Polynomial(x);
    else {
```

Listing 8.8 `Polynomial` implementation *(continued)*

```
        Polynomial ret(x);
        for (int i = 0; i <= x.ord; i++)
            ret.coeff[i] /= divby;
        return ret;
    }
}


// -----------------------------------------------------------
// Returns the derivative of a polynomial.
// -----------------------------------------------------------
Polynomial
Derivative(const Polynomial& x)
{
    Polynomial ret;

    for (int i = 1; i <= x.ord; i++)
        ret.AddElm(i-1, i*x.coeff[i]);
    return ret;
}


// -----------------------------------------------------------
// Returns (a+b)^x,
//     e.g. Triangle(1, 1, 2) returns x^2 + 2x + 1
// -----------------------------------------------------------
Polynomial
Triangle(double a, double b, int x)
{
    int i;
    double *coeff;
    double tempa = 1;
    double tempb = pow((double) b, x);
    double mulby = 1;
    double divby = 1;
    Polynomial ret;

    for (i = 1; i <= x; i++)
        mulby *= i;
    divby = mulby;
    coeff = new double[x+1];
    for (i = 0; i < x; i++) {
        coeff[i] = mulby*tempa*tempb/divby;
        tempa *= a;
        if (b != 0.0)
            tempb /= b;
        mulby /= i+1;
```

Listing 8.8 `Polynomial` implementation *(continued)*

```
            divby /= x-i;
        }
    coeff[i] = tempa;
    ret = Polynomial(x, coeff);
    delete[] coeff;
    return ret;
}

// ---------------------------------------------------------
// Add a polynomial to this one.
// ---------------------------------------------------------
Polynomial&
Polynomial::operator+=(const Polynomial& x)
{
    for (int i = 0; i <= x.ord; i++)
        AddElm(i, x.coeff[i]);
    return *this;
}

// ---------------------------------------------------------
// Multiply polynomial by another polynomial.
// ---------------------------------------------------------
Polynomial&
Polynomial::operator*=(const Polynomial& x)
{
    // Still zero if the polynomial has no coefficients yet.
    if (coeff) {
        double *newcoeff = new double[ord + x.ord + 2];
        memset(newcoeff, 0, (ord + x.ord + 2)*sizeof(double));
        for (int i = 0; i <= ord; i++)
            for (int j = 0; j <= x.ord; j++)
                newcoeff[i + j] += coeff[i] * x.coeff[j];
        delete[] coeff;
        coeff = newcoeff;
        ord += x.ord;
    }
    return *this;
}

// ---------------------------------------------------------
// Multiply polynomial by a constant.
// ---------------------------------------------------------
Polynomial&
Polynomial::operator*=(double x)
{
```

Listing 8.8 `Polynomial` implementation *(continued)*

```
    for (int i = 0; i <= ord; i++)
        coeff[i] *= x;
    return *this;
}


// ----------------------------------------------------------
// Binary + for polynomials.
// ----------------------------------------------------------
Polynomial
operator+(const Polynomial& A, const Polynomial& B)
{
    Polynomial ret(A);

    for (int i = 0; i <= B.ord; i++)
        ret.AddElm(i, B.coeff[i]);
    return ret;
}


// ----------------------------------------------------------
// Binary - for polynomials.
// ----------------------------------------------------------
Polynomial
operator-(const Polynomial& A, const Polynomial& B)
{
    Polynomial ret(A);

    for (int i = 0; i <= B.ord; i++)
        ret.AddElm(i, -B.coeff[i]);
    return ret;
}


// ----------------------------------------------------------
// Binary * for polynomials.
// ----------------------------------------------------------
Polynomial
operator*(const Polynomial& A, const Polynomial& B)
{
    Polynomial ret = A;
    ret *= B;
    return ret;
}


// ----------------------------------------------------------
// Scale polynomial by constant.
// ----------------------------------------------------------
```

Listing 8.8 `Polynomial` implementation *(continued)*

```
Polynomial
operator*(double x, const Polynomial& A)
{
    Polynomial ret(A);
    ret *= x;
    return ret;
}

// ----------------------------------------------------------
// Scale polynomial by constant.
// ----------------------------------------------------------
Polynomial
operator*(const Polynomial& A, double& x)
{
    Polynomial ret(A);
    ret *= x;
    return ret;
}

// ----------------------------------------------------------
// Output polynomial to stream.
// ----------------------------------------------------------
ostream&
operator<<(ostream& x, const Polynomial& y)
{
    int cnt = y.ord + 1;
    double *c = y.coeff + y.ord + 1;

    while (c > y.coeff+1)
        x << *--c << "x^" << --cnt << " + ";
    x << *--c;
    return x;
}

// ----------------------------------------------------------
// ModRF
//
// uses the modified regula-falsi method to evaluate
// the root in interval [a,b] of the polynomial described in
// coef. The root is returned is returned in *val.  The
// routine returns zero if it can't converge.
// ----------------------------------------------------------
int
Polynomial::ModRF(double a, double b, double *val)
{
```

Listing 8.8 `Polynomial` implementation *(continued)*

```
int its;
double fa, fb, x, fx, lfx;

fa = Evaluate(a);
fb = Evaluate(b);

/*
 * if there is no sign difference the method won't work
 */
if (fa * fb > 0.0)
    return 0;

if (fabs(fa) < RELERROR) {
    *val = a;
    return 1;
}

if (fabs(fb) < RELERROR) {
    *val = b;
    return 1;
}

lfx = fa;

for (its = 0; its < MAXIT; its++) {
    fx = Evaluate( x = ((fb * a - fa * b) / (fb - fa)) );

    if (fabs(x) > RELERROR) {
        if (fabs(fx / x) < RELERROR) {
            *val = x;
            return 1;
        }
    } else if (fabs(fx) < RELERROR) {
        *val = x;
        return 1;
    }

    if ((fa * fx) < 0) {
        b = x;
        fb = fx;
        if ((lfx * fx) > 0)
            fa /= 2;
    } else {
        a = x;
        fa = fx;
```

Listing 8.8 `Polynomial` implementation *(continued)*

```
            if ((lfx * fx) > 0)
                fb /= 2;
        }

        lfx = fx;
    }

//  fprintf(stderr, "modrf overflow %f %f %f\n", a, b, fx);

    return 0;
}


// -------------------------------------------------------
// modp
//
//    calculates the modulus of u(x) / v(x) leaving it in r,
//  it returns 0 if r(x) is a constant.
//  note: this function assumes the leading coefficient of v
//    is 1 or -1
// -------------------------------------------------------
Polynomial
operator%(const Polynomial& u, const Polynomial& v)
{
    int j, k;
    Polynomial ret = u;
    Polynomial nv = Normalize(v);

    if (nv.coeff[nv.ord] < 0.0) {
        for (k = u.ord - nv.ord - 1; k >= 0; k -= 2)
            ret.coeff[k] = -ret.coeff[k];

        for (k = u.ord - nv.ord; k >= 0; k--)
            for (j = nv.ord + k - 1; j >= k; j--)
                ret.coeff[j] = -ret.coeff[j] - ret.coeff[nv.ord + k] *
                    nv.coeff[j - k];
    } else {
        for (k = u.ord - nv.ord; k >= 0; k--)
            for (j = nv.ord + k - 1; j >= k; j--)
                ret.coeff[j] -= ret.coeff[nv.ord + k] * nv.coeff[j - k];
    }

    k = nv.ord - 1;
    while (k >= 0 && fabs(ret.coeff[k]) < Polynomial::SMALL_ENOUGH) {
        ret.coeff[k] = 0.0;
        k--;
```

Listing 8.8 Polynomial implementation *(continued)*

```
    }

    ret.ord = (k < 0) ? 0 : k;

    return ret;
}

// ---------------------------------------------------------
// Allocates and passes back the Sturm sequence array of
// polynomials for the given polynomial (*this).
// ---------------------------------------------------------
int
Polynomial::SturmSequence(Polynomial **passbk)
{
    Polynomial *ret;
    int i, numarr;

    ret = new Polynomial[ord+1];
    ret[0] = *this;
    ret[1] = Normalize(Derivative(*this));
    for (numarr = 2; ret[numarr - 1].ord > 0; numarr++) {
        ret[numarr] = Normalize(-(ret[numarr - 2] % ret[numarr - 1]));
    }
    *passbk = new Polynomial[numarr];
    for (i = 0; i < numarr - 1; i++)
        (*passbk)[i] = ret[i];
    (*passbk)[i] = -(ret[i - 2] % ret[i - 1]);
    delete[] ret;
    return numarr - 1;
}

// ---------------------------------------------------------
// Returns the number of real roots for the polynomial.
// ---------------------------------------------------------
int
NumRoots(Polynomial *sseq, int n, int *atneg, int *atpos)
{
    int i;
    int atposinf, atneginf;
    double f, lf;

    atposinf = atneginf = 0;

    /*
     * changes at positive infinity
```

Listing 8.8 Polynomial implementation *(continued)*

```
    */
    lf = sseq[0].coeff[sseq[0].ord];

    for (i = 1; i <= n; i++) {
        f = sseq[i].coeff[sseq[i].ord];
        if (lf == 0.0 || lf * f < 0)
            atposinf++;
        lf = f;
    }

    /*
     * changes at negative infinity
     */
    if (sseq[0].ord & 1)
        lf = -sseq[0].coeff[sseq[0].ord];
    else
        lf = sseq[0].coeff[sseq[0].ord];

    for (i = 1; i <= n; i++) {
        if (sseq[i].ord & 1)
            f = -sseq[i].coeff[sseq[i].ord];
        else
            f = sseq[i].coeff[sseq[i].ord];
        if (lf == 0.0 || lf * f < 0)
            atneginf++;
        lf = f;
    }

    *atneg = atneginf;
    *atpos = atposinf;

    return(atneginf - atposinf);
}

// -----------------------------------------------------------
// Returns the number of sign changes.
// -----------------------------------------------------------
int
NumChanges(Polynomial *sseq, int n, double a)
{
    int i;
    int changes;
    double f, lf;

    changes = 0;
```

Listing 8.8 `Polynomial` implementation *(continued)*

```
    lf = sseq[0].Evaluate(a);

    for (i = 1; i <= n; i++) {
        f = sseq[i].Evaluate(a);
        if (fabs(f) > Polynomial::SMALL_ENOUGH && (lf == 0.0 || lf * f <
            0))
            changes++;
        lf = f;
    }

    return changes;
}

// -------------------------------------------------------
// Finds roots in the given interval.
// -------------------------------------------------------
void
SBisect(Polynomial *sseq, int np,
        double min, double max,
        int atmin, int atmax,
        double *roots)
{
    double mid;
    int n1, n2, its, atmid, nroot;

    if ((nroot = atmin - atmax) == 1) {
        /*
         * first try a less expensive technique.
         */
        if (sseq[0].ModRF(min, max, roots))
            return;

        /*
         * if we get here we have to evaluate the root the hard
         * way by using the Sturm sequence.
         */
        for (its = 0; its < Polynomial::MAXIT; its++) {
            mid = (min + max) / 2;

            atmid = NumChanges(sseq, np, mid);

            if (fabs(mid) > Polynomial::RELERROR) {
                if (fabs((max - min) / mid) < Polynomial::RELERROR) {
                    roots[0] = mid;
```

Listing 8.8 `Polynomial` **implementation** *(continued)*

```
                return;
            }
        }
        else if (fabs(max - min) < Polynomial::RELERROR) {
            roots[0] = mid;
            return;
        }

        if ((atmin - atmid) == 0)
            min = mid;
        else
            max = mid;
    }

    if (its == Polynomial::MAXIT) {
        cerr << "SBisect: overflow min " << min << " max " << max;
        cerr << " diff " << max-min << " nroot " << nroot;
        cerr << " n1 " << n1 << " n2 " << n2 << '\n';
        roots[0] = mid;
    }

    return;
}

/*
 * more than one root in the interval, we have to bisect...
 */
for (its = 0; its < Polynomial::MAXIT; its++) {
    mid = (min + max) / 2;

    atmid = NumChanges(sseq, np, mid);

    n1 = atmin - atmid;
    n2 = atmid - atmax;

    if (n1 != 0 && n2 != 0) {
        SBisect(sseq, np, min, mid, atmin, atmid, roots);
        SBisect(sseq, np, mid, max, atmid, atmax, &roots[n1]);
        break;
    }

    if (n1 == 0)
        min = mid;
    else
        max = mid;
```

Listing 8.8 `Polynomial` implementation *(continued)*

```
    }

    if (its == Polynomial::MAXIT) {
        fprintf(stderr, "sbisect: roots too close together\n");
        fprintf(stderr, "sbisect: overflow min %f max %f diff %e\
            nroot %d n1 %d n2 %d\n",
            min, max, max - min, nroot, n1, n2);
        for (n1 = atmax; n1 < atmin; n1++)
        roots[n1 - atmax] = mid;
    }
}


// ------------------------------------------------------------
// Find roots of the polynomial.  This routine allocates an
// array of doubles for you and returns the number of roots.
// ------------------------------------------------------------
int
Polynomial::FindRealRoots(double **passbk)
{
    int ret = 0;
    double roots[4];
    switch (ord) {
        case 1:    // Linear
            *passbk = new double[1];
            **passbk = -coeff[0] / coeff[1];
            return 1;
        case 2:    // Quadratic
            ret = SolveQuadric(coeff, roots);
            if (ret) {
                *passbk = new double[ret];
                memcpy(*passbk, roots, ret*sizeof(double));
            }
            return ret;
        case 3:    // Cubic
            ret = SolveCubic(coeff, roots);
            if (ret) {
                *passbk = new double[ret];
                memcpy(*passbk, roots, ret*sizeof(double));
            }
            return ret;
        case 4:    // Quartic
            ret = SolveQuartic(coeff, roots);
            if (ret) {
                *passbk = new double[ret];
                memcpy(*passbk, roots, ret*sizeof(double));
```

Listing 8.8 `Polynomial` implementation *(continued)*

```
        }
        return ret;
    default:  // Higher order
        if (ord <= 0)
            return 0;
        break;
    }
// Find Sturm sequence
Polynomial norm = Normalize(*this);
Polynomial *sseq;
int sn = SturmSequence(&sseq);

// Find number of roots
int atmin, atmax;
int numroots = NumRoots(sseq, sn, &atmin, &atmax);

if (! numroots) {
    delete[] sseq;
    return 0;
}

// Bracket roots
double min = -1;
int nchanges = NumChanges(sseq, sn, min);
for (int i = 0; nchanges != atmin && i != MAXPOW; i++) {
    min *= 10;
    nchanges = NumChanges(sseq, sn, min);
}
if (nchanges != atmin) {
    cerr << "Polynomial::FindRealRoots: Unable to bracket all
        negative roots\n";
    exit(1);
}
double max = 1;
nchanges = NumChanges(sseq, sn, max);
for (i = 0; nchanges != atmax && i != MAXPOW; i++) {
    max *= 10;
    nchanges = NumChanges(sseq, sn, max);
}
if (nchanges != atmax) {
    cerr << "Polynomial::FindRealRoots: Unable to bracket all
        positive roots\n";
    exit(1);
}
*passbk = new double[numroots];
```

Listing 8.8 `Polynomial` implementation *(continued)*

```
    SBisect(sseq, sn, min, max, atmin, atmax, *passbk);

    delete[] sseq;

    return numroots;
}

#if 0
int
main()
{
    Polynomial p = Triangle(2, 1, 2);
    Polynomial q = Triangle(1, 1, 2);
    Polynomial r = Triangle(2, 2, 1);
    cout << p << " evaluated at 5 is " << p.Evaluate(5) << '\n';
    cout << q << " evaluated at 5 is " << q.Evaluate(5) << '\n';
    cout << p << " * " << q << " =\n" << p*q << "\n\n";
    cout << p << " - " << 4*q << " =\n" << p-4*q << "\n\n";
    cout << "Derivative(" << p*q << ") = " <<
        Derivative(p*q) << "\n\n";
    cout << p % q << "\n\n";
    cout << "    " << r << "\n % " << q << "\n = " << r%q << "\n\n";

    double *roots;
    Polynomial s = p*q*r;
    cout << s << '\n';

    Polynomial *sseq;
    int i, numarr;
    numarr = s.SturmSequence(&sseq);
    for (i = 0; i < numarr; i++)
        cout << sseq[i] << "\n\n";

    int numroots = s.FindRealRoots(&roots);
    for (i = 0; i < numroots; i++)
        cout << roots[i] << '\n';

    return 0;
}
#endif
```

Listing 8.8 `Polynomial` implementation *(continued)*

8.2.2   Finding Roots of a Polynomial

The root-finder in OORT, implemented by the `FindRoots` member function, is based on the work of Hook and McAree [HOOK90]. The public-domain code included with that work has been incorporated into the `Polynomial` class. In addition, for finding the roots of second-, third- and fourth-degree `Polynomial`s, public-domain code written by Schwartze [SCHW90] is used.

The algorithm to find the real roots of a polynomial uses the polynomial's Sturm sequence, as follows. The Sturm sequence is a series of polynomials f_1, f_2, ... where f_1 is the polynomial itself, $f_2 = f_1'$ (the derivative of f_1), $f_3 = -f_1 \% f_2$ where % denotes polynomial modulus. In general, $f_k = -f_{k-2} \% f_{k-1}$. The last polynomial in the sequence has degree 0 (i.e., is a constant only).

Once the Sturm sequence has been computed, it can be used to determine the number of real roots, and it can be used to isolate the intervals where they lie. This is done by applying Sturm's Theorem:

> The number of distinct real roots of $f(x)=0$ in the interval x=a to x=b is given by the difference $s(a)-s(b)$, where $s(a)$ and $s(b)$ are the number of sign changes in the Sturm sequence at x=a and x=b.

Thus, the number of negative real roots is given by applying Sturm's theorem to the interval $[-\infty, 0]$ and the number of positive real roots is given by applying Sturm's theorem to the interval $[0, +\infty]$. Although infinities are being thrown about with great abandon here, we can easily tell the sign of $f(\pm\infty)$ by examining the order of the polynomial and the sign of the coefficient of largest degree. The sign of $f(+\infty)$ is the same as the coefficient of largest degree. The sign of $f(-\infty)$ depends on whether the polynomial is of odd or even order. If the polynomial is of odd order, the sign is the opposite as the coefficient of largest degree. Otherwise, it is the same (since the $-\infty$ is made positive by having an even exponent applied to it).

From Hook and McAree [HOOK90], here is an example.

For the polynomial $f(x) = x^3 + 3x^2 - 1$, the Sturm sequence f_1, f_2, ... is as follows:

$$f_1(x) = f(x) = x^3 + 3x^2 - 1 \tag{8.7a}$$

$$f_2(x) = f'(x) = 3x^2 + 6x \tag{8.7b}$$

$f_1(x) / f_2(x)$ is $\dfrac{x}{3} + \dfrac{1}{3}$; the remainder from that division is $-2x - 1$. Thus,

$$f_3(x) = 2x + 1 \tag{8.7c}$$

$f_2(x) / f_3(x)$ is $\dfrac{3}{2}x + \dfrac{9}{4}$; the remainder from that division is $\dfrac{9}{4}$. Thus,

$$f_4(x) = \frac{9}{4} \tag{8.7d}$$

Since $f_4(x)$ is a constant, it is the last function in the Sturm sequence.

To determine the total number of roots in the range $(-\infty, \infty)$, examine the sign changes in $f_1...f_4$ at the two values:

	Value	Sign at $-\infty$	Sign at ∞
f_1	$x^3 + 3x^2 - 1$	$-$	$+$
f_2	$3x^2 + 6x$	$+$	$+$
f_3	$2x + 1$	$-$	$+$
f_4	$\dfrac{9}{4}$	$+$	$+$
	Sign changes:	3	0

Since $3 - 0 = 3$, there must be 3 distinct real roots of the polynomial.

`Polynomial::FindRealRoots`, which implements the above algorithm, is used by `Algebraic::NearestInt` and `Algebraic::FindAllIntersections` to compute parameters of intersection between a ray and an algebraic surface.

Further Work

The current implementation computes all intersections of the ray with the algebraic surface. To compute the nearest intersection, it would be more efficient to bracket the smallest positive root only and polish it using Newton's method, rather than bracketing and polishing all roots of the polynomial.

The current implementation does not do any subexpression elimination when computing the polynomial expression in t. For example, the equation for Steiner's surface $(x^2y^2 + y^2x^2 + z^2x^2 + xyz = 0)$ requires several expressions such as $(ray.\textbf{loc}.x + t\textbf{dir}.x)^2$ to be computed twice. Computing common subexpressions once and accessing them as needed to construct the polynomial would be much more efficient.

Appendix A
Introduction to C++

This chapter gives an overview of the C++ programming language. Since this book is not about C++ programming, it cannot go into too much depth; we will concentrate on the features of C++ that make it more suitable for ray tracing implementation than any other mainstream programming language. For more comprehensive coverage of the C++ programming language, see the Further Reading list at the end of this chapter.

A.1 Overview

C++ is a general-purpose programming language well-suited for implementing many different types of application. It derives from the popular C programming language. In fact, C++ compilers can compile well-written C code without modification. However, C++ is an infinitely more complex language than C. This complexity is a two-edged sword. While C++ lets programmers write expressive, powerful code, C++ programmers must cultivate an eye for trouble. Overdosing on a C++ feature can be fatal to a project. Meyers [MEY92] is an invaluable aid in discerning when to use which features of C++.

C++ is a *static* language, which means all the data types, function parameters, and other elements of the program must be described at compile time. In some languages, such as Smalltalk, new types can be defined at runtime; not so in C++. The C++ compiler requires you to describe everything so it can verify your code. For example, a C++ compiler will not compile code that calls a function for which the compiler hasn't seen a prototype.

C++ is a strongly-typed language. *Strong* typing means that only compatible types can be intermingled in expressions. Early versions of C treated integers and pointers identically; trying to do the same in C++ will cause the compiler to complain loudly. It knows enough to convert automatically between some types (for example, it will automatically promote an integer to a floating-point value), but will refuse to compile code that mixes incompatible types.

C++'s static, strongly-typed approach makes it more difficult to get code to compile in the first place, but that code is more likely to be correct once it compiles.

C++ is an object-oriented language. Object-oriented programming (or *OOP*) is a buzzword that has lost a lot of its original meaning, but we can safely say that it entails programming with *objects*, which are *instances* of *classes*. A few other buzzwords that we will get around to explaining are encapsulation, data hiding, inheritance, polymorphism, and templates (parameterized data types). These are all features of C++ that make it ideal for ray tracing implementation.

A.2   Enhancements Over C

A number of enhancements were added to C++ strictly to improve on the C programming language. These include inline functions, overloaded functions, default arguments, and the **const** storage qualifier.

Inline Functions

Inline functions cause the compiler to insert the equivalent code inline wherever the function is called, instead of generating a function call. Because inline functions can cause a formidable amount of object code to be generated, they are usually reserved for small tasks that take almost as little work as the call to the function itself. Efficiency is the sole motivation for inline functions: for small enough functions, avoiding the overhead of the function call is often a large performance win. To guarantee that the compiler knows what code to generate, inline functions are declared in headers rather than in implementation files.

The **inline** directive is a recommendation to the compiler, not an order. Compilers are free to impose restrictions on the generation of inline functions. Many compilers prefer to generate inline functions out-of-line when debugging information is being included in the object file, and most compilers cannot generate code in-line for functions that include loop constructs such as **while** or **for**.

Function Overloading

Function names can be overloaded. More than one function can have the same name, on one condition: they must take a different number of parameters, or the type of at least one of the parameters must differ. This restriction is intended to prevent programmers from writing ambiguous code. It is not sufficient for the return type to differ, nor may the parameters differ only by a storage qualifier. The only exception to this rule is that the reference parameters `T&`, `const T&`, and `volatile T&` are permitted to distinguish overloaded functions.

Although it is legal, explicit function overloading should be avoided. There's no reason to give two functions the same name just for the sake of it. Function overloading is difficult enough to avoid when programming in C++, because it occurs implicitly in certain situations (such as when overloading operators). We will see how function overloading applies to these situations later in this chapter.

Default Arguments

The arguments of a function can be declared with default values. This is done by giving an "= *value*" sequence after each argument that is to have a default value. Declaring

```
float Distance(float x=0, float y=0);
```

results in a function that can be called in any of three ways: `Distance(x, y)`; `Distance(x)`, which is equivalent to calling `Distance(x, 0)`; and `Distance()`, which is equivalent to calling `Distance(0, 0)`. Only the last arguments in the list can have default values; for example, the following declaration is illegal because the second argument does not have a default value:

```
float Distance(float x=0, float y);
```

Like most C++ features, default arguments should be used with care. They can add greatly to the clarity of code, especially for constructors with a large number of arguments. However, they can make code much less readable if used improperly.

const **Storage Qualifier**

Objects can be declared **const**; this is the case in C as well, but C++ takes the concept farther. Besides letting you declare standalone constants, it allows functions to promise not to modify objects passed to them, and allows member functions to promise not to modify the objects they operate on. For example, the Magnitude function is declared in `vector.h` as follows:

```
float Magnitude(const Vector3D& x);
```

The `const` qualifier means that `Magnitude` cannot modify the Vector3D passed to it. What good does this do? For one thing, Vectors that were declared **const** can now be passed to `Magnitude`. For another, compilers can use this information to generate more efficient code. But most importantly, declaring the parameter **const** establishes a contract between `Magnitude` and functions that call it. `Magnitude` promises not to modify Vector3Ds passed to it, and functions that call it can use that fact to their advantage. In particular, they can in turn promise not to modify Vector3Ds passed to *them*.

The compiler enforces the promises implied by **const**, so **const** must be used with care. C++ is willing to cast a non-**const** object to a **const** one, but never the other way around. Thus, it's fine to call `Magnitude` with a non-**const** Vector3D, but `Magnitude` cannot use any non-**const** functions to manipulate the Vector3D.

References

A reference is a name for another object. They are most useful when used as function return values and function parameter types. Declaring a standalone reference variable is allowed, but should be avoided; it is much too complicated to be worth the trouble.

One benefit of using references is efficiency. Like passing a pointer, passing a reference to an object is often more efficient than passing the whole object. Unlike passing a pointer, you do not need to take the address of the object when passing it.

Another benefit of references is that when declared as function return types, they allow the function return value to be used as an *lvalue*. For example, the function:

```
int&
SecondElement(int x[])
{
        return x[1];
}
```

can be used to modify the second element of the array passed to it:

```
int arr[5] = { 1, 2, 3, 4, 5 };
SecondElement(x) = 10;
```

```
// arr now contains {1, 10, 3, 4, 5}
```

A more practical example is the subscripting operator [] overloaded by Vector3D. If you have a Vector3D, you can subscript it from 0 to obtain the X, Y, and Z components.

```
Vector3D p(1, 2, 3);
float x = p[0];// x = 1
float y = p[1];// y = 2
float z = p[2];// z = 3
```

Since Vector3D::operator[] returns float& (reference to a **float**), you can use the subscripting operator to assign to the elements of the Vector3D as well as to read them.

new **and** delete

The **new** and **delete** operators largely supplant the dynamic memory allocation facilities offered by C (malloc and free). Instead of writing

```
int *newint = (int *) malloc(sizeof(int));
```

you can write:

```
int *newint = new int;
```

You can also declare arrays with **new**, as follows:

```
// Allocate an array of 10 integers
int *newints = new int[10];
```

To deallocate memory that was allocated with **new**, use the **delete** operator:

```
// Delete the integer allocated above with new
delete newint;
```

To deallocate an array, make sure to put square brackets [ ] after **delete**:

```
// Delete the array of integers allocated above
delete[] newints;
```

Besides offering type-safe dynamic memory allocation, the **new** and **delete** operators invoke constructors and destructors when used to allocate user-defined types. Constructors and destructors will be discussed in detail in the next section.

Most C++ compilers let you use malloc and free, as before, though the list of reasons to do so is very short (forward compatibility when porting from C is one). And although operators **new** and **delete** are usually implemented in terms of `malloc` and `free`, never mix the two paradigms. Never **delete** what you have `malloc`'d, and never `free` what you have **new**'d.

A.3 Classes (Encapsulation)

A *class* in C++ is a data type defined by the user. The class definition includes the following information:

- Data in the class (class members)

    These are declared like other data declarations in C++. Every instance of the class will contain this data. These members can be accessed using the `.` operator (for class member access) or the `->` operator (for access through a pointer), provided the client of the class has the right to access the member (see the discussion of scope restriction below).

- Functions in the class (member functions)

    These are declared like other functions in C++. There are two differences between a member function and other functions in C++. First, the member function can implicitly access members of the class instance by name. For instance, member functions of `Vector3D` can refer to implicitly declared variables `x`, `y`, and `z`, which refer to those members in the `Vector3D` that the function is being called on. Second, all member functions take an implicit parameter called **this**, which points to the class instance that the member function is being called for.

- Scope restriction of members (**private, protected,** or **public**)

    The scope of various members of the class can be restricted. **private** members can only be accessed by member functions of the class. **public** members can be accessed by anyone. **protected** members are a combination of the two: they are freely accessible by classes that inherit from the class being declared.

- Grants of access to the class (**friends**)

    A class may explicitly grant **private** access to itself by declaring **friends**. A function declared to be a **friend** may freely access **private** members of the class. If a class is declared a **friend**, then any member function of that class can access **private** members of the class. Friends are not inherited—that is, declaring a certain class a **friend** does not mean classes that inherit from it are also your **friends**. The next section will discuss inheritance in detail.

Once you have defined a class, you can declare *instances* of a class. This process is directly analogous to declaring instances of primitive data types. For example, after including `vector.h` you are free to write:

```
Vector3D point;        // Create a vector
Vector3D points[10];   // Create an array of vectors
```

When an instance of a class is created, the compiler calls a special member function called a *constructor*. Constructors have the same name as the class. A constructor should be thought of as a special member function that takes parameters and uses them to transform raw, uninitialized memory into a valid instance of the class. You can declare as many of them as you like, and they will be overloaded just like other overloaded functions (they will be distinguished by the parameters). Constructors are called not only when objects come into scope (as in the `Vector3D` examples given above), but also when the **new** operator is used to allocate an object dynamically.

See the `Vector3D` class for examples of constructors. `Vector3D(float)` takes a single `float` as input and initializes all three members of the class to that `float`. Thus, the declaration:

```
Vector3D org(0);
```

creates a `Vector3D` by calling `Vector3D::Vector3D(float)` with a parameter of 0. The constructor initializes the x, y, and z elements of the `Vector3D` to 0. Another constructor takes three `float`s and uses them to initialize the three members of the class. Writing:

```
Vector3D viewer(0, 0, -1000);
```

calls `Vector3D::Vector3D(float, float, float)`, which initializes the x, y, and z elements with the parameters.

Constructors cannot return a value. This means that there is no clean way to report an error (for example, out-of-memory) during execution of a constructor. The addition of exception handling to C++ should provide a clean solution to this problem.

There are several special constructors that are always created by the compiler, even if the programmer does not define them in the class. One is the *default constructor*, which takes no arguments. The default constructor is called when an object is created with no arguments:

```
Vector3D x;   // Vector3D::Vector3D() called on x.
```

The default constructor is also used when an array of objects is allocated with the **new** operator. In this case, the default constructor is called for every element in the array. Thus, if an object is going to be allocated in arrays frequently, it is best for default constructors to be as efficient as possible. If no default constructor is given by the programmer, the compiler assumes a default constructor that does nothing. The uninitialized bits given the constructor are left alone, and it is up to users of the class to ensure they are put into a stable state before use.

Another special constructor, called the *copy constructor*, takes an instance of a class and makes a duplicate. The default copy constructor is a member-wise copy, which suffices for most classes. However, copy constructors must be implemented for classes that are "deep," such as linked lists. The default copy constructor will merely copy the head of the linked list to the other linked list instance; once the first linked list is destroyed, the second will become invalid as well (since it pointed to nodes in the first linked list). To avoid this behavior, the copy constructor should create another linked list that contains copies of the nodes in the first.

The copy constructor takes a reference to the class as input. It then does what is necessary to make another instance of the class that is equivalent to the one given in the parameter list. The `SimpleList`, `SimpleStack`, and `Heap` class templates all implement copy constructors.

Classes that need a copy constructor also need to overload the *assignment operator*. This operation is similar to that of the copy constructor, in that it must convert the class instance into a duplicate of the class instance given. The difference is that the assignment operator operates on a viable instance of the class rather than on uninitialized memory. See the `SimpleList`, `SimpleStack`, and `Heap` class templates for examples of overloading the assignment operator. See also the later section on operator overloading.

A.4 Scope Restriction (Data Hiding)

Part of object-oriented programming is trying to treat objects as "black boxes." Allowing direct access to components of an object is inadvisable because it makes it more difficult to track the interactions between different parts of a program. C++ provides extensive facilities for scope restriction to help programmers enforce restricted access to class members. We have already seen some of those facilities in the **private, protected,** and **public** directives in the class definition. Declaring class members **public** means that anyone can access those members. Public access should be reserved for members that are deliberately available to everyone. Declaring class members **private** means only member functions of the class can access them. Declaring class members **protected** is a combination of the two: derived classes have direct access to the **protected** members of classes they inherit from.

A class can grant direct access to classes and non-member functions by declaring them **friends**. This is a direct violation of the principal of scope restriction, but is sometimes necessary in the face of other concerns.

Even **public** members of a class have restricted scope: they are restricted to the scope of the class. Class members can be accessed in only a few ways:

- With the . operator applied to an instance of the class (or a derived class).

- With the -> operator applied to a pointer to an instance of the class (or a derived class).

- With the scope resolution operator ::. For example, the Clear member function of Vector3D may be referred to as Vector3D:
  :Clear.

Restricting scope is important. Try to restrict the scope of class members to **private** when possible, **public** only when necessary. Try to define class relationships so that classes can treat each other as black boxes.

Restricting scope in other contexts is important, too. Make variables local to blocks or functions whenever possible. If a variable must persist between function calls, make it **static** to restrict its scope to the file it is declared in. If a variable must be made global, place it in a class to restrict its scope to that class. (See the Statistics class in stats.h for a group of global variables whose scope was restricted in this way.) In any program, there should be only a handful of truly global variables, if any.

A.5   Inheritance

A class can *inherit* from another class. The class that inherits is called the *derived class*; the class it inherits from is called the *base class*. When a class inherits from another, it inherits all of the members and member functions of the base class. In OOP-speak, the derived class bears an IS-A relationship to the base class. The most relevant example to ray tracing is the hierarchy of classes that inherit from Object3D.

Object3D roots a hierarchy of classes representing objects that can be ray traced by OORT. These include infinite planes, spheres, polygons, and other objects. The Object3D class contains only the minimum data needed by OORT to describe a generic, ray traceable object.

When a class inherits from another, it becomes that class. A Sphere *is* an Object3D. The C++ compiler knows that, so it will automatically convert instances of `Sphere` to `Object3D`, if necessary (for example, if you assign a `Sphere *` to an `Object3D *`). The converse does not hold: an `Object3D` is not necessarily a `Sphere`, so you must explicitly cast an `Object3D` to `Sphere` if you somehow know that it is a `Sphere` and want to deal with it as such.

Of course, other classes can inherit from derived classes in turn. These classes would include members that further distinguished them from their base classes. For example, the `BoundingVolume` class inherits from `Object3D`; another class called `BoundingBox` inherits from `BoundingVolume`. The principle that a derived class IS-A base class extends from `BoundingBox` through `BoundingVolume` to `Object3D`: a `BoundingVolume` is an `Object3D`, even though it does not inherit from it directly.

A group of classes related by inheritance is called a *class hierarchy*. The class hierarchy is *rooted* at the class which all the classes in it ultimately inherit from. OORT, the class library for ray tracing included with this book, has a number of class hierarchies rooted at different classes that interact in a variety of ways. The `Object3D` class is the root of a class hierarchy of all the different types of object that OORT can ray trace. The `Light` class is the root of another class hierarchy that includes all the different types of light source used by OORT. If you want to enable OORT to ray trace a new type of object, you would declare a class and have it inherit from `Object3D`. If you want to add a new type of light source to OORT, you would inherit a class from `Light`, and so on. The interactions between these classes are discussed in Appendix B.

Inheritance is a mechanism for code reuse, one of the hallmarks of object-oriented programming. While the OORT class library uses inheritance internally to a large extent, it is also designed to let you reuse its code by inheriting from the different classes it includes.

A.6 Polymorphism

Polymorphism is used heavily by OORT, so understanding it is important. Its utility is best illustrated by a real-life example. The `Object3D` class discussed above declares a number of member functions that reflect the operations you have to perform on objects when ray tracing. For example, `Object3D::NearestInt` computes the nearest intersection of an object with a ray. `Object3D::FindNormal` computes the normal to an object at a given point. There are many other member functions declared in `Object3D`, but they have one thing in common: they can't be implemented for `Object3D`. How can you compute the normal to an object when you don't know what type of object it is? In situations like this, we don't want an implementation; we just want

`Object3D` to say that `Object3D`s can `NearestInt` and `FindNormal`, and leave the implementation to classes that inherit from `Object3D`. In situations like this, we declare a *pure virtual* function by appending " = 0" to the declaration of the member function.

Any class that contains a pure virtual function is called an *abstract* class. You cannot declare instances of an abstract class; you can only declare pointers and references to one. This is because the definition of the abstract class is deliberately ambiguous—the `Object3D` class not only *doesn't know* how to intersect with a ray, it *doesn't want to know*. Now, when classes inherit from `Object3D`, they are required to either implement all the pure virtual functions declared by `Object3D`, or leave the pure virtual function unimplemented.

If a derived class leaves any pure virtual function unimplemented, it is an abstract class just like its parent. This "passes the buck" to classes that inherit farther down the line.

The former option, implementing all the pure virtual functions declared by the base class, results in a concrete (non-abstract) class that can be created. And since it inherits from `Object3D`, it inherits all of the members of `Object3D`, including the `NearestInt` member function. When `NearestInt` is called on the object pointed to by an `Object3D *`, the correct member function for the type of `Object3D` is called. If the `Object3D *` points to a `Sphere`, then `Sphere::NearestInt` is called; if the `Object3D *` points to a `Polygon`, then `Polygon::NearestInt` is called. In any case, the caller does not need to know the type of object that is pointed to; it just calls `NearestInt` and can be confident that the intersection calculation will be performed correctly.

Abstract classes make marvelous root classes for class hierarchies. In fact, almost every class hierarchy in OORT is rooted by an abstract class. `Object3D`, `Texture`, `Surface`, `BumpMap`, `Mapping`, and `NoiseMaker` are all abstract classes. They define the "shape" of the class, but do not have enough information to actually implement all of their member functions. They leave that to classes that inherit from them. For example, the `Sphere` class inherits from `Object3D` and implements all of the pure virtual functions. So `Sphere` is no longer an abstract class and can be created and destroyed with the best of them. Most of OORT does not care what type of object is being dealt with, so they use `Object3D *`'s. In fact, a lot of code in OORT assigns the result of **new** directly to a pointer to the base class. For example:

```
Object3D *obj = new Sphere(parameters);
```

Obviously, the expression to the right of the equal sign is a `Sphere *`. But a pointer to a `Sphere` is just as much a pointer to `Object3D`, since

`Sphere` inherits from `Object3D`. Once the `Sphere *` is converted to `Object3D *` and assigned to `obj`, its exact identity is lost—you still know it is an `Object3D`, but you forget that it is a `Sphere`. You can call `NearestInt`, `FindNormal` and other member functions on it, and the correct member functions will be called (`Sphere::NearestInt`, `Sphere::FindNormal`, etc.), but you never need to know it. The compiler takes care of the housekeeping for you.

Although this loss of identity is generally good, it can become a liability when the time comes to destroy the object. Destroying a `Sphere` is different than destroying a `Plane`, even though they are both `Object3D`s. For this reason, it is important always to declare the destructor for an abstract class **virtual**. Even if the destructor does nothing, it must be able to be overloaded so that the destructor for a derived class is called when the base class is destroyed. For example, `Object3D::~Object3D` does nothing, but is declared **virtual** so that classes that inherit from it can overload it. `Polygon::~Polygon`, which overloads `Object3D::~Object3D`, frees the dynamically allocated memory associated with the `Polygon`. This architecture for the `Object3D` class hierarchy lets you destroy a `Polygon` even if you don't know that it is a `Polygon`:

```
Object3D *obj = new Polygon(parameters);
// The Polygon just created has lost its identity.
// We only know it is an Object3D now.
delete obj;   // Destroy the object
// The above line calls Polygon::~Polygon
// because the destructor for Object3D
// was declared virtual.
```

Virtual functions do not need to be pure. For example, the `Object3D` member function `BBox`, which computes the bounding box of the object, assumes an unbounded object by default: it sets the object's bounds to the vectors (–MAXFLOAT, –MAXFLOAT) and (MAXFLOAT, MAXFLOAT). Classes that inherit from `Object3D` but do not overload `BBox` will be assumed to be unbounded objects.

A.7   Operator Overloading

Operator overloading is a C++ feature that lets you give your own definitions of uses of C++ operators. The most conspicuous use of operator overloading in

OORT is overloading operators for the `Vector3D` class. Once the operators have been declared correctly, you can write:

```
Vector3D a = b + c;
```

and the `Vectors` b and c will be added together correctly, and the result assigned to a.

The most difficult aspect of operator overloading is the syntax. The overloaded operator is implemented by a function called `operator`*op* (e.g., `operator+`, `operator<<`). Unary operators such as ~ and the unary + and – operators are defined either by global functions that take the object that is being operated on as a parameter, or by member functions that take no parameters (in which case the object being operated on is the implicit parameter to the member function). The most important difference between declaring the operator function as a member function and declaring it as a global function is that the member function can be declared **virtual** and overloaded by derived classes. Other than that, the implementation decision is a matter of taste.

The type of the operator's result is given by the return type of the `operator`*op* function. See `Vector3D::operator-` for an example of unary operator implementation. The return type is `Vector3D&`, because negating a `Vector3D` results in another `Vector3D`. The function operates on the `Vector3D` that the unary – is being applied to (it negates the `Vector3D` elements) and returns a reference to that same `Vector3D`.

Overloading binary operators such as + and && is more complex. They, too, can be implemented either by member functions or global **friend** functions. If the operator is implemented as a member function, the left-hand operand is pointed to by **this** (it is the implicit first parameter to the function) and the right-hand operand is given by the second parameter. If the operator is implemented as a global function, the function must take two parameters: the first and second correspond to the left- and right-hand operands. In either case, as with unary operators, the return value gives the result type of the function.

The `Vector3D` class overloads a multitude of binary operators. They happen to be implemented as global functions (**friends** of `Vector3D`). For example, the `Vector3D` class definition includes a declaration to overload the binary + operator for `Vectors`:

```
friend Vector3D operator+(const Vector3D&, const
    Vector3D&);
```

`vector.h` contains the inline implementation of `operator+` later in the file.

Adding two **ints** results in an **int**. Adding two `Vector3Ds` results in a `Vector3D`. When, you might ask, does it make sense for the result of an operator to be different than the parameters? One good example is `operator*` `(const Matrix&, const Vector3D&)`. In this case, the `Matrix` is postmultiplied by the `Vector3D` and the result is a `Vector3D` that has been transformed.

It often makes sense to implement overloaded operators as **inline** functions, as most of the operators for `Vector3D` are. If the operations being performed are simple enough, there's not only a significant time savings as the overhead of the function call is eliminated, but a space savings as well, because the amount of machine code to call the function is more than the amount to just perform the function in-line.

Limitations and Caveats

You cannot define new operators using the operator overloading mechanism, nor can you change the precedence or associativity of the existing operators in C++.

Be tasteful when overloading operators. Don't overload operators whose precedence is wrong. For example, don't overload the ^ operator for exponentiation, because the multiplication operator has higher precedence.

Model your operators' behavior after the behavior they exhibit during normal code development. The addition operator should take two objects, perform some operation akin to addition, and return another object of the same type. The `Vector3D` class overloads the multiplication operator to perform member-wise multiplication rather than dot product for exactly this reason.

Don't invent new meanings for operators without good reason. For example, the ~ operator does not have any particular meaning for `Vector3Ds`, so you are free to define one (`Magnitude` and `Normalize` come to mind). Yet the very fact that more than one option presents itself is a warning sign. Readers of your code shouldn't have to look in your header to figure out what the operator is doing.

Have some sympathy for the people who read your code. Resist the temptation to sacrifice readability for conciseness.

A.8 Parameterized Data Types

Templates and parameterized data types are a recent addition to the C++ programming language. They complement the mechanisms for code reuse provided by inheritance. A template describes the shape of a related family of functions or classes. After the template has been defined, functions or classes can be instantiated that make use of the template. For example, here is a function template that takes the minimum of two values:

```
template<class T>
T
Min(T x, T y)
{
return (x < y) ? x : y;
}
```

The above function template does not declare a function. Rather, it declares a family of functions that all take two instances of a class, compare them with the < operator, and returns the smaller one. If you call it with two **ints**, the compiler will declare a function `int Min(int, int)` that returns the minimum of two integers. If you call it with two **floats**, the compiler will declare a function `float Min(float, float)` that returns the minimum of two floating-point numbers. And if you call it with `UserDefinedClass`, the compiler declares a function `UserDefinedClass Min(UserDefinedClass, UserDefinedClass)` that will use `operator<(UserDefinedClass, UserDefinedClass)` to compare the two instances of `UserDefinedClass` and return the first if `operator<` returns a nonzero value. In the latter case, the programmer is under no obligation to the compiler or anyone else to guarantee intuitive operation of the < operator. Since the programmer overloads the operator for the user-defined class (or the compiler will be unable to generate the `Min` instance of the function template), he can define `operator<` to compare the two instances of the class in any way he wants.

One disadvantage of function templates is that every time the function is called with a different parameter for the template, another instance of the function is generated. As far as the object code of the program is concerned, the programmer might as well have written separate functions. Function templates are just a way to conserve source code without sacrificing efficiency.

Templates can be used to declare families of classes, too. The most obvious, and initially the most useful, application for class templates is in implementing container classes. The `SimpleList` class template, for example, implements an unordered linked list of objects. The parameter to the class template is the type that the list will contain. An abridged version of the template declaration is as follows:

```
template<class T>
class SimpleList {
```

```
template<class T> class SimpleList {
protected:
    class SimpleListNode {
    public:
T contents;
SimpleListNode *next;
SimpleListNode(const T& Contents, SimpleListNode *Next):
    contents(Contents), next(Next) { }
    };
    int n;
    SimpleListNode *head;
public:
    SimpleList();
    SimpleList(const T& x);
    SimpleList(const SimpleList& x);
    SimpleList& operator=(const SimpleList& x);
    virtual ~SimpleList();
// ... other member functions, other embedded classes
};
```

An *instance* of the class template is a class. Instances are declared using the same angle brackets that were used to declare the template: `Simple-List<int>` is a list of integers; `SimpleList<Object3D *>` is a list of `Object3D *`'s. These two classes have a lot in common. They both contain `SimpleListNode` classes, for example. (The names start getting ridiculously long—the default constructor for the `SimpleListNode` class contained in `SimpleListNode<int>` is `SimpleList<int>::SimpleListNode::SimpleListNode()`.) They both contain integers called n. They both have member functions with the same names.

Classes that are instantiations from class templates are just like other classes. They can be inherited from and their **virtual** functions can be overloaded. In fact, inheriting from an instance of a class template is often a good idea just because you can use the opportunity to give the class a more mnemonic name. For example, in OORT a class called `ObjectList` inherits from `SimpleList<Object3D *>`.

The biggest disadvantage to class templates is the same as the disadvantage to function templates: object code duplication. Although the source code does not contain multiple implementations of `SimpleList` classes for different types, it might as well from the standpoint of the resulting object code.

Incidentally, you *can* declare instances of class templates that instantiate other class templates. For example, `SimpleStack<int>` is a stack of integers. A list of such stacks may be declared as follows:

```
SimpleList<SimpleStack<int> > ListOfStacks;
```

There is a catch: the space between the right angle brackets > is absolutely necessary. If it is omitted, the compiler parses the >> as a right-shift token and generates a long list of confusing errors.

A.9 Design Issues

C++ has features and limitations that encourage similar solutions to common problems. This section describes some of these design issues and the approaches taken to resolve each in this book.

#define

The `#define` preprocessor construct is largely obsolete in C++. Macros that declare constants can be replaced by **const** objects; function-like macros can be replaced by **inline** functions. These constructs enforce type safety and allow the compiler to perform automatic type conversions, whereas preprocessor macros do not.

Iterators and Manipulators

Container classes are marvelous examples of the object-oriented paradigm in action. You declare a `SimpleList` class that keeps track of a list of objects in no particular order. You declare member functions for `SimpleList` with names like `Add` and `Query`; these functions have well-defined interfaces, and they perform well-defined tasks on instances of the `SimpleList` class. The `SimpleList` class is a "black box." However, this paradigm falls apart once you want to examine the list, or insert nodes in a particular order. You are faced with a difficult choice: should you make the elements of `SimpleList` **public** so users of the class can manipulate a `SimpleList` more effectively?

To avoid having to make the members of `SimpleList` **public**, which would obviate many of the benefits of an object-oriented approach, people typically define classes called *iterators* and *manipulators* that serve to examine and modify an instance of a `SimpleList`, respectively. Every instance of the `SimpleList` class template contains a class called `Iterator` (which, since it is declared within the scope of the SimpleList template, has the name

`SimpleList<T>::Iterator` in the global scope) that can be used to example the objects in the list. An instance of `SimpleList<T>::Iterator` has a pointer to one of the elements in the linked list.

Another class called `SimpleList<T>::Manipulator` lets you modify the list by adding and deleting elements at the location of the current pointer.

The `SimpleList` class has to cooperate with its iterators and manipulators. For the sake of safety, for example, it is illegal to have a `Manipulator` attached to a `SimpleList` when an `Iterator` or `Manipulator` is already attached to it. To ensure that nothing is already attached, every `SimpleList` has a count of `Iterators` and `Manipulators` attached to it. These counts are updated by the `Iterator` and `Manipulator` constructors and destructors.

Determining the Type of a Derived Class

Unlike many dynamic object-oriented languages, C++ does not contain a language construct to ask an object what type it is. For instance, you can't ask an `Object3D` whether it is a `Sphere`. This is because of the backward compatibility constraint that Stroustrup imposed on C++ when he designed the language. Concrete classes map directly to analogous C structures, so that C++ programs can call C programs without ill effects. This constraint makes it impossible to implement a dynamic type-checking facility.

It's easy to get around this restriction by implementing the feature yourself. For example, one of the only members of the `Object3D` class is a read-only integer called *flags*. Constructors for classes that inherit from `Object3D` set the flags—for instance, the constructor for `BoundingVolume` sets the `BOUNDING` flag. Then, users of the class can ask it whether it is a bounding volume by checking the `BOUNDING` bit in the flags for the object.

Read-Only Access to Class Members

Often, it is necessary for users of a class to access members of that class. The principle of scope restriction holds that providing this access is a violation of the class's integrity. A good compromise is to declare the class member **private** and provide a **public** access function that returns the member without allowing users of the class to modify it. The flags member of `Object3D` is made read-only in this way; the `Flags()` function returns the current state of the object's flags. However, `Object3D` does not provide any facility to modify the flags of an existing object. They are initialized by the various constructors for `Object3D`, but they cannot be modified thereafter. This allows users of `Object3D` to ask the object about itself without violating its integrity.

Creating "Instances" of Abstract Classes

It is often desirable to create an instance of an abstract base class based on some sort of input. For example, the parser for a ray tracing input language might contain a function that reads a description of an object and creates an `Object3D` based on that input. But actual *instances* of `Object3D` are illegal; only non-abstract classes derived from `Object3D` can be instantiated. A function that creates an "instance" of an abstract base class based on some input is often called a *virtual constructor*.

Virtual constructors can be built by writing a function that takes the input and returns a pointer to the abstract base class. The function can examine the input and decide which derived class is appropriate, allocate an instance of it, and return the pointer. As a case in point, look at the `Dup()` function in `Object3D`. It is a pure virtual function declared as follows:

```
Object3D *Dup() const = 0;
```

Classes that inherit from `Object3D` overload `Dup()` to create another instance of the object that the member function is being called for. `Sphere::Dup()` creates another instance of a `Sphere`, and `Plane::Dup()` creates another instance of a plane. In this way, an `Object3D` can be duplicated without knowing exactly what type of `Object3D` it is. The same approach can be applied to less trivial problems than making duplicates.

The static **Keyword**

static is a storage qualifier that means different things in different places. Many of its meanings are inherited from C, and C++ adds a few of its own.

When applied to a global variable, **static** restricts the scope of that variable to the file it is declared in. Similarly, when applied to a function, **static** restricts the scope of the function to the file. If a variable must be persistent across function calls, try to make it **static** so functions in other files cannot access it.

When applied to a data member of a class, **static** makes it persistent within the class; that is, not every instance of a class contains the member. Think of **static** data members as global variables belonging to the class. Static member functions do not take an implicit parameter; they must access members of class instances with **.** or `->`.

A.10 Conclusion and Further Reading

C++ is a complicated language, and one chapter is not enough to cover it in detail. With luck, the density of the material did not intimidate you. C++ isn't that bad, as long as you resist the temptation to overuse its features.

Programmers new to C++ may want to buy one of the many books that teach the language from scratch. For blooded C++ programmers (not necessarily experienced ones), I drew from my own bookshelf and came up with the following recommendations:

- Meyers [MEY92] is a must for every C++ programmer. I dearly wish I'd had this book when I began programming in C++.

- Stroustrup [STRO91] is a good reference to have in hand, and contains some good style guidelines.

- Coplien [COPL92] describes a number of standard C++ programming idioms.

- Ellis and Stroustrup [ELLI91] is targeted at compiler implementors and makes no effort to teach C++. I still occasionally find it useful to answer hair-splitting questions about the language.

Appendix B

The OORT Class Library and Utilities

The OORT Class Library, described in Section B.1, contains the classes needed to perform ray tracing. The Utilities library, described in Section B.2, contains functions and classes to create objects, textures, and surfaces.

B.1 Class Library

OORT is a complicated system consisting of more than 9000 lines of C++ code. Because of this complexity, it is difficult to absorb the entire system at once. But because it is object-oriented, we can concentrate on different parts of the system and how they interact. First, we will describe the class library from the top down, starting with the `World` class.

The `World` class performs ray tracing. An instance of `World` contains everything needed to ray trace a scene: a list of the objects and light sources in the scene, a description of the viewer location and the viewing frustrum, and member functions to compute pixel colors. When `World` casts a ray and computes the color of light arriving at the ray origin, it uses the `Object3D` class to determine the nearest object along the ray and to compute the shading equation at the intersection point.

The `Object3D` class roots the hierarchy of object types supported by OORT. `Object3D` provides a framework that allows clients of OORT to treat objects uniformly without ever knowing exactly what type of objects they are.

Object3D provides a member function called ShadeObject that shades an object at a given intersection point. Currently, ShadeObject is implemented only by Object3D; it is not overloaded by any class that derives from Object3D. ShadeObject fills in a ShadingInfo structure with such information as the intersection point, object intersected, and direction of the incident ray. It then uses the object's Surface to shade the object.

The Surface class roots a hierarchy of surface types. Surfaces implement shading equations, as described in Chapter 3. They determine the coefficients of reflection and transmission at the intersection point, then decide how many of each type of ray to use to evaluate the shading equation at the intersection point. Surface uses the BumpMap class to alter the local geometry at the intersection point before evaluating the shading equation; it uses the Texture class to determine coefficients of reflection and transmission at the intersection point.

The BumpMap class roots a hierarchy of bump/displacement maps. The definitive member function of BumpMap, PerturbNormal, displaces the intersection point, modifies the normal at the intersection point, or both.

The Texture class translates points in space to colors. Different Texture implementations use a variety of tools to compute color coefficients. Solid textures use noise functions (the NoiseMaker hierarchy) and color maps (the ColorMap hierarchy). Other textures use inverse mappings (the Mapping hierarchy), image files (the ImageFile hierarchy), and other textures.

Other classes, at an even lower level than ColorMap or Mapping, provide support for fundamental data structures and linear algebra. The SimpleList, SimpleStack and Heap class templates provide support for unordered linked lists, LIFO stacks, and binary heaps. The Vector3D and Matrix classes provide support for three-dimensional vectors and 4×4 transformation matrices.

All of the abstract classes, class templates and class hierarchies mentioned above are described in alphabetical order in the following section. Destructors for classes are not described in this section. All destructors, when defined, do something intuitive. (For example, Polygon::~Polygon deletes the array of vertices that make up the polygon.) Destructors for abstract classes are always declared **virtual** and generally do nothing—the classes they occupy usually do not even contain any data members. Declaring the destructor **virtual** allows base classes to override the behavior of the destructor (as Polygon::~Polygon overrides the behavior of Object3D::~Object3D), even when the exact type of the object is unknown.

Implicitly defined functions such as copy constructors and assignment operators are not described. For classes that contain dynamically allocated memory, the appropriate copy constructors and assignment operators are defined and behave exactly as you would expect.

Finally, for the sake of simplicity, member functions that derived classes inherit from their bases are not described. For example, `Sphere` inherits from `Object3D`, and overloads a plethora of `Object3D` member functions such as `NearestInt`, `FindNormal` and `BBox`. None of these member functions are described under `Sphere`; rather, the reader is referred to Chapter 4, where these operations are described and the source code is given.

This section of the book is intended as a reference. Every class contains a reference to a book section that describes in detail the concepts associated with the class.

`Aggregate` class	`object3d.h/aggreg.cpp`
	Hierarchy: `Object3D`

Encapsulates a group of objects, primarily so they can be transformed together. See Section 4.8 for a discussion of aggregate objects.

Data members

List	`ObjectList list;`
	List of the objects in the `Aggregate`.

Member functions

Add Object	`void AddObject(Object3D *);`
	Adds the object to the list of objects in the `Aggregate`.
List	`ObjectList& List();`
	Returns a reference to the list of objects.
New Surface	`void NewSurface(Surface *);`
	Replaces the `Surface` of all the objects in the list with the `Surface` given.

`Algebraic` class	`object3d.h/alg.cpp`
	Hierarchy: `Object3D`

Encapsulates a generalized algebraic surface, as described in Section 8.2. Algebraic surfaces have a canonical representation; before intersecting with one, the ray is transformed into the canonical coordinate system of the algebraic surface.

Data members	
Terms	`TermList terms;`
	Contains the terms in the implicit function for the algebraic surface.

Member functions	
Constructors	`Algebraic(Surface *clr);`
	Creates an instance of `Algebraic` with the surface characteristics given. Initially, the `Algebraic` does not contain any terms.
	`Algebraic(const Quadric& q);`
	Creates an algebraic surface that is equivalent to the given quadric. A `Quadric` is much faster to manipulate than the equivalent algebraic surface, so this is just a useful way to debug algebraic surfaces.
Add Term	`void AddTerm(double c, int i, int j, int k);`
	Adds $cx^i y^j z^k$ to the implicit function for the algebraic surface.

`Algebraic::Term` class   object3d.h/alg.cpp

This embedded class, declared **private** and accessible only by the `Algebraic` class, encapsulates a single term in the implicit function for an algebraic surface. An instance of `Algebraic::Term` contains a coefficient c and three exponents i, j, and k, and corresponds to the term $cx^i y^j z^k$.

Data members	
Coefficient	`double c;`
	Coefficient of the term.
Exponents	These are the exponents to the x, y, and z components of the term.

Member functions	
Constructors	`Term(double a, int I, int J, int K);`
	Creates an instance of `Algebraic::Term` with the given coefficient and exponents.

friend functions	
Equality	`int operator==(const Term&, const Term&);`
	Returns 1 if the exponents for the two terms are all equal, 0 otherwise.

`AxisAlignedBox` class	`object3d.h/bbox.cpp` Hierarchy: `Object3D`

Encapsulates a three-dimensional, six-sided box aligned with the coordinate axes. These boxes are used to bound primitives in OORT (see Section 4.7). When arranged in a hierarchy, these boxes can greatly increase the speed of ray tracing.

Member functions	
Constructors	`AxisAlignedBox();`
	Leaves the two vectors undefined.
	`AxisAlignedBox(const Vector& min, const Vector& max);`
	Assigns the two vectors to the `min` and `max` data members.
Include	`void Include(const Vector3D&);`
	`void Include(const AxisAlignedBox&);`
	These functions expand the bounding box, if necessary, to include the object given.
Intersection (ray)	`int ComputeMinMaxT(Ray& ray, float *tmin, float *tmax) const;`
	If the ray intersects the bounding box, this function returns nonzero and passes back the parameters of intersection in `tmin` and `tmax`. If the ray misses the bounding box, the function returns 0.

Min, Max	`Vector3D Min() const;`
	`Vector3D Max() const;`
	These functions provide read-only access to the minimum and maximum vectors for the bounding box.
Overlap	`int Overlap(const AxisAlignedBox&) const;`
	This function returns nonzero if this axis-aligned box overlaps the box given.
SurfaceArea	`virtual float SurfaceArea() const;`
	This function returns the surface area of the axis-aligned box.
Unbounded	`int Unbounded() const;`
	This function returns nonzero if the axis-aligned box is unbounded.

friend Functions

Intersection	`AxisAlignedBox Intersect(const AxisAlignedBox&, const AxisAlignedBox&);`
	This function computes the intersection of the two boxes given, and returns the result. If they are disjoint, there is no intersection, and it returns a bounding box with `min` and `max` set to the zero vector.
Transform	`AxisAlignedBox Transform(const AxisAlignedBox&, const Matrix&);`
	This function applies a transformation to each of the vertices of the axis-aligned box and returns the smallest axis-aligned box that encloses all of the transformed points.
Union	`AxisAlignedBox Union(const AxisAlignedBox&, const AxisAlignedBox&);`
	This function returns the union of the two axis-aligned boxes.

BoundingBox class	object3d.h/bbox.cpp
	Hierarchy: Object3D

Encapsulates an axis-aligned bounding box. As such, this class inherits from both `AxisAlignedBox` and `BoundingVolume`. Since `BoundingVolume` inherits from `Object3D`, `BoundingBox` is a type of `Object3D`.

Bounding boxes are described in Section 4.7.

Member functions

Constructors

`BoundingBox();`

Sets the bounding box to the opposite of an unbounded box (`min` = (MAXFLOAT, MAXFLOAT, MAXFLOAT); `max` = -MAXFLOAT, -MAXFLOAT, -MAXFLOAT). This guarantees that anything added to the box will update the `min` and `max` vectors.

`BoundingBox(const Vector3D& min, const Vector3D& max);`

Sets the `min` and `max` vectors of the bounding box to the parameters.

`BoundingBox(AxisAlignedBox&);`

Sets the bounding box to the same dimensions as the axis-aligned box given.

Surface Area

`virtual float SurfaceArea() const;`

Returns the surface area of the bounding box.

BoundingVolume abstract class	object3d.h/bbox.cpp
	Hierarchy: Object3D

Bounding volumes are invisible objects that enclose other objects. Usually, bounding volumes are more efficient to intersect with a ray than the objects they enclose (either because the objects are complex or because the bounding volume encloses many objects). If the ray misses the bounding volume, none of the objects it encloses have to be intersected with the ray. When arranged in a hierarchy, bounding volumes can very effectively speed up ray tracing. (Bounding volume hierarchies are discussed in Section 5.1.)

Data members	
Contents	`ObjectList contents;`
	A list of objects contained in the `BoundingVolume`.

Member functions	
Add Object	`virtual void AddObject(const Object3D& NewObj);`
	`virtual void AddObject(Object3D *NewObj);`
	Adds the given object to the list of objects in the bounding volume.
Constructor	`BoundingVolume();`
	Calls `Object3D::Object3D` to set `flags` to `BOUNDING`.
List	`virtual ObjectList *List();`
	Returns a pointer to the list of objects in the bounding volume.
NumChildren	`virtual int NumChildren();`
	Returns the number of objects enclosed by the bounding volume. Note: If the bounding volume contains other bounding volumes, their contents are not included in this count.
Surface Area	`virtual float SurfaceArea() const = 0;`
	Returns the surface area of the bounding volume.

`Bozo` class	`texture.h/texture.cpp` Hierarchy: `Texture`

`Bozo` maps the solid noise function directly into a color map. It can be used to very effectively model clouds (see the `Clouds` function in the Utilities library, which makes use of `Bozo`).

Data members	
Turbulence	`float turbulence;`

Turbulence applied to the noise function.

BumpMap abstract class	bump.h/bump.cpp

`BumpMap` roots a hierarchy of objects that alter the surface geometry at an intersection point (see Figure B.1). They optionally modify the position of the intersection point (displacement mapping), the normal at the intersection point (bump mapping), or both. See Section 6.2 for a discussion of bump mapping.

Derived classes of `BumpMap` frequently use solid noise functions (the `NoiseMaker` class hierarchy) to determine how to alter the surface geometry.

Member functions	
Dup	`virtual BumpMap *Dup() const = 0;`

Creates and returns a duplicate of the `BumpMap`.

Perturb Normal	`virtual void PerturbNormal(ShadingInfo& shade) = 0;`

Using the information in the ShadingInfo structure, this function modifies the local geometry of the point at `shade.p`.

See Also: `Texture` class hierarchy

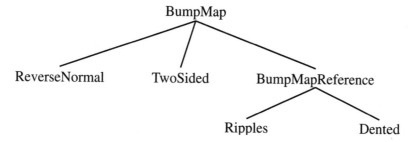

Figure B.1 BumpMap class hierarchy.

`Checkerboard` class	`texture.h/texture.cpp`
	Hierarchy: `Texture`

`Checkerboard` tiles a plane with two other textures. It uses an optional inverse mapping to map onto the plane.

Data members

Size

```
float xsize, ysize;
```
X and Y sizes of the rectangles that tile the plane.

Textures

```
Texture *text1, *text2;
```
These two `Textures` are used to tile the plane with rectangles of the given size.

Member functions

Constructor

```
Checkerboard(float XSize, float YSize,
Texture *Text1, Texture *Text2, const
Matrix& ref, Mapping *map = 0);
```
Constructs a `Checkerboard` with the given size, textures, reference matrix and inverse mapping.

`CircularMapping` class	`mapping.h/mapping.cpp`
	Hierarchy: `Mapping`

This class implements an inverse mapping into a circle. See Section 6.4.1 for a discussion of the circular inverse mapping.

Data members

Radius

```
float radius;
```
Radius of the circle being mapped onto.

Member functions

Constructor

```
CircularMapping(float r=1);
```
Creates a mapping that maps onto a circle of radius r centered about the origin.

`ColorMap` **class**   `colormap.h/texture.cpp`

`ColorMap` translates a floating-point value into a color. It is used by textures such as `Bozo` and `Wood` to determine the color of a point in space. Section 6.4.3 discusses color maps.

Data members	

Entries   `ColorMapEntry **entries;`

Array of entries in the `ColorMap`. Since `ColorMap-Entry` is an abstract class, each element in the array points to the instance of `ColorMapEntry`.

Num Entries   `int num_entries;`

The number of `ColorMapEntries` in the `ColorMap`.

Member functions	

Add Entry   `void AddEntry(ColorMapEntry *);`

Adds an entry to the color map.

Compute Color   `RGBColor ComputeColor(float value);`

Each entry in the `ColorMap` is asked in turn whether `value` is in its range. The first that responds in the affirmative is asked to translate the value to a color. If no entry in the color map can translate the value, this function returns black.

Constructor   `ColorMap();`

Creates a `ColorMap` with no entries.

`ColorMapEntry` **abstract class**   `colormap.h/texture.cpp`

The `ColorMapEntry` class helps `ColorMap` turn floating-point values into color coefficients. Every `ColorMap` contains an array of `ColorMapEntries` (see Figure B.2). See Section 6.4.3 for a discussion of color maps.

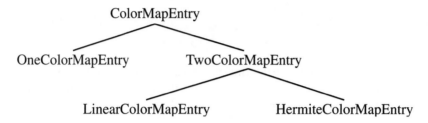

Figure B.2 `ColorMapEntry` class hierarchy.

Data members	
Interval	`float start, end;`
	Gives the interval of floating-point values that this `ColorMapEntry` is able to translate into colors.

Member functions	
Default Constructor	`ColorMapEntry();`
	Does nothing, but is provided because it has to be called when an array of `ColorMapEntry` is allocated by a `ColorMap`.
Constructor	`ColorMapEntry(float s, float e);`
	Creates a `ColorMapEntry` that spans the given interval.
Dup	`virtual ColorMapEntry *Dup() const = 0;`
	Creates a duplicate of the `ColorMapEntry` and returns a pointer to it.
IsInside	`virtual int IsInside(float value);`
	Returns nonzero if the given value falls within the `ColorMapEntry`'s interval.
Fraction	`float fract(float value);`
	Returns the fraction that the given value goes into the interval [`start`, `end`]. If `value` is equal to `start`, `fract` returns 0. If `value` is equal to `end`, `fract` returns 1. Otherwise `fract` returns a value between 0 and 1 indicating where `value` falls in the interval.

ConicalMapping class

`mapping.h/mapping.cpp`
Hierarchy: `Mapping`

Maps points onto a cone centered about the Y axis. See Section 6.4.1 for a discussion of the conical inverse mapping.

Data members

Height

```
float height;
```
Height of the cone.

Radius (height)

```
float radh;
```
Radius of the cone at the plane Y = height.

Radius (origin)

```
float rad0;
```
Radius of the cone at the origin.

Member functions

Constructor

```
ConicalMapping(float Rad0, float Radh,
float Height);
```
Creates a `ConicalMapping` with the given parameters.

CSGDifference class

`object3d.h/csg.cpp`
Hierarchy: `Object3D`

Encapsulates the CSG difference of two objects. The right-hand child of this CSG primitive is subtracted from the left-hand child. See Section 8.1 for a description of the CSG difference operation.

Member functions

Constructors

```
CSGDifference(Object3D *Left, Object3D
*Right);
```
Creates an object that is the right-hand object subtracted from the left-hand object.

`CSGObject` abstract class	`object3d.h/csg.cpp`
	Hierarchy: `Object3D`

`CSGObject` roots a hierarchy of CSG primitives. Functions common to the derived classes are implemented in `CSGObject`. For example, `CSGObject::ApplyTransform` applies a transform to the left and right children of the `CSGObject`. There is no need for derived classes of `CSGObject` to overload this behavior.

See Section 8.1 for a description of CSG operations.

Data members

Children   `Object3D *left, *right;`

The left and right children of the `CSGObject`.

Member functions

Constructors   `CSGObject(Object3D *Left, Object3D *Right);`

Creates a CSG object with the given left and right children.

`CSGUnion` class	`object3d.h/csg.cpp`
	Hierarchy: `Object3D`

Encapsulates the union of two objects. This CSG operation is described in Section 8.1.

Member functions

Constructors   `CSGUnion(Object3D *Left, Object3D *Right);`

Creates an object which is the union of the two objects given.

`CylindricalMapping` class	`mapping.h/mapping.cpp`
	Hierarchy: `Mapping`

Maps points onto a cylinder centered about the Y axis. The cylindrical mapping is described in Section 6.4.1.

Data members	
Height	`float height;`
	Height of the tiles being mapped onto.
Radius	`float radius;`
	Radius of the cylinder.

Member functions	
Constructor	`CylindricalMapping(float Radius, float Height);`
	Creates a `CylindricalMapping` with the given parameters.

`DirectLight` class	`light.h`/`light.cpp`
	Hierarchy: `Light`

`DirectLight` encapsulates a directional light source that is infinitely far away. Light emanating from a directional light source always comes from the same direction.

Member functions	
Constructor	`DirectLight(const Vector3D& dir, const RGBColor& clr);`
	`dir` points *toward* the direction the light is coming *from*. `clr` is the color of light emanated by the light source.

`Ellipsoid` class	`object3d.h`/`quadric.cpp`
	Hierarchy: `Object3D`

An ellipsoid is a bounded quadric surface. Figure 4.1 gives a taxonomy of quadric surfaces and contains an ellipsoid; Section 4.5 describes the operations supported with quadric surfaces.

Data members	
Radii	`float a, b, c;`
	a, b, and c are the X, Y, and Z radii of the ellipse.
Bounding Box	`BoundingBox bbox;`
	This bounding box starts out bounding the ellipse, and is updated whenever the ellipse is transformed. (It becomes less and less tight as more transformations are applied.)

Member functions	
Constructor	`Ellipsoid(float Xrad, float Yrad, float Zrad, Surface *NewColor);`
	Creates an ellipsoid with the given X, Y, and Z radii, centered about the origin. For ellipsoids that are not centered about the origin or aligned with the coordinate axes, transform this canonical ellipsoid.

`Granite` class   `texture.h/texture.cpp`
Hierarchy: `Texture`

This class encapsulates a granite texture after Upstill [UPST90, p. 354]. Both the ambient and diffuse components of a surface must use the coefficient of reflection returned by this texture, so the Utilities library provides a `MakeGranite` function that returns the surface.

Constructor	`Granite(const RGBColor _K, const Matrix& _reference = IdentityMatrix());`
	Creates a granite texture that reflects the given color.

`HallSurface` class   `surface.h/surface.cpp`
Hierarchy: `Surface`

`HallSurface` encapsulates a naive implementation of the Hall shading model, as described in Chapter 3. To shade a point, it uses a bump map to modify the local geometry of the point, then sums the ambient, diffuse, specular, reflected, and transmitted components of the shading equation to compute the color at the point.

Data members

Bump Map `BumpMap *NewNormal;`

If nonzero, this bump map is used to alter the local geometry of the intersection point before shading.

Ambient `Texture *Ambient;`

If nonzero, this `Texture` is used to compute the coefficient of ambient reflection for the `Surface`.

Diffuse `Texture *Diffuse;`

If nonzero, this `Texture` is used to compute the coefficient of diffuse reflection for the `Surface`.

Specular `Texture *Specular;`

If nonzero, this `Texture` is used to compute the coefficient of specular reflection for the `Surface`.

Specularity `float specnum;`

Gives the specularity, as described in Chapter 3.

Reflection `Texture *Reflect;`

If nonzero, this `Texture` is used to compute the coefficient of reflection for the `Surface`.

Transmission `Texture *Transmit;`

If nonzero, this `Texture` is used to compute the coefficient of transparency for the `Surface`.

IOR `float index;`

Index of refraction for the surface.

Shade Light `RGBColor diffuse, specular;`

Contain the precomputed coefficients of reflection required by `ShadeLight`.

Heap class template	heap.h

Binary heaps are described by Bentley [BENT86] and Cormen, Leiserson, and Rivest [CORM90]. They efficiently support the operations Insert, Min, and ExtractMin, and can be used to implement a sorting routine which, unlike Quicksort, has a worst-case performance of $O(N\lg N)$ rather than $O(N^2)$.

In many ways, a heap is like a binary tree. The heap has a root, and each node starting with the root has up to two children. However, the invariant for a binary heap is different than that for a binary tree: the children of a node in a binary heap are guaranteed to be greater than the node itself. With this invariant, the elements in the heap can be kept in a simple array; if the array is based at `elms`, the root is `elms[0]`. The children of any node `elms[i]` are `elms[i*2+1]` (the left child) and `elms[i*2+2]` (the right child).

Min

Because the heap property demands that every node in the heap be smaller than its children, the root node contains the smallest in the heap. Using the array representation described above, the root node is the first element in the array.

Insertion

When inserted into a binary heap, the new element is tacked onto the end of the array. This is likely to break the heap property for the heap, since the new element is not likely to be larger than its parents. To fix the heap, we perform an operation that Bentley calls SiftUp [BENT86]: as long as the new element's parent is larger than the new element, we swap the new element with its parent.

If the new element is the new minimum of the heap, we have to swap it with its parents all the way up until it is the root of the heap. In this worst case, only $O(\lg N)$ swaps will be made for a heap that contains N elements. Thus, inserting N elements into a heap requires $O(N\lg N)$ time.

ExtractMin

The minimum element of the heap is the first element in the heap's array. Extracting this minimum element breaks the heap property, because it leaves a void in the first element of the array. To fix the heap, the smaller of the root's children must be moved into the root position. This is the new minimum of the heap. However, moving the smaller of the root's children leaves a void where *it* was; the smaller of its children must be moved into this void. This process must be repeated until there is no more empty element in the heap. Bentley terms this process SiftDown.

Like SiftUp, SiftDown is an O(lgN) procedure, so for a heap with N elements, it takes O(NlgN) time to perform N ExtractMin operations.

The HeapSort algorithm combines Insert and ExtractMin to construct a sorting algorithm with worst-case running time of O(NlgN). First, insert the N elements to be sorted into a binary heap. Then perform N ExtractMin operations on the heap, placing the return values into the array in sorted order. Since the N insertions require O(NlgN) time and the N ExtractMin operations require O(NlgN) time, the worst-case performance of the algorithm is O(NlgN). HeapSort is more of theoretical interest than practical interest, however: for general purpose sorting, QuickSort is much faster on average.

Implementation

`heap.h` contains a class template for a generic family of binary heaps. `Heap<int>` is a "heap of integers" class; `Heap<UserDefinedClass>` is a "heap of `UserDefinedClass`" class. For more information on parameterized data types such as `Heap`, see Appendix A. Appendix A also gives references so you can read about them in books that concentrate on C++.

Although it's tempting to use `operator<` to order the objects in the `Heap`, this makes it slightly harder to place pointers to objects into the heap instead of the objects themselves. Using `operator<` directly on the pointers will cause the pointers themselves to be compared. That's not what we want at all! We want the *objects pointed to* to be compared. Instead of using `operator<`, the `Heap` class template uses a global function named `Compare` to order items in the heap. That way, the global `Compare` can be defined to take two pointers to the objects being ordered and dereference them to make the comparison.

`Compare` returns an `int` that tells how the two objects should be ordered. If the first object given to `Compare` is less than the second, `Compare` returns a negative integer. If the second is less than the first, `Compare` returns a positive integer. Otherwise, `Compare` returns 0. This interface is similar to using the `qsort` or `bsearch` library functions defined in ANSI C.

Data members	
Elements	`T *elms;`
	Points to the base of the array of heap contents.

Maximum size	`int maxsize;`
	The number of elements in `elms`. `maxsize` is greater than or equal to n, because only the first n elements of `elms` are the contents of the `Heap`. When `maxsize` objects have been inserted, the next insertion operation will cause `Heap` to reallocate `elms` and increase `maxsize`.
Number	`int n;`
	The number of elements in the array.

Member functions

Assignment	`Heap<T>& operator= (const Heap<T>&);`
	The assignment operator destroys the current contents of the `Heap` and replaces them with a copy of the parameter's contents.
Constructor	`Heap();`
	The default constructor allocates two empty elements (n = 0, `maxsize` = 2).
Extract Minimum	`T ExtractMin();`
	Extracts the minimum element from the `Heap` and returns it. It fixes the heap property for the `Heap` after extracting the minimum; this is an O(lgN) operation for a `Heap` that contains N elements. No error checking is performed to ensure that a minimum element is in the `Heap` to be extracted.
Insertion	`void Insert(const T& x);`
	Inserts a copy of x into the `Heap`. A global function `int Compare(T, T)` is used to order elements in the `Heap`. If the first parameter precedes the second in a sorted order, `Compare` returns a negative value; if the first parameter comes after the second in a sorted order, `Compare` returns a positive value. Otherwise, `Compare` returns 0.
Minimum	`T Min() const;`
	Returns a copy of the `Heap`'s minimum element. This is a constant-time operation.

Number	`int N() const;`

Returns the number of elements in the `Heap`.

SiftDown	`void SiftDown();`

Assumes that the heap property has been broken because the minimum element was extracted. To fix the heap property, the minimum of the root's children is moved into the root position. This element is the new minimum of the heap. Moving it into the root position leaves a void in its original spot, however, so the minimum of that position's two children must be moved into the newly vacated location in the heap. This process must be repeated $O(\lg N)$ times for a heap of size N.

`SiftDown` can only be called by other member functions of `Heap`.

SiftUp	`void SiftUp(int i);`

Assumes that the heap property has been broken because an out-of-order element was placed at the end. (`i` is the index of the new element.) To fix the heap property, the new element is compared with its parent; if smaller, the two are swapped to maintain the heap property. The new element is then compared with its new parent and the process is repeated, if necessary.

`SiftUp` can only be called by other member functions of `Heap`.

`ImageFile` **abstract class**   `texture.h/texture.cpp`

`ImageFile` provides a uniform way for the `ImageMap` texture uniformly deal with different file formats (see Figure B.3).

Data members

Size	`int width, height;`

Width and height of the image.

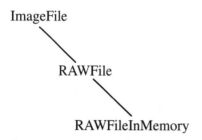

ImageFile

RAWFile

RAWFileInMemory

Figure B.3 `ImageFile` class hierarchy.

Member functions	
Constructor	`ImageFile();`
	The default constructor does nothing; constructors for derived classes are expected to fill in width and height.
GetPixel	`virtual RGBColor GetPixel(int x, int y) = 0;`
	Returns the pixel in the image at (x, y). The upper-left corner of the image is (0, 0), and the lower-right corner is (width–1, height–1). If (x, y) is outside this range, `GetPixel` returns black.
Width	`virtual int Width();`
	Returns the width of the image.
Height	`virtual int Height();`
	Returns the height of the image.

`ImageMap` class	`texture.h/texture.cpp` Hierarchy: `Texture`

This `Texture` maps images onto objects. It derives from `TextureMapping`, since it usually requires an inverse mapping to map the image properly.
Data members

File	`ImageFile *file;`
	The image to map.

Interpolate	`int interp;`
	If nonzero, bilinear interpolation is performed.
Once	`int once;`
	If nonzero, the image is mapped once rather than tiled.
Scale	`Vector3D scale;`
	This scale factor is applied to the vector after preprocessing.

Member functions

Constructors

```
ImageMap(const Matrix& ref, Mapping
*map, int Interp, int Once, char *file-
name, float xscale = 1, float yscale =
1);
```

```
ImageMap(const Matrix& ref, Mapping
*map, int Interp, int Once, ImageFile
*file, float xscale = 1, float yscale =
1);
```

These constructors both take the reference matrix (`ref`) and inverse mapping (`map`); `Interp` is nonzero if the texture is to linearly interpolate; `Once` is nonzero if the texture is to be mapped only once rather than tiled; `filename` or `file` gives the file that contains the image to be mapped; and the x and y scale factors to apply after the mapping are given.

InRange function template   oort.h

```
template<class T>
inline int
InRange(T min, T max, T candidate);
```

Returns nonzero if $min \leq candidate \leq max$.

`InverseRayObject` abstract class   `object3d.h/alg.cpp`
Hierarchy: `Object3D`

`InverseRayObject` encapsulates objects with a canonical representation. Instead of transforming the object, rays are transformed to the canonical coordinate system of the object. To that end, `InverseRayObject` contains two matrices, `mat` and `inv`. `mat` transforms rays to the canonical coordinate system of the object. `inv` transforms them back. Both `mat` and `inv` start out as identity matrices and are updated appropriately as `InverseRayObject::ApplyTransform` is called.

A number of **protected** member functions, described below, allow derived classes to easily transform rays and points between the world coordinate system and the object's canonical coordinate system.

Data members

Forward Matrix   `Matrix mat;`

This matrix is used to transform rays and points into the canonical coordinate system of the object.

Inverse Matrix   `Matrix inv;`

This matrix is used to transform rays and points from the canonical coordinate system of the object.

Member functions

Forward Transform   `Ray TransformRay(Ray&);`

`Vector3D TransformPt(const Vector3D&);`

`Vector3D RotatePt(const Vector3D&);`

These functions transform the given object from the world coordinate system to the object's canonical coordinate system.

Inverse Transform   `Ray InvertRay(Ray&);`

`Vector3D InvertPt(const Vector3D&);`

`Vector3D InvRotatePt(const Vector3D&);`

These functions transform the given object from the object's canonical coordinate system to the world coordinate system.

Transform	`virtual void ApplyTransform(const` `Matrix&);`

Applies a transform to the object by updating the `mat` and `inv` matrices.

`KayKajiyaNode` class	`oort.h/world.cpp`

This class is used to help traverse the bounding volume hierarchy to find the nearest intersection along a ray. It is named after the bounding volume hierarchy traversal algorithm of Kay and Kajiya [KAY86]. It contains information about bounding volumes that have been intersected but have not yet been "opened" for further intersection tests. The algorithm expects that closer bounding volumes are more likely to contain the nearest intersection. The bounding volumes that have been intersected are inserted into a heap and investigated in order of minimum parameter of intersection (using the ExtractMin feature of the heap data structure).

Data members

Object	`Object3D *obj;`

Pointer to the bounding volume intersected.

Parameter	`float t;`

This gives the parameter of intersection for the bounding volume with the ray.

friend Functions

Compare	`int Compare(KayKajiyaNode *,` `KayKajiyaNode *);`

This function is used by `Heap<KayKajiyaNode *>` to order the nodes when traversing the bounding volume hierarchy.

Light abstract class	light.h/light.cpp

The `Light` class encapsulates the different types of light source supported by OORT (see Figure B.4). Light sources account for the diffuse and specular components of the shading equation; when a shading equation is being evaluated and the diffuse or specular components is nonzero, one or more shadow rays must be cast at each light source in the scene to determine how much light is arriving at the intersection point. This amount of light is combined with the coefficients of diffuse and specular reflection as described in Chapter 3, to determine those components of the shading equation at the intersection point.

Data members

Color

`RGBColor Color;`

Color of the light emitted.

Attenuation

`float c1, c2, c3;`

These numbers describe the light source's attenuation by distance. The expression is as follows:

$$\frac{1}{c_1 + c_2 d + c_3 d^2}$$

where d is the distance to the light source. (Note: If the above expression yields a number greater than 1, the attenuation is 1.) If $c_1 = 1$ and $c_2 = c_3 = 0$, then the light source is not attenuated by distance. If c_1 and c_2 are 0, then the light source is attenuated in proportion to the square of the distance (the physically correct model).

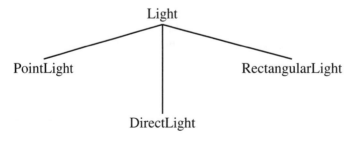

Figure B.4 `Light` class hierarchy

Shadow Cache	`Object3D *LastOpaque;`

Points to an opaque object that obscured the light source (if any). If an object obscures the light source for one shadow ray, there is a good chance it will also obscure the light source for subsequent shadow rays. So whenever an opaque object obscures the light source, `LastOpaque` is set to it. When casting shadow rays, if `LastOpaque` is nonzero, the shadow ray is intersected with it. If the ray hits `LastOpaque`, then we immediately know that the shadow ray's origin is in shadow and we need not perform any more intersection calculations.

Member functions

Constructor	`Light(const RGBColor& clr, float C1, float C2, float C3);`

Copies the parameters to data members and sets `LastOpaque` to 0.

Attenuation	`float DistAtten(Ray& ray, float maxt);`

Computes the attenuation due to distance of the ray.

Cache Check	`int HitCachedObject(Ray& ray, float maxt);`

Returns nonzero if `ray` hits `LastOpaque`. If it misses, `LastOpaque` is reset to 0.

Sample Light	`virtual RGBColor ShadowLight(ShadingInfo& shade, Surface *surf) = 0;`

Fires a collection of rays according to the type of light source. Point light sources, which are infinitely small, and directional light sources, which are infinitely far away, require only one shadow ray to sample; however, rectangular light sources are extended light sources that require multiple shadow rays to sample. The return value is the amount of light arriving from this light source.

Transform	`virtual void ApplyTransform(const Matrix&) = 0;`

Applies the transform to the `Light`.

Shadow Ray

```
virtual ShadowRay(ShadingInfo& shade,
Vector3D& target, Surface *Surf);
```

Casts a shadow ray from the origin `shade.p` at the vector `target`. This function is used by `Light::Shadow-Light` implementations to sample the light source.

Note: This member function is protected (accessible only by member functions and classes that inherit from `Light`).

`Limits` class	`limits.h/main.cpp`

`Limits` contains a number of related global variables. They all have to do with limits imposed by the inaccuracies of floating-point values.

Data members

Infinity

```
static float Infinity;
```

Numbers are guaranteed to be smaller than this member of `Limits`. The default value is `MAXFLOAT`.

Small

```
static float Small;
```

Numbers smaller than this member of `Limits` are considered to be zero (as when checking whether a divide-by-zero will occur).

Threshold

```
static float Threshold;
```

Threshold of no-intersection. Intersections with a positive parameter of intersection will still return no-intersection if the parameter is smaller than this member. This feature is to keep rays spawned off an object from immediately hitting the same object again.

`Matrix` class	`matrix.h/matrix.cpp`

`Matrix` encapsulates a 4×4 transformation matrix. They are used to apply transformations to 3D vectors, as described in Chapter 1. Besides operations such as matrix addition, subtraction and multiplication, a wide variety of **friend** functions provide ways to create transformation matrices.

Member functions

Addition

```
Matrix& operator+= (const Matrix&);
```

Adds the `Matrix` given.

Invert

```
void Invert();
```

Inverts the `Matrix` using Gaussian elimination.

Multiplication (matrix)

```
Matrix& operator*= (const Matrix&);
```

Multiplies the `Matrix` by the `Matrix` given.

Multiplication (scalar)

```
Matrix& operator*= (float);
```

Multiplies each element in the `Matrix` by the `float`.

Subtraction

```
Matrix& operator-= (const Matrix&);
```

Subtracts the `Matrix` given.

Transpose

```
void Transpose();
```

Transposes the `Matrix`.

friend Functions

Invert

```
Matrix Invert(const Matrix&);
```

Inverts the `Matrix` given and returns the result.

Transpose

```
Matrix Transpose(const Matrix&);
```

Transposes the `Matrix` given and returns the result.

Addition

```
Matrix operator+ (const Matrix&, const
Matrix&);
```

Adds the two matrices given and returns the result.

Subtraction

```
Matrix operator- (const Matrix&, const
Matrix&);
```

Subtracts the second `Matrix` from the first and returns the result.

Multiplication (matrix)	`Matrix operator* (const Matrix, const Matrix&);`
	Multiplies the first `Matrix` by the second and returns the result.
Multiplication (scalar)	`Matrix operator* (const Matrix&, float);`
	`Matrix operator* (float, const Matrix&);`
	Multiplies each element of the `Matrix` by the float and returns the result.
Transformation	`Vector3D operator* (const Vector3D&, const Matrix&);`
	Converts the 3D vector to its homogeneous representation (W = 1), multiplies it by the matrix, then converts the homogeneous representation back to 3D by dividing through by the W coordinate.
Rotate Only	`Vector3D operator* (const Vector3D&, const Matrix&);`
	Transforms the vector, but only applies the upper 3×3 submatrix. This rotates the vector without applying the translation or perspective portions of the matrix.

`Matrix`-creation functions

These functions create matrices according to the parameters given. They are all declared **friends** of `Matrix`.

Note: Angles are measured in radians.

Identity	`Matrix IdentityMatrix();`
	Returns the 4×4 identity matrix.
Mirror	`Matrix MirrorX();`
	`Matrix MirrorY();`
	`Matrix MirrorZ();`
	Creates a matrix that reflects about the X, Y, or Z axis.

Quadric	```Matrix QuadricMatrix(float a, float b, float c, float d, float e, float f, float g, float h, float j, float k);```
	Creates the matrix for the quadric with the given coefficients.
Rotation (any axis)	```Matrix RotationAxisMatrix(const Vector3D& axis, float angle);```
	Creates a matrix that rotates `angle` radians about the vector given by `axis`.
Rotation (general)	```Matrix GenRotation(const Vector3D& x, const Vector3D& y, const Vector3D& z);```
	Creates a matrix that rotates points into a coordinate system where the +X axis corresponds to `x`, the +Y axis corresponds to `y`, and the +Z axis corresponds to `z`. `x`, `y`, and `z` should be mutually perpendicular unit vectors.
Rotation (x axis)	```Matrix RotationXMatrix(float angle);```
	Creates a matrix to rotate about the X axis by the given angle.
Rotation (y axis)	```Matrix RotationYMatrix(float angle);```
	Creates a matrix to rotate about the Y axis by the given angle.
Rotation (yaw-pitch-roll)	```Matrix RotationYPRMatrix(float yaw, float pitch, float roll);```
	Creates a matrix that rotates `yaw` radians about the Y axis, then `pitch` radians in the plane defined by the first rotation, then `roll` radians about the axis defined by the first two rotations.
Rotation (z axis)	```Matrix RotationZMatrix(float angle);```
	Creates a matrix to rotate about the Z axis by the given angle.
Rotation Only	```Matrix RotationOnly(const Matrix&);```
	Extracts the upper-left `float` 3×3 submatrix of the matrix given, and returns the result.

Scale	`Matrix ScaleMatrix(float x, float y, float z);`
	Creates a matrix that scales by the given amounts in x, y, and z.
Translation	`Matrix TranslationMatrix(const Vector3D&);`
	Creates a translation matrix to translate by the given vector.
View transform	`Matrix ViewMatrix(const Vector3D& LookAt, const Vector3D& Viewer, const Vector3D& Up);`
	Creates a matrix that translates so that `Viewer` is at the origin, `LookAt` lies down the –Z axis from `Viewer` and `Up` corresponds to the Y axis. Applying this matrix to each object in the scene to be rendered places them in a uniform coordinate system that greatly simplifies ray tracing.
Zero	`Matrix ZeroMatrix();`
	Returns the zero matrix.

`Object3D` **abstract class**	`object3d.h/object3d.cpp`

`Object3D` provides an abstract definition of a primitive, ray traceable object supported by OORT. It contains a minimum of data members, and its member functions are designed to be overloaded by classes that inherit from `Object3D` to implement the behavior required of them (see Figure B.5). These functions are described in detail in Section 4.1.

Data members	
Flags	`int flags;`
	A limited amount of information about the object. The least significant bits of the integer are nonzero if the object meets certain criteria. For example, (`flags & BOUND-ING`) is nonzero if the object is a bounding box. For a

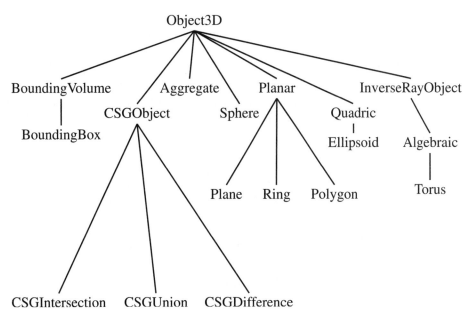

Figure B.5 `Object3D` class hierarchy.

complete list of the values that this variable can attain, see the table below.

Surface

`Surface *surf;`

Surface information for the object. Whenever a point on the object's surface must be shaded, this member is used to do it.

Definitions for `flags`:

Define	Value	Meaning
BOUNDING	1	Object is a bounding volume.
CSG	2	Object is a CSG primitive.
AGGREGATE	4	Object is an Aggregate.

Member functions

All Intersections

`virtual SpanList`
`*FindAllIntersections(Ray& ray) = 0;`

Computes all intersections of the object with the given ray. If there are none, it returns 0. Otherwise, it returns a

`SpanList` that contains the spans where the ray traverses the object.

BBox	`virtual AxisAlignedBox BBox() const;`

Returns the bounding box of the object. The return value is unbounded by default; the function must be overloaded to modify this behavior.

Constructors	`Object3D(int);`
	`Object3D(Surface *, int);`

These constructors copy the flags and surface information into the object.

CountMe	`virtual void CountMe() const = 0;`

Increments a global variable corresponding to the number of a certain type of object. For example, `Sphere::CountMe` increments `Statistics::Objects::Sphere`.

Describe	`virtual void Describe(int ind) const = 0;`

Writes a description of the object to `cout`, first indenting by `ind` spaces.

Dup	`virtual Object3D *Dup() const = 0;`

Creates a duplicate of the object and returns a pointer to it.

Flags	`int Flags();`

Provides read-only access to the `flags` member of `Object3D`.

HitAtAll	`virtual int HitAtAll(Ray& ray, float maxt);`

Returns nonzero if the given ray intersects the object with parameter of intersection less than `maxt`.

IsInside	`virtual int IsInside(Vector3D& v) = 0;`

Returns nonzero if the given point is inside the object, 0 if not.

Nearest Intersection	```virtual Object3D *NearestInt(Ray& ray, float& t, float maxt) = 0;```
	Intersects the object with the given ray. If the ray intersects the object and the parameter of intersection is greater than `Limits::Threshold` and smaller than `maxt`, then `t` is written with the smallest parameter of intersection and the function returns nonzero (a pointer to the object the ray intersects, usually this).
Normal	```virtual Vector3D FindNormal(const Vector3D&) = 0;```
	Returns the normal to the object at the given intersection point. The return value of this function is guaranteed to be normalized (have unit magnitude).
NumChildren	```virtual int NumChildren();```
	Returns the number of children the object has. This is defined to be 0, except for bounding volumes.
PtDistance	```virtual float PtDistance(Vector3D& v) = 0;```
	Returns a signed distance estimate of the given vector to the surface.
Shading	```virtual RGBColor ShadeObject(World& world, Ray& ray, Vector3D& NearestIntion, int depth);```
	This function shades the object at the given intersection point.
Surface Access	```Surface *ReturnColor() const;```
	```void OverrideColor(Surface *NewColor);```
	These member functions provide access to the object's surface information.
Transform	```virtual void ApplyTransform(const Matrix&) = 0;```
	Applies a 4×4 transformation matrix to the object.

Transform Surface
```
virtual void
TransformSurface(SurfaceList& clist,
const Matrix& tform);
```
Applies the transformation to the `Surface` associated with the object.

`OneColorMapEntry` class   `colormap.h/colormap.cpp`
Hierarchy: `ColorMapEntry`

Encapsulates a color map entry that translates all values given to it into one color. Color maps are discussed in Section 6.4.3.

Data members

Color
```
RGBColor clr;
```
Color returned by the color map entry.

Member functions

Constructor
```
OneColorMapEntry(float _start, float
_end, const RGBColor& _clr);
```
Creates a color map entry with the given interval and color.

`Planar` abstract class   `object3d.h/plane.cpp`
Hierarchy: `Object3D`

This class roots a hierarchy of planar objects. It implements much of the functionality needed by the objects that derive from it, such as intersection with a ray. Planar objects are discussed in Section 4.2.

Data members

Normal
```
Vector3D Normal;
```
Normal to the plane.

Distance
```
float d;
```
Signed distance of the plane from the origin.

Bad	`int bad;`

If the plane was created with a normal of zero length, this integer is set to nonzero and all intersection tests return no-intersection (rather than crashing the computer).

Member functions

Constructors	`Planar(Surface *);`

Creates a `Planar` object with the given surface characteristics. Presumably a derived class is going to set the data members.

```
Planar(float A, float B, float C, float
D, Surface *NewColor);
```

```
Planar(const Vector3D& norm, float D,
Surface *NewColor);
```

Creates a `Planar` object with the given plane equation and surface characteristics.

`Plane` class	`object3d.h/planar.cpp` **Hierarchy:** `Object3D`

Encapsulates an infinite plane. Planes are discussed in Section 4.2.

Data members

`Plane` inherits all of its data members from `Planar`.

Member functions

Constructors	`Plane(float A, float B, float C, float` `D, Surface *NewColor);`

```
Plane(const Vector3D& norm, float D,
Surface *NewColor);
```

Creates a plane with the given plane equation.

`PointLight` class	`light.h/light.cpp`
	Hierarchy: `Light`

`PointLight` encapsulates a point light source.

Constructor

`PointLight(const Vector3D& loc, const RGBColor& clr, float c1 = 1, float c2 = 0, float c3 = 0);`

`loc` gives the location that light emanates from. `clr` gives the color of the light emanated. `c1`, `c2` and `c3` give the attenuation due to distance of the light source (see `Light` for the formula for attenuation due to distance).

`Polynomial` class	`poly.h/poly.cpp`

`Polynomial` encapsulates a polynomial in one variable. It is used to compute the intersections of an arbitrary algebraic surface with a ray. See Section 8.2 for a discussion of algebraic surfaces.

Many operators have been overloaded for `Polynomial`, including unary + and −, addition, subtraction, multiplication, and remainder. The functions declared to overload these operators are not described below.

Data members

Coefficients

`double *coeff;`

Coefficients of the polynomial, in increasing degree.

Epsilon

`static double SMALL_ENOUGH;`

A coefficient of magnitude smaller than `SMALL_ENOUGH` is considered to be zero (default = 10^{-12}).

Maximum Iterations

`static int MAXIT;`

Maximum number of iterations permitted the root finder (default = 800).

Maximum Power	`static int MAXPOW;`

Maximum power of 10 to search for (default = 32). Roots outside the range $[-10^{MAXPOW}, 10^{MAXPOW}]$ will not be bracketed by the root finder.

Order	`int ord;`

Order of the polynomial (there are `ord+1` coefficients in the coefficients array).

Relative Error	`static double RELERROR;`

Smallest relative error we want (default is 10^{-8}).

Member functions

Add Element	`void AddElm(int deg, double x);`

Adds x^{deg} to the `Polynomial`.

Constructors	`Polynomial();`

Sets `ord` and `coeff` to 0. Does not allocate any memory.

`Polynomial(int, double *);`

Creates the `Polynomial` with the given order and set of coefficients.

Evaluate	`double Evaluate(double x) const;`

Evaluates the polynomial at the given point and returns the result.

Find Roots	`int FindRealRoots(double **passbk);`

Computes the real roots of the `Polynomial`. The roots are allocated using `new` and passed back in `passbk`. The return value gives the number of roots found.

Regula-Falsi	`int ModRF(double a, double b, double *val);`

Uses a modified regula-falsi technique to search for a root in the region bracketed by [a, b].

Sturm Sequence	`int SturmSequence(Polynomial **);`

Computes the Sturm sequence of the polynomial. Allocates the array of `Polynomials` using `new`, then assigns the pointer to the passback parameter. The return value gives the number of elements in the array.

friend Functions

Number of Roots	`int NumRoots(Polynomial *sseq, int n,` `int *neg, int *pos);`

Computes the number of positive and negative roots for a `Polynomial`. `sseq` points to an array of `n` `Polynomials` which are the Sturm sequence; the number of negative and positive roots are passed back in `neg` and `pos`.

Sign Changes	`int NumChanges(Polynomial *sseq, int n,` `double x);`

Computes the number of sign changes in the Sturm sequence. `sseq` and `n` give the array of polynomials that is the Sturm sequence, while `x` gives the value to use when evaluating the polynomials.

Bisection	`void SBisect(Polynomial *, int, double,` `double, int, int, double *);`

Bisects a polynomial over a given range. See the code for details.

Normalization	`Normalize(const Polynomial&);`

Divides through by the coefficient of highest degree to ensure that it is ± 1.

Derivative	`Polynomial Derivative(const` `Polynomial&);`

Returns the derivative of the given `Polynomial`.

Exponent	`Polynomial Triangle(double a, double b,` `int t);`

Computes the polynomial $(ax+b)^t$ using Pascal's Triangle.

Elementary Roots

```
int SolveQuadric(double[] coeff, dou-
ble[] roots);

int SolveCubic(double[] coeff, double[]
roots);

int SolveQuartic(double[] coeff, dou-
ble[] roots);
```

Find the roots of the second-, third- and fourth-degree polynomials given in the set of coefficients. The coefficients are given in order of increasing degree; the roots are returned in the array roots. The number of roots found is given by the return value.

`Mapping` **abstract class** `mapping.h/mapping.cpp`

Implements standard inverse mappings. They generally implement an inverse mapping for some canonical object (for example, a cylinder centered along the Y axis), so the input points must be transformed to the canonical coordinate system before performing the mapping (see Figure B.6).

Section 6.4.1 discusses the inverse mappings implemented in OORT.

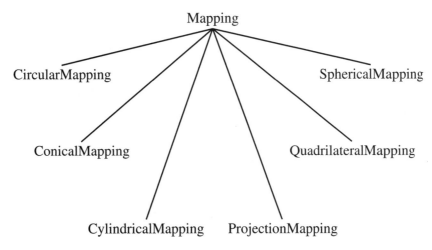

Figure B.6 `Mapping` class hierarchy.

Member functions	
Constructor	`Mapping();`
	Default constructor (does nothing, but has to be there to be called by classes that inherit from `Mapping`).
Dup	`virtual Mapping *Dup() const = 0;`
	Creates a duplicate of the `Mapping` and returns a pointer to it.
Map3DTo2D	`virtual Vector3D Map3DTo2D(const Vector3D&) = 0;`
	Maps the given vector from 3-dimensional space to 2-dimensional space. The return value is a 2-dimensional vector (it always has a Z coordinate of 0). Since the mapping is typically a canonical one, the input vector must be transformed into the canonical coordinate system before being passed to `Map3DTo2D`.

`MinDist` function	`distrib.h`/`distrib.cpp`

`float MinDist(const Vector3D& p, const Vector3D *arr, int n);`

Returns the distance from `p` to the nearest point in `arr`. `n` gives the number of elements in `arr`.

`MoreRays` global function	`distrib.h`/`distrib.cpp`

`int MoreRays(const RGBColor& min, const RGBColor& max, const RGBColor& tol);`

Called by adaptive supersampling schemes to decide whether to cast more rays. If it returns 1, more rays are needed; otherwise, it returns 0.

`MoreRays` computes the contrast of the colors given `min` and `max`. The function returns 1 if any component of the resulting contrast is higher than its corresponding component in `tol`.

`NoiseMaker` **abstract class**   `noise.h/noise.cpp`

`NoiseMaker` encapsulates a solid noise source. Solid noise functions are used by bump maps, displacement maps, and textures to vary colors and other parameters (see Figure B.7). For points that near each other, solid noise functions return similar values; however, for points that are far away, they return uncorrelated random values. See Section 6.4.2 for a discussion of solid noise functions.

Member functions	

DNoise	`virtual Vector3D DNoise(const Vector3D& x);`
	Vector-valued noise function. By default, this function implements Perlin's recommendation [PERL89]: it calls `Noise` with x, x + (some large displacement), and x − (some large displacement). The default displacement is (10000, 10000, 10000).
DTurbulence	`virtual Vector3D DTurbulence(const Vector3D& x);`
	Vector-valued turbulence function.
Noise	`virtual float Noise(const Vector3D& x) = 0;`
	Returns the noise value for the point given.

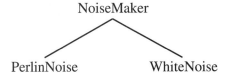

Figure B.7 `NoiseMaker` class hierarchy

Turbulence	`virtual float Turbulence(const Vector3D& x);`

This function uses `Noise` to return a model for turbulence after Perlin [PERL85]. The formula used by OORT is as follows:

$$Turbulence(\mathbf{x}) = \sum_{i=0}^{4} abs\left(\frac{1}{2^i} noise(2^i \mathbf{x})\right)$$

`PerlinNoise` class	`noise.h/noise.cpp` Hierarchy: `NoiseMaker`

Implements a solid noise function as described by Perlin [PERL89]. See Section 6.4.2 for a description of the implementation.

Member functions

Constructors	`PerlinNoise();`

Precomputes the values for the noise function using a random number seed garnered from the system clock.

`PerlinNoise(int seed);`

Precomputes the values for the noise function using the random number seed given.

`Polygon` class	`object3d.h/polygon.cpp` Hierarchy: `Object3D`

Encapsulates a planar polygon. Polygons are described in Section 4.6.

Data members

Bounding Rectangle	`float umin, umax, vmin, vmax;`

Bounding rectangle of projection. Intersection points that lie outside this bounding rectangle cannot intersect the polygon.

Num Verts	`int NumVerts;`
	Number of vertices in the polygon.
Vertices	`Vector3D *Vertices;`
	Dynamically allocated array of vertices in the polygon, listed in clockwise order.
Which	`int which;`
	Coordinate to ignore in projection (0 = X, 1 = Y, 2 = Z). Corresponds to the coordinate with the greatest magnitude in the polygon's normal vector.

Member functions

Constructors	`Polygon(int _NumVerts, Vector3D *_Vertices, Surface *NewColor);`
	Creates a `Polygon` with the given vertices and surface characteristics.
Precompute	`Precompute();`
	Precomputes parameters for the `Polygon` (e.g., the bounding rectangle).

ProjectionMapping class

`mapping.h/mapping.cpp`
Hierarchy: `Mapping`

`ProjectionMapping` applies an oblique parallel projection to 3D vectors onto the XY plane. This amounts to setting the Z coordinate to 0. See Section 6.4.1 for a discussion of the projection mapping.

Member functions

Default Constructor `ProjectionMapping` does not contain any member functions, so the constructor is a no-op.

PureColor class

`texture.h/texture.cpp`
Hierarchy: `Texture`

`PureColor` is a `Texture` that always returns the same color.

Data members	
Color	`RGBColor Color;`
	Color of this `Texture`.

`QuadrilateralMapping` class	`mapping.h/mapping.cpp`
	Hierarchy: `Mapping`

`QuadrilateralMapping` applies an inverse mapping to points in a convex quadrilateral. See Section 6.4.1 for a discussion of the quadrilateral mapping.

Data members	
Vertices	`Vector3D pts[4];`
	The vertices of the quadrilateral.
Precomputed Values	
	`Vector3D Na, Nb, Nc, Nd;`
	`float Du0, Du1, Du2, Dv0, Dv1, Dv2;`
	`int uaxespar, vaxespar;`
	`Vector3D Qux, Quy, Qvx, Qvy;`
	`float Dux, Duy, Dvx, Dvy;`
	These precomputed values help compute the mapping more efficiently.

`Quadric` class	`object3d.h/quadric.cpp`
	Hierarchy: `Object3D`

Encapsulates a generic quadric surface with equation

$$Ax^2 + By^2 + Cz^2 + 2Dxy + 2Eyz + 2Fxz + 2Gx + 2Hy + 2Jz + K = 0$$

Quadrics are discussed in Section 4.5.

Data members	
Coefficients	`double A, B, C, D, E, F, G, H, J;`

Matrix

```
Matrix mat;
```

4×4 matrix for the quadric. In general, this is used to transform the quadric.

`RandomValue` **function**   `oort.h`

```
inline float RandomValue(float a, float
b);
```

Returns a random number in the range [a, b]. Since the range is inclusive, the return value should occasionally be exactly a or b.

`RAWFile` **class**   `texture.h/texture.cpp`
Hierarchy: `ImageFile`

Encapsulates a RAW file, the same type of file that OORT generates as output. Because the color of any pixel can be found just by seeking to the right location on the disk, this class leaves the file on the disk. A primitive caching scheme helps keep access times down, but it is still much slower than accessing the image from memory.

Data members

File

```
FILE *fptr;
```

Pointer to the open image file.

Cached Scanline

```
int cachedscanl;
```

Gives the index of the upper scanline in the cache.

Scanlines

```
unsigned char *scanl[2];
```

Contents of the cache (two scanlines).

Member functions

Seek

```
void Seek(int y);
```

Seeks to the given scanline's position in the RAW file.

RAWFileInMemory class	texture.h/texture.cpp
	Hierarchy: ImageFile

Encapsulates a RAW file, just like the RAWFile class, except this class reads the entire file into memory. Pixel access is much faster using this technique, but it requires much more memory. (A DOS extender or Windows is almost a necessity for using this class.)

Data members

Scanlines

```
unsigned char **scanl;
```

Array of pointers to scanline. There are height unsigned char *'s in this array, and each one contains 3*width unsigned chars.

Ray class	oort.h

Encapsulates a ray used by OORT. Rays are discussed in Section 2.2.

Data members

Direction

```
Vector3D dir;
```

Unit vector pointing in the direction that the ray travels.

Origin

```
Vector3D org;
```

Point where the ray originates.

Precomputed

```
Vector3D ll, ld, dd;
```

Precomputed parameters for the ray.

Member functions

Constructors

```
Ray(const Vector3D& _org, const
Vector3D& _dir);
```

Creates a Ray with the given origin and direction.

Extrapolation

```
Vector3D Extrap(float t) const;
```

Computes a point on the ray, given a parameter.

Interpolation　　　`float Interp(Vector3D& p) const;`

Computes a parameter of the ray, given a point. The point must be on the ray for this function to work correctly.

Reflection　　　`Vector3D ReflectRay(const Vector3D& N) const;`

Returns the direction of perfect reflection given the normal.

Transform　　　`void ApplyTransform(const Matrix&);`

Applies the given 4×4 transformation matrix to the ray.

`RectangularLight` **class**　　　`light.h/light.cpp`
　　　　　　　　　　　　　　　　　Hierarchy: `Light`

`RectangularLight` encapsulates a rectangular, extended light source. These light sources are always centered about the origin upon creation, then get translated, rotated, and scaled until they are placed correctly in the scene.

Constructor　　　`RectangularLight(float width, float height, const RGBColor& clr = RGBColor(1, 1, 1), int min = 4, int max = 16, int numcandidates = 10, const RGBColor& cthreshold = RGBColor(0.4, 0.3, 0.6), float c1 = 1, float c2 = 0, float c3 = 0);`

The rectangular light source has the given color (`clr`) and attenuation due to distance (`c1`, `c2`, and `c3`; see `Light` for a description of the formula). Initially, the rectangular light source is located in the XY plane with the bounding rectangle `(-width/2, -height/2)-(width/2, height/2)`.

`min`, `max`, `numcandidates`, and `cthreshold` give the parameters to the adaptive supersampling algorithm used by OORT. (See Chapter 7 for details.)

New Sample

```
virtual Vector3D NewSample(Vector3D
*targs, int n);
```

Given an array of targets that have already been used, this function generates another one using the algorithm described in Section 7.3.

RGBColor class — vector.h/vector.cpp

RGBColor encapsulates a color value. "RGBColor" is a misnomer, because the class is intended to encapsulate color values without committing to a certain representation.

For the sake of convenience, RGBColor inherits from Vector3D. Many features of Vector3D are also used for RGBColor: operator[] is used to access the color components, member-wise multiplication is used for color attenuation, and so on.

friend Functions

NormalizeColor

```
RGBColor NormalizeColor(const RGBColor&
clr);
```

If any component of the color given is greater than 1.0, the three components of the color are divided by it. This reduces the color's intensity while preserving its hue.

Ring class — object3d.h/plane.cpp
Hierarchy: Object3D

Encapsulates a ring with a center and inner and outer radii. Rings are described in Section 4.3.

Like spheres, rings cannot be made non-circular by means of transformations.

Data members

Center

```
Vector3D center;
```

The center of the ring.

Radii	`float inner, float outer;`

The inner and outer radii of the ring.

Member functions

Constructors	`Ring(float A, float B, float C, float D, const Vector3D& _center, float _inner, float _outer);`
	`Ring(const Vector3D& norm, float D, const Vector3D& _center, float _inner, float _outer);`

Creates a `Ring` with the given plane equation, center, inner and outer radii, and surface characteristics.

`ShadingInfo` class   `surface.h`

This class contains everything needed to shade an intersection point. It is filled in by `Object3D::ShadeObject`, then passed around from `Object3D` to `Surface` to `World` to `Light` as the point is shaded.

Data members

Incident direction	`Vector3D incident;`

Direction of the incident ray at the intersection point.

Intersection point	`Vector3D p;`

The intersection point being shaded.

Normal	`Vector3D normal;`

Normal vector at the intersection point.

Object	`Object3D *obj;`

The object being shaded.

Ray	`Ray *ray;`

The incident ray that intersected the object.

Reflected direction	`Vector3D reflected;`
	Direction of perfect reflection for the incident ray.
World	`World *world;`
	The `World` that the intersection occurred in.

`SimpleList` class template	`list.h`

The `SimpleList` template in `list.h` supports Insert, Query, and other operations. Users can examine and modify linked lists using `Iterator` and `Manipulator` classes embedded in the template. Thus, a simple `list` of integers can be traversed as follows:

```
for (SimpleList<int>::Iterator sc(list); sc.Valid();
sc.GotoNext()) {
    // sc.Contents() will return the contents of the
    current item
}
```

This is a wordy way to traverse a linked list, but it can be made less so by deriving a class from `SimpleList<int>`. For example:

```
class IntList : public SimpleList<int> {
    // ...
};
```

Then traversing an IntList becomes:

```
for (IntList::Iterator sc(list); sc.Valid();
sc.GotoNext()) {
    // sc.Contents() returns contents of current item
}
```

Problems can result if a list changes while an iterator or manipulator is attached. For example, if the node that an iterator points to gets deleted, then calling `Contents` on the iterator will return an invalid pointer. To avoid this problem, each list keeps a count of how many iterators and manipulators are attached. Any number of iterators can be attached to a list at a time, but only one manipulator can be attached (and no iterators can be attached as long as a manipulator is attached).

Although iterators and manipulators may seem like more trouble than they're worth, they provide an important intermediary between the clients of a class and the internals of the class. Providing iterator and manipulator classes is much better than granting public access to the internals of the linked list.

Data members	
Count	`int n;`
	The number of elements in the list.
Head	`SimpleListNode *head;`
	Head of the linked list.
Iterator Count	`int icount;`
	The number of iterators currently attached to the list.
Manipulator Count	`int mcount;`
	The number of manipulators currently attached to the list.

Member functions	
Add To List	`virtual void AddToList(const SimpleList<T>& x);`
	Copies the contents of x into the list.
	`virtual void AddToList(const T& x);`
	Adds a copy of x to the list.
Constructors	`SimpleList();`
	Creates an empty list.
	`SimpleList(const T&);`
	Creates a list with one element containing a copy of the argument.
Empty	`virtual int Empty() const;`
	Returns nonzero if the list is empty.
Extract	`virtual T *Extract(const T& x);`
	Scans the list for an item equal to x. If one is found, a pointer to the item in the list is returned. Otherwise, the function returns 0.

Extract Head	`virtual T ExtractHead();`
	Removes the head item from the list and returns it. The return value is undefined if the list is empty.
Head	`virtual T *Head() const;`
	Returns a pointer to the head item in the list, or 0 if the list is empty.
List Count	`virtual int ListCount();`
	Returns the number of items in the list.
Query	`virtual int Query(T *passbk) const;`
	Scans the list for an item that tests equal to `*passbk`. If one is found, `*passbk` is replaced with the item found and `Query` returns 1. Otherwise, `Query` returns 0.
Modify Check	`void ModifyCheck();`
	This function is called before any operations are performed that might modify the list. If an iterator or manipulator is attached to the list, the function prints an error message to `cerr` and exits. This is because adding or deleting an item from the list while an iterator or manipulator is attached can have disastrous consequences.

`SimpleStack` class template   `stack.h`

The `SimpleStack` template implements a LIFO stack with Push, Pop, and Top operations. It can also traverse the stack from top to bottom using an embedded iterator class.

Data members

Top	`SimpleStackNode *top;`
	Points to the top element of the stack. `top` is 0 if the stack is empty.

Member functions	
Constructor	`SimpleStack();`
	Creates an empty stack.
Pop	`virtual T Pop();`
	Pops the topmost element off the stack and returns it. The return value is undefined if the stack is empty.
Pop Passback	`virtual int PopPassbk(T *passbk);`
	If the stack is empty, this function returns −1. Otherwise, it pops the topmost element and passes back a copy in `passbk`.
Push	`virtual void Push(const T&);`
	Pushes a copy of the parameter onto the top of the stack.
Top	`virtual T Top();`
	Returns a copy of the topmost element in the stack, without popping it. The return value is undefined if the stack is empty.
TOS	`SimpleStackNode *TOS() const;`
	Returns `top`.

`SimpleStack::Iterator` class   stack.h

`SimpleStack::Iterator` is used to traverse nondestructively the contents of a `SimpleStack`. When created, the iterator points at the topmost element of the stack. The iterator can then be moved toward the bottom of the stack.

Data members	
Pointer	`SimpleStackNode *ptr;`
	Points to the current stack node. When the `Iterator` is created, this element points to the topmost stack node.

Member functions	
Constructor	`Iterator(const SimpleStack<T>&);`
	Creates an iterator and points it at the top of the given stack.
Contents	`T Contents() const;`
	Returns the contents of the stack node currently pointed to by the iterator.
Goto Next	`void GotoNext();`
	Updates the iterator to point to the next stack node down.
Valid	`int Valid() const;`
	Returns nonzero if the iterator currently points to a valid stack node.

`SimpleStack::SimpleStackNode` class   stack.h

This class encapsulates a node in the linked list that comprises the stack.

Data members	
Contents	`T contents;`
	Contents of the node.
Next	`Node *next;`
	Points to the next node in the linked list. This element is 0 if this node is the last.

Member functions	
Constructor	`SimpleStackNode(const T& x, Node * _next);`
	Creates a `SimpleStackNode` with the given contents and `next` pointer.

`SolidTexture` abstract class	`texture.h/texture.cpp`
	Hierarchy: `Object3D`

Encapsulates solid textures such as `Bozo`, `Wood`, and `Marble`. Solid textures always contain a color map that helps determine the color of a point. Solid texturing is described in Section 6.5.

Data members	

Color Map

`ColorMap *cmap;`

Points to the texture's color map.

Member functions	

Constructors

`SolidTexture();`

`SolidTexture(const Matrix& ref, ColorMap *Cmap);`

Creates a solid texture with the given reference matrix and color map.

`SolveCubic` function	`poly.h/roots3an.c`

`int SolveCubic(double c[4], double s[3]);`

Finds the roots of the cubic equation

$$c[0] + c[1]x + c[2]x^2 + c[3]x^3 = 0.$$

Returns the number of roots N and passes them back in the first N elements of s.

This function and its relatives, `SolveQuadric` and `SolveQuartic`, are used by the `Polynomial` class to find the roots of small-order polynomials. In turn, the `Polynomial` class is used by `Algebraic` to intersect algebraic surfaces with rays. See the discussion of algebraic surfaces in Section 8.2.

SolveQuadric function	poly.h/roots3an.c

```
int SolveQuadric(double c[3], double
s[2]);
```

Finds the roots of the quadratic equation

$$c[0] + c[1]x + c[2]x^2 = 0$$

Returns the number of roots N and passes them back in the first N elements of s.

SolveQuartic function	poly.h/roots3an.c

```
int SolveQuartic(double c[5], double
s[4]);
```

Finds the roots of the quartic equation

$$c[0] + c[1]x + c[2]x^2 + c[3]x^3 + c[4]^4 = 0$$

Returns the number of roots N and passes them back in the first N elements of s.

Span class	object3d.h/span.cpp

Encapsulates the span of a ray across an object. This class is used in CSG (described in Section 8.1).

Data members	

Parameters	`float tmin, tmax;`

Parameters of intersection where the span enters and leaves the objects.

Objects	`Object3D *omin, *omax;`

Objects that the span enters and leaves.

Member functions	
Constructors	`Span(float _tmin, Object3D *_omin, float _tmax, Object3D *_tmax);`
	Creates a `Span` with the given parameters.

friend Functions	
Compare	`int Compare(const Span& x, const Span& y);`
	Orders the spans according to the minimum parameters of intersection (`tmin`).
Merge	`SpanList *MergeDifference(SpanList *, SpanList *);`
	`SpanList *MergeNearestIntion(SpanList *, SpanList *);`
	`SpanList *MergeUnion(SpanList *, SpanList *);`
	Computes the difference, intersection or union of the two `SpanLists` given. If the result is null, the function returns 0. Otherwise, it returns a `SpanList` that contains the new sets of spans. The two `SpanLists` given in the parameters are destroyed.
Overlap	`int Overlap(const Span& x, const Span& y);`
	Returns nonzero if the two `Spans` overlap.

`SpanList` class	`object3d.h/span.cpp`

Encapsulates a sorted list of `Spans`. The `Spans` are ordered using a `Heap`. `SpanList` is used in constructive solid geometry (CSG) operations. See Section 8.1 for a discussion of CSG.

Data members	
Spans	`Heap<Span> spans;`
	Binary heap of the spans in the `SpanList`.

Member functions	
AddSpan	`void AddSpan(const Span& x);`
	Adds a `Span` to the `SpanList`.
Constructor	`SpanList();`
	Creates a `SpanList` with no contents.
	`SpanList(const Span& x);`
	Creates a `SpanList` that contains the given `Span`.
ExtractMinSpan	`Span ExtractMinSpan();`
	Extracts the `Span` with the minimum parameter of intersection and returns it. The return value is undefined if the `SpanList` is empty.
NumSpans	`int NumSpans() const;`
	Returns the number of `Spans` in the `SpanList`.

Sphere class	`object3d.h/sphere.cpp` **Hierarchy:** `Object3D`

Encapsulates a sphere. Spheres are described in Section 4.4.

Data members	
Center	`Vector3D center;`
	Location of the sphere's center.
Radius	`float radius;`
	Radius of the sphere.
Radius^2	`float radiussq;`
	Radius of the sphere, squared. Precomputed for more efficient intersection calculations.

Member functions

Constructor	`Sphere(const Vector3D&, float, Surface *);`

Creates a `Sphere` with the given center, radius, and surface characteristics.

`SphericalMapping` class   `mapping.h/mapping.cpp`
Hierarchy: `Mapping`

Maps points onto a sphere that is centered about a given point. The spherical inverse mapping is described in Section 6.4.1.

Constructor	`SphericalMapping(const Vector3D&);`

Creates a `SphericalMapping` that maps points onto a sphere centered about the given point.

`Statistics` class   `stats.h/main.cpp`

This class contains a number of global statistics maintained by the ray tracer. The class restricts the scope of the globals, so only the `Statistics` name pollutes the global name space.

Data members

AppendTo	`static char *AppendTo;`

Filename to append the statistics to when done ray tracing. If the statistics are not to be appended to a file, this pointer is 0.

Ray Counts	`static long PrimaryRays;`
	`static long ShadowRays;`
	`static long ReflectedRays;`
	`static long TransmittedRays;`

Number of each type of ray cast.

Prep Time	`static long PrepTime;`
	Seconds spent preprocessing the scene.
Render Time	`static long RenderTime;`
	Seconds spent rendering the scene.
Shadow Caching	`static long ShadowTotal;`
	`static long ShadowHits;`
	Total number of shadow cache tests, and the number of successful ones.
Heuristic	`static float HierarchyHeuristic;`
	Heuristic of the bounding volume hierarchy's effectiveness.
Rays/pixel	`static long RayPixHist[16];`
	Histogram of rays per pixel. Each element of the array contains the number of pixels that required the corresponding number of rays to sample.

Surface abstract class	`surface.h/surface.cpp`

`Surfaces` know about the surface characteristics of objects. They can apply the shading equation at a given intersection point, and they can compute limited parts of the shading equation (such as the coefficient of transparency at a given point). The `Surfaces` in OORT all conform to the Hall shading model described in Chapter 3 (see Figure B.8). `HallSurface` implements a naive

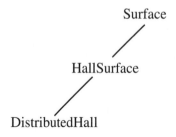

Figure B.8 `Surface` class hierarchy.

Hall shading model, while `DistributedHall` implements a distributed version of the same shading model.

Member functions	

ComputeColor

```
virtual RGBColor
ComputeColor(ShadingInfo& shade, int
depth) = 0;
```

Computes the shading equation at an intersection point using the given shading information. `depth` is the depth of recursion.

Dup

```
virtual Surface *Dup() const = 0;
```

Creates a duplicate of the `Surface` and returns a pointer to it.

Transform

```
void ApplyTransform(const Matrix&) = 0;
```

```
void PreMulTransform(const Matrix&) =
0;
```

Apply transforms to the `Textures` contained in the `Surface`.

Transparent

```
virtual int Transparent() = 0;
```

Returns nonzero if the `Surface` contains any transparent components.

Transmitted

```
virtual RGBColor Transmitted(Vector3D&)
= 0;
```

Returns the coefficient of transmission at the given location.

ShadeLight Begin

```
virtual void BeginShadeLight(Vector3D&
loc) = 0;
```

This function is called before using the `Surface` to compute the colors due to light sources at a given location. It should precompute the coefficients of reflection of light sources at the given intersection point. Currently, the `Surfaces` in OORT compute the diffuse and specular coefficients of reflection at the intersection point.

Shade Light

```
virtual RGBColor
ShadeLight(ShadingInfo& shade,
Vector3D& dir) = 0;
```

Computes the component due to light sources.

Swap function template   oort.h

```
template<class T> inline void Swap(T&
x, T& y);
```

Swaps the two values given as parameters.

Texture abstract class   texture.h/texture.cpp

A Texture translates locations into colors. Textures are used to compute the color coefficients for the five components of the shading equation (ambient, diffuse, specular, reflective, and transparent). Solid textures, such as Bozo, Wood, and Marble, are defined for all points. Other textures apply transformations to the input point to determine what color should be given to the point (see Figure B.9). Texture mapping is described in Chapter 6.

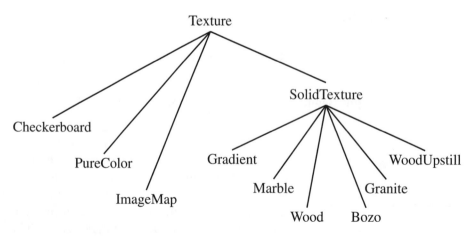

Figure B.9   Texture class hierarchy.

Data members	
Reference	`Matrix reference;`
	Reference matrix for the `Texture`. This matrix is applied to input points before they are used to compute the color.

Member functions	
Constructors	`Texture();`
	Sets the reference matrix to the identity matrix.
	`Texture(const Matrix&);`
	Sets the reference matrix to the matrix given.
Dup	`Texture *Dup() const = 0;`
	Creates a duplicate of the `Texture` and returns a pointer to it.
GetColor	`virtual RGBColor GetColor(const Vector3D&) = 0;`
	Computes the color at the intersection point given.
Preprocess Vector	`virtual Vector3D PreprocessVector(const Vector3D&) const;`
	Preprocesses the vector by multiplying it by the reference matrix. Derived classes can overload this behavior, if desired.
Transform	`virtual void ApplyTransform(const Matrix&);`
	`virtual void PreMulTransform(const Matrix&);`
	Post- or pre-multiplies the reference matrix by the matrix given.

`TextureMapping` abstract class	`texture.h/texture.cpp` Hierarchy: `Texture`

`TextureMapping` encapsulates a `Texture` that must apply an inverse mapping after applying the reference matrix.

Data members	
Mapping	`Mapping *mapping;`
	Points to the inverse mapping to apply while preprocessing the vector.

Member functions	
Constructor	`TextureMapping(const Matrix&, Mapping *map = 0);`
	Creates a `TextureMapping` with the given reference matrix and mapping.
Preprocess Vector	`virtual Vector3D PreprocessVector(const Vector3D& x) const;`
	Preprocess the vector given by multiplying it by the reference matrix, then applying the inverse mapping.

Torus class	object3d.h/alg.cpp Hierarchy: Object3D

A torus is a fourth-degree algebraic surface that looks like a donut. The `Torus` class encapsulates an elliptical torus—one whose cross-section may not be circular.

Data members	
Bounding Box	`BoundingBox bbox;`
	This bounding box is created when the `Torus` is created. Whenever the torus is transformed, the bounding box is transformed so that it always encloses the torus. (The bounding box gets less and less tight as more transformations are applied.)

Member functions	
Constructor	`Torus(float a, float b, float r, Surface *clr);`
	Creates an elliptical torus with minor radii a and b (in the X and Y axes), and major radius r.

Transform

```
virtual void ApplyTransform(const
Matrix&);
```

Applies the transform to the `Torus` and the bounding box that encloses it.

`Triangle` function   `poly.h/poly.cpp`

```
Polynomial Triangle(double a, double b,
int t);
```

Returns the polynomial $(ax + b)^t$.

`Vector3D` class   `vector.h/vector.cpp`

`Vector3D` encapsulates a three-dimensional vector. 3D vectors are described in Section 1.4.

Numerous operators have been overloaded for this class; they include unary + and –, addition, subtraction, memberwise multiplication, member-wise division, and equality. The * operator has also been overloaded for transformation by a 4×4 transformation matrix (see `Matrix`). **friend** functions include `DotProd` (dot product), `CrossProd` (cross product), `Normalize` (vector normalization), and `Magnitude`.

Data members

Coordinates

```
float x, y, z;
```

3D coordinates of the vector.

Member functions

Addition

```
Vector3D& operator+= (const Vector3D&);
```

Adds the vector given in the parameter list.

Constructors

```
Vector3D();
```

This constructor does nothing, so `Vectors` are uninitialized by default.

```
Vector3D(float X, float Y, float Z);
```

Creates a Vector3D with the coordinates given.

```
Vector3D(float X);
```

Creates a Vector3D with all three elements equal to the value given.

Division (memberwise)

```
Vector3D& operator/= (const Vector3D&);
```

Divides corresponding coordinates by those in the vector given in the parameter list.

Division (scalar)

```
Vector3D& operator/= (float);
```

Divides the vector by the scalar factor.

Multiplication (memberwise)

```
Vector3D& operator*= (const Vector3D&);
```

Multiplies corresponding coordinates by those in the vector given in the parameter list.

Multiplication (scalar)

```
Vector3D& operator*= (float);
```

Multiplies the vector by the scalar factor.

Projection

```
void ExtractVerts(float *px, float *py,
int which) const;
```

Passes back two of the vector coordinates in px and py; the component ignored corresponds to which. If which = 0, the Y and Z components are passed back (the X coordinate is ignored). If which = 1, the X and Z components are passed back (the Y coordinate is ignored). If which is any other value, the X and Y coordinates are passed back..

Subscripting

```
float& operator[] (int inx);
```

```
const float& operator[] (int inx)
const;
```

These functions both subscript into a vector; a subscript of 0 returns the X coordinate, 1 returns Y, and anything else (usually 2) returns Z. The two versions are provided so that both `const` and non-`const` functions can access the vector components this way.

Subtraction	`Vector3D& operator-= (const Vector3D&);`
	Subtracts the vector given in the parameter list.
Unary +	`Vector3D operator+() const;`
	Returns the vector untouched.
Unary −	`Vector3D operator-() const;`
	Negates the vector and returns it.

friend Functions

Addition	`Vector3D operator+ (const Vector3D&, const Vector3D&);`
	Returns the vector sum of the two parameters.
Cross Product	`Vector3D CrossProd(const Vector3D&, const Vector3D&);`
	Returns the cross product of the two vectors.
Division (memberwise)	`Vector3D operator/ (const Vector3D&, const Vector3D&);`
	Divides corresponding components of the two vectors and returns the result.
Division (scalar)	`Vector3D operator/ (const Vector3D&, float);`
	Divides each component of the vector by the float and returns the result.
Dominance	`int operator< (const Vector3D& p1, const Vector3D& p2);`
	Returns nonzero if p2 dominates p1 (i.e., if any component in p2 is greater than the corresponding component in p1).
Dot Product	`float DotProd(const Vector3D&, const Vector3D&);`
	Returns the dot product of the two vectors.

Equality	```int operator==(const Vector3D&, const Vector3D&);```
	Returns 1 if the two vectors are exactly equal.
Magnitude	```float Magnitude(const Vector3D&);```
	Returns the magnitude of the vector ($\sqrt{x^2 + y^2 + z^2}$).
Maximize	```void Maximize(Vector3D& max, const Vector3D& candidate);```
	Compares corresponding components of the two vectors; any components in ```candidate``` that are greater than the corresponding component in ```max``` replace the ```max``` component. This function is frequently used to compute objects' bounding boxes.
Minimize	```void Minimize(Vector3D& min, const Vector3D& candidate);```
	Compares corresponding components of the two vectors; any components in ```candidate``` that are less than the corresponding component in ```min``` replace the ```min``` component. This function is frequently used to compute objects' bounding boxes.
Multiplication (matrix)	```Vector3D operator* (const Matrix&, const Vector3D&);```
	Multiplies the matrix by the homogeneous representation of the vector, converts the result from a homogeneous vector to a 3D vector, and returns the result.
Multiplication (memberwise)	```Vector3D operator* (const Vector3D&, const Vector3D&);```
	Multiplies corresponding components of the two vectors and returns the result.
Multiplication (scalar)	```Vector3D operator* (const Vector3D&, float);```
	```Vector3D operator* (float, const Vector3D&);```
	Multiplies the vector by the scalar and returns the result.

Normalize	`Vector3D Normalize(const Vector3D&);`

Returns a vector with the same direction as the parameter, but with unit length.

Stream Output	`ostream& operator<< (ostream&, const Vector3D&);`

Prints the vector out to the given `ostream`.

Subtraction	`Vector3D operator- (const Vector3D&, const Vector3D&);`

Returns the vector difference of the two parameters.

`WoodUpstill` class	`texture.h/texture.cpp`
	Hierarchy: `Texture`

Encapsulates a solid texture that looks like dark wood. The table top in Plate 6 is rendered using this texture, which is derived from Upstill [UPST90, p. 351].

Data members

Scale	`float ringscale;`

Scale factor to apply.

Colors	`RGBColor light, dark;`

`dark` is the color of the dark wood; `light` is the color of the light wood.

Member functions

Constructor	`WoodUpstill(const Matrix& ref = IdentityMatrix(), float _ringscale = 10, const RGBColor& _light = RGBColor(0.3, 0.12, 0.03), const RGBColor& _dark = RGBColor(0.05, 0.01, 0.005));`

The constructor takes a reference matrix and parameters for the texture (the defaults are per Upstill [UPST90, p. 351]).

`World` class	`world.h/world.cpp`

The `World` class contains a list of objects and light sources, viewer parameters, and everything else needed to ray trace a scene. `World::RayTrace` will write a ray traced output file after all the objects have been placed in the `World`.

Data members

Ambient

`RGBColor Ambient;`

Ambient color. This light is equally incident from all directions in the `World` and is reflected in all directions.

Antialiasing

`enum AntiAliasModes mode;`

`Naive` or `Adaptive` antialiasing.

Background

`RGBColor Background;`

Background color. This color is assigned to rays that don't hit any objects.

Contrast Threshold   `RGBColor ContrastThreshold;`

Contrast threshold (higher contrasts than the threshold cause more rays to be cast). Default = (0.4, 0.3, 0.6) per Mitchell [MITC87].

Depth Limit

`int DepthLimit;`

Depth limit of recursion.

Lights

`LightList lights;`

List of the light sources in the `World`.

Num Candidates

`int NumCandidates;`

Number of candidates generated for each sample.

Num Pixels

`long NumPixels;`

Total number of pixels to be included in the trace. This value is computed by `World::RayTrace()`.

Objects

`ObjectList objects;`

`ObjectList unboundeds;`

These lists contain the bounded and unbounded objects in the `World`, respectively.

Output File
`char *Filename;`

Filename to send the ray traced output to.

Resolution
`int HorzRes, VertRes;`

Resolution of the target image.

Samples
`int MinSamples, MaxSamples;`

Minimum and maximum samples to take per pixel. If naive sampling is selected (see Antialiasing), these parameters are ignored.

Scanlines
`int StartScan, EndScan;`

Starting and ending scanlines to put out. `EndScan` is not inclusive: that is for a full-frame rendering of a 640×480 image, `EndScan` is set to 480.

Screen
`float ScreenHeight, ScreenWidth, ScreenDist;`

These parameters describe the viewing frustrum. At a distance of `ScreenDist` from the viewer, the viewing frustrum is `ScreenWidth` wide and `ScreenHeight` high. Thus, a given viewing frustrum can be described by an infinite number of `ScreenHeight/Screen-Width/ScreenDist` values.

View Transform
`Matrix ViewTransform;`

Transformation to apply to all the objects in the `World` to get them into a canonical coordinate system so that the viewer is on the origin looking down the –Z axis.

Viewer
`Vector3D ViewerLoc;`

`Vector3D LookAt;`

`Vector3D UpVector;`

These vectors give the location of the viewer, the point that he is looking at (this point is in the center of the rendered image), and the up vector (which points straight up in the rendered image). `LookAt` is typically set to the origin (0, 0, 0), and `UpVector` is usually set to the Y axis (0, 1, 0).

protected Member functions	
Build One Hierarchy	```static void BuildOneHierarchy(ObjectList& list, Object3D **objs, int n);```
	Replaces `list` with a bounding volume hierarchy that contains the n objects in the array pointed to by `objs`.
BuildHierarchy	```void BuildHierarchy(int tries);```
	Builds `tries` bounding volume hierarchies and retains the one with the smallest heuristic cost according to Goldsmith and Salmon's algorithm [GOLD87].
Count Objects (recursive)	```void CountObjectsRec(ObjectList& list);```
	Recursive assistant function to `CountObjects`. This function recursively traverses the bounding volume hierarchy to count the number of objects in the `World`.
Cull Singletons	```void CullSingletons(Object3D *bv, ObjectList *ParentList);```
	Replaces every bounding volume that contains only one object with the object itself.
Disband Aggregates	```void DisbandAggregates();```
	Replaces each `Aggregate` in the `World` with its list of objects. All `Aggregate` objects in the `World` are destroyed.
Draw Screen	```void DrawScreen(long beg, int start, int end);```
	The parameters are whatever is needed to draw the progress screen during ray tracing. For now, `beg` is the time that rendering began (as returned by the ANSI stan-

dard function `time`); `start` and `end` give the starting and ending scanlines that have been rendered so far.

Find Atten

```
Object3D *FindAtten(ObjectList& optr,
Ray& ray, RGBColor& Atten, float maxt);
```

`ray` is a shadow ray being cast in the `World`. This function casts it and replaces `Atten` with the attenuation of the light source due to objects that occlude it. If an opaque object occludes the light source, `Atten` is set to black (0, 0, 0). `maxt` gives the distance to the light source; intersections farther away than `maxt` do not affect the light arriving at the intersection point.

Find Nearest

```
Object3D *Find_Nearest(Ray& ray, float&
t);
```

Computes the nearest intersection along the ray. If an object is found, `t` is written with its nearest parameter of intersection and a pointer to the object is returned. Otherwise, `Find_Nearest` returns 0.

Hierarchy Cost (recursive)

```
static void
HierarchyCostRec(BoundingVolume *,
float&, float);
```

Recursive assistant function to `HierarchyCost`. This function recursively traverses the bounding volume hierarchy to compute the cost of the hierarchy per Goldsmith and Salmon's heuristic [GOLD87].

New Sample

```
Vector3D NewSample(Vector3D *arr, int
n);
```

Computes a sample in the unit square (x and y coordinates in the range [0, 1]). `NumCandidates` candidate samples are generated, and the one with the largest minimum distance to any vector in `arr` is returned.

Remove Unboundeds

```
void RemoveUnboundeds();
```

Moves all unbounded objects from the `Objects` list to the `Unboundeds` list.

public Member functions	
Add Light	`void AddLight(const Light&);`
	Adds a copy of the light source to the World.
	`void AddLight(Light *);`
	Adds the light source to the `World`.
Add Object	`void AddObject(const Object3D&);`
	Adds a copy of the object to the `World`.
	`void AddObject(Object *);`
	Adds the object given to the `World`.
Constructor	`World();`
	Sets all the `World`'s parameters to the default. The `World` contains no objects initially.
Count Objects	`void CountObjects();`
	Counts the number of each object in the hierarchy.
Diffuse Light	`RGBColor DiffuseLight(ShadingInfo& shade, Surface *surf);`
	Computes the light due to light sources in the world (in the Hall shading model, the diffuse and specular components) according to the shading information given.
Find Color	`RGBColor FindColor(Ray& ray, int depth);`
	Casts the given primary or secondary ray, finds the nearest object along the ray, and computes the shading equation at the nearest intersection point. If the ray does not intersect any object, this function returns the background color. `depth` gives the depth of recursion. It is incremented every time another level of recursion is undertaken. If the level of recursion hits `DepthLimit`, then recursion is halted.
Get Ambient Light	`RGBColor GetAmbientLight();`
	Returns the ambient light intensity for the `World`.

Hierarchy Cost	`static float HierarchyCost(const ObjectList&);`
	Computes the Goldsmith–Salmon heuristic cost of the bounding volume hierarchy in the `ObjectList`.
Hit Depth Limit	`int HitDepthLimit(int depth);`
	Returns nonzero if the depth limit for the `World` is exceeded by the given depth.
Parse Command Line	`void ParseCommandLine(int argc, char *argv[]);`
	Sets the `World` parameters according to the command line.
Parse NFF File	`void ParseNFFFile(const char *filename);`
	Parses the NFF file given, and sets the `World` according to the parameters given. NFF files are described in Appendix G.
Pixel Color	`RGBColor PixelColor(float xtarg, float ytarg);`
	Computes the color of the pixel given by (`xtarg`, `ytarg`). `xtarg` has the range [−`ScreenWidth`/2, `ScreenWidth`/2] and `ytarg` has the range [−`ScreenHeight`/2, `ScreenHeight`/2].
Ray Trace	`void RayTrace();`
	Using the parameters currently in effect in the `World`, renders an image and sends it to the output file.
Set Ambient Light	`void SetAmbientLight(RGBColor& NewAmbient);`
	Sets the ambient lighting.
Set Background Color	`void SetBackgroundColor(RGBColor& NewBackground);`
	Sets the background color. If the primary ray for a pixel does not hit any object, the pixel is assigned this color.

Set Contrast Threshold	`void SetContrastThreshold(const RGBColor& thresh);`
	Sets the contrast threshold to the given color. Pixels with any component of the contrast higher than the threshold will cause more samples to be taken, up to the maximum number of samples.
Set Depth Limit	`void SetDepthLimit(int NewDepthLimit);`
	Sets the depth limit of recursion.
Set End	`void SetEnd(int End);`
	Sets the scanline to end with. This value is exclusive—that is the scanline given is not rendered.
Set Horz Res	`void SetHorzRes(int NewHorzRes);`
	Set the horizontal resolution of the target output.
Set Number of Candidates	`void SetNumCandidates(int);`
	Sets the number of candidate vectors generated during the adaptive antialiasing.
Set Output File	`void SetOutputFile(char *NewFilename);`
	Sets the name of the output file to the given string. `World` allocates space for its own copy of the string.
Set Samples	`void SetSamples(int min, int max);`
	Sets the minimum and maximum samples per pixel to the values given.
Set Screen Distance	`void SetScreenDist(float NewScreenDist);`
	Sets the distance to the virtual screen.
Set Screen Height	`void SetScreenHeight(float NewScreenHeight);`
	Sets the height of the virtual screen.

Set Screen Width	`void SetScreenWidth(float` `NewScreenWidth);`
	Sets the width of the virtual screen.
Set Start	`void SetStart(int Start);`
	Sets the scanline to start with. This value is inclusive—that is the scanline given is rendered.
Set Vert. Res.	`void SetVertRes(int NewVertRes);`
	Sets the vertical resolution of the target output.

Set Viewer Parameters	`void SetViewerParameters(Vector3D&`
	`NewLookAt, Vector3D& NewViewerLoc,`
	`Vector3D& NewUpVector);`

	Sets the viewer parameters so that the viewer is located at `NewViewerLoc`, `NewLookAt` appears in the center of the rendered image, and `NewUpVector` appears to be pointing upward in the rendered image.
SetAntiAliasMode	`void SetAntiAliasMode(enum` `AntiAliasModes _mode);`
	Sets the antialiasing mode.
Shadow Atten	`Object3D *ShadowAtten(Ray& ray,` `RGBColor& Atten, float maxt);`
	The ray given is a shadow ray; this function casts the shadow ray by calling `FindAtten` first on the list of unbounded surfaces, then on the bounding volume hierarchy of bounded surfaces. If an opaque object is discovered, it is returned so the light sources can cache it. Otherwise, `Atten` (which must be set to (1, 1, 1) before calling this function) will be set to the color of light arriving from the light source. `maxt` should be set to the distance from the ray origin to the light source.

B.2 Utilities Library

The Utilities library contains mid-level utilities to do useful things like create textures, objects, and surfaces. The functions and classes in the Utilities library are declared in `utils.h`. The functions and classes are implemented in the UTILS subdirectory of OORT. See Appendix E, Development, for a description of how to build the Utilities library.

B.2.1 Textures

These functions all create solid textures. The reference matrix is used to translate, rotate, and scale the input points before applying the texture. If the function is called with no parameters, the identity matrix will be used by default.

Besides the reference matrix, all of these functions take a turbulence parameter. Increasing or decreasing the turbulence will change the appearance of the texture accordingly. (The greater the turbulence, the more chaotic the texture will look.)

Black Marble

```
Texture *BlackMarble(const Matrix& mat
= IdentityMatrix(), float turbulence =
1.0);
```

Creates a texture that looks like black marble.

Blue Marble

```
Texture *BlueMarble(const Matrix& mat =
IdentityMatrix(), float turbulence =
1.0);
```

Creates a texture that looks like blue marble.

Cherry Wood

```
Texture *CherryWood(const Matrix& mat =
IdentityMatrix(), float turbulence =
1.0);
```

Creates a reddish wood texture.

Clouds

```
Texture *Clouds(const Matrix& mat =
IdentityMatrix(), float turbulence =
1.0);
```

Creates a texture that looks like a cloudy blue sky.

Dark Wood

```
Texture *DarkWood(const Matrix& mat =
IdentityMatrix(), float turbulence =
1.0);
```

Creates a dark brown wood texture.

Pine Wood	`Texture *PineWood(const Matrix& mat = IdentityMatrix(), float turbulence = 1.0);`

Creates a yellow wood texture.

Red Marble	`Texture *RedMarble(const Matrix& mat = IdentityMatrix(), float turbulence = 1.0);`

Creates a texture that looks like red marble.

White Marble	`Texture *WhiteMarble(const Matrix& mat = IdentityMatrix(), float turbulence = 1.0);`

Creates a texture that looks like white marble.

B.2.2 Surfaces

These functions create surfaces. Many of these functions take parameters to let you override the default textures.

Clear	`Surface *MakeClear();`

Creates a perfectly clear surface with a index of refraction of 1.0. Objects shaded with this surface will not be visible. This `Surface` comes in handy when performing CSG— use it on objects that you need for CSG but don't want to be visible.

Shiny	`Surface *MakeShiny(Texture *ambient = 0, Texture *diffuse = 0, Texture *specular = 0, float specularity = 20);`

Creates a shiny surface (one that exhibits specular reflection). The default parameters allow you to use default values for the coefficients of ambient, diffuse, and specular reflection (0.3, 0.7, and 1.0).

Reflective	`Surface *MakeReflective(Texture *reflect = 0);`

Creates a reflective surface. The coefficient of reflection is white (perfectly reflective) by default, but can be overridden if desired.

Glass	`Surface *MakeGlass(Texture *transmit = 0, Texture *reflect = 0, Texture *specular = 0, float specularity = 100, Texture *diffuse = 0);`

Creates a surface that looks like glass. The coefficients can be overridden, or the default parameter will cause a default value to be used. The defaults are $k_t = 0.8$ for transmission; $k_r = 0.2$ for reflection; $k_s = 0.6$ for specular reflection, with a specularity of 100; and $k_d = 0.08$ for diffuse reflection. The index of refraction is set to 1.3.

Calling this function with no parameters will result in a fairly convincing glass surface (see Plate 7).

Granite	`Surface *MakeGranite(const Matrix& reference = IdentityMatrix(), const RGBColor& Ka = RGBColor(0.2), const RGBColor& Kd = RGBColor(0.8));`

Creates a surface that looks like granite. The coefficients of ambient and diffuse reflection can be overridden, if desired. After Upstill [UPST90, p. 354].

B.2.3 Objects

The functions in this section all create objects. OORT provides the primitive facilities to implement the objects (for example, the `Quadric` and `Algebraic` classes), while these functions make them much easier to use.

Note: most of these functions create unbounded objects. To bound them, use constructive solid geometry (CSG).

Also, you may want to refer to the `Torus` and `Ellipsoid` classes built into OORT. Since toruses and ellipsoids are bounded objects, they are implemented by inheritance so that the `BBox` member function can be overloaded, allowing them to participate in speedups due to a bounding volume hierarchy.

For examples of how to use the quadric- and algebraic-making functions, refer to the Quadrics and Algebraics examples (Appendix F).

Box	`Aggregate *MakeBox(const Vector3D& min, const Vector3D& max, Surface *surf);`

Creates an axis-aligned box with the given `min` and `max` vectors. The box is composed of polygons, so it can be translated, rotated, and scaled after creation. Each of the six polygons in the box has the surface characteristics of surf.

Cone	`Object3D *MakeCone(float a, float c, Surface *surf);`

Creates an elliptical cone aligned along the Y axis. The resulting cone will have X radius = a and Z radius = c at the planes Y = ±1. For a circular cone, just set a = c.

Cylinder	`Object3D *MakeCylinder(float a, float c, Surface *surf);`

Creates an elliptical cylinder aligned along the Y axis. The resulting cylinder will have X radius = a and Z radius = c. For a circular cylinder, just set a = c.

Hyperboloid	`Object3D *MakeHyperboloid(float a, float b, float c, Surface *surf);`

Creates an elliptical hyperboloid of one sheet. The hyperboloid has X radius = a and Z radius = c at the origin. The b parameter gives the slope of the asymptote.

Paraboloid	`Object3D *MakeParaboloid(float a, float c, float f, Surface *surf);`

Creates an elliptical paraboloid with X radius = a and Z radius = c at twice the focal distance f.

Cubic Catastrophe	`Algebraic *MakeCubicCusp(Surface *surf);`

Creates an algebraic surface with the equation
$$z^3 + xz + y = 0$$

Folium	`Algebraic *MakeFolium(Surface *surf);`

Creates an algebraic surface with the equation
$$2x^2 + y^2 + z^2 - 3xy^2 - 3xz^2 = 0$$

Kummer	`Algebraic *MakeKummer(Surface *surf);`

Creates an algebraic surface with the equation
$$\left(x^4 + y^4 + z^4 + 1\right) - \left(x^2 + y^2 + z^2 + y^2z^2 + x^2z^2 + x^2y^2\right) = 0$$

Lemniscate	`Algebraic *MakeLemniscate(Surface *surf);`
	Creates an algebraic surface with the equation $x^4 - x^2 + y^2 + z^2 = 0$
Piriform	`Algebraic *MakePiriform(Surface *surf);`
	Creates an algebraic surface with the equation $4x^4 - 4x^3 + y^2 + z^2 = 0$
Steiner	`Algebraic *MakeSteiner(Surface *surf);`
	Creates an algebraic surface with the equation $x^2 y^2 + y^2 z^2 + z^2 x^2 + xyz = 0$
Quartic Cylinder	`Algebraic *MakeQuarticCylinder(Surface *surf);`
	Creates an algebraic surface with the equation $x^2 y^2 + y^2 z^2 + \frac{1}{100} x^2 + \frac{1}{100} z^2 - \frac{1}{100} = 0$

B.2.4 Aggregates

Two classes implemented in the Utilities library inherit from the `Aggregate` class. They are `Sphereflake` and `STetrahedron`, recursively defined objects depicted in Plates 7 and 8.

`Sphereflake` class	`utils.h`

`Sphereflake` encapsulates a recursively defined object composed of spheres. To see what the `Sphereflake` looks like, see Plate 7.

Add Sphere	`void AddSphere(const Vector3D& center, float rad, const Vector3D& dir, int depth, Surface *surf);`
	This recursive function evaluates the depth and, if it is zero, creates a "leaf" sphere and terminates the recursion. Otherwise, it creates a larger, "internal" sphere and recurses. The resulting recursion will create nine smaller spheres attached to this internal sphere. Depending on the

depth, these smaller spheres may or may not have spheres attached to them.

| **Constructor** | `Sphereflake(const Vector& center, float rad, const Vector& dir, int depth, Surface *surf);` |

Creates a Sphereflake with the given depth. (The resulting Sphereflake will contain

$$\sum_{i=0}^{depth} 9^i$$

spheres.) The largest sphere, at the base of the Sphereflake, has radius `rad`. The Sphereflake extends away from this base sphere in the direction of `dir`. All spheres in the Sphereflake are given the surface characteristics of `surf`.

| **CreateObjSet** | `void CreateObjSet(Vector3D passbk[9]);` |

Precomputes a set of values needed to create a Sphereflake.

| `STetrahedron class` | `utils.h` |

`STetrahedron` encapsulates a recursively defined object composed of triangles. To see what Sierpinski's Tetrahedron looks like, see Plate 8.

| **Constructor** | `STetrahedron(int depth, const Vector3D& center, float mag, Surface *surf);` |

Creates a tetrahedron containing 4^{depth} spheres, centered about `center` and scaled by `mag`. Each triangle in the object is given the surface characteristics of `surf`.

| **CreateTetra** | `void CreateTetra(int depth, const Vector3D& center, float mag, Surface *surf);` |

This recursive function evaluates the depth, and then either continues the recursion or creates four "leaf" triangles and terminates the recursion.

Appendix C
Glossary

Algebraic surface   An implicit surface defined by the equation

$$\sum_i \sum_j \sum_k c_{ijk} x^i y^j z^k = 0$$

Quadric surfaces and planes are algebraic surfaces with equations of degree 2 and 1. *Related entries*: implicit surface, plane, quadric surface.

Aliasing   Undesirable artifacts in an image that arise from sampling a high-frequency signal at low frequencies. In ray tracing, aliasing artifacts are usually jagged-looking lines or missing objects. *Related entries*: antialiasing.

Antialiasing   A catch-all term for techniques designed to combat the undesirable artifacts caused by aliasing. *Related entries*: aliasing.

Attenuation   The selective reduction of a color's intensity, usually achieved by multiplying the color's RGB components by the corresponding components of another color. Thus, white light with RGB=(0.8, 0.8, 0.8) becomes blue light with RGB=(0.1, 0.1, 0.8) when attenuated by blue glass with a coefficient of transmission of (0.125, 0.125, 1.0).

Bounding box   A rectangular box aligned with the coordinate axes. This type of bounding volume is used by OORT. *Related entries*: bounding volume, bounding volume hierarchy.

Bounding volume An invisible object used to speed up ray tracing. If a ray misses a bounding volume (presumably, this is most of the time), it misses all of the objects inside it. *Related entries*: bounding box, bounding volume hierarchy.

Bounding volume hierarchy A tree-like structure composed of bounding volumes nested within one another. The entire hierarchy is contained in a bounding volume called the *root*; objects that are not bounding volumes are usually called *leaf objects* in the context of a bounding volume hierarchy.

Bump mapping Systematically changing the surface normal of an object to make it look more complicated (e.g., rippled or wrinkled). *Related entries*: texture mapping.

Candidate list A list of objects associated with some entity (bounding volume in a bounding volume hierarchy, voxel in a spatial subdivision scheme, or hypercube in a ray classification scheme). The candidate list contains every object that must be considered if a ray pierces the entity.

Canonical object An object in a coordinate system that it is easy to describe. For example, an axis-aligned ellipsoid has a much simpler equation than one that has been rotated. In OORT, some objects (algebraic surfaces) are so difficult to transform that they are kept in their canonical forms. The transformations applied are accumulated so that input parameters (e.g., rays) can be transformed into the canonical coordinate system, and output parameters (e.g., surface normals) can be transformed back.

Coherence A general concept used to speed up 3D rendering. The basic idea is that parts of the image that are near each other tend to be similar to each other.

Constructive solid geometry (CSG) A ray tracing primitive that lets two objects be combined with a Union, Intersection or Difference operation (see Section 8.1).

Cross product An operation that takes two vectors V_1 and V_2 and generates another vector perpendicular to the first two, oriented according to the right-hand rule, and with magnitude $\| V_1 \| \| V_2 \| \sin \theta$, where θ is the angle between the two vectors.

Depth limit The maximum number of levels of recursion that are allowed in a ray tracer. This limit is needed because certain scenes result in infinite recursion (two reflective objects facing each other, for instance).

Direction vector   A vector that has been normalized to contain a direction rather than a location.

Distribution ray tracing   A technique that extends the number of effects that can be rendered by ray tracing. The effects made possible by distribution ray tracing include antialiasing, soft shadows, blurry reflection and transmission, depth of field, and motion blur.

Dot product   The sum of the products of corresponding elements of a vector. This can be thought of as the length of the projection of one vector onto the other. *Related entries*: Law of cosines.

Implicit surface   Surface defined by an equation in x, y, and z. For example, a sphere centered at (x_0, y_0, z_0) and with radius r is an implicit surface with the equation $(x - x_0)^2 + (y - y_0)^2 + (z - z_0)^2 = r^2$.

Incident light   Light arriving at a point.

Incident ray   A ray arriving at a point. The direction of this ray is used to compute the directions of reflected or transmitted rays.

Law of Cosines $\mathbf{v}_1 \cdot \mathbf{v}_2 = |\mathbf{v}_1| \, |\mathbf{v}_2| \cos\theta$. The Law of Cosines is most useful when the vectors are normalized, so that the dot product of two vectors is equal to the cosine of the smallest angle between them.

Magnitude   Length of a vector. For a 3D vector (x, y, z), the magnitude is $\sqrt{x^2 + y^2 + z^2}$.

Normalize   Force a vector to be unit length by dividing by the magnitude.

Normal vector   A normalized vector perpendicular to a surface at a given point.

Plane   A first-degree algebraic surface. A plane with normal (A, B, C) has the equation $Ax + By + Cz + D = 0$. If (A, B, C) is normalized, then D is the distance of the nearest point to the origin.

Primary ray   A ray fired through the virtual screen to determine the color of a pixel.

Quadric surface   A second-degree algebraic surface. Quadric surfaces include spheres, ellipsoids, cones, cylinders, paraboloids and hyperboloids.

Radiosity   A photorealistic rendering technique developed more recently than ray tracing. Radiosity gives a much better approximation of interobject reflections, and is able to generate more realistic scenes in many cases.

Ray classification   A technique of ray tracing acceleration described by Arvo and Kirk [ARVO89].

Recursive ray tracing   Ray tracing that uses recursion to help evaluate the shading equation. In general, this is ray tracing that supports reflective and transparent objects.

Reflected ray   A secondary ray fired to evaluate the reflective component of the shading equation.

Secondary ray   Ray recursively cast from an intersection point to help evaluate the shading equation. *Related entries*: reflected ray, transmitted ray.

Shading equation   The set of calculations that must be performed to implement a given shading model.

Shading model   A model of light transport that tells how to compute the color of a point.

Shadow ray   A ray fired from an intersection point toward a light source to determine how much light is reaching the intersection point from that light source.

Sphere   The set of points equidistant from a given point. *Related entries:* implicit surface, quadric surface.

Texture mapping   Systematically changing the color of an object for different points—for instance, making it look like wood or marble. *Related entries*: bump mapping.

Traditional ray tracing   Ray tracing as pioneered by Whitted [WHIT80]. In this text, the term is used to contrast with distribution ray tracing and radiosity through ray tracing.

Transmitted ray   A secondary ray fired to evaluate the transparent component of the shading equation.

Viewing frustrum   The pyramid that extends from the eye in the direction the eye is *looking*, when perspective projection is being performed.

Appendix D
Bibliography

D.1 Abbreviations

IEEE CG&A   IEEE Computer Graphics and Applications

SIGGRAPH 78   *Proceedings of SIGGRAPH 78* (Atlanta, Georgia, August 23–25, 1978). In *Computer Graphics* 12 (3), August 1978, ACM SIG-GRAPH, New York.

SIGGRAPH 82   *Proceedings of SIGGRAPH 82* (Boston, Massachusetts, July 26–30, 1982). In *Computer Graphics* 16 (3), July 1982, ACM SIGGRAPH, New York.

SIGGRAPH 84   *Proceedings of SIGGRAPH 84* (Minneapolis, Minesota, July 23–27, 1984). In *Computer Graphics* 18 (3), July 1984, ACM SIGGRAPH, New York.

SIGGRAPH 85   *Proceedings of SIGGRAPH 85* (San Francisco, California, July 22–26, 1985). In *Computer Graphics* 19 (3), July 1985, ACM SIGGRAPH, New York.

SIGGRAPH 86   *Proceedings of SIGGRAPH 86* (Dallas, Texas, August 18–22, 1986). In *Computer Graphics* 20 (4), August 1986, ACM SIG-GRAPH, New York.

SIGGRAPH 87   *Proceedings of SIGGRAPH 87* (Anaheim, California, July 27–31, 1987). In *Computer Graphics* 21 (4), July 1987, ACM SIG-GRAPH, New York.

SIGGRAPH 89   *Proceedings of SIGGRAPH 89* (Boston, Massachusetts, July 31–August 4, 1989). In *Computer Graphics* 23 (3), July 1989, ACM SIGGRAPH, New York.

SIGGRAPH 91   *Proceedings of SIGGRAPH 91* (Las Vegas, Nevada, July 28–August 2, 1991). In *Computer Graphics* 25 (4), August 1991, ACM SIGGRAPH, New York.

D.2   Works Cited

[AKIM91]   Akimoto, Takaaki, Kenji Mase, and Yasuhito Suenaga. Pixel-selected ray tracing. *IEEE CG&A* 11 (4), 14–22, July 1991.

[ARNA87]   Arnaldi, Bruno, Thierry Priol, and Kadi Bouatouch. A new space subdivision method for ray tracing CSG modelled scenes. *The Visual Computer* 3, Springer-Verlag, 98–108, 1987.

[ARVO87]   Arvo, James and David Kirk. Fast ray tracing by ray classification. *SIGGRAPH 87*, 55–64.

[ARVO89]   Arvo, James and David Kirk. A survey of ray tracing classification techniques. In *An Introduction to Ray Tracing*, Andrew Glassner, ed. Boston: Academic Press, 1989.

[ARVO91]   Arvo, James, ed. *Graphics Gems II*. Boston: Academic Press, 1991.

[BENT86]   Bentley, Jon. *Programming Pearls*. Reading, MA: Addison–Wesley, 1986.

[BLIN78]   Blinn, James F. Simulation of wrinkled surfaces. *SIGGRAPH 78*, 286–292.

[COOK84a]   Cook, Robert L., Timothy Porter and Loren Carpenter. Distributed ray tracing. *SIGGRAPH 84*, 137–145.

[COOK84b]   Cook, Robert L. Shade trees. *SIGGRAPH 84*, 223–231.

[COOK89]   Cook, Robert L. Stochastic sampling and distributed ray tracing. In *An Introduction to Ray Tracing*, Andrew Glassner, ed. Boston: Academic Press, 1989.

[COPL92]   Coplien, James O. *Advanced C++ Programming Styles and Idioms*. Reading, MA: Addison–Wesley, 1992.

[CORM90]   Cormen, Thomas, Charles Leiserson and Ronald Rivest. *Introduction to Algorithms*. Cambridge, MA: MIT Press, 1990.

[CYCH91]   Cychosz, Joseph M. Intersecting a ray with an elliptical torus. In *Graphics Gems II*, James Arvo, ed. Boston: Academic Press, 1991.

[CYCH92]   Cychosz, Joseph M. and Warren N. Waggenspack, Jr. Intersecting a ray with a quadric surface. In *Graphics Gems III*, David Kirk, ed. Boston: Academic Press, 1992.

[DIPP85]   Dippe, Mark A. Z. and Erling Henry Wold. Antialiasing through stochastic sampling. *SIGGRAPH 85*, 69–78.

[ELLI90]   Ellis, Margaret and Bjarne Stroustrup. *The Annotated C++ Reference Manual*. Reading, MA: Addison–Wesley, 1990.

[FOLE90]   Foley, James D., Andries van Dam, Steven K. Feiner and John F. Hughes. *Computer Graphics*. Reading, MA: Addison–Wesley, 1990.

[FUJI86]   Fujimoto, A., T. Tanaka, and K. Iwata. ARTS: Accelerated Ray Tracing System. *IEEE CG&A* 6 (4), 16–26, April 1986.

[GLAS84]   Glassner, Andrew S. Space subdivision for ray tracing. *IEEE CG&A* 4 (10), 15–22, October 1984.

[GLAS89a]   Glassner, Andrew, ed. *An Introduction to Ray Tracing*. London: Academic Press, 1989.

[GLAS89b]   Glassner, Andrew S. Surface physics for ray tracing. In *An Introduction to Ray Tracing*, Andrew Glassner, ed. London: Academic Press, 1989.

[GLAS90]   Glassner, Andrew, ed. *Graphics Gems*. Boston: Academic Press, 1990.

[GLAS92]   Glassner, Andrew S. Darklights. In *Graphics Gems III*, David Kirk, ed. Boston: Academic Press, 1992.

[GOLD87]   Goldsmith, Jeffrey and John Salmon. Automatic creation of object hierarchies for ray tracing. *IEEE CG&A* 7 (5), 14–20, May 1987.

[HAIN87]   Haines, Eric. A proposal for standard graphics environments. *IEEE CG&A* 7 (11), 3–5, November 1987.

[HAIN86]   Haines, Eric A. and Donald P. Greenberg. The light buffer: a shadow-testing accelerator. *IEEE CG&A* 6 (9), 6–16, September 1986.

[HAIN89]   Haines, Eric. Essential ray tracing algorithms. In *Graphics Gems*, Andrew Glassner, ed. Boston: Academic Press, 1989.

[HALL83]   Hall, Roy and Donald Greenberg. A testbed for realistic image synthesis. *IEEE CG&A* 3 (10), 10–20, November 1983.

[HALL89]   Hall, Roy. *Illumination and Color in Computer-Generated Imagery*. New York: Springer-Verlag, 1989.

[HANR83]   Hanrahan, Pat. Ray tracing algebraic surfaces. *SIGGRAPH 83*, 83–90.

[HANR89]   Hanrahan, Pat. A survey of ray-surface intersection algorithms. In *An Introduction to Ray Tracing*, Andrew Glassner, ed. London: Academic Press, 1989.

[HART89]   Hart, John, Daniel Sandin and Louis Kauffman. Ray tracing deterministic 3D fractals. *SIGGRAPH 89*, 289–296.

[HART91]   Hart, John and Thomas DeFanti. Efficient antialiased rendering of 3D linear fractals. *SIGGRAPH 91*, 91–100.

[HECK82]   Heckbert, Paul. Color quantization for frame buffer display. *SIGGRAPH 82*, 297.

[HECK86]   Heckbert, Paul. Survey of texture mapping. *IEEE CG&A* 6 (11), 56–67, November 1986.

[HOOK90]   Hook, D.G. and McAree, P.R. Using Sturm sequences to bracket real roots of polynomial equations. In *Graphics Gems*, Andrew Glassner, ed. Boston: Academic Press, 1990.

[JEVA89]   Jevans, David and Brian Wyvill. Adaptive voxel subdivision for ray tracing. In *Proceedings of Graphics Interface '89*. Toronto: Canadian Information Processing Society, June 1989, pp. 164–172.

[KAJI83]   Kajiya, James T. New techniques for ray tracing procedurally defined objects. *SIGGRAPH 83*, 91–102.

[KAJI86]   Kajiya, James T. The rendering equation. *SIGGRAPH 86*, 143–150.

[KAY86]   Kay, Timothy L. and James T. Kajiya. Ray tracing complex scenes. *SIGGRAPH 86*, 269–278.

[KIRK92]   Kirk, David, ed. *Graphics Gems III*. Boston: Academic Press, 1992.

[LEE85]   Lee, Mark E., Richard A. Redner and Samuel P. Uselton. Statistically optimized sampling for distributed ray tracing. *SIGGRAPH 85*, 61–67.

[LEW89]   Lewis, J.P. Algorithms for solid noise synthesis. *SIGGRAPH 89*, 263–270.

[MEY92]   Meyers, Scott. *Effective C++*. Reading, MA: Addison–Wesley, 1992.

[MITC87]   Mitchell, Don P. Generating antialiased images at low sampling densities. *SIGGRAPH 87*, 65–72.

[MITC91]   Mitchell, Don P. Spectrally optimal sampling for distributed ray tracing. *SIGGRAPH 91*, 157–164.

[PEAC85]   Peachey, Darwyn R. Solid texturing of complex surfaces. *SIGGRAPH 85*, 279–286.

[PERL85]   Perlin, Ken. An image synthesizer. *SIGGRAPH 85*, 287–296.

[PERL89]   Perlin, Ken. Hypertexture. *SIGGRAPH 89*, 253–262.

[PREP85]   Preparata, Franco P. and Michael I. Shamos. *Computational Geometry*. New York: Springer-Verlag, 1985.

[ROTH82]   Roth, Scott D. Ray casting for modelling solids. *Computer Graphics and Image Processing* 18, 109–144, 1982.

[SCHW90]   Schwartze, Jochen. Cubic and quartic roots. In *Graphics Gems*, Andrew Glassner, ed. Boston: Academic Press, 1990.

[SEGG93]   von Seggern, David H. *CRC Standard Curves and Surfaces*. Boca Raton, FL: CRC Press, 1993.

[SNYD87]   Snyder, John M. and Alan H. Barr. Ray tracing complex models containing surface tessellations. *SIGGRAPH 87*, 119–128.

[SPEER91]   Speer, L.R. A cross-indexed guide to the ray tracing literature. *Computer Graphics Forum* 10 (2), 145–174, June 1991.

[STON75]   Stone, L. *Theory of Optimal Search*. New York: Academic Press, 1975, pp. 27–28.

[STRO91]   Stroustrup, Bjarne. *The C++ Programming Language*, 2nd ed. Reading, MA: Addison–Wesley, 1991.

[UPST90]   Upstill, Steve. *The RenderMan Companion*. Reading, MA: Addison–Wesley, 1990.

[WHIT80]   Whitted, Turner. An improved illumination model for shaded display. *Communications of the ACM* 23 (6), 343–349, June 1980.

[WOO90]   Woo, Andrew. Fast ray-polygon intersection. In *Graphics Gems*, Andrew Glassner, ed. Boston: Academic Press, 1990.

[YELL83]   Yellott, J.I., Jr. Spectral consequences of photoreceptor sampling in the Rhesus retina. *Science* 221, 382–385, 22 July 1983.

Appendix E

Development

E.1 Installation

To develop with OORT, you need:

- A PC-class machine, preferably a 386 or 486. A floating-point coprocessor is highly recommended, since ray tracing is floating-point intensive.
- Besides the 35M of disk space required by Borland C++, you will need at least 10M of space for the ray tracer's development directories.
- Borland C++ v3.1 or another C++ compiler that supports templates. If you want to use a different C++ compiler, you will have to modify the makefiles for the class library and examples.

Before doing any development with OORT, you must build it from the disk set included with the book. OORT is freely available, though it may not be distributed for profit; if you did not purchase the book with disk set included, you may be able to download OORT from a local bulletin board service or CompuServe. If you have access to FTP, OORT can probably be found on an FTP site dedicated to computer graphics, such as princeton.edu or the graphics archives on SIMTEL20.

Developing with OORT can be done under DOS or Windows. OORT was developed with the Borland C++ compiler. Although no other cfront 3.0-compliant compilers were used, OORT is intended to be portable and should be easy to move to other environments. DOS development is subject to the traditional limitations of DOS: 640K memory: no multi-tasking or virtual memory. Some of the large data sets included in the examples cannot be rendered using DOS because they require too much memory.

Windows development is supported using Borland's EasyWin library. EasyWin basically reduces Windows to the status of DOS extender. Programs developed using it are native Windows applications and can access all of the virtual memory available to Windows, but they look and act like DOS applications running in a window. Other DOS extenders could conceivably be used to give OORT access to more memory, as well.

For now, you must write in C++ to use OORT. No user interface or input language has been provided. This is surprisingly painless; see the code for the example images (included on the code disk). You just have to make calls to `World` member functions to add objects and lights to the `World`, and to set other parameters that will affect the image.

Before you can develop OORT or use it to generate images, you must follow a sequence of steps:

1. Install OORT.

   This can be done from the code disk, or from the freeware distribution downloaded from an information service.

2. Build the ray tracing class library.

   At this point, you must choose between developing under DOS or Windows. Windows development is easier than DOS development because Windows is not subject to DOS-style memory constraints (640K).

3. Build the utilities library.

   Again, this build may be done for DOS or for Windows.

4. Build the examples, if desired. The examples are described individually in Appendix F.

These steps are outlined in detail below.

1. Install OORT.

This disk contains everything you need to begin ray tracing with OORT.

To use OORT, you must first install it using the installation program included on the disk. Insert the diskette into a 3.5" diskette drive on the system and run INSTALL off the diskette. For example, if drive B: is the 3.5" diskette drive, type the following:

```
b:install
```

The installation program lets you choose the directory to install OORT into. It also lets you choose which parts of OORT to install. The four parts are as follows:

OORT   This is the class library. It must be installed.

RAW2GIF   This program converts ray tracer output files to the popular GIF format for viewing. It should probably be installed.

SPLICE   This program splices together ray tracer output files that each contain a portion of an image. This is useful if you divide the task between multiple computers. There's no need to install SPLICE if you're not going to use multiple computers for ray tracing.

VUIMAGE   This is a shareware GIF viewer by Offe Enterprises. If you already have a GIF viewer, you do not need to install VUIMAGE.

Compressed Archive   If you downloaded OORT from CompuServe or some other online service, it should have come in the form of a compressed archive, such as a .ZIP file. The file should contain the OORT, RAW2GIF and SPLICE directories listed above. You can unpack the .ZIP file as follows:

```
pkunzip -d oort10.zip c:\
```

Like the XCOPY command shown above, this will unpack the contents of the ZIP file into the root directory of your hard drive. Note: If you want to use a hard drive other than C: to develop with OORT, you will have to specify that hard drive's signature (D:, E:, etc.) in the commands shown above.

After installing OORT, you should modify your PATH environment variable (declared in AUTOEXEC.BAT) to include the directories for any of the utilities that you wish to use (e.g., RAW2GIF, SPLICE, and VUIMAGE).

2. Build the ray tracing class library.

The Borland Make utility must be used to make the library. Change directories to the OORT source directory (\OORT\SOURCE) and type:

```
make -fmakefile.dos
```

to build the DOS version of the library, or:

```
make -fmakefile.win
```

to build the Windows version.

Most likely, the Makefiles can be used unmodified to build the library satisfactorily. If not, however, you may want to customize the Makefiles by changing the following variables which are defined therein:

INCLUDES   Gives –I command line options as needed, to specify directories where the compiler can find include files. The default is "..\include," which will work as long as you are using the default directory structure.

LIBDIR   Gives the directory to write the library to. The default is "..\lib."

WARNS   Turns off some of the more tiresome compiler warnings, such as "possibly incorrect assignment."

MODEL   Memory model to use. The default is large (–ml).

OPTS   Optimizations to use. The default is maximum optimization, as follows:

–vi	Enable inline functions.
–Ox	Maximum optimization.
–3	386 or better target machine.
–DASM	Enable assembler.
–f87	Coprocessor in target machine.

Remove "–3" if you are targeting 286 or earlier machines.

Remove "–f87" if you want OORT to run on machines without coprocessors (a masochistic endeavor).

To disable optimizations completely, sets OPTS=–Od.

The only variable you are likely to modify is OPTS. OORT hasn't been tested in any other directory structure or memory model, so if you modify the INCLUDES, LIBDIR or MODEL variables, you are on your own.

3. Build the utilities library.

The utilities library contains primitives which are higher-level than those in OORT, but lower-level than the Examples. For example, the utilities library contains a function called `MakeSteiner` that creates an algebraic surface with the equation for Steiner's surface. The utilities library also contains functions to create `Textures` such as `PineWood` and `DarkWood` using the `Wood` texture built into OORT. For `MakeSteiner`, the `Algebraic` class is used as a primitive to create a picture of Steiner's surface. For `PineWood`, the `Wood` class is used as a primitive to create a texture that looks like pine. The Utilities library contains functions at this mid-level between the primitives provided by OORT and the functionality required by the user.

Build the utilities library by switching the directory to \OORT\UTILS and typing:

```
make -fmakefile.dos
```

for the DOS version, or

```
make -fmakefile.win
```

for the Windows version. These Makefiles are almost identical to the ones that build OORT. If it is necessary to modify the OORT makefiles, you will probably want to change these makefiles, as well. Refer to the preceding section for particulars on how to modify the makefiles if necessary.

4. Build the examples.

Each example has its own directory. The directory contains:

- Source file. These are listed in Appendix F.
- Two Makefiles, one for DOS and one for Windows.
- A module definitions file (for the Windows version).
- A project file for the Windows-hosted Borland C++ IDE.

After building the example, the directory will contain an executable file that generates a ray traced image. You can run the application as-is, or with command-line options to change the output resolution, antialiasing and other parameters. See Table E.1 for a list of the valid command-line options for an OORT application. Note: OORT does not expect a space between the option and the parameter to the option. For example, to render the CSG Demo example at 1024×768 resolution, you would type:

```
csgdemo -w1024 -h768
```

with no space between -w and 1024, and no space between -h and 768.

Antialiasing	
–anti	Antialias the image.
–min*val*	Minimum number of samples to take for each pixel. If this option is not specified, the minimum is set to 4.
–max*val*	Maximum number of samples to take for each pixel. If this option is not specified, the maximum is set to 16.

Rendering	
–e*scanl*	Gives ending scanline. The default is equal to the height of the image (i.e., the default is to render the entire image).
–h*height*	Height of the output image. The default is 200.
–s*scanl*	Gives starting scanline. The default is 0.
–w*width*	Gives width of the output image. The default is 320.

Miscellanous	
–S*filename*	Append statistics to the given file.
–o*filename*	Sends image to the given file. The default is set by the OORT application calling `World::SetOutputFile`, but can be overridden by this option.
–D*depth*	Set the depth limit for recursion.

Table E.1   Valid command-line options for an OORT application

E.2 The Application Template

Currently, all programs that generate images using OORT have a common structure. The `main` routine creates a few global objects needed by OORT and calls a function called `PopulateWorld` to add objects to the `World`, place the viewer, and perform other tasks that describe the scene to be rendered. Then it parses the command line using `World::ParseCommandLine`, so that command-line options take precedence over parameters set from within the program. `World::RayTrace` is then called to render the scene to an output file. During this time, the program prints status information to the screen, including the number of pixels computed so far, average time per pixel, and estimated remaining rendering time. When the trace finishes, the statistics for the scene are printed out. In the OORT distribution, the SKELETON subdirectory of EXAMPLES contains the application template given in Listing E.1. I strongly suggest starting from the application template when rendering with OORT at first. After you've become more familiar with the workings of the ray tracer, you can move on to more ambitious projects than merely rendering a single scene.

```
// =====================================================================
// skeleton.cpp
//     Skeleton OORT application.
// Copyright (C) 1993 by Nicholas Wilt.  All rights reserved.
// =====================================================================

#include "oort.h"
#include "world.h"
#include "colors.h"
#include "utils.h"

void
PopulateWorld(World& world)
{
    // The calls here are pretty much mandatory (though the
    // parameters may obviously change).  Calls to World::AddLight
    // and World::AddObject have to made, also, to place
    // light sources and objects in the World.  See the Examples
    // for how to do this.
    world.SetDepthLimit(3);
    world.SetOutputFile("quadrics.raw");

    world.SetViewerParameters(Vector3D(0), Vector3D(0, 0, 10),
        Vector3D(0, 1, 0));
    world.SetScreenWidth(40);
    world.SetScreenHeight(30);
    world.SetScreenDistance(10);
    world.SetAmbientLight(RGBColor(0.3, 0.3, 0.3));

    world.SetBackgroundColor(RGBColor(0));

}

int
main(int argc, char *argv[])
{
    World TheWorld;

    // Say hello
```

Listing E.1 skeleton.cpp (application template)

```
cout << "OORT: The Object-Oriented Ray Tracer  Version 1.0\n";
cout << "Copyright (C) 1992 by Nicholas Wilt.  All rights
reserved.\n\n";

// Allocate global noise sources.
if (! GlobalNoise::Noise)
   GlobalNoise::Noise = new PerlinNoise;
if (! GlobalNoise::Waves)
   GlobalNoise::Waves = new WaveSource(10, GlobalNoise::Noise);
if (! GlobalNoise::Freqs)
   GlobalNoise::Freqs = new FreqSource(10, GlobalNoise::Noise);

PopulateWorld(TheWorld);

// Parse the command line; options given on the command line sub-
sume
// stuff specified in the input file.
TheWorld.ParseCommandLine(argc, argv);

// Write RAW output file.
TheWorld.RayTrace();

// Report on statistics gathered.
Report(cout);
if (Statistics::AppendTo) {
     ofstream app(Statistics::AppendTo, ios::ate);
     if (! (! app)) {
        Report(app);
        app.close();
     }
}

// Delete global noise sources.
delete GlobalNoise::Noise;
delete GlobalNoise::Waves;
delete GlobalNoise::Freqs;

return 0;
}
```

Listing E.1   `skeleton.cpp` (application template) *(continued)*

E.3 ■ Splicing RAW Files Together

Because ray tracing is compute-intensive but trivially parallelizable, different pixels can be computed by different computers with no communication during the computation. As long as both computers are rendering the same model, the different parts of the image can be spliced together, resulting in the same image as if one computer had crunched it alone. Large traces can currently be distributed among computers using "sneakernet": the program linked against OORT can be put on a floppy disk and executed on a variety of computers with different starting and ending scanlines so that different portions of the image are rendered by each computer. The resulting output files can then be consolidated on one computer and spliced using the Splice program.

Splice takes two sets of parameters: the list of files to splice and an output file. The output file is given with the −o parameter (which is required). As with other command-line arguments in OORT, there is no space between the command-line option and the filename. The following command line illustrates how to execute Splice:

```
splice eggs1 eggs2 eggs3 -oeggs4.raw
```

This causes splice to read in the files `eggs1.raw`, `eggs2.raw`, and `eggs3.raw`. The files are spliced together, and the resulting file is written to `eggs4.raw`.

Splice knows to append the .RAW extension to the filenames if no extension is given. Its task is very disk-intensive, so be patient. You might also want to get a cup of coffee so you don't need to listen to the grinding noises coming from your disk drive.

Once the files have been spliced, the output file can be quantized and displayed.

```
/* splice.c:
 *    program to splice multiple RAW files in OORT/DKB/QRT format.
 *    Copyright (C) 1993 by Nicholas Wilt.  All rights reserved.
 */

#include <stdlib.h>
#include <string.h>
#include <alloc.h>
#include <stdio.h>
```

Listing E.2   `splice.c`

```
#define SPLICE_ER_MEMORY      1
#define SPLICE_ER_READOPEN      2
#define SPLICE_ER_WRITEOPEN      3
#define SPLICE_ER_BADDIMS      4

struct rawfile {
    short ymin;
    struct rawfile *next;
    char filename[1];
};

short width = 0, height = 0;
unsigned char *buffer;
static struct rawfile *files = NULL;
static char inbuf[32767];

int
splice_newfile(char *filename)
{
    struct rawfile *newfile;
    FILE *inp;
    short wid, hgt;

    newfile = (struct rawfile *) malloc(sizeof(struct rawfile) +
    strlen(filename));
    if (! newfile)
        return -SPLICE_ER_MEMORY;
    newfile->next = files;
    files = newfile;
    inp = fopen(filename, "rb");
    if (! inp)
        return -SPLICE_ER_READOPEN;
    fread(&wid, sizeof(short), 1, inp);
    if (! width) {
        width = wid;
        buffer = (unsigned char *) malloc((2 + 3 * width) *
                                        sizeof(unsigned char));
    }
    else if (wid != width)
        return -SPLICE_ER_BADDIMS;
    fread(&hgt, sizeof(short), 1, inp);
    if (! height)
        height = hgt;
    else if (hgt != height)
        return -SPLICE_ER_BADDIMS;
```

Listing E.2 splice.c *(continued)*

```
      fread(&newfile->ymin, sizeof(short), 1, inp);
      strcpy(newfile->filename, filename);
      fclose(inp);
      return 0;
}

int
splice_readfile(char *infile, FILE *outfile, int stopscanl)
{
   FILE *inp = fopen(infile, "rb");
   int i;
   printf("Reading %s...\n", infile);
   setvbuf(inp, inbuf, _IOFBF, 32767);
   for (i = 0; i < 4; i++)        /* Skip header */
      (void) fgetc(inp);
   while (! feof(inp)) {
      fread(buffer, 1, 2 + 3*width, inp);
      fwrite(buffer, 1, 2 + 3*width, outfile);
      if ((stopscanl-1) == ((short *) buffer)[0])
         break;
   }
   fclose(inp);
   return 0;
}

void
splice_findmin(struct rawfile **pmin, struct rawfile **pminfoll)
{
   struct rawfile *sc, *foll;
   struct rawfile *min, *minfoll;

   sc = min = files;
   minfoll = foll = NULL;
   for (; sc; foll = sc, sc = sc->next) {
      if (sc->ymin < min->ymin) {
         min = sc;
         minfoll = foll;
      }
   }
   if (pmin)
      *pmin = min;
   if (pminfoll)
      *pminfoll = minfoll;
}
```

Listing E.2 splice.c *(continued)*

```
int
main(int argc, char *argv[])
{
    char *outfilename = NULL;
    FILE *outp;
    struct rawfile *min, *sc;

    argc--;
    argv++;
    while (argc--) {
        if (argv[0][0] == '-' && argv[0][1] == 'o') {
            if (! argv[0][2]) {
                outfilename = argv[0];
                argv++;
                argc--;
                continue;
            }
            outfilename = argv[0] + 2;
        }
        else {
            char newfile[256];
            strcpy(newfile, argv[0]);
            if (! strchr(newfile, '.'))
                strcat(newfile, ".RAW");
            if (splice_newfile(newfile)) {
                fprintf(stderr, "Error opening %s for input", argv[0]);
                exit(-1);
            }
        }
        argv++;
    }
    if (! outfilename) {
        fprintf(stderr, "No output file specified\n");
        exit(-1);
    }
    outp = fopen(outfilename, "wb");
    fwrite(&width, sizeof(short), 1, outp);
    fwrite(&height, sizeof(short), 1, outp);
    if (! outp) {
        fprintf(stderr, "Error opening %s for output\n", outfilename);
        exit(-1);
    }
    while (files) {
        struct rawfile *min, *minfoll, *min2;
        splice_findmin(&min, &minfoll);
```

Listing E.2 splice.c *(continued)*

```
    if (minfoll)
        minfoll->next = min->next;
    else
        files = min->next;
    splice_findmin(&min2, NULL);
    splice_readfile(min->filename, outp, (min2) ? min2->ymin :
height);
    free(min);
    }
    fclose(outp);
    return 0;
}
```

Listing E.2 `splice.c` *(continued)*

E.4 Color Quantization: RAW2GIF

Color quantization is the process of choosing a limited number of colors to represent a full-color image. There are several reasons to perform color quantization on an image. One is compression: if you quantize a 24-bit image to an image with less precision, you get a corresponding decrease in size. The primary reason to quantize an image, however, is for display.

Many computers, including most PC compatibles with VGA and SuperVGA, are limited to displaying 256 or fewer colors at once. For such computers, images must be quantized before they can be displayed. A program called RAW2GIF has been provided that takes an output file from the ray tracer (whose extension defaults to RAW), quantizes the image, and writes out a file using the Graphics Interchange Format (GIF).

GIF is an image file format used by CompuServe that has many advantages for our application. Many public domain or shareware programs can read and display GIF images, so displaying our output images is not a problem. Also, GIF has built-in LZW compression, and ray traced images tend to be *very* compressible. The GIF file resulting from a call to RAW2GIF is often an order of magnitude smaller than the original RAW file.

RAW2GIF uses the popular median-cut quantization algorithm, as described by Heckbert [HECK82]. The command-line options are given in Table E.2.

The source code for RAW2GIF has been provided on the code disk. Compiled versions have been provided for DOS (`raw2gif.exe`) and Windows (`raw2gifw.exe`). The Windows version is compiled using the EasyWin library, so it looks like the DOS application and is run using the same command-line parameters.

–num	Specify the number of colors to quantize to. This number must be a power of 2 in the range 2–256.
–d	Perform Floyd-Steinberg dithering on the image. Turning on this option will significantly increase the time required to write the image, but it may reduce objectionable artifacts in the image due to aliasing.
–ifile	Specify an input file. The default extension is .RAW.
–ofile	Specify an output file. The default extension is .GIF.

Table E.2   RAW2GIF usage

E.5 Displaying GIF Files

Dozens of computer programs are capable of reading, displaying and manipulating GIF files. Many are dedicated simply to displaying GIF files on the screen; they are called *GIF viewers*. Many public-domain and shareware GIF viewers are available through shareware houses, or can be downloaded from graphics-related information services. A shareware GIF viewer called VUIMAGE, from Offe Enterprises, has been included on the disk set for this book. Those of you who did not buy the disk set with the book must find a GIF viewer yourselves. It should be easy to get a GIF viewer from the same place you got OORT. Including VUIMAGE rather than any of a dozen other GIF viewing utilities does not constitute an endorsement of the product; I simply didn't want readers to have to download or purchase a GIF viewer in order to look at their ray traced images.

Like any shareware, you should register VUIMAGE if you use it.

Please see the documentation files for VUIMAGE to understand how the program works. The most important command-line argument is –v, which specifies the video driver. VESA-compliant VGA and SuperVGA cards will work fine if you launch VUIMG with no command-line arguments. If you have another type of display adapter or your VGA adapter does not comply with the VESA standard, read the documentation for VUIMG included on the disk to determine which video driver you should use.

E.6 Hints

- Don't dive into creating images from the application template all at once. Get at least one of the examples to work from start to finish before striking out on your own.

- Be careful running GIF viewers from a DOS shell under Windows. The DOS shell knows about standard VGA modes such as $640 \times 480 \times 16$ and $320 \times 200 \times 256$, but it will not know how to save and restore the screen in a nonstandard SuperVGA mode like $1024 \times 768 \times 256$.

- By default, all the Makefiles and project files generate programs with symbolic information. Turbo Debugger can then open the source files so that OORT, as well as the scene being rendered, can be examined during execution. The drawback is that the objects and executables are extremely large. You can conserve disk space by removing $-v$ and $-vi$ command-line options from the Makefiles in \OORT\SOURCE. This will prevent Borland C++ from writing debugging information in the objects (and, of course, will make it so you can't debug the executables).

- When using Turbo Debugger to debug an OORT application that linked against OORT and the UTILS library, you must use the Change Directory command in the File menu to switch the directory to the same as the OORT source (\OORT\SOURCE) or, if you are debugging the Utilities library, the Utilities library source (\OORT\UTILS). If Turbo Debugger cannot find the source code of the application being debugged, it will display the assembler code instead. Switching directories and hitting the F7 or F8 (steps/trace) keys should fix the problem.

Under Windows:

- If the Borland C++ IDE complains that it can't find OORT include files, select the Directories option from the Options menu and add the OORT include directory.

- One nice way to launch RAW2GIF easily from Windows is to define a Program Item with the desired command line (choose New from the File menu, then type the command line). This will create an icon in the Program Manager that you double-click whenever you want the .RAW file in a certain directory to be quantized.

A Few Troubleshooting Tips

1. The compiler can't find OORT include files.

   If you are using the command-line compiler, you should specify the OORT include directory (\OORT\INCLUDE by default) using the –I command-line option.

If you are using the Borland C++ IDE, pull down the Directories option from the Options menu and make sure the OORT include directory is listed there.

2. The OORT and UTILS libraries are both built properly, but the Borland C++ IDE is still getting link errors.

Make sure the compiler is set to generate code for the Large model. Go into the Options menu and select Code Generation from the Compiler>> pop-up menu. The resulting dialog box has a group of radio buttons to select the memory model.

3. The image being generated is wrong. Why?

Check for the following symptoms:
- Make sure there are light sources in the World.
- Make sure `World::AddObject` is being called for all the objects that are supposed to appear in the scene.
- For one-sided, planar objects, make sure the surface normals are pointing the right direction.

Use Turbo Debugger if the problem persists. Set a breakpoint in `HallSurface::ComputeColor`. If the breakpoint never triggers, then no object is being intersected for some reason. If the breakpoint triggers, watch the five components of the shading equation. Which ones should contribute? Are they failing to contribute because the surface normals are backward, because everything is in shadow, or because the coefficients of reflection or transmission are all zero?

You may want to practice on a working examples, such as the ones described in Appendix F, before trying to debug your own.

Appendix F

Examples

Each Example is in its own subdirectory in \OORT\EXAMPLES. Besides the source file listed in this chapter, each Example directory contains the following files:

File	Description
`makefile.dos`	Makefile to use if OORT was built for DOS. Type: `make -fmakefile.dos` from the DOS prompt to build the example.
`makefile.win`	Makefile to use from the command line if OORT was built for Windows. Type: `make -fmakefile.win` from the DOS prompt to build the example.
example`.prj`	Project file for the example. This can be opened from the Windows-hosted Borland C++ IDE. Once this is done, BC++ will create other related files, such as *example*.dsk (the desktop file).
example`.def`	Module definitions file for the example. This is used by the linker under Windows. For OORT applications, all the module definitions file does for OORT is set the stack size to 40K (a ludicrously high number, but one that most Windows machines can certainly afford).

F.1 Specular

The Specular example is intended to illustrate how different coefficients of specular reflection and Phong exponents affect the appearance of an object. Plate 1 shows the image generated by this program. From left to right, the spheres have increasing specular exponents (3, 5, 10, 27, 200). From top to bottom, the spheres have increasing coefficients of specular reflection, so that they reflect more brightly (0.1, 0.25, 0.5).

```
// =====================================================================
// SPECULAR.CPP
//     Scene derived from Figure 16.10 in Foley, van Dam, Feiner
//     and Hughes, figure by David Kurlander.  Used by permission.
// Copyright (C) 1993 by Nicholas Wilt.  All rights reserved.
// =====================================================================

#include "oort.h"
#include "world.h"

void
PopulateWorld(World& world)
{
    float specularities[5] = {3.0, 5.0, 10.0, 27.0, 200.0};
    float sattens[3] = {0.1, 0.25, 0.5};

    world.SetDepthLimit(3);
    world.SetOutputFile("specular.raw");

    world.SetViewerParameters(Vector3D(0), Vector3D(0, 0, 50),
    Vector3D(0, 1, 0));
    world.SetScreenWidth(8);
    world.SetScreenHeight(4);
    world.SetScreenDistance(10);

    world.SetAmbientLight(RGBColor(1));
    world.SetBackgroundColor(RGBColor(0));

    world.AddLight(new PointLight(Vector3D(-20, 40, 80), RGBColor(1),
                   1, 0, 0));

    for (int i = 0; i < 5; i++) {
```

Listing F.1 specular.cpp

```
    for (int j = 0; j < 3; j++) {
        HallSurface *sphsurf = new HallSurface;
        sphsurf->SetAmbient(new PureColor(RGBColor(0.1)));
        sphsurf->SetDiffuse(new PureColor(RGBColor(0.45)));
        sphsurf->SetSpecular(new PureColor(RGBColor(sattens[j])),
                            specularities[i]);
        Sphere *addme = new Sphere(Vector3D( (i-2) * 6.0, (j-1) *
                                   6.0, 0), 2.0, sphsurf);
        world.AddObject(addme);
    }
  }
}

int
main(int argc, char *argv[])
{
    World TheWorld;

    // Say hello
    cout << "OORT: The Object-Oriented Ray Tracer  Version 1.0\n";
    cout << "Copyright (C) 1992 by Nicholas Wilt.  All rights
    reserved.\n\n";

    // Allocate global noise sources.
    if (! GlobalNoise::Noise)
       GlobalNoise::Noise = new PerlinNoise;
    if (! GlobalNoise::Waves)
       GlobalNoise::Waves = new WaveSource(10, GlobalNoise::Noise);
    if (! GlobalNoise::Freqs)
       GlobalNoise::Freqs = new FreqSource(10, GlobalNoise::Noise);

    PopulateWorld(TheWorld);

    // Parse the command line; options given on the command line
    subsume
    // stuff specified in the input file.
    TheWorld.ParseCommandLine(argc, argv);

    // Write RAW output file.
    TheWorld.RayTrace();

    // Report on statistics gathered.
    Report(cout);
    if (Statistics::AppendTo) {
         ofstream app(Statistics::AppendTo, ios::ate);
```

Listing F.1 specular.cpp *(continued)*

```
        if (! (! app)) {
            Report(app);
            app.close();
        }
    }

    // Delete global noise sources.
    delete GlobalNoise::Noise;
    delete GlobalNoise::Waves;
    delete GlobalNoise::Freqs;

    return 0;
}
```

Listing F.1 `specular.cpp` *(continued)*

F.2 CSG Demo

The CSG Demo example illustrates the three fundamental CSG operations: Union, Intersection and Difference. On the left, it shows the overlapping objects to be combined; on the right, the objects are combined using Union (bottom), Intersection (middle), and Difference (top).

The lowest spheres, which are combined using the Union operator, are transparent to better show the effects of the Union. The two separate, overlapping spheres on the left interact to cast a darker shadow, and many rays are refracted to reflect background. In contrast, the object on the right is truly one object, so it casts a uniform shadow and refracts rays in a more well-behaved way.

```
// ======================================================================
// CSGDEMO.CPP
//    Illustrate constructive solid geometry.
// Copyright (C) 1993 by Nicholas Wilt.  All rights reserved.
// ======================================================================


#include "oort.h"
#include "world.h"
#include "colors.h"
#include "utils.h"

void
```

Listing F.2 `csgdemo.cpp`

```
PopulateWorld(World& world)
{
    world.SetDepthLimit(3);
    world.SetOutputFile("csgdemo.raw");

    world.SetViewerParameters(Vector3D(0), Vector3D(0, 5, 12),
    Vector3D(0, 1, 0));
    world.SetScreenWidth(4);
    world.SetScreenHeight(3);
    world.SetScreenDistance(2);

    world.SetBackgroundColor(RGBColor(0));

    world.AddLight(new PointLight(Vector3D(0, 10, 20), RGBColor(1./3),
                                  1, 0, 0));
    world.AddLight(new DirectLight(Vector3D(0, 1, 0), RGBColor(1./3)));
    world.AddLight(new PointLight(Vector3D(0, 5, 12), RGBColor(1./3),
                                  1, 0, 0));

    Texture *ChessBoard = new Checkerboard(5, 5,
                                  new PureColor(0, 0, 0.5),
                                  new PureColor(0, 0.5, 0.5),
                                  RotationXMatrix(-90*M_PI/180));

    HallSurface *surf = new HallSurface;
    surf->SetBumpMap(new TwoSided);
    surf->SetDiffuse(new PureColor(Blue));

    HallSurface *sph2surf = new HallSurface;
    surf->SetBumpMap(new TwoSided);
    sph2surf->SetDiffuse(new PureColor(Red));

    {
        Sphere sph1(Vector3D(0), 2, surf);
        Sphere sph2(Vector3D(1.5, 0, 0), 2, sph2surf);
        Aggregate *addme = new Aggregate;
        addme->AddObject(sph1);
        addme->AddObject(sph2);
        addme->ApplyTransform(TranslationMatrix(Vector3D(-4, 0, 0)));
        world.AddObject(addme);
        CSGIntersection *inter = new CSGIntersection(sph1.Dup(),
                                                     sph2.Dup());
        inter->ApplyTransform(TranslationMatrix(Vector3D(4, 0, 0)));
        world.AddObject(inter);
    }
```

Listing F.2   `csgdemo.cpp` *(continued)*

```
    {
        Object3D *right = new CSGIntersection(new Plane(Vector3D(0, 1,
    0), -2, surf), new Plane(Vector3D(0, -1, 0), -2, surf));
        right = new CSGIntersection(right, MakeCylinder(0.5, 0.75,
                                    surf));
        right->ApplyTransform(RotationXMatrix(90*M_PI/180) *
                            RotationYMatrix(30*M_PI/180));
        Object3D *left = new Sphere(Vector3D(0), 1.5, surf);

        Aggregate *nodiff = new Aggregate;
        nodiff->AddObject(left->Dup());
        nodiff->AddObject(right->Dup());
        nodiff->ApplyTransform(TranslationMatrix(Vector3D(-5, 5, 0)));
        world.AddObject(nodiff);

        Object3D *diff = new CSGDifference(left, right);
        diff->ApplyTransform(TranslationMatrix(Vector3D(5, 5, 0)));
        world.AddObject(diff);
    }

    {
        Aggregate *addme = new Aggregate;
        addme->AddObject(new Sphere(Vector3D(0), 1, MakeGlass()));
        addme->AddObject(new Sphere(Vector3D(-0.5, 0, 0), 1,
                        MakeGlass()));
        addme->ApplyTransform(TranslationMatrix(Vector3D(-3, 0, 7)));
        world.AddObject(addme);
        Sphere *sph1 = new Sphere(Vector3D(0), 1, MakeGlass());
        Sphere *sph2 = new Sphere(Vector3D(-0.5, 0, 0), 1, MakeGlass());
        CSGUnion *uni = new CSGUnion(sph1, sph2);
        uni->ApplyTransform(TranslationMatrix(Vector3D(3, 0, 7)));
        world.AddObject(uni);
    }

    HallSurface *checks = new HallSurface;
    checks->SetDiffuse(/*new PureColor(CornflowerBlue)*/ChessBoard);
    world.AddObject(new Plane(Vector3D(0, 1, 0), 5.0, checks));
}

int
main(int argc, char *argv[])
{
    World TheWorld;
```

Listing F.2   csgdemo.cpp *(continued)*

```
    // Say hello
    cout << "OORT: The Object-Oriented Ray Tracer  Version 1.0\n";
    cout << "Copyright (C) 1992 by Nicholas Wilt.  All rights
reserved.\n\n";

    // Allocate global noise sources.
    if (! GlobalNoise::Noise)
        GlobalNoise::Noise = new PerlinNoise;
    if (! GlobalNoise::Waves)
        GlobalNoise::Waves = new WaveSource(10, GlobalNoise::Noise);
    if (! GlobalNoise::Freqs)
        GlobalNoise::Freqs = new FreqSource(10, GlobalNoise::Noise);

    PopulateWorld(TheWorld);

    // Parse the command line; options given on the command line
subsume
    // stuff specified in the input file.
    TheWorld.ParseCommandLine(argc, argv);

    // Write RAW output file.
    TheWorld.RayTrace();

    // Report on statistics gathered.
    Report(cout);
    if (Statistics::AppendTo) {
        ofstream app(Statistics::AppendTo, ios::ate);
        if (! (! app)) {
            Report(app);
            app.close();
        }
    }

    // Delete global noise sources.
    delete GlobalNoise::Noise;
    delete GlobalNoise::Waves;
    delete GlobalNoise::Freqs;

    return 0;
}
```

Listing F.2 csgdemo.cpp *(continued)*

F.3   Blurry Reflection

This demo illustrates blurry reflection. It depicts five spheres that reflect more blurrily from left to right. The spheres and the viewer are enclosed in a checkered sphere. The checks are distorted because of the perspective projection: checks that are near the viewer appear larger.

```cpp
// =======================================================================
// RBLURRY.CPP
//    Illustrate blurry reflection.
// Copyright (C) 1993 by Nicholas Wilt.  All rights reserved.
// =======================================================================


#include "oort.h"
#include "world.h"
#include "colors.h"

Texture *
RedMarble()
{
   ColorMap *cmap = new ColorMap;
   cmap->AddEntry(new LinearColorMapEntry(0, 0.8,
                                 RGBColor(0.8, 0.8, 0.6),
                                 RGBColor(0.8, 0.4, 0.4)));
   cmap->AddEntry(new LinearColorMapEntry(0.8, 1.0,
                                 RGBColor(0.8, 0.4, 0.4),
                                 RGBColor(0.8, 0.2, 0.2)));
   return new Marble(IdentityMatrix(), 1.0, cmap);
}

Texture *
BlueMarble()
{
   ColorMap *cmap = new ColorMap;
   cmap->AddEntry(new OneColorMapEntry(0, 0.5, RGBColor(0.3, 0.3,
      0.5)));
   cmap->AddEntry(new LinearColorMapEntry(0.5, 0.55, RGBColor(0.3,
      0.3, 0.5), RGBColor(0.2, 0.2, 0.3)));
   cmap->AddEntry(new LinearColorMapEntry(0.55, 0.6, RGBColor(0.2,
      0.2, 0.3), RGBColor(0.25, 0.25, 0.35)));
   cmap->AddEntry(new LinearColorMapEntry(0.6, 0.7, RGBColor(0.25,
      0.25, 0.35), RGBColor(0.15, 0.15, 0.26)));
```

Listing F.3   `rblurry.cpp`

```
   cmap->AddEntry(new LinearColorMapEntry(0.7, 0.8, RGBColor(0.15,
      0.15, 0.26), RGBColor(0.1, 0.1, 0.2)));
   cmap->AddEntry(new LinearColorMapEntry(0.8, 0.9, RGBColor(0.1, 0.1,
      0.2), RGBColor(0.3, 0.3, 0.5)));
   cmap->AddEntry(new LinearColorMapEntry(0.9, 1.0, RGBColor(0.3, 0.3,
      0.5), RGBColor(0.1, 0.1, 0.2)));
   return new Marble(ScaleMatrix(0.3, 0.3, 0.3), 0.3, cmap);
}

Texture *
WhiteMarble()
{
   ColorMap *cmap = new ColorMap;
   cmap->AddEntry(new OneColorMapEntry(0, 0.3, White));
   cmap->AddEntry(new LinearColorMapEntry(0.3, 0.7, White,
      RGBColor(0.6)));
   cmap->AddEntry(new LinearColorMapEntry(0.7, 0.9, RGBColor(0.6),
      RGBColor(0.45)));
   cmap->AddEntry(new LinearColorMapEntry(0.9, 1.0, RGBColor(0.45),
      RGBColor(0.3)));
   return new Marble(ScaleMatrix(0.2, 0.2, 0.2), 1.0, cmap);
}

extern void printhist();

void
PopulateWorld(World& world)
{
   world.SetDepthLimit(3);
   world.SetOutputFile("rblurry.raw");

   // The World is lit by ambient light only, so no shadow rays are
   cast.

   world.SetViewerParameters(Vector3D(0), Vector3D(0, 1, 12),
   Vector3D(0, 1, 0));
   world.SetScreenWidth(3);
   world.SetScreenHeight(1.5);
   world.SetScreenDistance(2);
   world.SetAmbientLight(RGBColor(1));
   world.SetBackgroundColor(RGBColor(0, 1, 0));

   float angs[] = {0.04, 0.08, 0.12, 0.16, 0.2};
   for (int i = 0; i < 5; i++) {
      DistributedHall *surf = new DistributedHall;
```

Listing F.3 rblurry.cpp *(continued)*

```
        surf->SetReflect(new PureColor(RGBColor(0.8)));
        surf->SetReflectParms(DistributedHall::DistribParms(4, 8, 10,
            angs[i]));
        world.AddObject(new Sphere(Vector3D(3 * (i - 2), 0, 0), 1.0,
            surf));
    }

    Texture *ChessBoard = new Checkerboard(0.1, 0.1,
                                        new PureColor(Aquamarine),
                                        new PureColor(CornflowerBlue),
                                        IdentityMatrix(),
                                        new SphericalMapping(Vector3D(0, 0,
                                        12)));
    HallSurface *checks = new HallSurface;
    checks->SetBumpMap(new ReverseNormal);
    checks->SetDiffuse(ChessBoard);
    checks->SetAmbient(ChessBoard);
    world.AddObject(Sphere(Vector3D(0, 0, 12), 15, checks));
}

int
main(int argc, char *argv[])
{
    World TheWorld;

    // Say hello
    cout << "OORT: The Object-Oriented Ray Tracer  Version 1.0\n";
    cout << "Copyright (C) 1992 by Nicholas Wilt.  All rights
    reserved.\n\n";

    // Allocate global noise sources.
    if (! GlobalNoise::Noise)
        GlobalNoise::Noise = new PerlinNoise;
    if (! GlobalNoise::Waves)
        GlobalNoise::Waves = new WaveSource(10, GlobalNoise::Noise);
    if (! GlobalNoise::Freqs)
        GlobalNoise::Freqs = new FreqSource(10, GlobalNoise::Noise);

    PopulateWorld(TheWorld);

    // Parse the command line; options given on the command line
    subsume
    // stuff specified in the input file.
    TheWorld.ParseCommandLine(argc, argv);
```

Listing F.3 rblurry.cpp *(continued)*

```
    // Write RAW output file.
    TheWorld.RayTrace();

    // Report on statistics gathered.
    Report(cout);
    if (Statistics::AppendTo) {
        ofstream app(Statistics::AppendTo, ios::ate);
        if (! (! app)) {
            Report(app);
            app.close();
        }
    }

    // Delete global noise sources.
    delete GlobalNoise::Noise;
    delete GlobalNoise::Waves;
    delete GlobalNoise::Freqs;

    return 0;
}
```

Listing F.3 `rblurry.cpp` *(continued)*

F.4 Quadrics

This example illustrates five quadric surfaces: the ellipsoid, cone, cylinder, paraboloid, and hyperboloid of one sheet. Since only the ellipsoid is a bounded primitive, CSG was used to bound the other primitives by intersecting them with planes.

```
// ======================================================================
// quadrics.cpp
//     Illustrate the various quadric surfaces.
// Copyright (C) 1993 by Nicholas Wilt.  All rights reserved.
// ======================================================================

#include "oort.h"
#include "world.h"
#include "colors.h"
#include "utils.h"

void
```

Listing F.4 `quadrics.cpp`

```
PopulateWorld(World& world)
{
    world.SetDepthLimit(3);
    world.SetOutputFile("quadrics.raw");

    world.SetViewerParameters(Vector3D(0), Vector3D(0, 0, 10),
    Vector3D(0, 1, 0));
    world.SetScreenWidth(40);
    world.SetScreenHeight(30);
    world.SetScreenDistance(10);
    world.SetAmbientLight(RGBColor(0.3, 0.3, 0.3));

    world.SetBackgroundColor(RGBColor(0));

    Limits::Threshold = 0.01;
    Limits::Small = 0.001;

    world.AddLight(new PointLight(Vector3D(0, 5, 10), RGBColor(0.8), 1,
        0, 0));

    Texture *ChessBoard = new Checkerboard(5, 5,
                        new PureColor(58623/65535., 31092/65535.,
                            2921/65535.),
                        new PureColor(58623/65535., 53948/65535.,
                            12894/65535.),
                        Matrix(RotationXMatrix(-90)));

    HallSurface *surf = new HallSurface;
    surf->SetBumpMap(new TwoSided);
    surf->SetDiffuse(new PureColor(Blue));
    surf->SetAmbient(new PureColor(Blue));

    Object3D *addme = new Algebraic(Ellipsoid(4, 2, 1, surf));
    addme->ApplyTransform(TranslationMatrix(Vector3D(10, 0, 0)));
    addme->ApplyTransform(RotationZMatrix(0*2*M_PI/5));
    world.AddObject(addme);

    addme = new CSGIntersection(new Plane(Vector3D(0, 1, 0), 0, surf),
        MakeCone(0.5, 0.5, surf));
    addme = new CSGIntersection(addme, new Plane(Vector3D(0, -1, 0),
        -6, surf));
    addme->ApplyTransform(RotationXMatrix(60*M_PI/180) *
        TranslationMatrix(Vector3D(10, 0, 0)));
    addme->ApplyTransform(RotationZMatrix(1*2*M_PI/5));
    world.AddObject(addme);
```

Listing F.4 `quadrics.cpp` *(continued)*

```
    addme = new CSGIntersection(new Plane(Vector3D(0, 1, 0), -3, surf),
        new Plane(Vector3D(0, -1, 0), -3, surf));
    addme = new CSGIntersection(addme, MakeCylinder(1, 1, surf));
    addme->ApplyTransform(RotationXMatrix(-30*M_PI/180) *
        RotationZMatrix(-20*M_PI/180));
    addme->ApplyTransform(TranslationMatrix(Vector3D(5, 0, 0)));
    addme->ApplyTransform(RotationZMatrix(2*2*M_PI/5));
    world.AddObject(addme);

    addme = new CSGIntersection(new Plane(Vector3D(0, 1, 0), -2, surf),
        new Plane(Vector3D(0, -1, 0), -2, surf));
    addme = new CSGIntersection(addme, MakeHyperboloid(1, 1, 0.5,
        surf));
    addme->ApplyTransform(RotationZMatrix(90*M_PI/180));
    addme->ApplyTransform(TranslationMatrix(Vector3D(-10, 0, 0)));
    world.AddObject(addme);

    addme = MakeParaboloid(1, 1, 0.2, surf);
    addme->ApplyTransform(MirrorY());
    addme = new CSGIntersection(new Plane(Vector3D(0, -1, 0), -5,
        surf), addme);
    addme->ApplyTransform(TranslationMatrix(Vector3D(0, 2, 0)));
    world.AddObject(addme);

    HallSurface *checks = new HallSurface;
    checks->SetDiffuse(ChessBoard);
    checks->SetDiffuse(new PureColor(0.2, 0.6, 0.7));
    checks->SetAmbient(new PureColor(0.2, 0.6, 0.7));
    world.AddObject(new Plane(Vector3D(0, 1, 0), 11.0, checks));
}

int
main(int argc, char *argv[])
{
    World TheWorld;

    // Say hello
    cout << "OORT: The Object-Oriented Ray Tracer  Version 1.0\n";
    cout << "Copyright (C) 1992 by Nicholas Wilt.  All rights
    reserved.\n\n";

    // Allocate global noise sources.
    if (! GlobalNoise::Noise)
        GlobalNoise::Noise = new PerlinNoise;
```

Listing F.4 quadrics.cpp *(continued)*

```
if (! GlobalNoise::Waves)
    GlobalNoise::Waves = new WaveSource(10, GlobalNoise::Noise);
if (! GlobalNoise::Freqs)
    GlobalNoise::Freqs = new FreqSource(10, GlobalNoise::Noise);

PopulateWorld(TheWorld);

// Parse the command line; options given on the command line
subsume
// stuff specified in the input file.
TheWorld.ParseCommandLine(argc, argv);

// Write RAW output file.
TheWorld.RayTrace();

// Report on statistics gathered.
Report(cout);
if (Statistics::AppendTo) {
    ofstream app(Statistics::AppendTo, ios::ate);
    if (! (! app)) {
        Report(app);
        app.close();
    }
}

// Delete global noise sources.
delete GlobalNoise::Noise;
delete GlobalNoise::Waves;
delete GlobalNoise::Freqs;

return 0;
}
```

Listing F.4 `quadrics.cpp` *(continued)*

F.5 Algebraic Surfaces

This example generates an image of five algebraic surfaces: Steiner's surface, the quartic cylinder, Kummer's surface, the piriform, and the Lemniscate of Gerano.

```
// =====================================================================
// algs.cpp
//     Illustrate a variety of algebraic surfaces.
// Copyright (C) 1993 by Nicholas Wilt.  All rights reserved.
// =====================================================================

#include "oort.h"
#include "world.h"
#include "colors.h"
#include "utils.h"

void
PopulateWorld(World& world)
{
    world.SetAmbientLight(RGBColor(1/3.));
    world.SetDepthLimit(3);
    world.SetOutputFile("steiner.raw");

    // Important: set threshold of no-intersection to a
    // much smaller value than the default.
    Limits::Threshold = 0.01;
    Limits::Small = 0.001;

    world.SetViewerParameters(Vector3D(0), Vector3D(0, 0, -8),
    Vector3D(0, 1, 0));
    world.SetScreenWidth(4);
    world.SetScreenHeight(3);
    world.SetScreenDistance(2);

    world.SetBackgroundColor(RGBColor(0));

    world.AddLight(new PointLight(Vector3D(2, 0, -2.5), RGBColor(1/3.),
        1, 0, 0));
    world.AddLight(new PointLight(Vector3D(-2, 2, -2), RGBColor(1/3.),
        1, 0, 0));

    HallSurface *surf = new HallSurface;
    surf->SetBumpMap(new TwoSided);
    surf->SetAmbient(new PureColor(0, 0.5, 1));
    surf->SetDiffuse(new PureColor(0, 0.5, 1));
    surf->SetSpecular(new PureColor(0.8), 100);

    Object3D *addme = new CSGIntersection(MakePiriform(surf),
        new Plane(-1, 0, 0, -0.1, surf));
    addme->ApplyTransform(RotationZMatrix(-90*M_PI/180));
```

Listing F.5 algs.cpp

```
addme->ApplyTransform(RotationXMatrix(30*M_PI/180));
addme->ApplyTransform(TranslationMatrix(Vector3D(-3, 0, 0)));
world.AddObject(addme);

addme = new CSGIntersection(new Sphere(Vector3D(0), 2, surf),
                            MakeLemniscate(surf));
addme->ApplyTransform(RotationYMatrix(-25*M_PI/180));
addme->ApplyTransform(RotationZMatrix(-40*M_PI/180));
addme->ApplyTransform(TranslationMatrix(Vector3D(-6, 0, 0)));
world.AddObject(addme);

addme = new CSGIntersection(new Sphere(Vector3D(0), 1.1, surf),
                            MakeSteiner(surf));
addme->ApplyTransform(RotationYMatrix(45*M_PI/180));
addme->ApplyTransform(TranslationMatrix(Vector3D(6, 0, 0)));
world.AddObject(addme);

Object3D *qcyl = MakeQuarticCylinder(surf);
qcyl->ApplyTransform(RotationYMatrix(45*M_PI/180));
addme = new CSGIntersection(new Sphere(Vector3D(0), 4, surf),
                            qcyl);
addme->ApplyTransform(TranslationMatrix(Vector3D(3, 0, 0)));
world.AddObject(addme);

Object3D *kummer = MakeKummer(surf);
kummer->ApplyTransform(RotationYMatrix(25*M_PI/180));
kummer->ApplyTransform(TranslationMatrix(Vector3D(0, 0, 5)));
world.AddObject(kummer);
}

int
main(int argc, char *argv[])
{
    World TheWorld;

    // Say hello
    cout << "OORT: The Object-Oriented Ray Tracer  Version 1.0\n";
    cout << "Copyright (C) 1992 by Nicholas Wilt.  All rights
    reserved.\n\n";

    // Allocate global noise sources.
    if (! GlobalNoise::Noise)
        GlobalNoise::Noise = new PerlinNoise;
    if (! GlobalNoise::Waves)
        GlobalNoise::Waves = new WaveSource(10, GlobalNoise::Noise);
```

Listing F.5   `algs.cpp`   *(continued)*

```
    if (! GlobalNoise::Freqs)
        GlobalNoise::Freqs = new FreqSource(10, GlobalNoise::Noise);

    PopulateWorld(TheWorld);

    // Parse the command line; options given on the command line
    subsume
    // stuff specified in the input file.
    TheWorld.ParseCommandLine(argc, argv);

    // Write RAW output file.
    TheWorld.RayTrace();

    // Report on statistics gathered.
    Report(cout);
    if (Statistics::AppendTo) {
        ofstream app(Statistics::AppendTo, ios::ate);
        if (! (! app)) {
            Report(app);
            app.close();
        }
    }

    // Delete global noise sources.
    delete GlobalNoise::Noise;
    delete GlobalNoise::Waves;
    delete GlobalNoise::Freqs;

    return 0;
}
```

Listing F.5 `algs.cpp` *(continued)*

F.6 Textures

This demo showcases a variety of textures available in OORT. It shows a table on a tiled floor, with textured spheres on it. One sphere is reflective; one is transparent; one is solid red; and the others have various textures, including granite, wood, marble, and cloudy sky. The table uses a texture derived from Upstill's wood texture ([UPST90, p. 351). The floor is checkered with white and blue marble textures.

```
// =====================================================================
// TEXTS.CPP
//     Illustrates a number of textures.
// Copyright (C) 1993 by Nicholas Wilt.  All rights reserved.
// =====================================================================

#include "oort.h"
#include "world.h"
#include "colors.h"
#include "utils.h"

void
PopulateWorld(World& world)
{
   world.SetDepthLimit(3);
   world.SetOutputFile("texts.raw");

   world.SetViewerParameters(Vector3D(0), Vector3D(0, 3.5, 15),
      Vector3D(0, 1, 0));
   world.SetScreenWidth(8);
   world.SetScreenHeight(4);
   world.SetScreenDistance(4);

   world.SetAmbientLight(RGBColor(1));
   world.SetBackgroundColor(RGBColor(0));

   // Three light sources.
   world.AddLight(new PointLight(Vector3D(-20, 40, -80),
      RGBColor(1./3), 1, 0, 0));
   world.AddLight(new DirectLight(Vector3D(0, 1, 0), RGBColor(1./3)));
   world.AddLight(new PointLight(Vector3D(30, 40, 80), RGBColor(1./3),
      1, 0, 0));

   // Create a table textured with WoodUpstill, then put a white ring
   on it.
   {
      float min = -20;
      float max = 20;
      float legdiff = 2, legwid = 3;

      legwid += legdiff;

      // Table surface.
      HallSurface *newsurf = new HallSurface;
      newsurf->SetDiffuse(new
```

Listing F.6 texts.cpp

```
WoodUpstill(RotationYMatrix(45*M_PI/180), 0.2));
    newsurf->SetSpecular(new PureColor(RGBColor(0.6)), 40);

    // Create the table
    Aggregate *table = new Aggregate;
    table->AddObject(MakeBox(Vector3D(min, -6, min), Vector3D(max, -
        5, max), newsurf));
    newsurf = new HallSurface;
    newsurf->SetDiffuse(new WoodUpstill(RotationXMatrix(M_PI/2) *
        RotationYMatrix(45*M_PI/180), 0.2));
    newsurf->SetSpecular(new PureColor(RGBColor(0.6)), 10);
    table->AddObject(MakeBox(Vector3D(min + legdiff, -20, min +
        legdiff), Vector3D(min + legwid, -5, min + legwid), newsurf));
    table->AddObject(MakeBox(Vector3D(min + legdiff, -20, max -
        legwid), Vector3D(min + legwid, -5, max - legdiff), newsurf));
    table->AddObject(MakeBox(Vector3D(max - legwid, -20, min +
        legdiff), Vector3D(max - legdiff, -5, min + legwid), newsurf));
    table->AddObject(MakeBox(Vector3D(max - legwid, -20, max -
        legwid), Vector3D(max - legdiff, -5, max - legdiff), newsurf));
    table->ApplyTransform(RotationYMatrix(45*M_PI/180) *
        TranslationMatrix(Vector3D(0, 0, -15)));
    world.AddObject(table);

    // Ring surface: off-white diffuse reflector.
    HallSurface *surf = new HallSurface;
    surf->SetDiffuse(new PureColor(0.8));

    // Add ring to world.
    world.AddObject(new Ring(Vector3D(0, 1, 0), 4.9, Vector3D(0, 0,
        -15), 17, 18, surf));
}

// Use the random number generator to place NumSpheres spheres
// in the ring.
const int NumSpheres = 12;
Sphere *sphs[NumSpheres];
Vector3D centers[NumSpheres];
{
    srand(19);
    for (int i = 0; i < NumSpheres; i++) {
        int goti = 0;
        do {
            float mag = RandomValue(0, 15);
            float ang = RandomValue(0, 2 * M_PI);
            centers[i] = RotationYMatrix(ang) * Vector3D(1, 0, 0) *
```

Listing F.6   texts.cpp   *(continued)*

```
                    mag;
             centers[i] -= Vector3D(0, 4, 15);
             goti = (! i) || (MinDist(centers[i], centers, i - 1) > 5);
        } while (! goti);
    }
    HallSurface *surf = new HallSurface;
    surf->SetDiffuse(new PureColor(1, 0, 0));
    for (i = 0; i < NumSpheres; i++) {
        world.AddObject(sphs[i] = new Sphere(centers[i], 1, surf));
    }
}
// Now override the surfaces of the various spheres.
{
    HallSurface *surf = new HallSurface;
    surf->SetDiffuse(RedMarble());
    surf->SetSpecular(new PureColor(RGBColor(0.6)), 100);
    sphs[0]->OverrideColor(surf);

    surf = new HallSurface;
    surf->SetDiffuse(BlueMarble());
    surf->SetSpecular(new PureColor(RGBColor(0.6)), 100);
    sphs[1]->OverrideColor(surf);

    surf = new HallSurface;
    surf->SetDiffuse(WhiteMarble());
    surf->SetSpecular(new PureColor(RGBColor(0.6)), 100);
    sphs[2]->OverrideColor(surf);

    surf = new HallSurface;
    surf->SetDiffuse(BlackMarble());
    surf->SetSpecular(new PureColor(RGBColor(0.6)), 100);
    sphs[3]->OverrideColor(surf);

    surf = new HallSurface;
    surf->SetDiffuse(CherryWood(IdentityMatrix(), 0.3));
    surf->SetSpecular(new PureColor(RGBColor(0.6)), 100);
    sphs[4]->OverrideColor(surf);

    surf = new HallSurface;
    surf->SetDiffuse(PineWood(IdentityMatrix(), 0.3));
    surf->SetSpecular(new PureColor(RGBColor(0.6)), 100);
    sphs[5]->OverrideColor(surf);

    surf = new HallSurface;
    surf->SetDiffuse(DarkWood(IdentityMatrix(), 0.3));
```

Listing F.6 texts.cpp *(continued)*

```
            surf->SetSpecular(new PureColor(RGBColor(0.6)), 100);
            sphs[6]->OverrideColor(surf);

            surf = new HallSurface;
            surf->SetDiffuse(Clouds(IdentityMatrix(), 0.5));
            surf->SetSpecular(new PureColor(RGBColor(0.6)), 100);
            sphs[7]->OverrideColor(surf);
            sphs[8]->OverrideColor(MakeReflective());
            sphs[9]->OverrideColor(MakeGranite());
            surf = new HallSurface;
            surf->SetDiffuse(new PureColor(Red));
            surf->SetSpecular(new PureColor(RGBColor(0.6)), 100);
            sphs[10]->OverrideColor(surf);
            sphs[11]->OverrideColor(MakeGlass());
        }
        {
            Texture *check1 = WhiteMarble(ScaleMatrix(0.1, 0.1, 0.1));
            Texture *check2 = BlueMarble(ScaleMatrix(0.35, 0.35, 0.35) *
                RotationYMatrix(M_PI/2) * TranslationMatrix(Vector3D(1000, 0,
                    0)));
            Texture *checks = new Checkerboard(20, 20, check1, check2,
                RotationXMatrix(M_PI/2));
            HallSurface *newsurf = new HallSurface;
            newsurf->SetDiffuse(checks);
            Object3D *backplane = new Plane(0, 1, 0, 20, newsurf);
            world.AddObject(backplane);
        }
    }
}

int
main(int argc, char *argv[])
{
    World TheWorld;

    // Say hello
    cout << "OORT: The Object-Oriented Ray Tracer  Version 1.0\n";
    cout << "Copyright (C) 1993 by Nicholas Wilt\n";
    cout << "See COPYRGHT.DOC for details on copyright
    restrictions.\n\n";

    // Allocate global noise sources.
    if (! GlobalNoise::Noise)
        GlobalNoise::Noise = new PerlinNoise;
    if (! GlobalNoise::Waves)
        GlobalNoise::Waves = new WaveSource(10, GlobalNoise::Noise);
```

Listing F.6 texts.cpp *(continued)*

```
if (! GlobalNoise::Freqs)
   GlobalNoise::Freqs = new FreqSource(10, GlobalNoise::Noise);

PopulateWorld(TheWorld);

// Parse the command line; options given on the command line subsume
// stuff specified in the input file.
TheWorld.ParseCommandLine(argc, argv);

// Write RAW output file.
TheWorld.RayTrace();

// Report on statistics gathered.
Report(cout);
if (Statistics::AppendTo) {
      ofstream app(Statistics::AppendTo, ios::ate);
      if (! (! app)) {
         Report(app);
         app.close();
      }
}

// Delete global noise sources.
delete GlobalNoise::Noise;
delete GlobalNoise::Waves;
delete GlobalNoise::Freqs;

return 0;
}
```

Listing F.6   `texts.cpp`   *(continued)*

F.7 Balls

This example illustrates the Sphereflake, a recursively defined object composed of spheres. The Sphereflake is composed of a sphere with nine smaller spheres adjacent to it, each of which has nine smaller spheres adjacent to it, each of which has...

Because the Sphereflake can be made as complex as desired, the Sphereflake class takes a *depth*, or measure of the complexity to put into the model.

A Sphereflake of depth N contains $\sum_{i=0}^{N} 9^i$ spheres (1+9=10 for a depth of 1, 1+9+81=91 for a depth of 2, etc.).

The Sphereflake is not symmetrical; it has an orientation. In this scene, the Sphereflake is pointing upward (along the +Y axis). To illustrate the effects made possible by lenses, the Sphereflake is enclosed in a spherical lens in front of the background plane.

```cpp
// ====================================================================
// BALLS.CPP
//     Illustrate the SphereFlake.
// Copyright (C) 1993 by Nicholas Wilt.  All rights reserved.
// ====================================================================

#include "oort.h"
#include "world.h"
#include "colors.h"
#include "utils.h"

void
PopulateWorld(World& world)
{
    world.SetDepthLimit(3);
    world.SetOutputFile("balls.raw");

    world.SetViewerParameters(Vector3D(0), Vector3D(0, 0, 1000),
        Vector3D(0, 1, 0));
    world.SetScreenWidth(4000);
    world.SetScreenHeight(3000);
    world.SetScreenDistance(1000);

    world.SetBackgroundColor(RGBColor(0));

    world.AddLight(new PointLight(Vector3D(500, 500, 1000),
    RGBColor(0.5), 1, 0, 0));
    world.AddLight(new PointLight(Vector3D(0, 500, 2000),
    RGBColor(0.5), 1, 0, 0));

    HallSurface *surf = new HallSurface;
    surf->SetDiffuse(new PureColor(Blue));

    world.AddObject(new SphereFlake(Vector3D(0), 300.0, Vector3D(0, 1,
        0), 4, surf));

    Texture *ChessBoard = new Checkerboard(500, 500,
                                new PureColor(White),
                                new PureColor(LightBlue),
                                IdentityMatrix());
```

Listing F.7 balls.cpp

```
    HallSurface *checks = new HallSurface;
    checks->SetDiffuse(ChessBoard);
    world.AddObject(new Plane(Vector3D(0, 0, 1), 0.0, checks));
    HallSurface *glass = new HallSurface;
    glass->SetDiffuse(new PureColor(RGBColor(0.08)));
    glass->SetSpecular(new PureColor(RGBColor(0.6)), 100);
    glass->SetReflect(new PureColor(RGBColor(0.2)));
    glass->SetTransmit(new PureColor(RGBColor(0.8)), 1.3);

    world.AddObject(new Sphere(Vector3D(0), 750, glass));
}

int
main(int argc, char *argv[])
{
    World TheWorld;

    // Say hello
    cout << "OORT: The Object-Oriented Ray Tracer  Version 1.0\n";
    cout << "Copyright (C) 1992 by Nicholas Wilt.  All rights
    reserved.\n\n";

    // Allocate global noise sources.
    if (! GlobalNoise::Noise)
        GlobalNoise::Noise = new PerlinNoise;
    if (! GlobalNoise::Waves)
        GlobalNoise::Waves = new WaveSource(10, GlobalNoise::Noise);
    if (! GlobalNoise::Freqs)
        GlobalNoise::Freqs = new FreqSource(10, GlobalNoise::Noise);

    PopulateWorld(TheWorld);

    // Parse the command line; options given on the command line
    subsume
    // stuff specified in the input file.
    TheWorld.ParseCommandLine(argc, argv);

    // Write RAW output file.
    TheWorld.RayTrace();

    // Report on statistics gathered.
    Report(cout);
    if (Statistics::AppendTo) {
        ofstream app(Statistics::AppendTo, ios::ate);
        if (! (! app)) {
```

Listing F.7   `balls.cpp` *(continued)*

```
            Report(app);
            app.close();
        }
    }

    // Delete global noise sources.
    delete GlobalNoise::Noise;
    delete GlobalNoise::Waves;
    delete GlobalNoise::Freqs;

    return 0;
}
```

Listing F.7 `balls.cpp` *(continued)*

F.8 Sierpinski's Tetrahedron

This example illustrates Sierpinski's Tetrahedron, a recursively defined object composed of triangles. The Tetrahedron is composed of four tetrahedra arranged in a tetrahedron, each of which may also consist for four tetrahedra...

Like the Sphereflake, the Tetrahedron can be made arbitrarily complex, so the STetrahedron constructor takes a depth parameter. For a depth of N, the tetrahedron contains 4^N triangles.

```
// =====================================================================
// tetra.cpp
//     Implementation file for Tetrahedron example.
//     The code for this file is derived from tetra.c in Eric
//     Haines's public domain Standard Procedural Database (SPD).
//     For more information on the SPD, see his article "A Proposal
//     For Standard Graphics Environments" in the November 1987
//     issue of IEEE Computer Graphics & Applications.
//
//     Copyright (C) 1993 by Nicholas Wilt.  All rights reserved.
// =====================================================================

#include "oort.h"
#include "world.h"
#include "utils.h"

void
```

Listing F.8 `tetra.cpp`

```
PopulateWorld(World& world)
{
    world.SetDepthLimit(3);
    world.SetOutputFile("tetra.raw");

    Vector3D LookAt(-0.004103, -0.004103, 0.216539);
    Vector3D Viewer = 1.5 * Vector3D(1.02285, -3.17715, -2.17451);
    Vector3D Up(-0.816497, -0.816497, 0.816497);
    world.SetViewerParameters(LookAt, Viewer, Up);

    world.SetScreenWidth(asin(45*M_PI/180));
    world.SetScreenHeight(asin(45*M_PI/180));
    world.SetScreenDistance(1);

    // Important: set threshold of no-intersection to a
    // much smaller value than the default.
    Limits::Threshold = 0.01;
    Limits::Small = 0.001;

    world.SetBackgroundColor(RGBColor(0));
    world.AddLight(new PointLight(Vector3D(1.87607, -18.1239, -
        5.00042), Vector3D(0.5), 1, 0, 0));
    world.AddLight(new PointLight(Vector3D(-5, -6, -5), Vector3D(0.5),
        1, 0, 0));

    HallSurface *tetracolor = new HallSurface;
    Texture *tetratext = new PureColor(1, 0.2, 0.2);
    tetracolor->SetDiffuse(tetratext);

    Object3D *tetra = new STetrahedron(5, 1, tetracolor);
    tetra->ApplyTransform(RotationAxisMatrix(Normalize(Vector3D(-1, -1,
        1)), 45*M_PI/180));
    world.AddObject(tetra);

    HallSurface *checks = new HallSurface;

    Matrix ref = Invert(ViewMatrix(LookAt, Viewer, Up));
    checks->SetBumpMap(new TwoSided);//(new Waves(2000, 0, 0.025, ref *
    ScaleMatrix(1/1000., 1/100., 1/1000.) * Invert(ref))));

    checks->SetDiffuse(new PureColor(0, 0.4, 0.8));

    Plane *facing = new Plane(-Up, -7, checks);
    world.AddObject(facing);
}
```

Listing F.8 `tetra.cpp` *(continued)*

```
int
main(int argc, char *argv[])
{
    World TheWorld;

    // Say hello
    cout << "OORT: The Object-Oriented Ray Tracer  Version 1.0\n";
    cout << "Copyright (C) 1992 by Nicholas Wilt.  All rights
    reserved.\n\n";

    // Allocate global noise sources.
    if (! GlobalNoise::Noise)
       GlobalNoise::Noise = new PerlinNoise;
    if (! GlobalNoise::Waves)
       GlobalNoise::Waves = new WaveSource(10, GlobalNoise::Noise);
    if (! GlobalNoise::Freqs)
       GlobalNoise::Freqs = new FreqSource(10, GlobalNoise::Noise);

    PopulateWorld(TheWorld);

    // Parse the command line; options given on the command line
    subsume
    // stuff specified in the input file.
    TheWorld.ParseCommandLine(argc, argv);

    // Write RAW output file.
    TheWorld.RayTrace();

    // Report on statistics gathered.
    Report(cout);
    if (Statistics::AppendTo) {
        ofstream app(Statistics::AppendTo, ios::ate);
        if (! (! app)) {
           Report(app);
           app.close();
        }
    }

    // Delete global noise sources.
    delete GlobalNoise::Noise;
    delete GlobalNoise::Waves;
    delete GlobalNoise::Freqs;

    return 0;
}
```

Listing F.8   tetra.cpp *(continued)*

Appendix G
File Formats

O ORT uses a number of file formats. The RAW file format is the output file format for the ray tracer. The Neutral File Format (NFF) is used to describe test scenes from the Standard Procedural Database. This chapter describes these file formats.

G.1 RAW File Format

The .RAW file format is a popular format for ray tracing output files. Besides OORT, it is used by DKBTrace and QRT. The file format consists of a header followed by a series of scanlines, as follows:

Header:
> **Width**, 16 bits, least significant byte first.
> **Height**, 16 bits, least significant byte first.

Scanlines:
> Y coordinate, range 0 to **Height** – 1 (16 bits, least significant byte first).
> **Width** bytes, the red component of each pixel in the scanline.
> **Width** bytes, the green component of each pixel in the scanline.
> **Width** bytes, the blue component of each pixel in the scanline.

`World::RayTrace` and `World::PutScanline` implement the output of this file format.

Note that the scanlines need not start at 0, and need not end at **Height**–1. If only a portion of the image was rendered, the scanlines in the file will reflect the scanlines that were rendered. This comes in handy for extremely large traces, for which multiple computers each rendered part of the image. This generates one output file for each computer. Before quantizing or displaying the image, these files must be spliced together. See Section E.3.

G.2 NFF (File Format)

The Neutral File Format was created by Eric Haines as a medium to create images for speed comparisons of different ray tracing implementations. Programs in his Standard Procedural Database (SPD), described in [HAIN87], write NFF files as output. The complete SPD may be downloaded via anonymous FTP from princeton.edu (directory: /pub/Graphics). OORT implements an NFF parser in the form of `World::ParseNFFFile`, which takes the filename of an NFF file and modifies the `World` accordingly.

The elements of an NFF file are as follows:

- Perspective frustrum.
- Background color.
- Point light sources.
- Surface properties description.
- Objects (polygons, polygonal patches, cylinders, cones, and spheres are supported).

OORT supports all of these elements except polygonal patches, cylinders, and cones.

An NFF file consists of lines of text which enumerate these entities. The first line of each item tells the type. It may be one of the following:

v	Viewer parameters
b	Background color
l (ell)	Point light
f	Object material properties
c	Cone or cylinder
s	Sphere
p	Polygon
pp	Polygonal patch

Each of these is described below.

Viewer parameters

v	Header.
from *Fx Fy Fz*	The eye location.
at *Ax Ay Az*	This point will be in the center of the output image.
up *Ux Uy Uz*	This direction vector points toward the top of the output image.
angle *angle*	In degrees. This is the angle from the center of the top pixel row to the bottom pixel row, and the left column to the right column. (Note: The aspect ratio is always 1.0.)
hither *hither*	Distance of the hither plane from the eye. This parameter is not used by OORT.
resolution *xres yres*	Width and height of the output image in pixels.

A view entity must be defined before any objects are defined.

Background color

$$b \ R \ G \ B$$

Gives the background color. If no background color is set, it is assumed to be black (0, 0, 0).

Light

$$l \ X \ Y \ Z \ [R \ G \ B]$$

Gives the location and, optionally, the color output of a point light source.

Shading parameters

$$f \ \text{red green blue Kd Ks Shine T index}$$

red, *green*, and *blue* specify the color reflected by the object. *Kd* and *Ks* give the diffuse and specular coefficients of reflection. *Shine* is the Phong cosine power for highlights. *T* is the coefficient of transmission. *index* is the index of refraction for the object.

Transmitting objects ($T > 0$) are considered to have two sides for algorithms that need these. (Normally, objects have one side.)

The fill color is used to color the objects following it until a new color is assigned.

Sphere

```
s center.x center.y center.z radius
```

This places a sphere with the given center point and radius in the scene. The NFF definition specifies that if the radius is negative, then only the sphere's inside is visible (essentially that the normal vectors of the sphere are reversed). OORT does not support this capability, since no SPD scene makes use of negative radii.

Polygon

```
p total_vertices
vert1.x vert1.y vert1.z
[etc. for total_vertices vertices]
```

A polygon is defined by a set of vertices. A polygon has only one side, with the order of the vertices being counterclockwise as you face the polygon (right-handed coordinate system). The first two edges must form a nonzero convex angle, so that the normal and side visibility can be determined by using just the first three vertices.

Polygonal patch

```
pp total_vertices
vert1.x vert1.y vert1.z norm1.x norm1.y
norm1.z
[etc. for total_vertices vertices]
```

A patch is defined by a set of vertices and their normals. A patch has only one side, with the order of the vertices being counterclockwise as you face the patch (right-handed coordinate system). The first two edges must form a nonzero convex angle, so that the normal and side visibility can be determined.

OORT does not yet support smooth polygons, so it ignores the normal.

Comment

```
# [ string ]
```

As soon as a "#" character is detected, the rest of the line is considered a comment.

Cones and cylinders

```
c
base.x base.y base.z base_radius
apex.x apex.y apex.z apex_radius
```

The NFF parser for OORT does not yet support cones or cylinders, but they are included here for the sake of completeness.

The base and apex points define the axis of the cone or cylinder, as well as its height. The difference between cones and cylinders is that a cone has different base and apex radii (the NFF specification holds that the apex radius is always smaller than the base radius). The base and apex points may not be coincident.

A negative value for both radii means that only the inside of the object is visible.

Index

OBJECT-ORIENTED RAY TRACING IN C++
programs are available on a 3½" high-density disk.
The companion diskette contains all of the code
for the example programs in the book
plus the C++ Class Library for Object-Oriented Ray Tracing (OORT).

3½" HIGH-DENSITY DISKETTE. Please send me _____ copy(ies) of the diskette for use with the book **OBJECT-ORIENTED RAY TRACING IN C++** at $33.00 each, **WILT/OBJECT-ORIENTED RAY TRACING IN C++ DISK,** ISBN 0-471-30416-6.

BOOK. Please send me _____ copy(ies) of the book **WILT/OBJECT-ORIENTED RAY TRACING IN C++** at $36.95, ISBN 0-471-30415-8.

BOOK/DISK SET. Please send me _____ copy(ies) of the book/disk set for **WILT/OBJECT-ORIENTED RAY TRACING IN C++** at $69.95, ISBN 0-471-30414-X.

☐ Payment enclosed ☐ Visa ☐ MasterCard ☐ American Express

Card Number_____ Expiration Date_____

Signature_____

NAME_____

COMPANY NAME _____

ADDRESS _____

CITY/STATE _____ ZIP CODE_____

BUSINESS REPLY MAIL
FIRST CLASS   PERMIT NO. 2277   NEW YORK, N.Y.

POSTAGE WILL BE PAID BY ADDRESSEE

JOHN WILEY & SONS, INC.
Attn: Continuation Department
P.O. Box 6792
Somerset, N.J. 08875-9976